Google SketchUp® 8
FOR DUMMIES®

by Aidan Chopra

WILEY

Wiley Publishing, Inc.

Google SketchUp® 8 For Dummies®

Published by

Wiley Publishing, Inc.
111 River Street
Hoboken, NJ 07030-5774
www.wiley.com

Copyright © 2011 by Wiley Publishing, Inc., Indianapolis, Indiana

Published by Wiley Publishing, Inc., Indianapolis, Indiana

Published simultaneously in Canada

WILEY

About the Author

Aidan Chopra has always had a thing for computers — his parents thoughtfully sent him to Apple camp instead of hockey lessons like every other eight-year-old in Montreal — but he learned to draft and build physical models the old-fashioned way, working for his architect father. These days, Aidan is a Product Evangelist at Google, where he's been since that company bought SketchUp in the first part of 2006. In the six years since he graduated with a Master of Architecture degree from Rice University, he's done a lot of writing and lecturing about the way software is used in design. Aidan writes the SketchUpdate, a monthly e-mail newsletter that reaches over a million SketchUp users worldwide. At Google, he works on ways to mediate between power and usability; he believes the best software in the world isn't worth a darn if nobody can figure out how it works. Aidan is based in Boulder, Colorado, even though he is what many would consider to be the diametric opposite of a world-class endurance athlete.

Dedication

For my parents, Jenny and Shab, and my brother, Quincy, because I love them very much.

Acknowledgments

For helping in all the ways that it is possible to help with a book — offering technical advice, lending a critical ear, providing moral support and encouragement — I'd like to thank my wife, Sandra Winstead. It's rare to find everything you need in a single person, and I can't imagine having written this book without her.

I'd like to thank Chris Dizon for agreeing to be the Technical Editor for this volume; I can't think of anyone who brings more enthusiasm and curiosity to everything he does. As a dyed-in-the-wool SketchUpper who uses the software even more than I do, I knew he'd do a bang-up job of keeping me honest, and he did.

I thank Kyle Looper, Becky Huehls, and Jen Riggs, my editors at Wiley, for making what I fully expected to be a painful process not so at all. It was a delight to work with a team of such intelligent, thoughtful, and well-meaning professionals; I only hope I'm half as lucky on the next book I write.

Finally, I need to thank the very long list of individuals who provided critical help. From clearing the way for me to be able to write this book to patiently explaining things more than once, I owe the following people (and almost certainly a few more) a whole lot: Tommy Acierno, Brad Askins, John Bacus, Brian Brewington, Brian Brown, Todd Burch, Chris Campbell, Mark Carvalho, Chris Cronin, Tasha Danko, Steve Dapkus, Jonathan Dormody, Bil Eberle, Joe Esch, Rich Feit, Jody Gates, Toshen Golias, Scott Green, Adam Hecht, Barry Janzen, Alex Juhola, Tyson Kartchner, Chris Keating, Patrick Lacz, Mark Limber, Scott Lininger, Catherine Moats, Allyson McDuffie, Millard McQuaid, Tyler Miller, Parker Mitchell, Simone Nicolo, Steve Oles, Bruce Polderman, Alok Priyadarshi, Peter Saal, Brad Schell, Gopal Shah, Matt Simpson, Mike Springer, Tricia Stahr, Bryce Stout, Vicky Tait, Daniel Tal, James Therrien, Mason Thrall, Nancy Trigg, Tushar Udeshi, John Ulmer, David Vicknair, Greg Wirt, and Tom Wyman.

Publisher's Acknowledgments

We're proud of this book; please send us your comments at http://dummies.custhelp.com. For other comments, please contact our Customer Care Department within the U.S. at 877-762-2974, outside the U.S. at 317-572-3993, or fax 317-572-4002.

Some of the people who helped bring this book to market include the following:

Acquisitions, Editorial, and Media Development

Project Editor: Rebecca Huehls

Acquisitions Editor: Kyle Looper

Copy Editor: Jen Riggs

Technical Editor: Chris Dizon

Editorial Manager: Leah P. Cameron

Media Development Assistant Project Manager: Jenny Swisher

Editorial Assistant: Amanda Graham

Sr. Editorial Assistant: Cherie Case

Cartoons: Rich Tennant
(www.the5thwave.com)

Composition Services

Project Coordinator: Katherine Crocker

Layout and Graphics: Carl Byers, Lavonne Roberts

Proofreaders: Melissa Cossell, Rebecca Denoncour, Toni Settle

Indexer: BIM Indexing & Proofreading Services

Publishing and Editorial for Technology Dummies

    Richard Swadley, Vice President and Executive Group Publisher

    Andy Cummings, Vice President and Publisher

    Mary Bednarek, Executive Acquisitions Director

    Mary C. Corder, Editorial Director

Publishing for Consumer Dummies

    Diane Graves Steele, Vice President and Publisher

Composition Services

    Debbie Stailey, Director of Composition Services

Contents at a Glance

Table of Contents

Introduction

A few years ago, I was teaching a workshop on advanced SketchUp techniques to a group of extremely bright middle and high school (or so I thought) students in Hot Springs, Arkansas. As subject matter went, I wasn't pulling any punches — we were breezing through material I wouldn't think of introducing to most groups of adults. At one point, a boy raised his hand to ask a question, and I noticed he looked younger than most of the others. Squinting, I read a logo on his T-shirt that told me he was in elementary school. "You're in sixth grade?" I asked, a little stunned. These kids were *motoring,* after all. The boy didn't even look up. He shook his head, double-clicked something, and mumbled, "Third." He was 8 years old.

SketchUp was invented in 1999 by a couple 3D industry veterans (or refugees, depending on your perspective) to make it easier for people to see their ideas in three dimensions. That was it, really — they just wanted to make a piece of software that anyone could use to build 3D models. What I saw in Arkansas makes me think they were successful.

Before SketchUp was acquired in 2006 by Google, it cost $495 a copy, and it was already a mainstay of architects' and other designers' software toolkits. No other 3D modeler was as easy to understand as SketchUp, meaning that even senior folks (many of whom thought their CD/DVD trays were cup holders) started picking it up. These days, SketchUp is being used at home, in school, and at work by anyone with a need to represent 3D information the way it's meant to be represented: in 3D. Google SketchUp (as it's now called) is available in at least 15 languages and is just as popular internationally as it is in North America.

About This Book

The thing I like least about software is figuring out how it works. I once saw a movie where the main character acquired knowledge by plugging a cable (a rather fat cable, actually) into a hole in the back of his head. A computer then uploaded new capabilities — languages, martial arts, and fashion sense (apparently) — directly into his brain. Afterward, the character ate a snack and took a nap. *That's* how I wish I could get to know new software.

This book, on the other hand, is a fairly analog affair. In it, I do my best to guide you through the process of building 3D models with SketchUp. I wrote this book for people who are new to 3D modeling, so I don't assume you know anything about polygons, vertices, or linear arrays. The nice thing is that the people who make SketchUp don't assume you know any of those things, either. That means I don't have to spend many words explaining theoretical concepts, which I think we both can appreciate.

I don't think many people want to use software just for the sake of using software. You probably didn't learn to drive just because you thought seatbelts and turn signals were cool; I'm betting you wanted to be able to get around in a car. People use SketchUp so that they can build 3D models. As such, most of this book focuses on what *you can do* with SketchUp, and not *what SketchUp does.* Naturally, this emphasis has a few implications:

- ✔ **I use the word *you* a lot.** You're reading this book because you have something you want to build in 3D on your computer, and you think SketchUp can help you do that. I try to keep this in mind by letting you know how you can use the features I talk about to do what you want to do.

- ✔ **I err on the side of architecture.** The fact is, a lot of people want to use SketchUp to model buildings, so I assume that a good many of you (the collective *you,* in this case) want to do the same. You can use SketchUp to build just about anything you want, but to ignore the fact that it's extra-great for architecture would be silly.

- ✔ **I don't cover everything SketchUp can do.** If this book were about SketchUp, and not modeling *with* SketchUp, I'd list every feature, every tool, and every command in exhaustive detail. I'd tell you exactly what all the radio buttons and slider bars are for. I'd, in effect, just copy the documentation in SketchUp's online Help Center and call it a day. In writing this book, I had to make a tough choice: I had to figure out what to show you and, more importantly, what to leave out. The Table of Contents I settled on is a list of what most people want to know, most of the time.

Just in case you're interested, here's what didn't make the cut (and why):

- • *The Dimension and Label tools:* I left these out because they're so simple to use that I didn't think they needed any explanation. That's not to say they're not great — they are. It's just that this book can be only so long.

- • *The 3D Text tool:* Why'd I leave out this one? Like the Dimension and Label tools, it's too easy to use. Just try it, and you'll see what I mean.

- • *Style Builder:* Because it's a separate program that comes with SketchUp Pro 8, I decided not to dive into Style Builder. You use it to create your own Styles for SketchUp; read more about Styles in Chapter 9.

- *Ruby:* Actually, I do talk a little bit about Ruby, but only in Chapter 17, which is practically at the end of the book. Ruby is a scripting (programming) language that you (maybe) can use to code your tools for SketchUp. I think that says it all, don't you?

One more thing: Because SketchUp is a *cross-platform* program (it's available for both Windows and Macintosh computers), I make reference to both operating systems throughout this book. In most cases, SketchUp works the same in Windows and on a Mac, but where it doesn't, I point out the differences. Just so you know, any figures in this book that show the SketchUp user interface show the Windows version.

Foolish Assumptions

I mention earlier that I don't presume you know anything about 3D modeling, much less 3D modeling with SketchUp, in this book. That's true — you're safe even if you call SketchUp "Sketch'em-Up" (which I've heard more than once, believe it or not). If you happen to know a thing or two about SketchUp, I think you'll still find plenty of useful stuff in this book. Even though I write with beginners in mind, I include a lot that definitely isn't beginner-level information. I mean for this book to be useful for people with just about any level of SketchUp skill.

That said, I assume you're familiar with a few important concepts. To begin with, I assume you know how to work your computer well enough to understand how to do basic things like saving and opening files. I don't cover those things in this book because SketchUp handles them just like every other program does. If you're trying to model with SketchUp *and* figure out how to use a computer at the same time, Wiley has some excellent books that can help you out, such as *Windows 7 For Dummies,* by Andy Rathbone, or *Mac OS X Snow Leopard For Dummies,* by Bob LeVitus, just to name two; visit www. dummies.com for other options.

Next, I take for granted that you have, and know how to work, a mouse with a scroll wheel. SketchUp all but requires you to have a scroll wheel mouse — especially when you're just starting out. The good news for folks who don't have one is that they're fairly cheap. Just look for something with a left button, a right button, and a little scroll wheel in the middle.

Finally, I assume you have at least occasional access to the Internet. Don't panic! Unlike most Google applications, you don't have to be online to use

SketchUp — I do most of my best work on airplanes, in fact. You can find great resources on the Web, though, and I point them out when I think they're important.

How This Book Is Organized

Tell me if you think this is strange: I read most computer books in completely random order. I *never* start at the beginning and work my way through. In fact, I only pick them up for two reasons:

- ✔ **To figure something out:** I like to have a book on hand when I begin something new because I like the way books *work*. If I need help, I look it up, but something else invariably happens — I end up reading more than I needed to, and I usually end up finding out something I didn't even know I didn't know. That almost never happens when I use digital media; it's too good at providing me with just the answer to my question. Computers are lousy for browsers like me.

- ✔ **To kill time:** I hate to admit this, but I don't usually keep my computer books anywhere near my computer. I keep them in the bathroom because my bathroom has excellent light for reading and because I'm afraid that a television would fall in the bathtub and electrocute me. When I'm just killing time, I open my book to a random page and start reading.

Despite these two facts, this book *does* have structure. Basic concepts are grouped in the first few chapters, and more advanced material appears toward the end. Chapter 3 is devoted entirely to a step-by-step approach to getting started, just for those who like to get to know software that way.

In general, though, this book is intended to be a reference. If you keep reading from this page on, right to the end of the index, you'll have a pretty good idea of how to use SketchUp to make 3D models — but that isn't what I expect you to do. I recommend that you start with Chapters 1 and 2, just to get your bearings. After that, use the Table of Contents or the index to find what you're looking for; then proceed from there.

To make it easier to understand how certain chapters are related, this book lumps them together into parts. Check out the following summaries to get an idea of what's in each part.

Part 1: Getting Started with SketchUp

If you're completely new to SketchUp and 3D modeling, this is the most important part in this book. Start here, lest you get frustrated and decide to use these pages to line your rabbit coop. Chapter 1 talks about how SketchUp fits into the bigger 3D modeling picture. Chapter 2 lays out all — that's 100 percent — of the basic concepts you need to understand to do anything useful with SketchUp. Chapter 3 offers a basic end-to-end workflow for creating and sharing a model. You can skip it, but I think it's a nice way to ease into the program.

Part II: Modeling in SketchUp

SketchUp is a 3D modeling tool, so this part is, in Shakespeare's eternal words, "where it's at." Chapter 4 dives right into using SketchUp to make buildings, with an emphasis on drawing and extruding simple plans, modeling stairs, and constructing roofs. Making buildings isn't easy, mind you, but it's what a lot of people want to do in SketchUp, so I put it right at the beginning.

Chapter 5 deals with using groups and components, two of the most important elements in any SketchUp model you make. Chapter 6 lays out advanced techniques for modeling things like terrain, characters, and other non-boxy objects, whereas Chapter 7 deals with tools and techniques you can use to manage big models. In Chapter 8, I talk about using photographs in SketchUp. The second part of the chapter is all about SketchUp's photo-matching feature, which I guarantee will make you smile.

Part III: Viewing Your Model in Different Ways

Making models in SketchUp is only half the fun. The chapters in this part present some of this software's truly unique presentation features. Chapter 9 dives in to Styles and Shadows. Also, don't skip the last part of Chapter 10 on using sections to create animations — it's easy and more rewarding than almost anything else you can do in SketchUp.

Part IV: Sharing What You've Made

These chapters are dedicated to getting your models into the world. In Chapter 11, I talk about using SketchUp with Google Earth, which, if you haven't tried it, is reason in itself to have a fast Internet connection. Chapters 12 and 13 deal with printing and exporting images and movies from your model files. Chapters 14 and 15 provide an introduction to LayOut. This relatively new program, which is included as part of SketchUp Pro, is for creating 2D presentation documents that automatically link to your 3D models.

Part V: The Part of Tens

My favorite thing about books in the *For Dummies* series is the way they embrace people's love of lists. I *could* have spread the information contained in these ultra-short chapters throughout the entire book, but it's so much easier to read when it's all in one place, don't you think?

Chapter 16 is a list of ten things that you'll definitely struggle with when you're first using SketchUp; remember to check here before you do anything drastic. Chapter 17 lists great add-ons that'll make your SketchUping more enjoyable, and Chapter 18 is all about where to turn when the information you need isn't in this book.

On the Web site

I created a little online presence for this book so I could share more information with you. This book's Web site (www.dummies.com/go/SketchUp8FD) includes lots of useful stuff:

✔ **Bonus chapters:** A previous edition of *Google SketchUp For Dummies* included a whole chapter on exporting 2D and 3D vector information with SketchUp Pro. That information is still relevant, but I cut it out of this book to make room for new features. The good news is that you can get the whole chapter in digital form on the Web site.

You also find a mini chapter on creating your own Dynamic Components with SketchUp Pro. *DCs* are programmable, configurable pieces of SketchUp content that can make your workflow a lot more efficient.

✔ **Videos:** I recorded about six dozen videos and put them up on YouTube. They're pretty basic (just me talking and modeling), but seeing SketchUp in action is often very helpful — black-and-white pictures can convey only so much. All my videos are also embedded in this book's Web site, and they're organized by chapter and section to make them easy to find.

✔ **Color images:** It often helps to be able to see a figure in color, so I put color versions of some images in this book online.

✔ **SketchUp files:** These are actually stored on the Google 3D Warehouse (which you can find out about in Chapters 5 and 11), but I link to them to make them easier to find.

✔ **Links to other cool resources:** There's a world of great SketchUp material — plugins, components, models, and blogs — out there, and you can find direct links to many of them on my Web site.

Icons Used in This Book

This icon indicates a piece of information I think will probably save you time.

When you're working in SketchUp, you need to know a lot of things. I use the Remember icon to remind you of something I cover earlier in the book, just in case you may have forgotten (or skipped) it.

Everyone's a little bit of a nerd sometimes, and paragraphs that bear this icon indulge that nerdiness. You can skip them without fear of missing anything important, but reading them can give you something to annoy your SketchUp friends with later.

When you see this icon, pay special attention. It occurs rarely, but when it does, something you do could harm your work.

This icon denotes a spot where you can find supporting material on this book's companion Web site, including videos, sample files, and links to helpful material, which you can find at www.dummies.com/go/SketchUp8FD.

I revised this book to cover SketchUp 8, but instead of adding a section at the beginning that lists everything that's new, I added the information throughout — I think it makes more sense that way. This icon denotes what's new or different in the new version.

If you want to see a complete list of new features and improvements in SketchUp 8, open your Web browser of choice and do a Google search for *new in SketchUp 8* — something gloriously list-like will no doubt appear.

Part I
Getting Started with SketchUp

In this part . . .

This part of the book is dedicated to helping you get your bearings. It's not a step-by-step guide to starting a new file in SketchUp; instead, it provides a little bit of information about what SketchUp is, what you can use it to do, and how to get the most out of it.

Chapter 1 is a very general overview of Google SketchUp. I try not to bore you with too much background information, but here's where you can read about what the software is supposed to let you do, how it compares to other 3D modeling applications, and where everything is.

In Chapter 2, I jump right in. There are a few things about SketchUp you absolutely need to know when you're just getting started, and here's where I lay them out. I think this is the most important chapter in this book; read it, and you'll know more about SketchUp than millions of other folks who already use it every day.

The contents of Chapter 3 are included for the benefit of those readers who like to figure out software by getting their hands dirty right away. The whole chapter is a workflow that takes you through the process of making a simple model, changing the way it looks, and creating an image of it that you can keep forever.

Chapter 1

Meeting Google SketchUp

*O*nce upon a time, software for building three-dimensional (3D) models of thing like buildings, cars, and other stuff was hard to use. I mean *really* hard — people went to school for years to learn it. And if that wasn't bad enough, 3D modeling software was expensive — so expensive that the only people who used it were professionals and software pirates (people who stole it, basically). Then along came SketchUp.

Operating under the assumption that lots of people may want — and need — to make 3D models, the folks who invented SketchUp decided to design a program that worked more intuitively. Instead of making you think about 3D models as complex mathematical constructs (the way computers think), they created an interface that lets you build models using elements you're already familiar with: lines and shapes.

So do you need to know how to draw to use SketchUp? In the latest version of the software, not really. Traditional drawing is about *translating* what you see onto a flat piece of paper: going from 3D to 2D, which is hard to do for most people. In SketchUp, you're always in 3D, so no translation is involved — you just *build*, and SketchUp takes care of stuff like perspective and shading for you.

This first chapter is about putting SketchUp in context: why Google offers it for free, how it compares to other 3D software, and what you can (and can't) do with it. In the last part of the chapter, I give a quick tour of the program, just to let you know where things are.

Things You Ought to Know Right Away

Before I continue, here's some information you may need:

- ✔ **You get SketchUp by downloading it from the Internet.** Just type http://sketchup.google.com into your Web browser and read through the first page of the Google SketchUp Web site. Click the links to download the application to your computer and then follow the installation instructions on the Web.

- ✔ **SketchUp works in Windows and Mac OS X.** Google SketchUp is available for both operating systems, and it looks (and works) about the same way on both.

- ✔ **A Pro version is available.** Google offers a Pro version of SketchUp *(Google SketchUp Pro)* that you can buy if you need it. The Pro version includes a few terrific features that folks like architects, production designers, and other design professionals need for exchanging files with other software. SketchUp Pro also includes a whole separate application — dubbed *LayOut* — for creating presentation documents with your SketchUp models; it's the subject of Chapters 14 and 15. If you think you may need Pro, you can download a free trial version at http://sketchup.google.com.

Where SketchUp Fits in Google's World

A long time ago, somebody invented photography (hey — this isn't a history book), and suddenly people could make pictures of things that didn't involve drawing, engraving, or painting. Nowadays, you can't throw a rock without hitting a photograph of something. *Everything* (it seems) can take pictures, including people's phones. Photography is the main way that visual information is communicated.

But what comes after photography? Google (and just about every science-fiction writer who ever lived) thinks it's 3D, and here's why: You live in 3D. The furniture you buy (or build) is 3D, and so is the route you take to work. Because so many of the decisions you need to make (buying a couch, finding your way) involve 3D information, wouldn't it be nice to experience that information in 3D?

Software like SketchUp lets you see 3D information on a 2D screen, which is good, but affordable 3D printers and holography (yep, holograms) are just over the horizon. All that's left is to build a model of every single thing in the world — and guess who's going to do it?

You. By making SketchUp free for everyone, Google is leading the 3D charge. Rather than relying on a small number of 3D nerds to get around to modeling everything in the universe, Google made SketchUp available to anyone who wants to participate. Sometimes the best way to solve a hard problem (like modeling millions of buildings and other objects) is to get lots and lots of people working on it.

Comparing SketchUp to Other 3D Modeling Programs

If you're reading this book, I presume you're at least interested in two things: building 3D models and using SketchUp to do so. The following sections tell you something about how SketchUp compares to other 3D modeling programs — how long it takes to figure out how to use it and what kind of models it produces.

Jumping right in

When it comes to widely available 3D modeling software, it really doesn't get any easier than SketchUp. This software has been successful for one reason: People can get good enough at SketchUp to build something within a couple hours of launching it for the first time. You have no thick manuals to read, and no special geometric concepts to understand. Modeling in SketchUp is about grabbing your mouse and making something.

So how long should it take you to discover how SketchUp works? That depends on your background and experience, but in general, you can expect to make something recognizable in less than four hours. That's not to say you'll be a whiz — it just means that SketchUp's learning curve is extremely favorable. You don't need to know much to get started, and you'll still pick up things years from now. In fact, I've discovered a couple things just writing this book.

But is SketchUp *easy?* Lots of people say so, but I think it's all relative. SketchUp is without a doubt easi*er* than any other modeling program I've tried, but 3D modeling itself can be tricky. Some people catch on right away, and some folks take longer. But I can say this for sure: If you want to build 3D models and you have an afternoon to spare, there's no better place to start than SketchUp (and this book of course). Chapter 3 walks you through the basics to help you start modeling in SketchUp quickly.

Understanding the difference between paper and clay

Three-dimensional modeling software comes in two basic flavors: *solids* and *surfaces.* Figure 1-1 and the following points illustrate the difference:

Surface models are hollow   Solid models are solid

 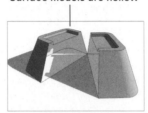 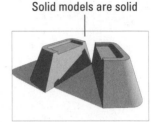

- ✔ **SketchUp is a surfaces modeler.** Everything in SketchUp is basically made up of thin (infinitely thin, actually) surfaces — dubbed *faces.* Even things that look thick (like cinder-block walls) are actually hollow shells. Making models in SketchUp is a lot like building things out of paper — really, really thin paper.

  Surface modelers like SketchUp are great for making models quickly because all you really need to worry about is modeling what things *look* like. That's not to say that they're less capable; it's just that they're primarily intended for visualization.

- ✔ **Using a solids modeler is more like working with clay.** When you cut a solid model in half, you create new surfaces where you cut; that's because objects are, well, solid. Programs like SolidWorks, form·Z, and Autodesk Inventor create solid models.

  People who make parts — like mechanical engineers and industrial designers — tend to work with solid models because they can use them to do some pretty precise calculations. Being able to calculate the volume of an object means that you can figure how much it will weigh, for example. Also, special machines can produce real-life prototypes directly from a solid-model file. These prototypes are handy for seeing how lots of little things are going to fit together.

An important point to reinforce here is that there's no "best" type of modeling software. It all depends on three things: how you like to work, what you're modeling, and what you plan to do with your model when it's done.

Despite what I just said about SketchUp being only a surfaces modeler, one of the niftiest new features in SketchUp Pro 8 (the non-free version of the software) is a set of tools that lets you manipulate special solid objects in your models. The Solid Tools feature offers a whole new way to work in SketchUp — you can read all about it in Chapter 6.

Yet another caveat: When I said (a few paragraphs ago) that 3D modeling programs come in two basic flavors, I sort of lied. The truth is, you can split them into two groups another way: by the kind of math they use to produce 3D models. You can find *polygonal* modelers (of which SketchUp is an example) and *curves-based* modelers. The former type uses straight lines and flat surfaces to define everything — even things that *look* curvy, aren't. The latter kind of modeler uses true curves to define lines and surfaces. These yield organic, flowing forms that are much more realistic than those produced by polygonal modelers, but that put a lot more strain on the computers that have to run them — and the people who have to figure out how to use them. Ultimately, it's a trade-off between simplicity and realism.

What You Should (And Shouldn't) Expect SketchUp to Do

Have you ever been to a hardware store and noticed the multitool gizmos on the racks next to the checkout stands? I once saw one that was a combination screwdriver, pliers, saw, tape measure, and (I swear) hammer. I sometimes wonder whether the hardware store people put them there as a joke, just to make you feel better about standing in line.

I generally don't like tools that claim to do everything. I much prefer *specialists* — tools that are designed for doing one thing *really* well. In the case of SketchUp, that one thing is building 3D models.

Here's a list of things (all model-building-related) that you can do with SketchUp:

✔ **Start a model in lots of ways:** With SketchUp, you can begin a model in whatever way makes sense for what you're building:

 • *From scratch:* When you first launch SketchUp, you see nothing except a little person standing in the middle of your screen. If you want, you can even delete him, leaving you a completely blank slate on which to model anything you want.

 • *From a photograph:* The second part of Chapter 8 talks all about how you can use SketchUp to build a model based on a photo of the thing you want to build; it's not really a beginner-level feature, but it's there.

- *With another computer file:* SketchUp can import images that you can use as a starting point for what you want to make. SketchUp Pro can even import CAD (computer-aided drawing) files that give you even more of a head start.

- *From a geo-location snapshot:* If you've ever used Google Earth, you know that Google has amazing aerial imagery and 3D terrain data for the whole world. In SketchUp 8, it's easy to grab a geo-location snapshot (a small chunk of the planet, basically) to use as a site for your model; read all about it in Chapter 11.

- *From Building Maker:* Google has an easy-as-pie, super-specialized tool for modeling real-world structures — Building Maker. You can start a model in Building Maker and modify it in SketchUp 8. If you're modeling existing buildings, this is a great way to save time — read more in Chapter 11.

✔ **Work loose or work tight:** One of my favorite things about SketchUp is that you can model without worrying about exactly *how big* something is. You can make models that are super-sketchy, but if you want, you can also make models that are absolutely precise. SketchUp is just like paper in that way; the amount of detail you add is entirely up to you.

✔ **Build something real or make something up:** *What* you build with SketchUp really isn't the issue. You work only with lines and shapes — or in SketchUp, *edges* and *faces* — so how you arrange them is your business. SketchUp isn't intended for making buildings any more than it is for creating other things. It's just a tool for drawing in three dimensions.

✔ **Share your models:** After you make something you want to show off, you can do a number of things, which you can discover in detail in Part IV:

- *Print:* Yep, you can print from SketchUp.

- *Export images:* If you want to generate an image file of a particular view, you can export one in any of several popular formats.

- *Export movies:* Animations are a great way to present three-dimensional information, and SketchUp can create them easily.

- *Export other 3D model formats:* With the Pro version of SketchUp, you can share your model with other pieces of software to create CAD drawings, generate photorealistic renderings, and more.

- *Upload to the 3D Warehouse:* This is a giant, online repository of SketchUp models. Add (or take) all the models you want.

- *Contribute to Google Earth:* Models you make of actual buildings that are efficient, accurate, and *photo-textured* (painted with photographs of the building itself) are welcome on Google Earth's default 3D Buildings layer. If you like, you can submit your work for consideration; if it's accepted, it goes live in a place where millions of people can see it.

Is this model a toaster or a bungalow?

SketchUp models are made from two basic kinds of *geometry:* edges (which are straight lines) and *faces* (which are 2D surfaces bound by edges). That's it. When you use SketchUp to draw a bunch of edges and faces in the shape of a staircase, all SketchUp knows is how many edges and faces it has to keep track of, and where they all go. There's no such thing as a *stair* in SketchUp — just edges and faces.

That said, the previous version of SketchUp introduced an exciting new development: *Dynamic Components* are pre-programmed objects that know what they are. A dynamic staircase, for example, is smart enough to know that it should add or subtract steps when you make it bigger or smaller. Dynamic Components are a big step for SketchUp; all of a sudden, there's a class of stuff in the program that has (what software types would call) *intelligence*. What's that mean for you? For starters, SketchUp is easier to pick up than it's ever been. I go on and on about Dynamic Components in Chapter 5.

With the exception of Dynamic Components, though, things in SketchUp don't have any idea what they're supposed to represent. Coming to this realization has the tendency to freak out some people. If you want a model of something, you have to make it out of edges and faces. The thing to remember is that SketchUp was created to let you model *anything,* not just buildings, so its tools are designed to manipulate geometry. That's good news, believe it or not, because you're not restricted in any way; you can model anything you can imagine.

What *can't* SketchUp do? A few things, actually — but that's okay. SketchUp was designed from the outset to be the friendliest, fastest, and most useful modeler available — and that's it, really. Fantastic programs are available that do the things in the following list, and SketchUp can exchange files with most of them:

- ✔ **Photorealistic rendering:** Most 3D modelers have their own, built-in photo renderers, but creating model views that look like photographs is a pretty specialized undertaking. SketchUp has always focused on *non-photorealistic rendering (NPR)* instead. NPR (as it's known) is essentially technology that makes things look hand-drawn — sort of the opposite of photorealism. If you want to make realistic views of your models, I talk about renderers that work great with SketchUp in Chapter 17.

- ✔ **Animation:** A few paragraphs ago, I mention that SketchUp can export animations, but that's a different thing. The movies that you can make with SketchUp involve moving your "camera" around your model. True animation software lets you move things around *inside* your model. SketchUp doesn't do that, but the Pro version lets you export to a number of different programs that do.

Taking the Ten-Minute SketchUp Tour

The point of this portion of the chapter is to show you where everything is — kind of like the way a parent shows a new babysitter around the house before leaving for a couple hours. Here I don't explain what anything *does,* per se. I just want you to feel like you know where to start looking when you find yourself hunting around for something.

Just like most programs you already use, SketchUp has five main parts. Figure 1-2 shows them all, in both the Windows and Mac versions of the program. I describe these parts, plus an additional feature, in the following list:

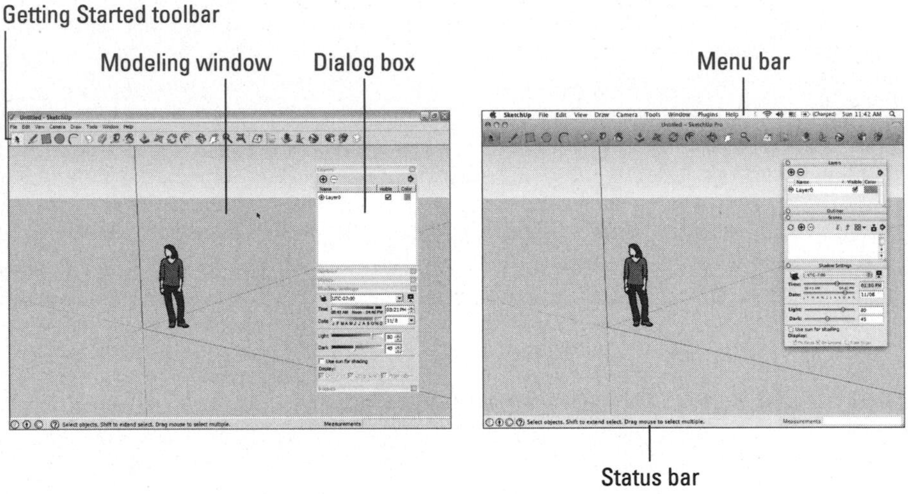

Getting Started toolbar

Modeling window　　Dialog box　　　　　　　　　　Menu bar

Figure 1-2:
All
SketchUp's
parts: in
Windows
(left) and on
the Mac.

Status bar

✔ **Modeling window:** See the big area in the middle of your computer screen? That's your modeling window, and it's where you spend 99 percent of your time in SketchUp. You build your model there; it's sort of a frame into a 3D world inside your computer. What you see in your modeling window is *always* a 3D view of your model, even if you happen to be looking at it from the top or side.

✔ **Menu bar:** For anyone who has used a computer in the last 30 years, the menu bar is nothing new. Each menu contains a long list of options, commands, tools, settings, and other goodies that pertain to just about everything you do in SketchUp.

✔ **Toolbars:** These contain buttons that you can click to activate tools and commands; they're faster than using the menu bar. SketchUp has a few toolbars, but only one is visible when you launch it the first time: the Getting Started toolbar.

If your modeling window is too narrow to show all the tools on the Getting Started toolbar, you can click the arrow on the right to see the rest of them.

✔ **Dialog boxes:** Some programs call them palettes and some call them inspectors; SketchUp doesn't call them anything. Its documentation (the SketchUp Help document you can get to in the Help menu) refers to some of them as managers and some as dialog boxes, but I thought I'd keep things simple and just call them all the same thing: dialog boxes.

✔ **Status bar:** You can consider this your SketchUp dashboard, I suppose. The status bar contains contextual information you use while you model.

✔ **Context menus:** Right-clicking things in your modeling window usually causes a context menu of commands and options to open. These are always relevant to whatever you happen to right-click (and whatever you're doing at the time), so the contents of each context menu are different.

Although the following items aren't part of the SketchUp user interface (like all the stuff in the preceding list), they're a critical part of modeling in SketchUp:

✔ **A mouse with a scroll wheel:** You usually find a left button (the one you use all the time), a right button (the one that opens the context menus), and a center *scroll wheel* that you both roll back and forth and click down like a button. You should get one if you don't already have one — it'll improve your SketchUp experience more than any single other thing you can buy.

✔ **A keyboard:** This sounds silly, but some people have tried to use SketchUp without one; it's just not possible. So many of the things you need to do all the time (such as make copies) involve your keyboard, so you'd better have one handy if you plan to use SketchUp.

Hanging out at the menu bar

SketchUp's menus are a pretty straightforward affair; you won't find anything surprising like "Launch Rocket" in any of them, unfortunately. All the same, here are the menus:

✔ **File:** Includes options for creating, opening, and saving SketchUp files. The File menu is also where to go if you want to import or export a file, or make a printout of your model view.

✔ **Edit:** Has all the commands that affect the bits of your model that are selected.

✔ **View:** This one's a little tricky. You'd think it'd contain all the options for flying around in 3D space, but it doesn't — that stuff's on the Camera menu. Instead, the View menu includes all the controls you use to affect the appearance of your model itself: what's visible, how faces look, and so on. View also contains settings for turning on and off certain elements of SketchUp's user interface.

✔ **Camera:** Contains controls for viewing your model from different angles. In SketchUp, your "camera" is your point of view, literally.

✔ **Draw:** Includes tools for drawing edges and faces in your modeling window.

✔ **Tools:** Most of SketchUp's tools are contained here, except of course for the ones you use for drawing.

✔ **Window:** If you're ever wondering where to find a dialog box you want to use, this is the place to look; they're all right here.

✔ **Plugins:** You can get extra tools for SketchUp — little programs that "plug in" to it and add functionality. Some of them show up here after they're installed. Chapter 17 introduces a few of my favorites.

✔ **Help:** When you're stuck, and this book isn't helping (heaven forbid), check out the Help menu; it's the gateway to SketchUp salvation.

Checking the status bar

The narrow strip of information below the modeling window is packed with information goodness:

✔ **Context-specific instructions:** Most of the time, you check here to see what options may be available for whatever you're doing. *Modifier keys* (keyboard strokes that you use in combination with certain tools to per-form additional functions), step-by-step instructions, and general infor-mation about what you're doing all show up in one place: right here.

✔ **The Measurements box:** The Measurements box is where numbers show up (to put it as simply as I can). Chapter 2 goes into more detail, but the basic purpose of the Measurements box is to enable you to be precise while you model.

✔ **Status indicator icons:** These three little icons appear in the lower-left corner of your screen. They change to tell you things about your model, and you can click them to find out what they do. The most important one to note (this early on in your SketchUp tutelage) is the one that looks like a question mark. When you click this icon, it opens the Instructor dialog box, which contains information about the tool you're currently using.

Where are all the tools?

The Getting Started toolbar contains a small subset of the tools that you can use in SketchUp. The thinking (which I agree with, incidentally) is that seeing all the tools right away tends to overwhelm new users, so having a limited selection helps people.

To get access to more tools (through toolbars, anyway — you can always access everything through the menus), you do different things, depending on which operating system you use:

✔ **Windows:** Choose View➪Toolbars. The mother lode! I recommend starting off with

the Large Tool Set to begin with and then adding toolbars as you need them (and as you figure out what they do).

✔ **Mac:** Choose View➪Tool Palettes➪Large Tool Set. To add even more tools, right-click the Getting Started toolbar (the one right above your modeling window) and choose Customize Toolbar. Now drag whatever tools you want onto your toolbar and click the Done button.

Taking a peek at the dialog boxes

Most graphics programs have a ton of little controller boxes that float around your screen, and SketchUp is no exception. After the dialog boxes are open, you can "dock" them together by moving them close to each other, but most people I know end up with them all over the place — me included. Dialog boxes in SketchUp contain controls for all kinds of things; here are the ones that I think deserve special attention:

✔ **Preferences:** While the Model Info dialog box (see the next point) contains settings for the SketchUp file you have open right now, the Preferences dialog box has controls for how SketchUp behaves *no matter what* file you have open. Pay particular attention to the Shortcuts panel, where you can set up keyboard shortcuts for any tool or command in the program.

On the Mac, the Preferences dialog box is on the SketchUp menu, which doesn't exist in the Windows version of SketchUp.

Some changes to the Preference settings don't take effect until you open another file or restart SketchUp altogether, so don't worry if you can't see a difference right away.

✔ **Model Info:** This dialog box is, to quote the bard, the mother of all dialog boxes. It has controls for everything under the sun; you should definitely open it and take your time going through it. Chances are, the next time you can't find the setting you're looking for, it's in Model Info.

✔ **Entity Info:** This little guy is small, but it shows information about *entities* — edges, faces, groups, components, and lots of other things — in your model. Keeping it open is a good idea because it helps you see what you've selected.

✔ **Instructor:** The Instructor does only one thing: It shows you how to use whatever tool happens to be activated. While you're discovering SketchUp, keep the Instructor dialog box open off to the side. You can also open it at any time by clicking the little ? icon in the status bar, at the bottom of your screen.

Chapter 2

Establishing the Modeling Mind-Set

*W*hen you were learning how to drive a car, you probably didn't just get behind the wheel, step on the gas, and figure it out as you went along. (If you did, you probably have bigger things to worry about than getting started with SketchUp.) My point is, you should really know several things before you get started. This chapter introduces those things — concepts, really — that can make your first few hours with SketchUp a lot more productive and fun.

So here's the deal: I've divided this chapter into three main parts:

✔ The first part talks about edges and faces — the basic *stuff* that SketchUp models are made of.

✔ The second part deals with how SketchUp lets you work in 3D (three dimensions) on a 2D (flat) surface — namely, your computer screen. Understanding how SketchUp represents depth is everything when making models. If you've never used 3D modeling software before, pay close attention to the middle part of this chapter.

✔ The final part of this chapter is all about the things you need to do all the time — things like navigating around your model, drawing lines, selecting objects, and working with accurate measurements.

All about Edges and Faces

In SketchUp, everything is made up of one of two kinds of things: edges and faces. They're the basic building blocks of every model you'll ever make.

Collectively, the edges and faces in your model are *geometry*. When someone (including me) refers to geometry, she's talking about edges and faces. Other modeling programs have other kinds of geometry, but SketchUp is pretty simple. That's a good thing — there's less to keep track of.

The drawing on the left in Figure 2-1 is a basic cube drawn in SketchUp; it's composed of 12 edges and 6 faces. The model on the right is a lot more complex, but the geometry's the same; it's all just edges and faces.

Edge   Face   Face   Edge

Figure 2-1:
SketchUp
models are
made from
edges and
faces.

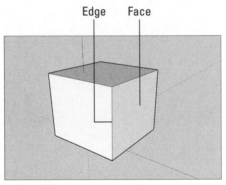 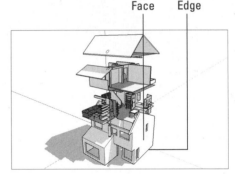

Living on (with, actually) the edge

Edges are lines. You can use lots of tools to draw them, erase them, move them, hide them, and even stretch them. Here are some things you ought to know about SketchUp edges:

- **Edges are always straight.** Not only is everything in your SketchUp model made up of edges, but all those edges are also perfectly straight. Even arcs and circles are made of small straight-line segments, as shown in Figure 2-2.

- **Edges don't have a thickness.** This one's a little tricky to get your head around. You never have to worry about how thick the edges in your model are because that's just not how SketchUp works. Depending on how you choose to *display* your model, your edges may look like they have different thicknesses, but your edges themselves don't have a built-in thickness. You can read more about making your edges look thick in Chapter 9.

✓ **Just because you can't see the edges doesn't mean they're not there.**
Edges can be hidden so that you can't see them; doing so is a popular
way to make certain forms. Take a look at Figure 2-3. On the left is a
model that looks rounded. On the right, I've made the hidden edges visible as dashed lines — see how even surfaces that look smoothly curved
are made of straight edges?

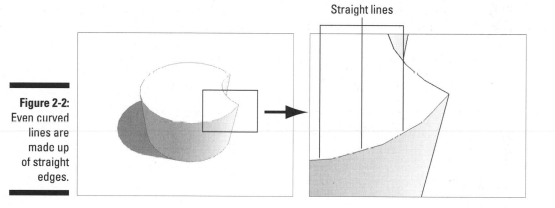

Straight lines

Figure 2-2:
Even curved
lines are
made up
of straight
edges.

These edges are smoothed, but still there

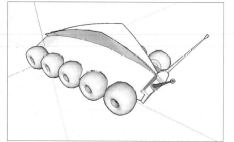
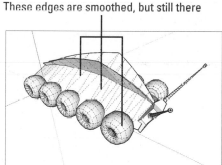

Figure 2-3:
Even
organic
shapes and
curvy forms
are made up
of straight
edges.

Facing the facts about faces

Faces are surfaces. If you think of SketchUp models as being made of toothpicks and paper (which they kind of are), faces are basically the paper.
Here's what you need to know about them:

✔ **You can't have faces without edges.** To have a face, you need to have at least three *coplanar* (on the same plane) edges that form a loop. In other words, a face is defined by the edges that surround it, and those edges all have to be on the same, flat *plane*. Because you need at least three straight lines to make a closed shape, faces must have at least three sides. There's no limit to the number of sides a SketchUp face can have, though. Figure 2-4 shows what happens when you get rid of an edge that defines one or more faces.

✔ **Faces are always flat.** In SketchUp, even surfaces that look curved are made up of multiple, flat faces. In the model shown in Figure 2-5, you can see that what looks like organically shaped surfaces (on the left) are really just lots of smaller faces (on the right). To make a bunch of flat faces look like one big, curvy surface, the edges between them are *smoothed;* you can find out more about smoothing edges in Chapter 6.

✔ **Just like edges, faces don't have any thickness.** If faces are a lot like pieces of paper, they're *infinitely thin* pieces of paper — they don't have any thickness. To make a thick surface (say, like a 6-inch-thick wall), you need to use two faces side by side.

Figure 2-4:
You need at least three edges to make a face.

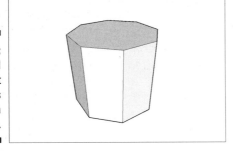
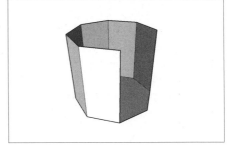

Each of these triangles is perfectly flat

Figure 2-5:
All faces are flat, even the ones that make up larger, curvy surfaces.

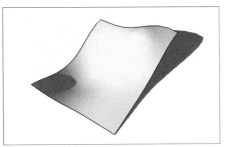
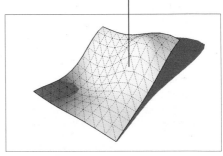

Understanding the relationship between edges and faces

Now that you know that models are made from edges and faces, you're most of the way to understanding how SketchUp works. Here's some information that should fill in the gaps (and also check out additional resources on this book's companion Web site; see the *Introduction* for details about the site):

- ✔ **Every time SketchUp can make a face, it will.** There's no such thing as a "Face tool" in this software; SketchUp just automatically makes a face every time you finish drawing a closed shape out of three or more coplanar edges. Figure 2-6 shows this in action: As soon as I connect the last edge that I draw to the first one to close the loop, SketchUp creates a face.

- ✔ **You can't stop SketchUp from creating faces, but you can erase them if you want.** If SketchUp creates a face you don't want, just right-click the face and choose Erase from the context menu. That face is deleted, but the edges that defined it remain. (See Figure 2-7.)

- ✔ **If you delete an edge that defines a face, that face will be deleted, too.** When I erase one of the edges in the cube (with the Eraser tool, in this case), *both* the faces that were defined by that edge disappear. This happens because it's impossible to have a face without also having all its edges.

- ✔ **Retracing an edge re-creates a missing face.** If you already have a closed loop of coplanar edges but no face (because you erased it, perhaps), you can *redraw* one of the edges to make a new face. Just use the Line tool to trace over one of the edge segments, and a face reappears. (See Figure 2-8.)

Figure 2-6: SketchUp automatically makes a face whenever you create a closed loop of coplanar edges.

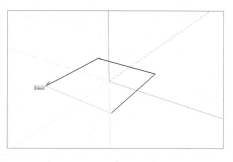 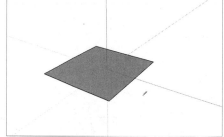

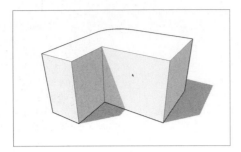
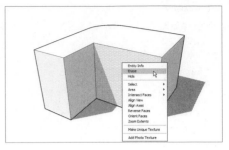

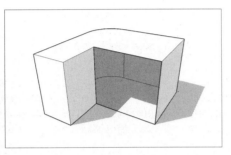

Figure 2-7:
You can delete a face without deleting the edges that define it.

✔ **Drawing an edge all the way across a face splits the face in two.** When you draw an edge (like with the Line tool) from one side of a face to another, you cut that face in two. The same thing happens when you draw a closed loop of edges (like a rectangle) on a face — you end up with two faces, one "inside" the other. In Figure 2-9, I split a face in two with the Line tool and then I extrude one of them out a little bit with the Push/Pull tool.

✔ **Drawing an edge that crosses another edge automatically splits both edges where they touch.** In this way, you can split simple edges you draw with the Line tool, as well as edges that are created when you draw shapes like rectangles and circles. Most of the time, this auto-slicing is desirable, but if it's not, you can always use groups and components to keep things separate. Flip to the first part of Chapter 5 for more information.

Figure 2-8:
Just retrace any edge on a closed loop to tell SketchUp to create a new face.

Drawing an edge from here...

...to here...

...causes this face to be created

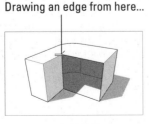
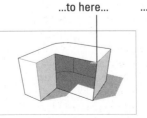
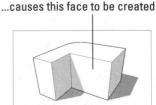

Figure 2-9:
Splitting a
face with an
edge, and
then extrud-
ing one of
the new
faces.

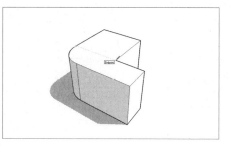 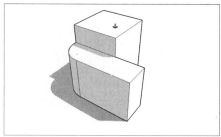

Drawing in 3D on a 2D Screen

For computer programmers, letting you draw 3D objects on your screen is a difficult problem. You wouldn't think it'd be such a big deal; after all, people have been drawing in perspective for a very long time. If some old guy could figure it out 500 years ago, why should your computer have problems?

The thing is, human perception of depth on paper is a trick of the eye. And of course, your computer doesn't have eyes that enable it to interpret depth without thinking about it. You need to give your computer explicit instructions. In SketchUp, this means using drawing axes and inferences, as I explain in the sections that follow.

Don't worry about drawing in perspective

Contrary to popular belief, modeling in SketchUp doesn't involve drawing in perspective and letting the software figure out what you mean. This turns out to be a very good thing for two reasons:

✔ **Computers aren't very good at figuring out what you're trying to do.** This has probably happened to you: You're working away at your computer, and the software you're using tries to "help" by guessing what you're doing. Sometimes it works, but most of the time it doesn't, and eventually, it gets really annoying. Even if SketchUp *could* interpret your perspective drawings, you'd probably spend more time correcting its mistakes than actually building something.

✔ **Most people can't draw in perspective anyway.** I can see you nodding because even if you're one of the few folks who *can,* you know darn well that most people couldn't draw an accurate 3D view of the inside of a room if their life depended on it — drawing just isn't one of the things people are taught, unfortunately. So even if SketchUp *did* work by turning your 2D perspective drawings into 3D models (which it most certainly doesn't), the vast majority of those who "can't draw" couldn't use it. And that would be a shame because building 3D models is a real kick.

Giving instructions with the drawing axes

Color Plate 1 is a shot of the SketchUp modeling window, right after you create a new file. See the three colored lines that cross in the lower-left corner of the screen? These are the *drawing axes,* and they're the key to understanding how SketchUp works. Simply put, you use SketchUp's drawing axes to figure out where you are (and where you want to go) in 3D space. When you're working with the color axes, you need to keep three important things in mind:

✔ **The red, green, and blue drawing axes define 3D space in your model.** If you were standing at the spot where all three axes meet (the *axis origin*), the blue axis would run vertically, passing through your head and feet. The red and green axes define the ground plane in SketchUp; you'd be standing on top of them. The axes are all at right angles to one another, and extend to infinity from the origin.

✔ **When you draw, move, or copy something parallel to one of the colored axes, you're working in that color's direction.** Take a look at Color Plate 2. In the first image, I'm drawing a line parallel to the *red* axis, so I would say I'm drawing "in the *red* direction." I'm sure that the line I'm drawing is parallel to the red axis because it turns red to let me know. In the second image, I'm moving a box parallel to the *blue* axis, so I'm "moving in the *blue* direction." I know I'm parallel to the blue axis because a dotted, blue line appears to tell me so.

✔ **The whole point of using the red, green, and blue axes is to let SketchUp know what you mean.** Remember that the big problem with modeling in 3D on a computer is the fact that you're working on a 2D screen. Consider the example shown in Color Plate 3: If I click the cylinder with the Move tool and move my cursor *up,* how is SketchUp supposed to know whether I mean to move it *up* in space (above the ground) or *back* in space? That's where the colored axes come into play: If I want to move it *up,* I go in the *blue* direction. If I want to move it *back,* I follow the *green* direction (because the green axis happens to run from the front to the back of my screen).

When you work in SketchUp, you use the colored drawing axes *all the time.* They're not just handy; they're what make SketchUp work. Having colored axes (instead of ones labeled *x, y,* and *z*) lets you draw in 3D space without typing commands to tell your computer where you want to draw. They make modeling in SketchUp quick, accurate, and relatively intuitive. All you have to do is make sure that you're working in your intended color direction as you model by lining up your objects with the axes and watching the screen tips that tell you what direction you're working in. After your first couple hours with the software, paying attention to the colors becomes second nature — I promise.

Keeping an eye out for inferences

If you've spent any time fiddling with SketchUp, you've noticed all the little colored circles, squares, dotted lines, yellow tags, and other doodads that show up as you move your cursor around your modeling window. All this stuff is referred to collectively as SketchUp's *inference engine,* and its sole purpose is to help you while you build models. Luckily, it does. Without inferences (the aforementioned doodads), SketchUp wouldn't be very useful.

Point inferences

Generally, SketchUp's inferences help you be more precise. *Point* inferences (see Color Plate 4) appear when you move your cursor over specific parts of your model. They look like little colored circles and squares, and if you pause for a second, a yellow label appears. For example, watching for the little green Endpoint inference (which appears whenever your cursor is over one of the ends of an edge) helps you accurately connect an edge you're drawing to the end of another edge in your model. Here's a list of them (I don't give descriptions because I think they're pretty self-explanatory):

- ✔ Endpoint (green circle)
- ✔ Midpoint (cyan or light blue circle)
- ✔ Intersection (red X)
- ✔ On Edge (red square)
- ✔ Center (of a circle or arc, dark blue)
- ✔ On Face (dark blue square)

In SketchUp, lines are called *edges,* and surfaces are called *faces.* Everything in your model is made up of edges and faces.

Linear inferences

As you've probably already noticed, color plays a big part in SketchUp's *user interface* (the way it looks). Maybe the best example of this is in the software's *linear* inferences — the "helper lines" that show up to help you work more precisely. Color Plate 5 is an illustration of them all in action, and here's a description of what they do:

- ✔ **On Axis:** When an edge you're drawing is parallel to one of the colored drawing axes, the edge turns the color of that axis.

- ✔ **From Point:** This one's a little harder to describe. When you move your cursor, sometimes you see a colored, dotted line appear. The dotted line means that your cursor is "lined up" with the point at the other end of the dotted line. Naturally, the color of the From Point inference corresponds to whichever axis you're lined up "on." Sometimes From Point inferences show up on their own, and sometimes you have to *encourage* them; see the section "Encouraging inferences," later in this chapter, for details.

🖝 **Perpendicular:** When you draw an edge that's perpendicular to another edge, the one you're drawing turns magenta (reddish purple).

🖝 **Parallel:** When the edge you're drawing is parallel to another edge in your model, it turns magenta to let you know. You tell SketchUp which edge you're interested in "being parallel to" by *encouraging* an inference.

🖝 **Tangent at Vertex:** This one applies only when you draw an arc (using the Arc tool) that starts at the endpoint of another arc. When the arc you're drawing is *tangent* to the other one, the one you're drawing turns cyan. *Tangent,* in this case, means that the transition between the two arcs is smooth.

One of the most important inferences in SketchUp is one that you probably didn't even realize was an inference: Unless you specifically start on an edge or a face in your model, you always draw on the ground plane by default. That's right — if you just start creating stuff in the middle of nowhere, SketchUp just assumes that you mean to draw on the ground.

Using inferences to help you model

A big part of using SketchUp's inference engine involves *locking* and *encouraging* inferences — sometimes even simultaneously. At first, these actions seem a little like that thing where you pat your head and rub your stomach at the same time, but with practice, they get easier.

Locking inferences

If you hold down the Shift key when you see any of the first four types of linear inferences described previously, that inference gets *locked* — and stays locked until you release Shift. When you lock an inference, you constrain whatever tool you're using to work only in the direction of the inference you locked. Confused? Check out the following example for some clarity.

In Color Plate 6, locking a blue On Axis inference while I'm using the Line tool would be useful. I want to draw a vertical line that's exactly as tall as the peak of the house's roof, so here's what I do:

1. Click once to start drawing an edge.

2. Move my cursor up until I see the edge I'm drawing turn blue.

   This is the blue On Axis inference that lets me know I'm exactly parallel to the blue drawing axis.

3. Hold down the Shift key to lock the inference I see.

   My edge gets thicker to let me know it's locked, and now I can draw only in the blue direction (no matter where I move my cursor).

4. Click the peak of the roof to make my vertical edge end at exactly that height.

5. Release Shift to unlock the inference.

Encouraging inferences

Sometimes, an inference you need doesn't show up on its own — when this happens, you have to *encourage* it. To encourage an inference, just hover your cursor over the part of your model you want to "infer" from and then slowly go back to whatever you were doing when you decided you could use an inference. The following example demonstrates how to encourage an inference.

Color Plate 7 shows a model of a cylinder. I want to start drawing an edge that lines up perfectly with the center of the circle on top of the cylinder, but I don't want it to start at the center itself. Follow these steps:

1. **Hover (don't click) over the edge of the circle for about two seconds.**

2. **Move slowly toward the middle of the circle until the Center Point inference appears.**

3. **Hover (still don't click) over the center point for a couple seconds.**

4. **Move your cursor slowly in the direction of where you want to start drawing your edge.**

    A dotted From Point inference appears.

5. **Click to start drawing your edge.**

Warming Up Your SketchUp Muscles

I can think of seven activities you need to do every time you use SketchUp. Formal-education types would probably call them *core competencies,* but I find language like that tends to put people to sleep. Whatever you care to call these activities, I introduce them all in the following sections, so you can come back and get a quick refresher whenever you want.

Getting the best view of what you're doing

Using SketchUp without learning how to orbit, zoom, and pan is like trying to build a ship in a bottle. In the dark. With your hands tied behind your back. Using chopsticks. Get the picture?

Fully half of modeling in SketchUp uses the aforementioned navigation tools, which let you change your view so that you can see what you're doing. Most people who try to figure out SketchUp on their own take too long to understand this; they spend hours squinting, grunting, and having an all-around miserable time trying to "get at" what they're working on. The following sections help you avoid the headache (literally).

SketchUp has three tools that are dedicated to letting you get a better view of your model. I usually call them the Big Three, but I'm a little afraid of lawsuits from big companies in Detroit, so I'll just refer to them collectively as the navigation tools.

Going into orbit

Hold a glass of water in your hand. Now twist and turn your wrist around in every direction so that the water's all over you and the rest of the room. Stop when the glass is completely empty. I think that's a pretty memorable way to find out about the Orbit tool, don't you?

Just as your wrist helps you twist and turn a glass to see it from every angle, think of using Orbit as the way to fly around your work. Figure 2-10 shows Orbit in all its glory.

Here's some stuff you need to know about using Orbit:

- ✔ **It's on the Camera menu.** By far the least productive way to use Orbit is to choose it from the Camera menu.

- ✔ **It's also on the toolbar.** The second-least productive way to activate Orbit is to click its button on the toolbar; it looks like two blue arrows trying to form a ball.

- ✔ **You can orbit with your mouse.** Here's how you should *always* orbit: Click the scroll wheel of your mouse and hold it down. Now move your mouse around. See your model swiveling around? Release the scroll wheel when you're done. Using your mouse to orbit means that you don't have to switch tools every time you want a better view, which saves you *truckloads* of time.

Zooming in and out

Hold your empty glass at arm's length. Close your eyes and then bring the glass rushing toward you, stopping right when it smashes you in the nose. Now throw the glass across the room, noticing how it shrinks as it gets farther away. That, in a nutshell, describes the Zoom tool.

You use Zoom to get closer to (and farther from) your model. If you're working on something small, you zoom in until it fills your modeling window. To see everything at once, zoom out. Figure 2-11 is a demonstration. I can think of a couple things to tell you about Zoom:

- ✔ **Just like Orbit, you can activate the Zoom tool in several ways.** The worst way is from the Camera menu; the next-worst way is to click the Zoom tool button in the toolbar. If you use Zoom either of these two ways, you actually zoom in and out by clicking and dragging up and down on your screen.

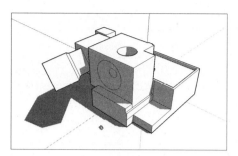

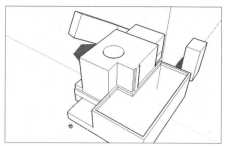

Figure 2-10: The Orbit tool lets you see your model from any angle.

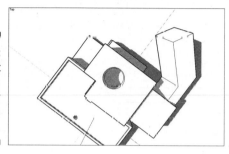

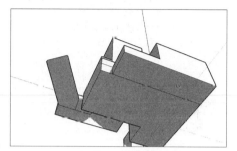

Zoomed in   Zoomed in even more

Figure 2-11: Use the Zoom tool to get closer to the action.

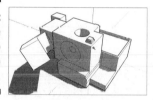

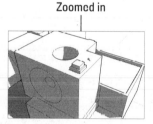

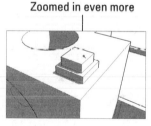

The best way to zoom is to roll your finger on the scroll wheel of your mouse to zoom in and out. Instead of clicking the scroll wheel to orbit, just roll your scroll wheel back and forth to zoom. And just like Orbit, using your mouse to zoom means that you don't have to switch tools — as soon as you stop zooming, you revert to whatever tool you were using before.

✔ **Use Zoom Extents to see everything.** Technically, Zoom Extents is a separate tool altogether, but I think it's related enough to mention here. If you want your model to fill your modeling window (which is especially useful when you "get lost" with the navigation tools — trust me, it happens to everyone), just choose Camera➪Zoom Extents.

When you use the Zoom tool, SketchUp zooms in on your cursor; just position it over whatever part of your model you want to zoom in on (or zoom out from). If your cursor isn't over any of your model's geometry (faces and edges), the Zoom tool doesn't work very well — you end up zooming either really slowly or really quickly.

Just panning around

Using the Pan tool is a lot like washing windows — you move the paper towel back and forth, but it stays flat and it never gets any closer or farther away from you. The Pan tool is basically for sliding your model view around in your modeling window. To see something that's to the right, you use Pan to slide your model to the left. It's as simple as that. You need to know these three things about Pan:

- ✔ **Pan is on the Camera menu.** But that's not where you should go to activate it.

- ✔ **Pan is also on the toolbar.** You *can* access the Pan tool by clicking its button on the toolbar (it looks like a severed hand), but there's a better way....

- ✔ **Hold down your mouse's scroll wheel button and press the Shift key.** When you do both at the same time — basically, Orbit+Shift — your cursor temporarily turns into the Pan tool. When your cursor does so, move your mouse to pan.

Drawing edges with ease

Being able to use the Line tool without having to think too much about it is *the* secret to being able to model anything you want in SketchUp. You use the Line tool to draw individual edges, and because SketchUp models are really just fancy collections of edges (carefully arranged, I'll admit), anything you can make in SketchUp, you can make with the Line tool.

SketchUp models are made up of edges and faces. Anytime you have three or more edges that are *connected* and *on the same plane,* SketchUp creates a face. If you erase one of the edges that *defines* (or borders) a face, the face disappears, too. Take a look at the section "All about Edges and Faces," earlier in this chapter, for more information on the relationship between edges and faces.

Drawing edges is simple. Just follow these steps:

1. **Select the Line tool (some people call it the Pencil tool).**

2. **Click where you want your line to begin.**

3. **Move your cursor to the desired endpoint for your line and click again to end.**

   Figure 2-12 demonstrates the basic idea.

   When you draw a line segment with the Line tool, notice how SketchUp automatically tries to draw another line? This is called *rubber banding* — the Line tool lets you continue to draw edge segments, automatically starting each new one at the end of the previous one you drew.

4. **When you want the Line tool to stop drawing lines, press the Esc key to snip the line at the last spot you clicked.**

SketchUp lets you draw lines in two ways: You can either use the click-drag-release method or the click-move-click one. They both work, of course, but I highly recommend training yourself to do the latter. You'll have more control, and your hand won't get as tired. When you draw edges by clicking and *dragging* your mouse (click-drag-release), you're a lot more likely to "drop" your line accidentally. Because the Line tool draws only straight lines, think about using it less like a pencil (even though it looks like one) and more like a spool of sticky thread.

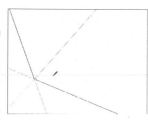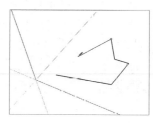

Figure 2-12: Use the Line tool to draw edges.

The Eraser tool is specifically designed for erasing edges; use it by clicking the edges you don't like to delete them. You can also *drag* over edges with the Eraser, but I think that's a little harder to get used to.

Injecting accuracy into your model

It's all well and fine to make a model, but most of the time, you need to make sure that it's accurate. Without a certain level of accuracy, the model isn't as useful. The key to accuracy in SketchUp is the little text box that lives in the lower-right corner of your SketchUp window — the one I point out in Figure 2-13.

This box is the Measurements box, and here are some things you can do with it:

- ✔ Make a line a certain length.
- ✔ Draw a rectangle a certain size.
- ✔ Push/pull a face a certain distance.
- ✔ Change the number of sides in a polygon.
- ✔ Move something a given distance.
- ✔ Rotate something by a certain number of degrees.
- ✔ Make a certain number of copies.
- ✔ Divide a line into a certain number of segments.
- ✔ Change your field of view (how much you can see).

Turning off rubber-banding lines

Depending on what you're making and on how you work, you may want to turn the Line tool's rubber-banding behavior off. To do so, follow these steps:

1. **Choose Window⇨Preferences (SketchUp⇨ Preferences on the Mac).**

2. **Choose the Drawing panel from the list on the left in the Preferences dialog box.**

3. **Deselect the Continue Line Drawing check box.**

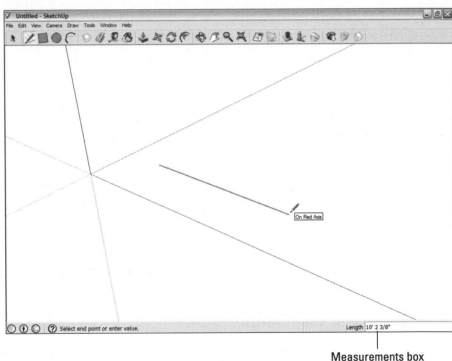

Figure 2-13: SketchUp's Measurements box is the key to working precisely.

Measurements box

Here's what you need to know about the Measurements box:

✔ **You don't have to click in the Measurements box to enter a number.** This one's a big one: SketchUp beginners often assume that they need to click in the Measurements box (to select it, presumably) before they can start typing. They (and you) don't — just start typing, and whatever you type shows up in the box automatically. When being precise, SketchUp always "listens" for you to type something in this box.

✓ **The Measurements box is context-sensitive.** What this box controls depends on what you happen to be doing at the time. If you're drawing an edge with the Line tool, it knows that whatever you type is a length; if you're rotating something, it knows to listen for an angle.

✓ **You the set the default units for the Measurements box in the Model Info dialog box.** Perhaps you want a line you're drawing to be 14 inches long. If inches are your default unit of measurement, just type **14** into the Measurements box and press Enter — SketchUp assumes that you mean 14 inches. If you want to draw something 14 *feet* long, type **14'**, just to let SketchUp know that you mean feet instead of inches. You can override the default unit of measurement by typing any unit you want. If you want to move something a distance of 25 meters, type **25m** and press Enter. You set the default units for the Measurements box in the Units panel of the Model Info dialog box (which is on the Window menu).

✓ **Sometimes, the Measurements box does more than one thing.** In certain circumstances, you can change its mode (what it "listens for") by typing a unit type after a number. For example, when you draw a circle, the default "value" in the Measurements box is the radius — if you type **6** and press Enter, you end up with a circle with a radius of 6 inches. But if you type **6s**, you're telling SketchUp that you want 6 *sides* (and not inches), so you end up with a circle with 6 sides. If you type **6** and press Enter, and then type **6s** and press Enter again, SketchUp draws a hexagon (a 6-sided circle) with a radius of 6 inches.

✓ **The Measurements box lets you change your mind.** As long as you don't do anything after you press Enter, you can always type a new value and press Enter again; there's no limit to the number of times you can change your mind.

✓ **You can use the Measurements box *during* an operation.** In most cases, you can use the Measurements box to be precise *while* you're using a tool. Here's how that works:

   1. Click once to start your operation (such as drawing a line or using the Move tool).

   2. Move your mouse so that you're going in the correct color direction. Be sure not to click again.

   If you're using the Line tool and you want to draw parallel to the green axis, make sure that the edge you're drawing is green.

   3. Without clicking the Measurements box, type the dimension you want.

   The dimension appears in the box.

   4. Press Enter to complete the operation.

✓ **You can also use the Measurements box *after* an operation.** Doing this revises what you've just done. These steps give you an idea of what I'm talking about:

   1. Complete your operation.

This may be drawing a line, moving something, rotating something, or any of the other things I mention at the beginning of this section.

2. *Before you do anything else, type whatever dimension you* intended *and then press Enter.*

Whatever you did is redone according to what you typed.

To give you a more concrete example, say I want to move my box (as shown in Figure 2-14) a total of 5 meters in the red direction (parallel to the red axis). Here's what I'd do:

1. With the Move tool, I click the box once to pick it up.

2. I move my mouse until I see the linear inference that tells me I'm moving in the red direction.

3. I type **5m** and then I press Enter. My box is positioned exactly 5 meters from where I picked it up.

4. On second thought, I don't think I'm happy with the 5 meters, so I decide to change it. I type **15m** and then press Enter again.

   The box moves another 10 meters in the blue direction.

5. I can keep changing the box's position until I'm happy (or bored).

Selecting what you mean to select

If you want to move (rotate, copy, and so on) something in your model, you need to select it first. When you select elements, you're telling SketchUp that *this* is the stuff you want to work with. To select things, you use (drum roll, please) the Select tool, which looks exactly the same as the Select tool in every other graphics program on the planet — it's an arrow. That's a good thing because selecting isn't the sort of thing you should have to relearn every time you pick up a new program. Here's everything you need to know about selecting things in SketchUp:

✔ **Just click anything in your model to select it (while you're using the Select tool, of course).**

✔ **To select more than one thing, hold down the Shift key while you click all the things you want to select. (See Figure 2-15.)**

The Shift key works both ways when it comes to the Select tool. You can use it to *add* to your set of selected objects (which I mention earlier), but you can also use it to *subtract* an object from your selection. In other words, if you have a bunch of stuff selected and you want to deselect something in particular, just hold down Shift while you click it — it isn't selected anymore.

Resizing everything with the Tape Measure tool

Consider that you've been working away in SketchUp, not paying particular attention to how big anything in your model is, when you suddenly decide that you need what you've made to be a specific size. SketchUp has a terrific trick for taking care of this exact situation: You can use the Tape Measure tool to resize your whole model based on a single measurement.

Here's how this tool works: In the following figure, I started to model a simple staircase, and now I want to make sure that it's the right size; doing so will make it easier to keep working on it. I know I want the *riser height* (the vertical distance between the steps) to be 7 inches, so this is what I do:

1. Select the Tape Measure tool (choose Tools⇨Tape Measure).

2. Make sure that the Tape Measure is in Measure mode by pressing the Ctrl key (Option on the Mac) until I don't see a plus sign (+) next to the Tape Measure cursor.

3. To measure the distance I want to change (in this case, the riser height), I click once to start measuring and click again to stop.

4. I type the dimension I *want* what I just measured to be: **7** (for 7 inches).

5. In the dialog box that appears, asking me whether I want to resize my whole model, I click the Yes button.

When I click the Yes button, my whole model is resized proportionately to the dimension I entered.

Measure from here...   ...to here

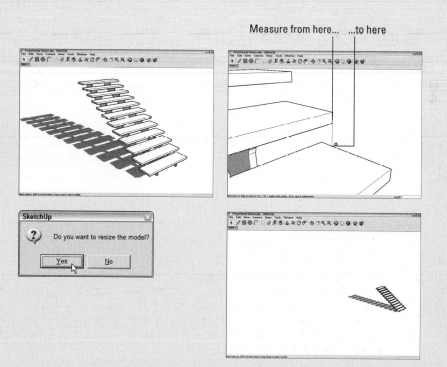

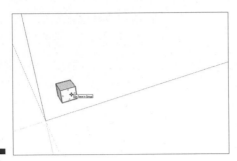 

Figure 2-14:
I move
the box 5
meters,
and then
I change
my mind
and move
it 15 meters
instead.

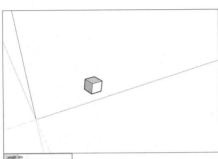 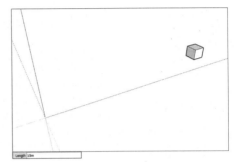

✔ **Selected objects in SketchUp look different depending on what kind of objects they are:**

• Selected edges and guides turn blue.

• Selected faces look covered in tiny blue dots.

• Selected groups and components (which you can read about in Chapter 5) get a blue box around them.

• Selected section planes (see Chapter 10 for more info on these) turn blue.

✔ **A much fancier way to select things in your model is to double- and triple-click them.** When you double-click a face, you select that face and all the edges that define it. Double-clicking an edge gives you that edge plus all the faces that are connected to it. When you *triple*-click an edge or a face, you select the whole object that it's a part of. Figure 2-16 shows what I mean.

✔ **You can also select several things at once by dragging a box around them.** You have two kinds of selection boxes; the one you use depends on what you're trying to select (see Figure 2-17):

• *Window selection:* If you click and drag from *left to right* to make a selection box, you create a window selection. In this case, only things that are *entirely* inside your selection box are selected.

• *Crossing selection:* If you click and drag from *right to left* to make a selection box, you create a crossing selection. With one of these, anything your selection box touches (including what's inside) is selected.

Click to select a face

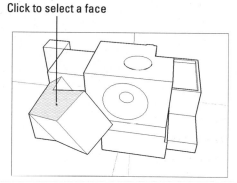

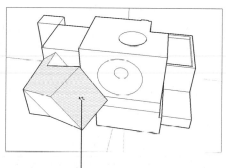

Figure 2-15: Click things with the Select tool to select them. Hold down Shift to select more than one thing.

Shift+click to add another face to your selection

Figure 2-16: Try single-, double-, and triple-clicking edges and faces in your model to make different kinds of selections.

Single-click selects a face

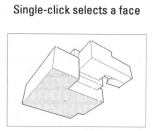

Double-click selects the face and edges

Triple-click selects the whole object

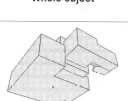

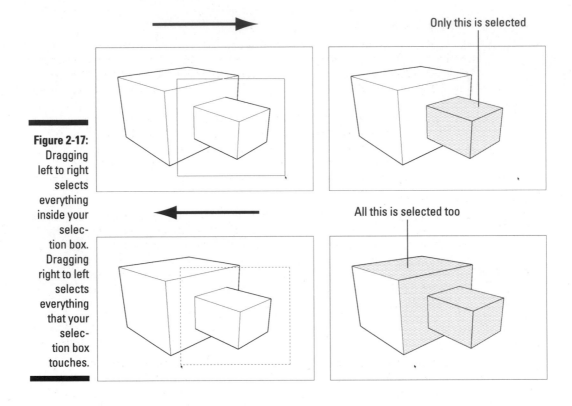

Only this is selected

Figure 2-17:
Dragging left to right selects everything inside your selection box. Dragging right to left selects everything that your selection box touches.

All this is selected too

I keep saying that selected stuff turns blue in SketchUp, but you can make it turn any color you want. Blue is just the default color for new documents you create. The "selected things" color is one of the settings you can adjust in the Styles dialog box; if you're interested, you can read all about styles in Chapter 9.

Just because you can't see something doesn't mean it isn't selected. Whenever you make a selection, it's a very good idea to orbit around to make sure you have only what you intended to get. Accidentally selecting too much is an easy mistake to make.

Moving and copying like a champ

To move things in SketchUp, use the Move tool. To make a copy of something, use the Move tool in combination with a button on your keyboard: the Ctrl key in Windows and the Option key on a Mac. It's really that simple.

Moving things

The Move tool is the one that looks like crossed red arrows. Using this tool involves clicking the entity you want to move, moving it to where you want it to be, and clicking again to drop it. The maneuver isn't complicated, but getting the hang of it takes a bit of time. Here are tips for using Move successfully:

✔ **Click, move, and click. Don't drag your mouse.** Just like using the Line tool, try to avoid the temptation to use the Move tool by clicking and dragging with your mouse; doing so makes things a lot harder. Instead, practice clicking once to pick things up, moving your mouse without any buttons held down, and clicking again to put down whatever you're moving.

✔ **Click a point that will let you position whatever you're trying to move** *exactly* **where you want when you drop it (instead of just clicking anywhere on the thing you're trying to move to pick it up).** Figure 2-18 shows two boxes that I want precisely to stack on top of each other. If I just click anywhere on the first box and move it over the other one, I can't place it where I want; SketchUp just doesn't work that way.

To stack the boxes precisely, I have to click the *bottom corner* of the soon-to-be top box to grab it there and then move my cursor over the *top corner* of the bottom box to drop it. Now my boxes are lined up perfectly.

✔ **Press the Esc key to cancel a move operation.** Here's something beginners do all the time: They start to move something (or start moving something accidentally) and then they change their minds. Instead of pressing Esc, they try to use Move to put things back the way they were. Inevitably, they don't, and things get messed up.

If you change your mind in the middle of moving something, just press Esc, and everything goes back to the way it was.

✔ **Don't forget about inferences.** To move something in one of the colored directions, just wait until you see the dotted On Axis linear inference appear; then hold down Shift to lock yourself in that direction. For more information about using SketchUp's inference engine, check out the section "Keeping an eye out for inferences," earlier in this chapter.

✔ **Don't forget about the Measurements box.** You can move things precise distances with the Measurements box; have a look at the section "Injecting accuracy into your model," earlier in this chapter.

Modeling with the Move tool

In SketchUp, the Move tool is very important for modeling; it's not just for moving whole objects. You can also use this tool to move just about anything, including *vertices* (edges' endpoints), edges, faces, and combinations of any of these. By moving only certain *entities* (all the things I just mention), you can change the shape of your geometry pretty drastically. Figure 2-19 shows what I mean.

Picking it up here...

...doesn't let you stack properly

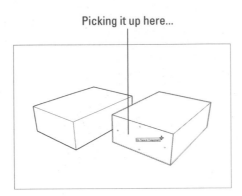
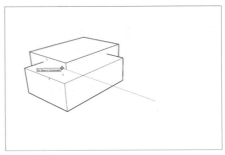

Figure 2-18:
To move
things
precisely,
choose
precise
points to
grab things
and put
them down.

Picking it up here...

...lets you stack precisely

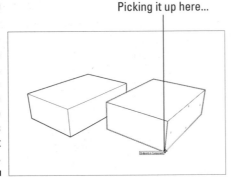
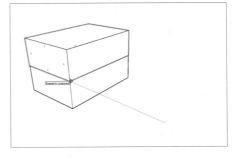

 Using the Move tool to create forms (instead of just moving them around) is an incredibly powerful way to work but isn't particularly intuitive. After all, nothing in the physical world behaves like the Move tool — you can't just grab the edge of a hardwood floor and move it up to turn it into a ramp in real life. In SketchUp, you can — and should.

To preselect or not to preselect

The Move tool works in two different ways; you eventually need to use them both, depending on what you're trying to move:

- **Moving a selection:** When you have a selection of one or more entities, the Move tool moves only the things you've selected. This comes in handy every time you need to move more than one object; Figure 2-20 shows how to move selected items with the Move tool.

- **Moving without a selection:** If you don't have anything selected, you can click anything in your model with the Move tool to move it around. Only the thing you click moves, as shown in Figure 2-21.

Moving a vertex

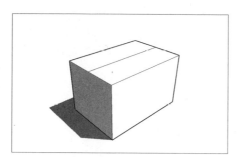

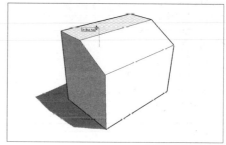

Moving an edge

Moving a face

Figure 2-19:
You can use
the Move
tool on verti-
ces, edges,
and faces
to model
different
forms.

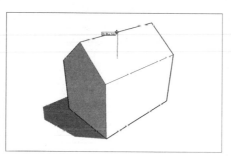

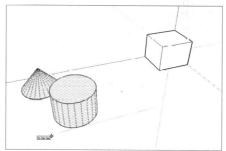

This isn't selected

...so it doesn't move with the rest

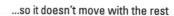

Figure 2-20:
Using the
Move tool
when you
have a
selection
moves only
the things
in that
selection.

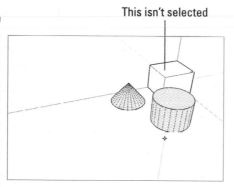

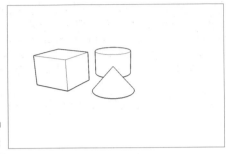
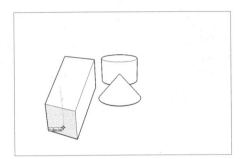

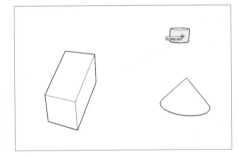

Figure 2-21:
Without
anything
selected,
you can
click any-
thing in your
model with
the Move
tool to start
moving it.

Making copies with the Move tool

Lots of folks spend time hunting around in SketchUp, trying to figure out how to make copies. It's very simple: You just press a *modifier key* (a button on your keyboard that tells SketchUp to do something different) while you're using the Move tool. Instead of moving something, you move a copy of it. Here are a couple things to keep in mind:

- ✓ **Press the Ctrl key to copy in Windows, and press the Option key to copy on a Mac.** This tells SketchUp to switch from Move to Copy while you're moving something with the Move tool. Your cursor shows a little + next to it, and your copy moves when you move your mouse. Figure 2-22 shows this in action.

  If you decide you don't want to make a copy, just press the Ctrl key (Option on a Mac) again to toggle back to Move; the + sign disappears.

- ✓ **Copying is just like moving, except you're moving a copy.** This means that all the same rules that apply to using the Move tool apply to making copies, too.

TIP

You can make more than one copy at a time. Perhaps I want to make five equally spaced copies of a column, as shown in Figure 2-23. All I have to do is move a copy to where I want my last column to be; then I type **5/** and press Enter. This makes five copies of my column and spaces them evenly between the first and last column in the row. Neat, huh?

If I know how far apart I want my copies to be, I can move a copy that distance, type **5x**, and press Enter. My five copies appear equally spaced in a *row*. (See Figure 2-24.)

Figure 2-22:
Press Ctrl
(Option on a
Mac) to tell
SketchUp
to make a
copy while
you move
something.

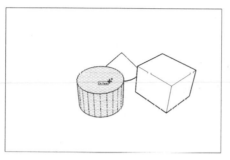 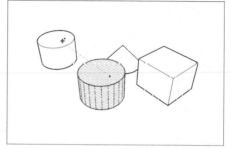

Figure 2-23:
Make evenly
spaced
copies by
typing the
number
of copies
you want
followed by
a slash (/)
and press
Enter.

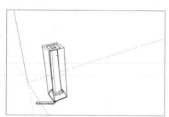 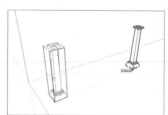

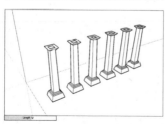

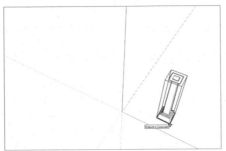

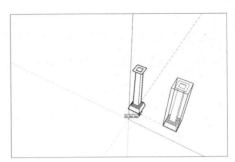

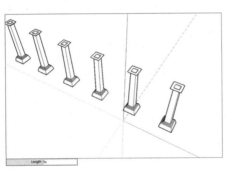

Figure 2-24:
To make multiple copies in a row, type the number of copies you want, type an x, and press Enter.

Rotating the right way

Using SketchUp's Rotate tool is a lot like using the Move tool. Despite the fact that rotation is pretty straightforward, I include a section about it in this chapter for one specific reason: The Rotate tool has a trick up its sleeve that most new modelers don't discover until hours after they could've used it. First things first, though:

- ✔ **It's better to preselect.** As with the Move tool, rotating something you've already selected is usually easier.

- ✔ **The Rotate tool can make copies, too.** Press the Ctrl key (Option on a Mac) to switch between rotating your original or rotating a copy. You can also make several copies at once; check out the earlier section "Making copies with the Move tool" in this chapter, to read about using *x* and / to create multiples while you rotate.

- ✔ **You can be precise.** Feel free to use your keyboard and the Measurements box to type exact angles while you're rotating. Take a look at "Injecting accuracy into your model" (earlier in this chapter) to find out more.

ON THE WEB

Telling SketchUp who's boss with Auto-Fold

This will happen to you sooner or later: As you try to move a vertex, an edge, or a face, you can't go in the direction you want. SketchUp doesn't like to let you create *folds* (when extra faces and edges are created in place of a single face) with the Move tool, so SketchUp constrains your movement to directions that won't add folds. To force the move, press and hold down the Alt key (Command on a Mac) while you move. When you do this, you're telling SketchUp that it's okay to proceed — to create folds if it has to. This is called *Auto-Fold,* and the following figure shows how it works.

Click once with the Move tool
to start moving

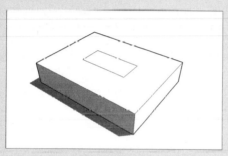

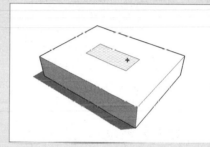

Hold down Alt (⌘ on a Mac)
and move your mouse

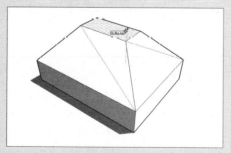

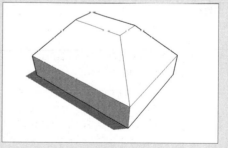

Using Rotate: The basic method

Follow these steps to rotate objects in your model:

1. **Select everything you want to rotate.**

2. **Activate the Rotate tool.**

   The default keyboard shortcut for Rotate is *Q,* just in case you're wondering.

3. **Click once to establish an axis of rotation.**

   Your *axis of rotation* is the theoretical line around which your selected objects will rotate; picture the axle of a wheel. Although it'd be nice if SketchUp drew the axis of rotation in your model, you just have to imagine it.

   As you move the Rotate tool's big protractor cursor around your screen, notice that the cursor sometimes changes orientation and color. When you hover over a face, the cursor re-aligns itself to create an axis of rotation that's perpendicular to that face. When the cursor is red, green, or blue, its axis of rotation is currently parallel to that colored axis.

   You can (and should) use *inference locking* when you're using the Rotate tool. Just hover over any face in your model that's perpendicular to the axis of rotation you want, hold down the Shift key to lock in that orientation, and click where you want your axis to be. See "Using inferences to help you model" (earlier in this chapter) to read all about it.

4. **Click again to start rotating.**

   Clicking part of the thing you're rotating is helpful, especially if you're rotating visually instead of numerically (by typing an angle).

5. **Move your mouse; then click again to finish rotating.**

   If you like, now is a good time to type a rotation angle and press Enter. As with everything else in SketchUp, you can be as precise as you want — or need — to be.

Using Rotate: The not-so-basic method

The basic method of using Rotate is fine when you need to rotate something on the ground plane, but this method isn't as useful when your axis of rotation isn't vertical. Finding a face to use to orient your cursor can be tricky or impossible, and that's where a lot of SketchUp modelers get hung up.

In version 6 of SketchUp, the software's designers introduced a feature that pretty much everybody realizes is great: You can establish a precise axis of rotation (the invisible line around which you're rotating) *without having any preexisting faces to use for orientation.* This makes rotating things about a million times easier, and those who use SketchUp a lot danced little jigs (albeit awkwardly) when we heard the news.

In this case, using Rotate goes from being a five-step operation to a seven-step one (check out Figure 2-25 for a visual explanation):

1. **Select everything you want to rotate.**

2. **Activate the Rotate tool.**

3. **Click once to establish your axis of rotation, but *don't let go* — keep your finger on your mouse button.**

4. **Drag your cursor around (still holding down the mouse button) until your axis of rotation is where you want it.**

   As you drag, notice your Rotate protractor changes orientation; the line from where you clicked to your cursor is the axis of rotation.

5. **Release your mouse button to set your axis of rotation.**

6. **Click (but don't drag) the point at which you want to "pick up" whatever you're rotating.**

7. **Click again to drop the thing you're rotating where you want it.**

Making and using guides

Sometimes you need to draw temporary lines while you model. These temporary lines, or *guides,* are useful for lining up things, making things the right size, and generally adding precision and accuracy to what you're building.

In previous versions of SketchUp, guides were called *construction geometry* because that's basically what they are: a special kind of entity that you create when and where you need them. They aren't part of your model because they're not edges or faces. This means that you can choose to hide them or delete them — they don't affect the rest of your geometry.

Figure 2-26 shows an example of guides in action. I use guides positioned 12 inches from the wall and 36 inches apart to draw the sides of a doorway. I use another guide 6 feet, 8 inches from the floor to indicate the top, and then I draw a rectangle, bounded by my guides, which I know is exactly the right size. When I'm done, I erase my guides with the Eraser tool, as I explain in a moment.

Click   Drag to locate axis of rotation

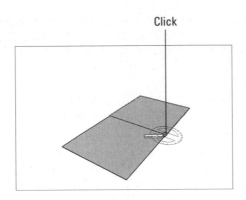

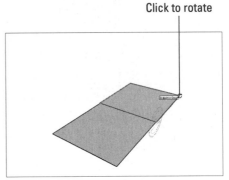

Release mouse to define axis   Click to rotate

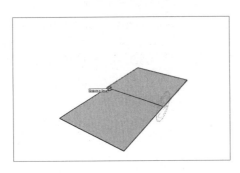

Click to finish rotating

Figure 2-25:
Define a
custom axis
of rotation
by click-
dragging
your mouse.

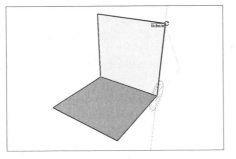

Creating guides with the Tape Measure tool

You can create three kinds of guides, and you use the Tape Measure tool to
make them all. (See Figure 2-27.)

✔ **Parallel guide lines:** Clicking anywhere (except the endpoints or mid-point) along an edge with the Tape Measure tool tells SketchUp that you want to create a guide parallel to that edge. (See Figure 2-27.) Just move your mouse, and you see a parallel, dashed line; click again to place the line wherever you want.

✔ **Linear guide lines:** To create a guide along an edge in your model, click one of the endpoints or the midpoint once, and then click again some-where else along the edge.

✔ **Guide points:** You may want to place a point somewhere in space; you can do exactly that with guide points. With the Tape Measure tool, click an edge's midpoint or endpoint, and then click again somewhere else in space. A little *x* appears at the end of a dashed line — that's your new guide point.

Here's an important point about the Tape Measure tool: It has two modes, and it creates guides in only one of them. Pressing the Ctrl key (Option on a Mac) toggles between the modes. When you see a + next to your cursor, your Tape Measure can make guides; when there's no +, it can't.

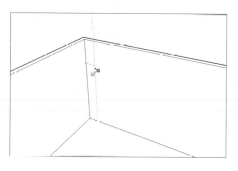
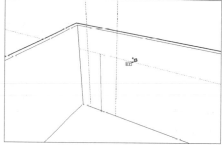

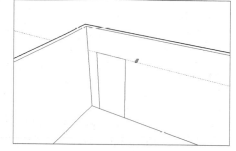

Figure 2-26:
Use guides to measure things before you draw.

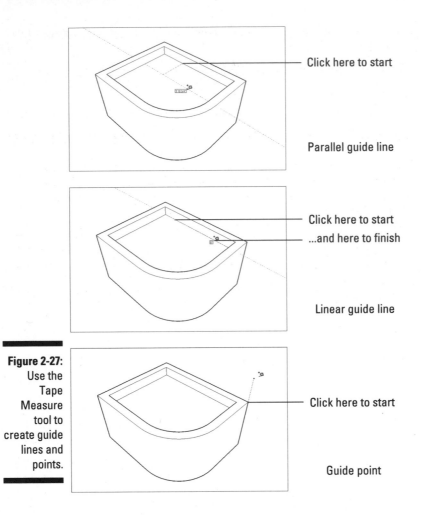

Click here to start

Parallel guide line

Click here to start

...and here to finish

Linear guide line

Figure 2-27:
Use the
Tape
Measure
tool to
create guide
lines and
points.

Click here to start

Guide point

Using guides to make your life easier

As you're working along in this software, you'll find yourself using guides all the time; they're an indispensable part of the way modeling in SketchUp works. Here's what you need to know about using them:

- ✔ **Position guides precisely using the Measurements box.** Check out the section "Injecting accuracy into your model," earlier in this chapter, to find out how.

- ✔ **Erase guides one at a time.** Just click or drag over them with the Eraser tool to delete guides individually. You can also right-click them and choose Erase from the context menu.

- ✔ **Erase all your guides at once.** Choosing Edit➪Delete Guides does just that.

- ✔ **Hide guides individually or all at once.** Right-click a single guide and choose Hide to hide it, or deselect View➪Guides to hide them all. It's a good idea to hide your guides instead of erasing them, especially while you're still modeling.

✔ **Select, move, copy, and rotate guides just like any other entity in your model.** Guides aren't edges, but you can treat them that way a lot of the time.

Painting your faces with color and texture

When adding colors and textures — collectively referred to in SketchUp as *materials* — to your model, there's really only one place you need to look, and one tool you need to use — the Materials dialog box and the Paint Bucket tool, respectively.

The Materials dialog box

To open the Materials dialog box (or Colors dialog box on the Mac), choose Window⇨Materials. Figure 2-28 shows what you see when you do. The Materials dialog box is radically different in the Windows and Mac versions of SketchUp, but that's okay — they do basically the same thing.

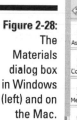

Figure 2-28:
The
Materials
dialog box
in Windows
(left) and on
the Mac.

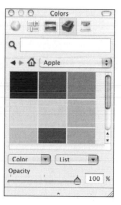

In SketchUp, you can choose from two kinds of materials to apply to the faces in your model:

✔ **Colors:** These are simple — colors are always solid colors. You can't have *gradients* (where one color fades into another), but you can pretty much make any color you want.

✔ **Textures:** Basically, a SketchUp texture is a tiny image — a photograph, really — that gets tiled over and over to cover the face you apply it to. If you paint a face with, say, a brick texture, what you're really doing is telling SketchUp to cover the surface with however many "brick photo" tiles it takes to do the job. The preview image you see in the Materials dialog box is actually a picture of a single texture image tile.

SketchUp comes with a whole bunch of textures, and you can always go online and choose from thousands more available for sale. And if that's *still* not enough, you can make your own (though the process is well beyond the scope of this humble tome).

On the Mac, you have to click the little brick icon in the Materials dialog box to see the textures libraries that ship with SketchUp; it's the drop-down list next to the little house icon.

The following facts about SketchUp materials are also handy to know as you work with them:

✔ **Materials can be translucent.** Sliding the Opacity slider makes the material you've selected more or less translucent, which makes seeing through windows in your model a lot easier.

✔ **Textures can have transparent areas.** If you take a look at the materials in the Fencing library, you'll notice that a lot of them look kind of strange; they have areas of black that don't seem right. These black areas are areas of transparency: When you paint a face with one of these textures, you can see through the areas that look black.

✔ **You can edit materials, and even make your own.** I'd consider this to be a pretty advanced use of SketchUp, so I don't talk about it in this book, but I thought you should at least know it's possible.

There's actually a third thing (besides colors and textures) you can apply to the faces in your models: photos. In fact, *photo-texturing* is an incredibly important part of some SketchUp workflows — especially those that relate to building models for Google Earth. As such, I dedicate Chapter 8 to the subject of modeling with photographs.

The Paint Bucket tool

The Paint Bucket tool looks just like — you guessed it — a bucket of paint. Activating it automatically opens the Materials dialog box so it's handy. Here's everything you need to know about the Paint Bucket tool:

✔ **You fill it by clicking in the Materials dialog box.** Just click a material to load your bucket and then click the face you want to paint. It's as simple as that.

✔ **Holding down the Alt key (Command on a Mac) switches to the Sample tool.** With the Sample tool, you can click any face in your model to load your Paint Bucket with that face's material. Release the Alt key to revert to the Paint Bucket tool.

✔ **Holding down the Shift key paints all similar faces.** If you hold down Shift when you click to paint a face, all faces in your model that match the one you click are painted, too. If things don't turn out the way you want, just choose Edit➪Undo to go back a step.

Chapter 3

Getting Off to a Running Start

In This Chapter

▶ Starting at the right place in SketchUp

▶ Building a simple model

▶ Changing the way the model looks

▶ Exporting a JPEG file that you can e-mail

*I*f you can't wait to get your hands dirty (so to speak), you've come to the right chapter. Here, I help you make a simple model step by step, spin it around, paint it, and even apply styles and shadows. You don't need to read another word of this book to be able to follow along, although I do refer you to chapters where you can find out more. Above all, these pages are about *doing* and about the basics of putting together the various SketchUp features to produce a knockout model in no time.

So what are you going to build? Perhaps a doghouse. The nice thing about doghouses is that they're a lot like peoplehouses in the ways that count: They have doors and roofs, and just about everybody has seen one.

One last thing: Just about every other piece of this book is written so that you can jump around to the bits you need; you don't have to follow a particular order. I'm afraid this chapter is the exception to that rule. If you want to follow along, start on this page and work your way to the end. Otherwise, the steps just won't make sense.

Setting Things Up

I know — setup is boring. Who wants to flip through menus and options dialog boxes instead of jumping in? I completely agree, so I keep this short and sweet. This section is just about making sure that you start at the right place. That's it.

Follow these steps to get ready:

1. **Launch Google SketchUp.**

2. **Choose your default settings.**

   If you've never launched SketchUp on your computer before, the Welcome to SketchUp dialog box appears. (See Figure 3-1.) Here's what to do if it pops up:

   a. *Click the Choose Template button.*

   b. *Choose one of the Architectural Design templates — it doesn't matter if you prefer Feet and Inches or Millimeters.*

   c. *Click the Start using SketchUp button to close the dialog box and open a new SketchUp file.*

   If the Welcome to SketchUp dialog box doesn't appear, someone (maybe you) has told the dialog box not to show up automatically on startup. Don't worry — just follow these steps to set things straight:

   a. *Choose Help➪Welcome to SketchUp from the menu bar.*

   b. *Follow Steps a and b in the preceding steps list.*

   c. *Open a new file by choosing File➪New.*

   If you're using the Pro version of SketchUp 8, the Welcome to SketchUp dialog box looks a little different — it includes information about your software license. The best place to go for help when you're having trouble with your license is the SketchUp Help Center. Choose Help➪Online Help Center to go there directly from SketchUp.

3. **Make sure that you can see the Getting Started toolbar.**

   Figure 3-2 shows the Getting Started toolbar. If it's not visible in your modeling window, choose View➪Toolbars➪Getting Started to make it show up. If you're on a Mac, choose View➪Show Toolbar.

4. **Clear your modeling window.**

   If this isn't the first time your computer has run SketchUp, you may see dialog boxes all over the place. If that's the case, just open the Window menu and deselect each window to close it.

Figure 3-1:
The Welcome to SketchUp dialog box, which pops up the first time you launch SketchUp.

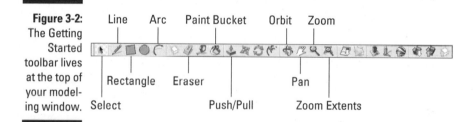

Figure 3-2:
The Getting Started toolbar lives at the top of your modeling window.

Line   Arc   Paint Bucket   Orbit   Zoom

Rectangle   Eraser   Pan

Select   Push/Pull   Zoom Extents

Making a Quick Model

Figure 3-3 shows what your computer screen looks like at this point. You should see a row of tools across the top of your modeling window, a little person, and three colored *modeling axes* (red, green, and blue lines).

Follow these steps to build a doghouse (and check this book's companion Web site at `www.dummies.com/go/SketchUp8FD` for additional help):

1. **Delete the little person on your screen.**

   Using the Select tool (the arrow on the far left of your toolbar), click the little person to select her (her name is Susan, in case that matters to you) and then choose Edit➪Delete.

2. **Choose Camera➪Standard Views➪Iso.**

   This command switches you to an *isometric* (3D) view of your model, which allows you to build something without having to "move around."

3. **Draw a rectangle on the ground.**

   Use the Rectangle tool (between the pencil and the circle on your toolbar) to draw a rectangle by doing the following:

   a. *Click once to place one corner on the left side of your screen.*

   b. *Click again to place the opposite corner on the right side of your screen.*

   Remember that you're in a 3D, *perspective,* view of the world, so your rectangle looks more like a diamond — 90-degree angles don't look like 90-degree angles in perspective. Figure 3-4 shows what you should aim for in this step.

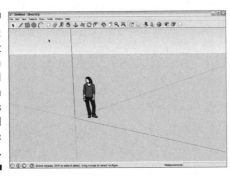 

Figure 3-3: This is what your screen should look like in Windows (left) and on a Mac (right).

It's important to draw the right kind of rectangle for this example (or for any model you're trying to create in Perspective view), so try it a few times until it looks like the rectangle in Figure 3-4. To go back a step, choose Edit➪Undo Rectangle; the last thing you did is undone. You can use Undo to go back as many steps as you like.

4. **Use the Push/Pull tool to extrude your rectangle into a box.**

   Use this tool (it looks like a brown box with a red arrow coming out the top) to pull your rectangle into a box by following these steps:

   a. *Click the rectangle once to start the push/pull operation.*

   b. *Click again, somewhere above your rectangle, to stop pushing/pulling.*

At this point, you should have something that looks like Figure 3-5; if you don't, use Push/Pull again to make your box look about the right height.

Click here to start drawing   Finish drawing here

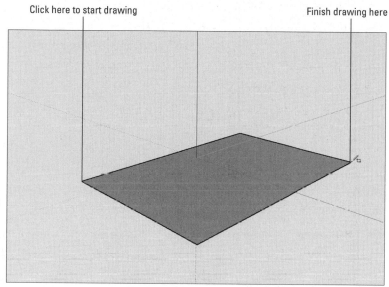

Figure 3-4:
Draw a 3D
rectangle on
the ground.

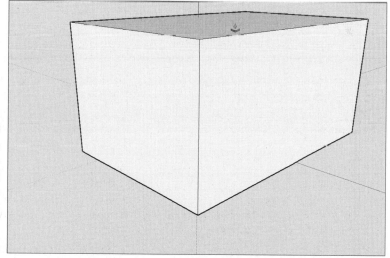

Figure 3-5:
Use the
Push/Pull
tool to
extrude your
rectangle
into a box.

If you're happily pushing/pulling away on your box and everything suddenly disappears, you pushed/pulled the top of your box all the way to the ground. Just choose Edit⇨Undo and keep going.

5. Draw a couple diagonal lines for your roof.

Use the Line tool (it's shaped like a pencil) to draw two diagonal edges (lines) that will form your peaked roof, as shown in Figure 3-6. Follow these steps:

Click here to start drawing   Click here to finish your first edge

Figure 3-6:
Draw two diagonal lines that will become your peaked roof.

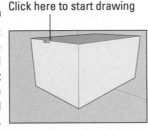 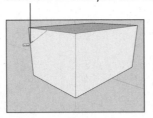 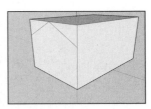

    a. *Click once at the midpoint of the top of your box's front face to start your line.*

    You know you're at the midpoint when you see a small, light blue dot and *Midpoint* appears. Move slowly to make sure that you see it.

    b. *Click again somewhere along one of the side edges of your box's front face to end your line.*

    Wait until you see a red *On Edge* square (just like the Midpoint one in the last step) before you click; if you don't, your new line won't end on the edge like it's supposed to.

    c. *Repeat the previous two steps to draw a similar (but opposite) line from the midpoint to the edge on the other side of the face.*

    Don't worry about making your diagonal lines symmetrical; for the purposes of this exercise, it's not important that they are.

6. Push/pull the triangles away to leave a sloped roof.

Use the Push/Pull tool (the same one you used back in Step 4) to get rid of the triangular parts of your box, leaving you with a sloped roof. Have a look at Figure 3-7 to see this in action and then follow these steps:

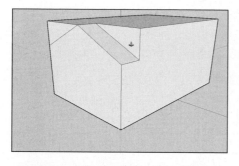 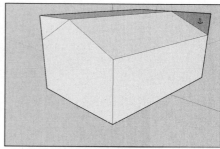

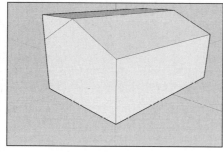 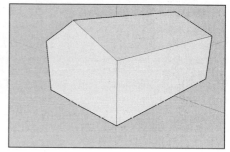

Figure 3-7:
Use the
Push/Pull
tool to form
a peaked
roof on
your box.

a. *Select the Push/Pull tool and then click the right triangular face once to start the push/pull operation.*

b. *Move your cursor to the right to push the triangle as far as it will go (even with the end of your box).*

c. *Click again (on the triangle) to end the push/pull operation and to make the triangular face disappear.*

d. *Still using the Push/Pull tool, double-click the left triangular face to repeat the previous push/pull operation, making that face disappear as well.*

7. Draw a rectangle on your front face.

Switch back to the Rectangle tool (which you use in Step 3) and draw a rectangle on the front face of your pointy box. Make sure that the bottom of your rectangle is flush with the bottom of your box by watching for the red On Edge hint to appear before you click. Check out Figure 3-8 to see what it looks like when you're done.

Finish here

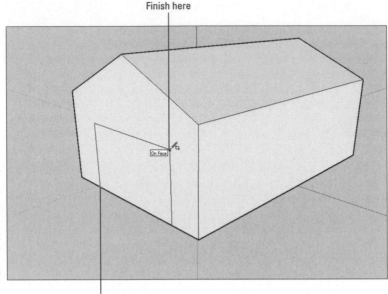

Figure 3-8:
A rectangle
drawn on
the front
of your
pointy box.

Click here to start drawing

Using the Rectangle tool is a two-step process: You click once to place one corner and again to place the opposite corner. Try not to draw lines and shapes in SketchUp by *dragging* your cursor; doing so makes things more difficult. Practice clicking once to start an operation, such as drawing a rectangle, and clicking again to stop.

8. Draw an arc on top of the rectangle you just drew.

Use the Arc tool (to the right of the Circle tool) to draw an arc on top of your rectangle (see Figure 3-9). Follow these steps to draw an arc:

a. *Click the upper-left corner of the rectangle to place one endpoint of your arc. Make sure that you see the green Endpoint hint before you click.*

b. *Click the upper-right corner of the rectangle to place the other endpoint of your arc.*

c. *Move your cursor up to bow out the line you're drawing into an arc and then click when you're happy with how it looks.*

9. Select the Eraser tool and then click the horizontal line between the rectangle and the arc to erase that line.

10. Push/pull the doorway inward.

Use the Push/Pull tool (which you're an old hand with by now) to push in the "doorway" face you created in Steps 7–9 just a bit.

Click here to start   Click here second

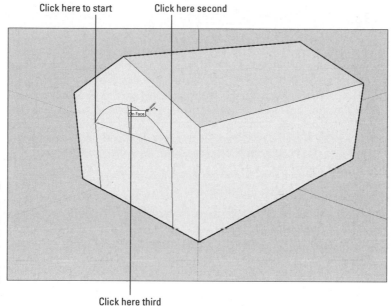

Click here third

Figure 3-9:
Draw an
arc on top
of your
rectangle.

Use Push/Pull by clicking a face once to start, moving your cursor to push/pull it in or out, and then clicking again to stop.

11. **Erase the horizontal line at the bottom of the doorway by clicking it with the Eraser tool.**

    This makes the line (and the whole face above it) disappear. Figure 3-10 shows what your finished doghouse looks like.

For a more detailed introduction to drawing lines and working with mid-points, angles, and more, flip to Chapter 2.

Figure 3-10:
Create
the door
opening
by erasing
its bottom
edge.

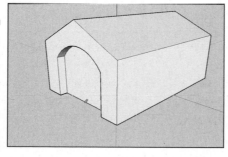
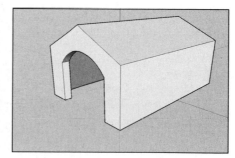

Slapping on Some Paint

I have an ulterior motive for getting you to paint your doghouse: To color it, you have to understand how to spin it around first. Moving around your model is *the most important* skill to develop when you're first figuring out SketchUp. Run through these steps to apply colors (and textures) to the faces in your model, and to find out about moving around while you're doing it:

1. **Choose Window⇨Materials to open the Materials dialog box (see Figure 3-11) and then click a color or texture you like.**

   When you do, you automatically pick up the Paint Bucket tool and fill it with your chosen material.

2. **Paint some of the faces in your model by clicking any face with the Paint Bucket tool.**

3. **Switch materials.**

   Choose another material from the Materials dialog box by clicking it.

4. **Paint the rest of the faces you can see. (See Figure 3-12.)**

   Loop through Steps 2 to 4 for as long as you like. Finding the Materials dialog box in SketchUp is just like getting a brand-new box of crayons when you were little (you know, the *big* box, with the built-in sharpener).

Click here to see your materials libraries

Figure 3-11: The Materials dialog box in Windows (left) and on a Mac.

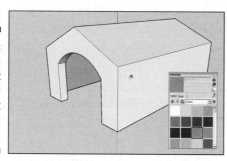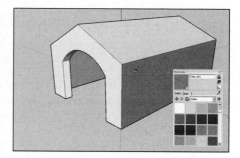

Figure 3-12:
Use the
Paint
Bucket tool
to paint
everything
you can see.

5. **Choose the Orbit tool; it's just to the left of the creepy white hand on the toolbar.**

6. **Click somewhere on the left side of your screen and *drag* your cursor over to the right (see Figure 3-13). Release your mouse button when you're done.**

   Your model spins, or *orbits!* Orbit around some more, just to get the hang of it.

If you're orbiting, and you've dragged your cursor over as far as it will go, and you haven't orbited as much as you wanted to, don't fret. Just release the mouse button, move your cursor over to where it was when you started orbiting, and orbit some more by clicking and dragging. You usually can't see what you want to see with a single orbit; you need a bunch of separate drags (separate orbits, I guess) to get things looking the way you want them to.

Figure 3-13:
Choose the
Orbit tool
and drag
your cursor
to spin your
model.

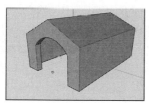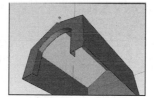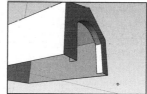

7. **Zoom in and out if you need to by selecting the Zoom tool and dragging your cursor up and down in your modeling window.**

   The Zoom tool looks like a magnifying glass, and it's on the other side of the creepy white hand. Dragging up zooms in, and down zooms out.

8. **If needed, move around in two dimensions with the Pan tool by selecting it and then clicking and dragging the Pan cursor inside your modeling window.**

   The Pan tool is the creepy white hand between Orbit and Zoom. Use Pan to slide your model around inside your modeling window without spinning it or making it look bigger or smaller. You can pan in any direction.

9. **Use the Orbit, Zoom, Pan, and Paint Bucket tools to finish painting your doghouse.**

   Now that you know how to move around your model, here's how I want you to paint it (Color Plate 8 shows what it should look like):

   • Paint the exterior walls red-brown.

   • Paint the roof light blue.

   • Paint the interior yellow-orange.

When you're just starting out, it's easy to get a little lost with the navigation tools (Orbit, Zoom, and Pan); it happens to everybody. If you find yourself in a pickle, just choose Camera➪Zoom Extents. When you do, SketchUp automatically plunks your model right in front of you; check out Figure 3-14 to see Zoom Extents in action.

Figure 3-14: Use Zoom Extents anytime you can't figure out where your model went.

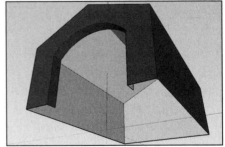

Chapter 2 is the place to look for extra tips and tricks on orbiting, zooming, and panning, as well as for details about using the Materials dialog box to paint the faces of an object.

Giving Your Model Some Style

SketchUp Styles allow you to change your model's appearance — the way it's drawn, basically — with just a few clicks of your mouse. You can create your own styles, of course, but SketchUp also comes with a library of pre-made ones that you can use without knowing anything about how they work.

Follow these steps to try a couple styles on your doghouse:

1. **Choose Window⇨Styles.**

   The Styles dialog box opens.

2. **Click the Select tab to show the Select pane.**

3. **In the Libraries drop-down list (see Figure 3-15), choose the Assorted Styles library.**

4. **Click through the different styles to see what they're about.**

   When you click a style in the Styles dialog box, that style is applied to your model. Figure 3-16 shows the doghouse with a few styles applied — can you figure out which ones?

5. **Go back to your original style.**

   Click the little house icon in the Styles dialog box to see a list of all the Styles you've applied to your model. Find the Architectural Design Style (it should be first in the list) and click to choose it. Chapter 9 explains styles in more detail.

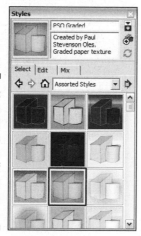

Figure 3-15: The Assorted Styles library is a sampler of ready-mixed SketchUp styles.

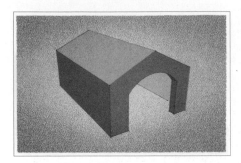

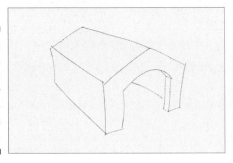
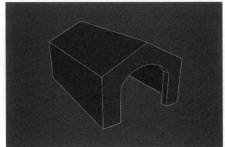

Figure 3-16:
The same doghouse with four very different styles applied to it.

Switching on the Sun

You're about to use what I consider to be one of SketchUp's best features: shadows. When you turn on shadows, you're activating SketchUp's built-in sun. The shadows you see in your modeling window are *accurate* for whatever time and location you set. For the purposes of this example, though, don't worry about accuracy. Go through these steps to let the light shine in:

1. **Use Orbit, Zoom, and Pan to get an aerial, three-quarter view of your doghouse, sort of like the one shown in Figure 3-17.**

2. **Choose Window⇨Shadows.**

   This opens the Shadow Settings dialog box (as shown in Figure 3-18).

3. **Select the Display Shadows check box to turn on the sun.**

   Your doghouse casts a shadow on the ground.

4. **In the Shadow Settings dialog box, move the Time slider back and forth.**

   Changing the time of day means that you're moving SketchUp's sun around in the sky. When the sun moves around, so do your shadows. Chapter 9 explains what I mean and explains more about fine-tuning light and shadows.

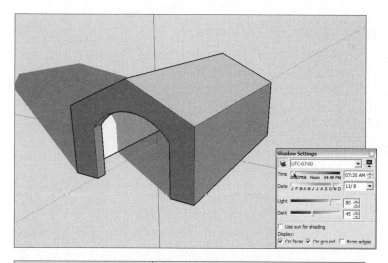

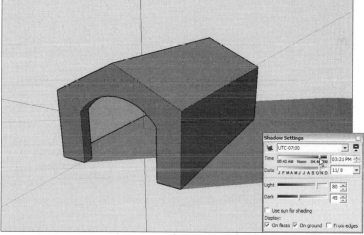

Figure 3-17:
Use Orbit, Zoom, and Pan to navigate around until your model looks something like this.

Slide back and forth

Figure 3-18:
The Shadow Settings dialog box controls the position of SketchUp's built-in sun.

Sharing Your Masterpiece

Now that you have a model that looks about the way you want it to, you probably want to show it to someone. The easiest way is to export a JPEG image that you can attach to an e-mail. Follow these steps, and you're on your way:

1. **Navigate around (using Orbit, Zoom, and Pan) until you like the view of your model that you see in your modeling window.**

2. **Choose File⇨Export⇨2D Graphic.**

3. **In the Export dialog box that opens, choose JPEG from the Export Type drop-down list.**

4. **Pick a location on your computer system and give your exported image a name.**

5. **Click the Export button to create a JPEG image of what's visible in your modeling window.**

Exporting a JPEG file is just one way to share models. To find out about all your options, see Part IV, which explains how to share your model on the Google 3D Warehouse, in Google Earth, as a printout, as an image or animation, or as a slick presentation that will (hopefully) impress all your friends.

Part II
Modeling in SketchUp

The 5th Wave   By Rich Tennant

"My brother built the barn, but the silo came from
a design I did in Google SketchUp."

In this part . . .

When all is said and done, SketchUp is about making 3D models. Sure, you can paint them, make animations with them, print them, and e-mail images of them to your friends, but first you have to actually create them.

Chapter 4 makes the assumption that, sooner or later, you're going to want to use SketchUp to make a model of a building. Starting with drawing simple floor plans and proceeding into the transition from 2D to 3D, modeling stairs and creating roofs, this chapter does its best to get you started.

Don't want to use SketchUp to just model buildings? Chapters 5 and 6 describe how to use things like components and the Follow Me and Scale tools to create some pretty advanced models.

In Chapter 7, I go over all the ways you can organize your model; doing so improves your modeling efficiency, your computer's performance, and ultimately, your sanity. You don't have to be a tidy person to "work clean" in SketchUp — I'm living proof.

Chapter 8 talks about how you can use photographs in SketchUp, both to "paint" your faces and to create whole models based on photographs of objects like buildings and furniture.

Chapter 4

Building Buildings

Even though SketchUp lets you make (just about) anything you can think of, certain forms are easier to make than others. Fortunately, these kinds of shapes are exactly the ones that most people want to make with SketchUp, most of the time. That's no accident; SketchUp was designed with architecture in mind, so the whole *paradigm* — the models made of faces and edges, and the kinds of tools SketchUp offers — is perfect for making things like buildings.

But what about curvy, swoopy buildings? You can use SketchUp to make those, too, but they're a little harder, so I don't think they're a good place to start. Because *most* people live in boxy places with right-angled rooms and flat ceilings, that kind of architecture is relatively easy to understand.

In this chapter, I introduce you to some of the fundamentals of SketchUp modeling in terms of making simple, rectilinear buildings. By writing about how to build certain kinds of things, instead of just describing what the individual tools do, I hope to make it easier for you to get started. Even if you're not planning to use SketchUp to model any of the things I describe, you can still apply these concepts to your creations.

One more thing: Just about every page in this chapter relies heavily on the stuff I introduce in Chapter 2. Working with the colored drawing axes, selecting objects, navigating around your model, and drawing things accurately are pretty key to making anything in SketchUp, so be prepared to flip back and forth while you're getting used to how things work. I like to use paper clips as bookmarks, but I'm sure you have your own method. . . .

Drawing Floors and Walls

Most floors and walls are flat surfaces, so it's easy to model them with straight edges and flat faces in SketchUp. In fact, chances are good that the first thing you ever model in SketchUp looks a lot like the floor and walls of a building.

I can think of two kinds of architectural models that most people want to create in SketchUp; how you approach modeling floors and walls depends entirely on the type of model you're making:

- ✔ **Exterior:** An exterior model of a building is basically just an empty shell; you don't have interior walls, rooms, or furniture to worry about. This type of model is a slightly simpler proposition for folks who are just starting out.

- ✔ **Interior:** An interior model of a building is significantly more complicated than an exterior-only one; dealing with interior wall thicknesses, floor heights, ceilings, and furnishings involves a lot more modeling prowess.

Here's the thing: Because everything in SketchUp is made of super-flat faces (they have no thickness), the only way to model a wall that's, say, 8 inches thick is to use two faces side by side and 8 inches apart. For models where you need to show wall thicknesses — namely, interior models — you have to use this two-face approach. Exterior models are easier to make because you can use single faces to represent walls. Figure 4-1 shows what I mean.

Single-face walls   Double-face walls

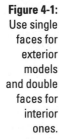

Figure 4-1:
Use single faces for exterior models and double faces for interior ones.

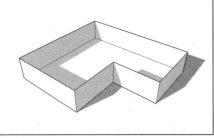
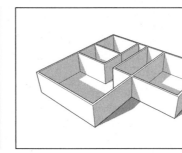

One of the biggest mistakes new SketchUp users make is attempting an inside-outside model right off the bat. Making a model that shows both the interior and the exterior of a building at the same time is, to be honest, *way* too hard when you're just getting started. Instead, build two separate models if you need both interior and exterior views. If you need a combination model later on, you can build it in a quarter of the time it took you to build either of the first two — I guarantee it.

Starting out in 2D

Of course, you can make a 3D model of a building's interior in lots of ways, but I'm going to show you the one I think makes the most sense. Basically, you draw a two-dimensional floorplan that includes all your interior and exterior walls, and then pull it up to the right height. In my method, you don't worry about doors, windows, or stairs until after your model is extruded; you put them in after, which I think is an easier and more logical way to work.

If you're using SketchUp Pro to import a floorplan from another piece of software like AutoCAD or Vectorworks, I think you'll appreciate this approach, which lets you take 2D information and make it 3D, regardless of where it comes from.

The thing to keep in mind is that SketchUp isn't a full-fledged drafting program, and it probably never will be.

If you're an architect-type who needs to do heavy-duty CAD (computer-aided drawing) work, you should probably be drafting in another piece of software and importing your work into SketchUp when you need 3D. If you're just drawing your house or the place where you work, look no further — SketchUp should do just fine.

Switching to a 2D view

If you're going to use SketchUp to draw a 2D plan, the first thing you need to do is orient your point of view. It's easiest to draw in 2D when you're directly above your work, looking down at the ground plane. You also want to make sure that you're not seeing things in perspective, which distorts your view of what you have.

Follow these simple steps to set up things (and find additional help on this book's companion Web site at www.dummies.com/go/SketchUp8FD):

1. **Create a new SketchUp file.**

   Depending on the template you have set to open when you create a new SketchUp file, you may already be in a 2D view. If all you see are the red and green axes on a white background, you can skip Step 2. Remember that you can always switch templates by choosing Help➪Welcome to SketchUp and clicking the Templates section of the dialog box that pops up.

2. **Choose Camera➪Standard➪Top.**

   This changes your viewpoint so that you're looking directly down at the ground.

3. **Choose Camera⇨Parallel Projection.**

Switching from Perspective to Parallel Projection makes it easier to draw plans in 2D. At this point, your modeling window should look like the one shown in Figure 4-2.

Feel free to delete Susan. That little diagonal line that's visible in your modeling window when you're in Top view is a top view of Susan — the 2D person who appears in every new SketchUp file you create. To get rid of Susan, just right-click her and choose Erase.

Dusting off SketchUp's drafting tools

Here's some good news: You don't need many tools to draft a 2D plan in SketchUp. Figure 4-3 shows the basic toolbar; everything you need is right there:

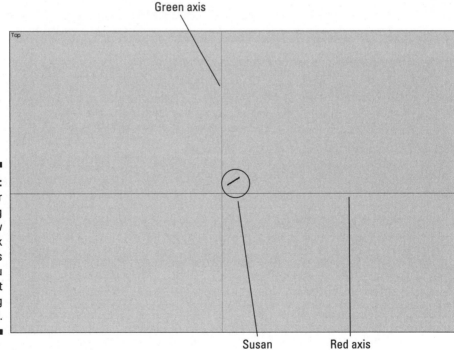

Green axis

Top

Figure 4-2: Your modeling window should look like this before you start drawing in 2D.

Susan   Red axis

Figure 4-3:
All the tools
you need to
draft in 2D
in SketchUp
are on the
basic
toolbar.

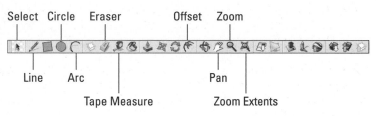

Select Circle Eraser   Offset Zoom

Line   Arc   Pan

Tape Measure   Zoom Extents

 ✔ **Line tool:** You use the Line tool (which looks like a pencil) to draw
   edges, which are one of the two basic building blocks of SketchUp
   models. Fundamentally, you click to start drawing an edge and click
   again to finish it. (You can find lots more information about drawing
   lines in Chapter 2.)

 ✔ **Eraser tool:** Use the Eraser to erase edges; see Figure 4-4. Keep in mind
   that you can't use the Eraser to delete faces, though erasing one of the
   edges that defines a face automatically erases that face, too. Take a look
   at the section about edges and faces at the beginning of Chapter 2 for
   more detail on using the Eraser tool on edges. You can use the Eraser in
   two ways:

   • *Clicking:* Click edges to erase them one at a time.

   • *Dragging:* Click and drag over edges to erase them; this is faster if
     you have lots of edges you want to erase.

Eraser tool   Edge has been erased

Figure 4-4:
Use the
Eraser tool
to erase
edges.
Erasing an
edge that
defines a
face erases
that face,
too.

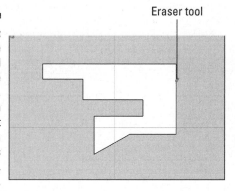
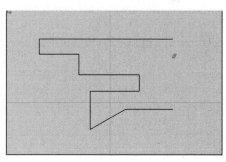

✔ **Circle tool:** Drawing circles in SketchUp is pretty easy: Click once to define the center and again to define a point on the circle (which also defines the radius). To enter a precise radius, just draw a circle, type a radius, and press Enter (see Figure 4-5). For more information on typing while you draw, check out the section on model accuracy in Chapter 2.

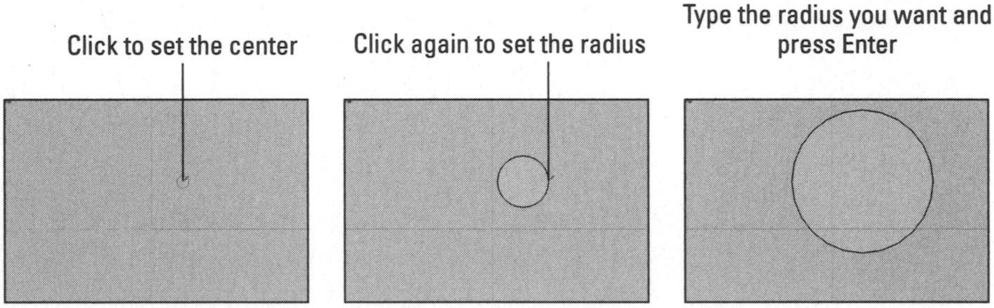

Click to set the center   Click again to set the radius   Type the radius you want and press Enter

Figure 4-5:
Drawing circles is easy with the Circle tool.

✔ **Arc tool:** To draw an arc, click once to define one end, again to define the other end, and a third time to define the *bulge* (how much the arc sticks out). If you want, you can type a radius after you draw your arc by entering the radius, the units, and the letter *r.* If you want an arc with a radius of 4 feet, draw it however big, type **4'r**, and press Enter. This is shown in Figure 4-6.

✔ **Offset tool:** The Offset tool helps you draw edges that are a constant distance apart from edges that already exist in your model. Pictures are usually better than words, so take a look at Figure 4-7. Using Offset on the shape I've drawn lets me create another shape that's exactly 6 inches bigger all the way around (middle image), or 6 inches *smaller* all the way around (right image). Offsetting edges is a useful way to create things like doorways and window trim.

You can use Offset in two ways; for both ways you click once to start offsetting and again to stop:

• *Click a face to offset all its edges.* If nothing is selected, clicking a face with the Offset tool lets you offset all that face's edges by a constant amount (as shown in Figure 4-7).

• *Preselect one or more coplanar (on the same plane) edges and then use Offset.* If you have selected edges, you can use Offset on just those edges; this comes in handy for drawing things like doorframes and balconies, as shown in Figure 4-8.

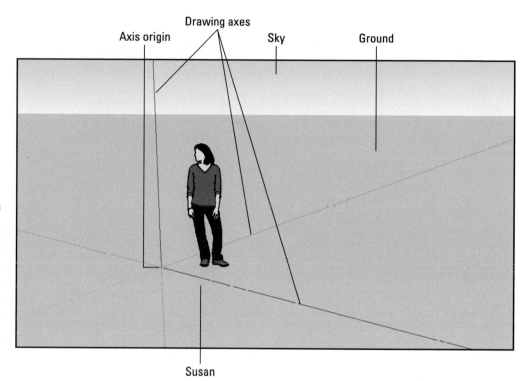

Axis origin   Drawing axes   Sky   Ground

Susan

Color Plate 1: The colored drawing axes are the key to how SketchUp works (Chapter 2).

Drawing in the red direction

Moving in the blue direction

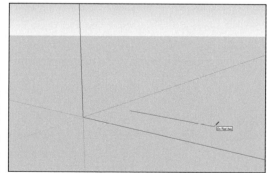

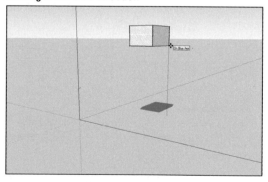

Color Plate 2: Going in the right color direction (Chapter 2).

To go up, move in the blue direction

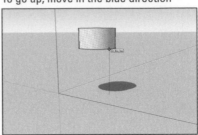

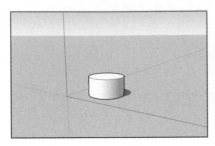

To go back, move in the green direction

Color Plate 3:
Moving an
object in
3D on a
2D screen
(Chapter 2).

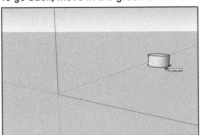

Color Plate 4:
Point
inferences
are colored
by type and
help you
model more
precisely
(Chapter 2).

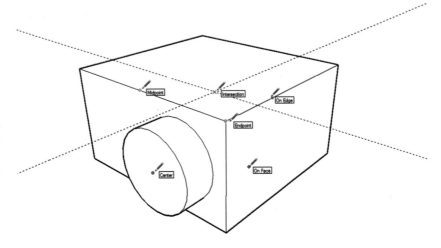

Color Plate 5:
Linear
inferences
are color
coded and
help you draw
in 3D, too
(Chapter 2).

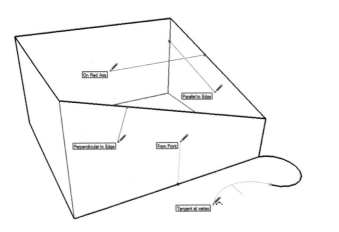

Hold down Shift to lock
yourself in the blue direction

Hover over the point to which
you want to infer; then click to
end your edge

Color Plate 6:
Locking an
inference
helps you
draw in the
right direction
(Chapter 2).

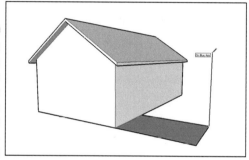
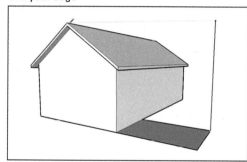

Hover over the center point
inference

Move slowly away in the red
direction

Color Plate 7:
Encouraging
an inference
(Chapter 2).

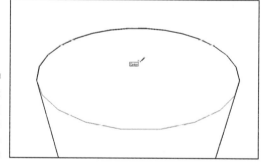
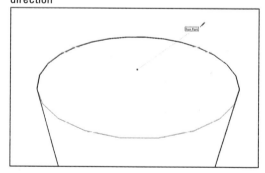

Color Plate 8:
Orbit (spin)
your model
to paint all
the faces
(Chapter 3).

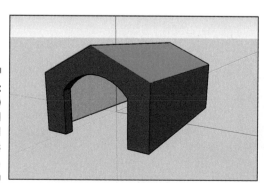
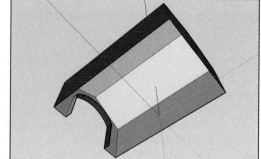

Anatomy of a Completed House Model

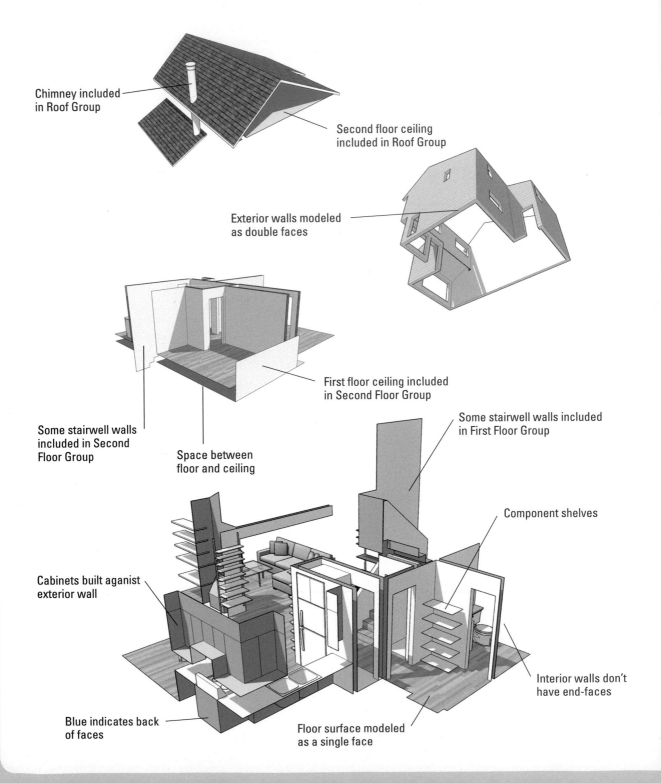

Chimney included in Roof Group

Second floor ceiling included in Roof Group

Exterior walls modeled as double faces

First floor ceiling included in Second Floor Group

Some stairwell walls included in First Floor Group

Some stairwell walls included in Second Floor Group

Space between floor and ceiling

Component shelves

Cabinets built aganist exterior wall

Blue indicates back of faces

Floor surface modeled as a single face

Interior walls don't have end-faces

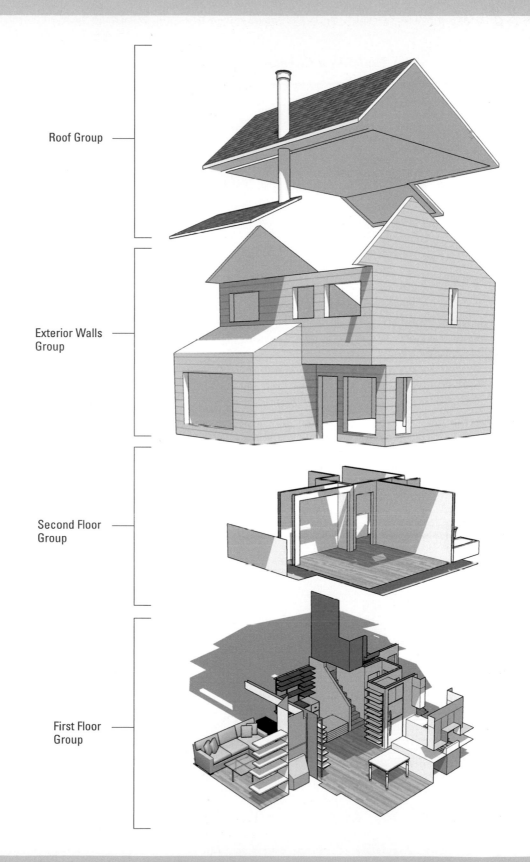

Roof Group

Exterior Walls
Group

Second Floor
Group

First Floor
Group

Building a Circular Stair with Components

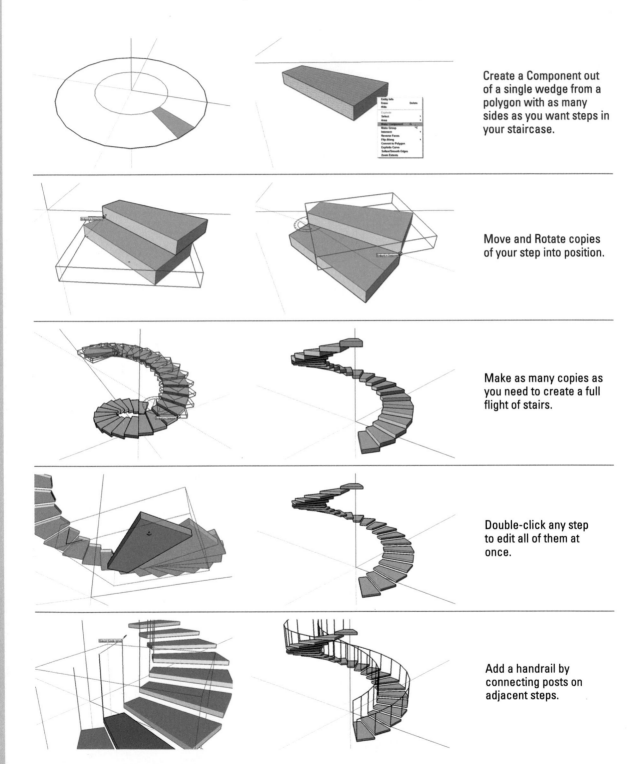

Create a Component out of a single wedge from a polygon with as many sides as you want steps in your staircase.

Move and Rotate copies of your step into position.

Make as many copies as you need to create a full flight of stairs.

Double-click any step to edit all of them at once.

Add a handrail by connecting posts on adjacent steps.

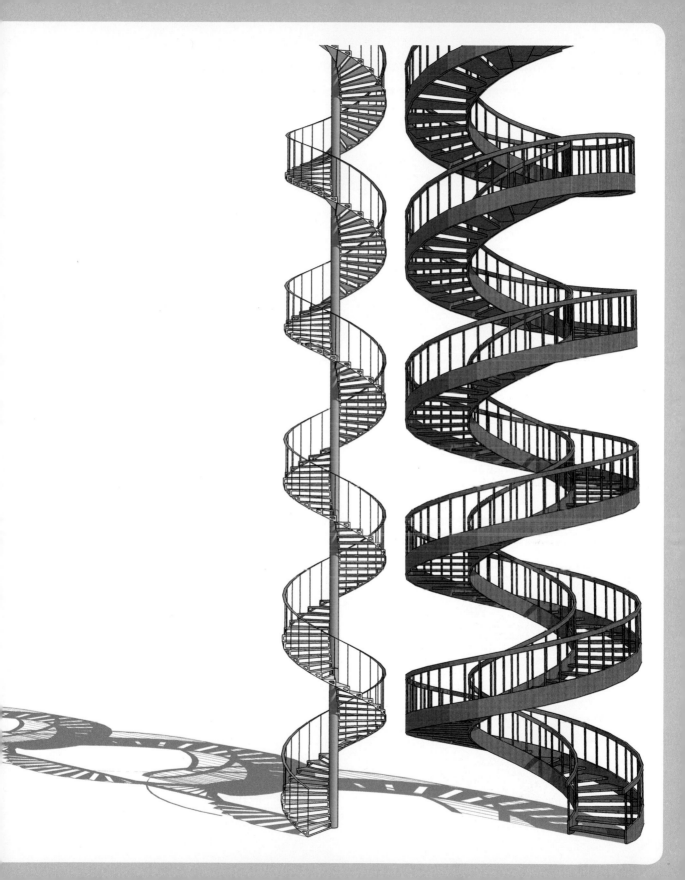

Building a Simple Boat with Mirrored Components and the Scale Tool

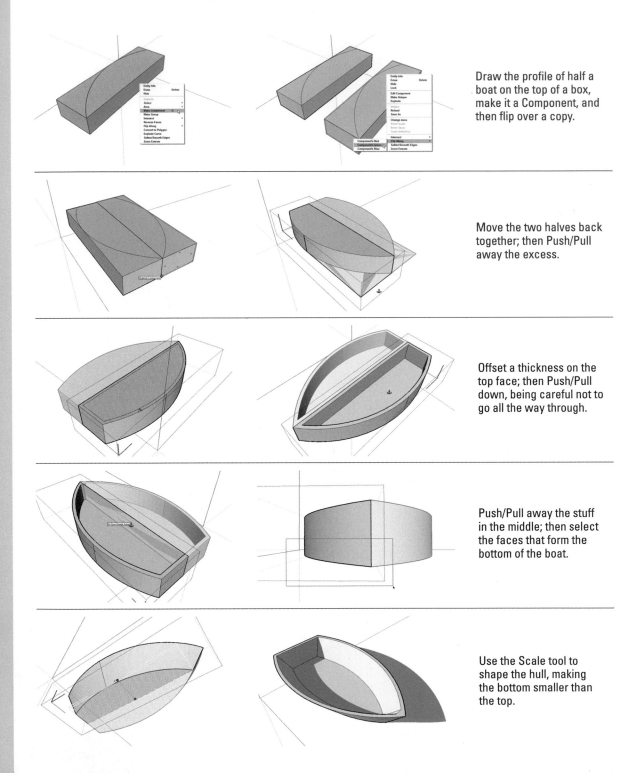

Draw the profile of half a boat on the top of a box, make it a Component, and then flip over a copy.

Move the two halves back together; then Push/Pull away the excess.

Offset a thickness on the top face; then Push/Pull down, being careful not to go all the way through.

Push/Pull away the stuff in the middle; then select the faces that form the bottom of the boat.

Use the Scale tool to shape the hull, making the bottom smaller than the top.

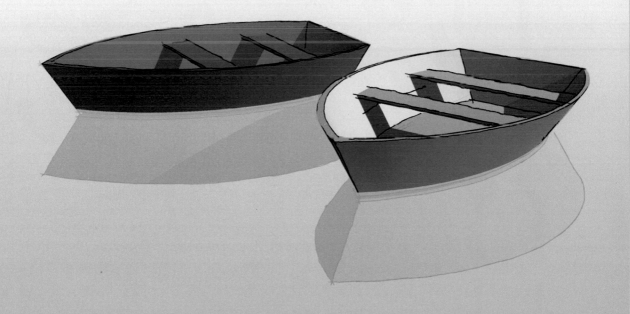

Combine Smaller, Simpler Models to Build Complicated Ones

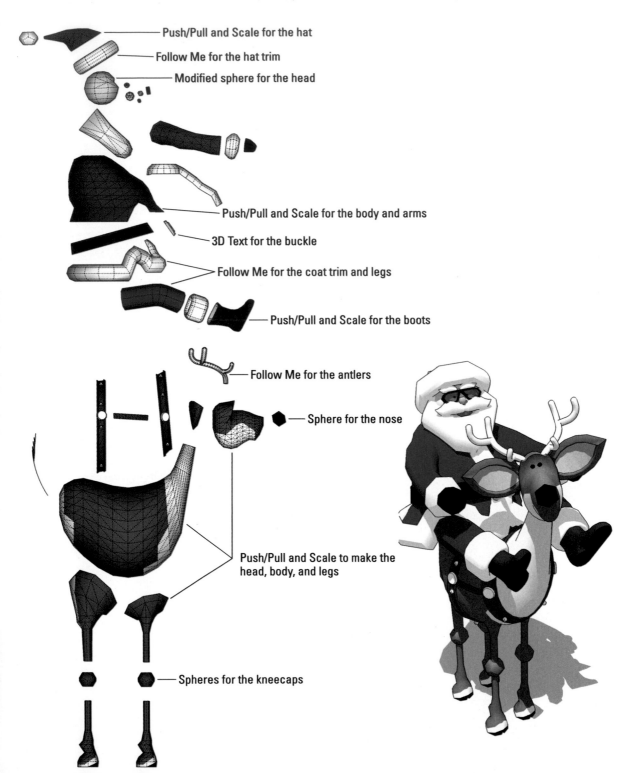

Push/Pull and Scale for the hat

Follow Me for the hat trim

Modified sphere for the head

Push/Pull and Scale for the body and arms

3D Text for the buckle

Follow Me for the coat trim and legs

Push/Pull and Scale for the boots

Follow Me for the antlers

Sphere for the nose

Push/Pull and Scale to make the head, body, and legs

Spheres for the kneecaps

Color Plate 9: A transparent version of your image, along with four colored pins, appear when editing textures (Chapter 8).

Scale Line/Vertical Axis

Photograph

Vanishing Point Grip

Perspective bars

Match Photo dialog box

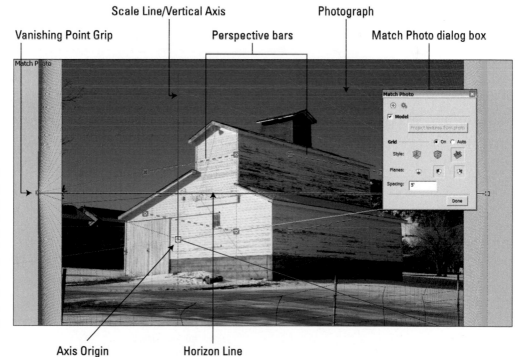

Color Plate 10: The Match Photo interface shows your picture, plus tools to create a model from it (Chapter 8).

Axis Origin

Horizon Line

Line up each Perspective Bar with an edge in your photograph

Color Plate 11: Lining up the Perspective bars (Chapter 8).

Color Plate 12: All four Perspective bars, properly lined up with edges in the picture (Chapter 8).

Perspective bars lined up

Color Plate 13: Placing the Axis Origin in a good spot (Chapter 8).

Move the Axis Origin to a logical place

Color Plate 14: Using the grid lines to give your picture an approximate scale (Chapter 8).

4 grid lines high (approx.)

Draw an edge from here . . .   . . . to here

Color Plate 15: Tracing an edge in one of the three main directions (Chapter 8).

Color Plate 16: Creating a face to match a surface in the photograph (Chapter 8).

Color Plate 17:
Projecting textures from a picture onto a face; then Orbiting around to see the result (Chapter 8).

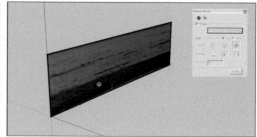

Draw this diagonal edge by connecting the endpoints

Edge

Color Plate 18:
Using the endpoints of perpendicular edges to draw a diagonal (Chapter 8).

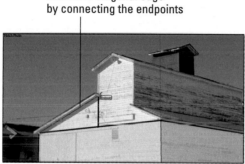
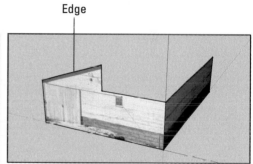

Color Plate 19:
A model created from two matched photos (Chapter 8).

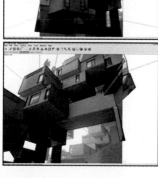
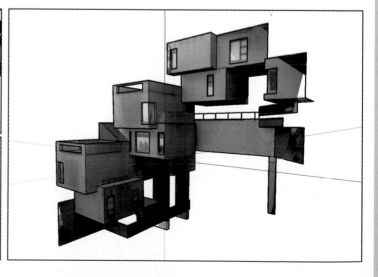

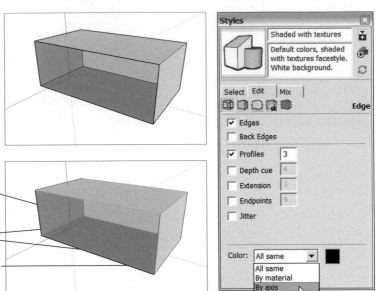

Color Plate 20: Turning on Color by Axis helps you track down edges that aren't what they seem (Chapter 16).

This edge should be blue

Their color tells me these edges aren't right

This edge should be green

Color Plate 21: Use Styles to make your model look any way you want (Chapter 9).

2. then click here...

1. Click here to start...   3. then click here.

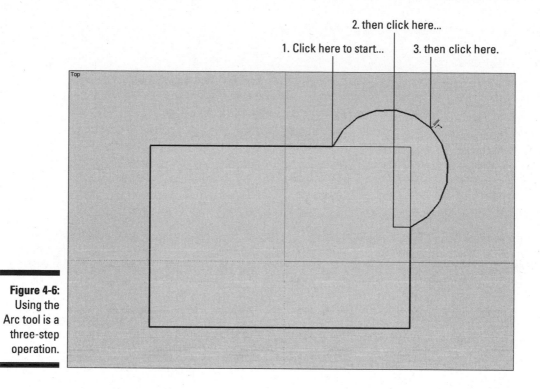

Figure 4-6:
Using the
Arc tool is a
three-step
operation.

Click to start drawing; then
move your cursor

6 inch *outside* offset

6 inch *inside* offset

Figure 4-7:
Offset lets
you
create
edges
based on
other edges.

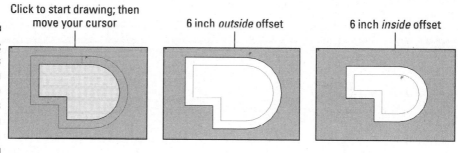

Select the edges you want to offset

Use Offset to create more edges

Figure 4-8:
Using Offset
on a set of
preselected
edges is
handy for
drawing
things like
doorframes.

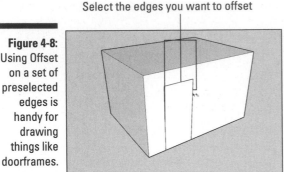
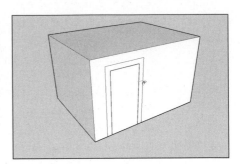

✔ **Tape Measure tool:** The Tape Measure is one of those tools that does a bunch of things. To measure distances with it, click any two points in your model to measure the distance between them. The distance readout is in the Measurements box, in the lower-right corner of your modeling window. You can also use it to size a model and to create guides, as I explain in Chapter 2.

Coming up with a simple plan

If all you're trying to do is model an exterior view of a building, just measure around the perimeter, draw the outline of the building in SketchUp, and proceed from there. (See Figure 4-9.) Your walls will be only a *single-face thick* (meaning paper-thin), but that's okay — you're interested only in the outside, anyway.

Figure 4-9:
To make
an exterior
model, just
measure the
outside of
your build-
ing to draw
an outline in
SketchUp.

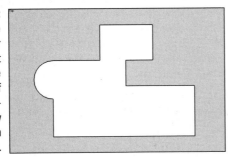
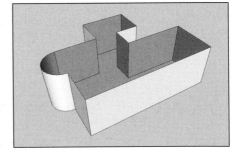

If, on the other hand, you want to create an *interior* view, your life is a little bit more complicated. The business of measuring an existing building so that you can model it on the computer is easier said than done — even experienced architects and builders often get confused when trying to create *as-builts,* which are drawings of existing buildings. Closets, ventilation spaces, interior walls, and all kinds of other obstructions inevitably get in the way of getting good measurements; most of the time, you just have to give it your best shot and then tweak things a bit to make them right.

Drawing an interior outline

Because the main goal of making an interior model of a building is to end up with accurate interior spaces, you need to work from the inside out. If your tape measure is long enough, try to figure out a way to get the major dimensions first — this means the total interior width and length of the inside of your building. You may not be able to, but do your best. After that, just work your way around, using basic arithmetic and logic to figure out things.

Before you start drawing an interior outline in SketchUp make a paper drawing. The drawing helps you know what you need to draw so you can focus all your concentration for drafting on the computer. Figure 4-10 shows the paper sketch I used when modeling my house.

From this paper drawing, here's how you draw a basic interior outline of this house:

1. **Switch to a 2D overhead view.**

    The section "Switching to a 2D view," earlier in this chapter, explains how.

2. **Using the Line tool, draw an edge 17 feet long (see Figure 4-11, top left), representing the eastern wall of the house.**

    To draw it, click once to start the edge, move my cursor up until you see the green linear inference (indicating that I'm drawing parallel to the green axis), and click again to end the line. To make the edge 17 feet long, type **17'** and then press Enter — the line resizes itself automatically to be exactly 17 feet in length. If you wanted to, you could use the Tape Measure to double-check what you did.

3. **Draw an edge 11 feet 10 inches long, starting at the end of the first edge, heading to the right in the red direction. (See Figure 4-11, bottom right.)**

    To do this, do exactly what you did to draw the first edge, except that you move parallel to the red axis this time, type **11'10** and then press Enter.

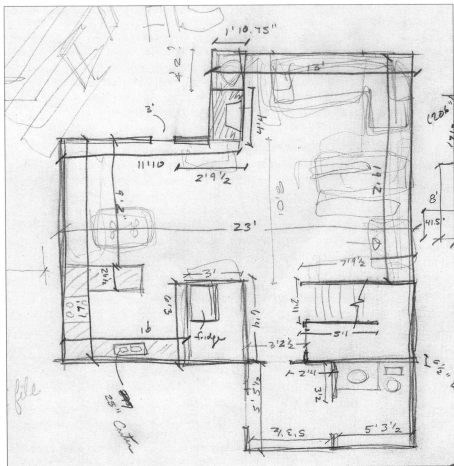

Figure 4-10:
This is
the paper
sketch I
used to
model my
house in
SketchUp.

4. **Keep going all the way around the house, until you get back to where you started. (See Figure 4-12.)**

   If you make a mistake, either use the Eraser to get rid of edges you're unhappy with or choose Edit⇨Undo to go back a step or two.

5. **If all your measurements don't add up, adjust things so that they do — a few extra inches here and there never killed anyone, after all.**

   After you complete the outline (forming a closed loop of edges that were all on the same plane), a face automatically appears. Now you have a total of 11 edges and 1 face.

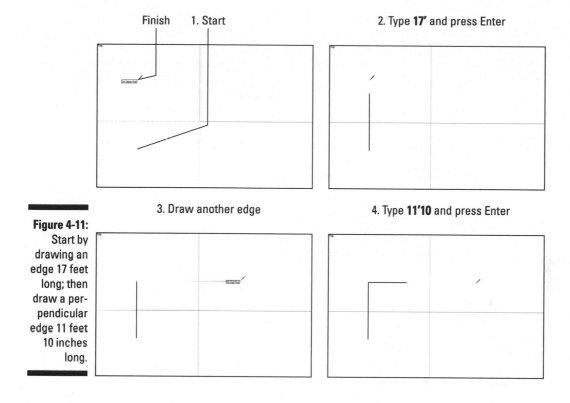

Figure 4-11:
Start by
drawing an
edge 17 feet
long; then
draw a per-
pendicular
edge 11 feet
10 inches
long.

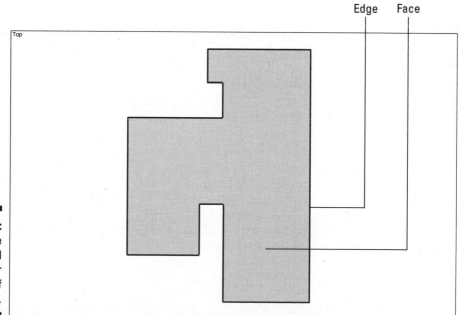

Figure 4-12:
The
completed
interior
perimeter of
my house.

When you draft in 2D, whatever you do, don't use the Orbit tool. Because you work in 2D, you need only to use Zoom and Pan to navigate around your drawing (see Chapter 2). If you accidentally orbit your model into a 3D view, follow the steps in the section "Switching to a 2D view," earlier in this chapter, to get things back in order.

If you get lost, and no amount of zooming and panning gets you back to a view of your floorplan, choose Camera⇨Zoom Extents — think of it as an emergency lever you can pull to fill your modeling window with your geometry.

Offsetting and grouping an exterior wall

I decided to *offset* (using the Offset tool) an exterior wall thickness, just to make it easier to visualize my spaces. Here's how you do it:

1. **Using the Offset tool, offset your closed shape by 8 inches to the outside. (See Figure 4-13, upper-left.)**

   An offset of 8 inches is a pretty standard thickness for an exterior wall, especially for houses in my neck of the woods. This is how you use the Offset tool:

   a. Make sure that nothing is selected by choosing Edit⇨Select None.

   b. Click once inside your shape.

   c. Click again outside your shape to make a second, bigger shape.

   *d. Type **8** and then press Enter.*

2. **Because no alcoves are on the exterior, use the Line tool to close them off, creating pockets of wall that are thicker than the rest. (See Figure 4-13, middle-left.)**

3. **Use the Eraser tool to get rid of the extra edges. (See Figure 4-13, lower-left.)**

   By deleting the extra edges, you have only two faces: one that represents the floor and one that represents the wall.

4. **With the Line tool, draw edges that define the thickness of your exterior wall. (See Figure 4-13, upper-right.)**

   In the case of this house, this means separating the *bulges* (which actually represent a fireplace and a mechanical closet) from the part of the wall that goes all the way up to the roof, two stories up.

   When you're done, you end up with several faces: one for the floor, one for the exterior wall (whose thickness should be more or less uniform), and a few for the bulges.

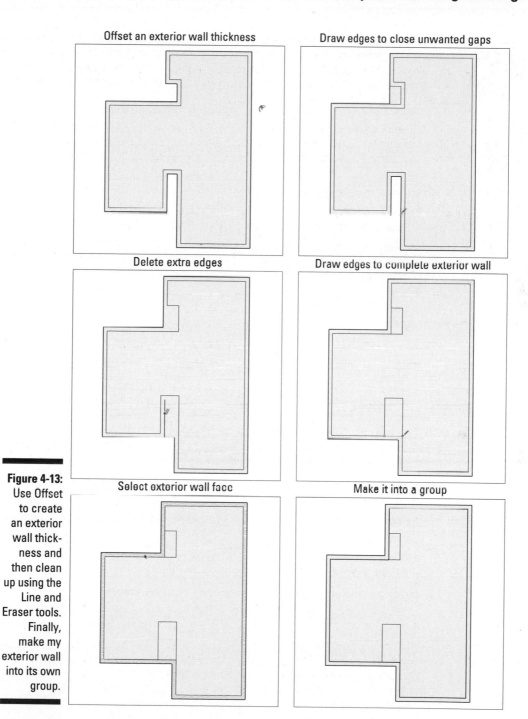

Offset an exterior wall thickness

Draw edges to close unwanted gaps

Delete extra edges

Draw edges to complete exterior wall

Select exterior wall face

Make it into a group

Figure 4-13:
Use Offset to create an exterior wall thickness and then clean up using the Line and Eraser tools. Finally, make my exterior wall into its own group.

5. **Select the face that defines the exterior wall. (See Figure 4-13, middle-right.)**

   The easiest way to do this is to click once on the face with the Select tool.

6. **Make the face you just selected into a group. (See Figure 4-13, lower-right.)**

   Chapter 5 is all about these groups (and their über-useful cousins, components), but here's all you need to know for now: Making groups lets you separate different parts of your model. Turning your exterior wall into a separate group makes it easier to edit, hide, and move. Groups also simplify the process of adding more levels to your building, if that becomes necessary.

   To turn the face you selected in Step 5 into a group, choose Edit⇨Make Group. You see a perimeter of blue lines around your face; that's the group you just created. Congratulations — you're now officially an intermediate SketchUp user.

Putting in the interior walls

For this part of the process, I use guides a lot. If you haven't done so already, check out the section on guides in Chapter 2. There, you find a full description of guides and how to use them.

When I draft a floorplan in SketchUp, I find it really helps to ignore things like doors and windows — where a doorway should be in a wall, I just draw a solid wall. I like to add doors and windows after I extrude my floorplan into a 3D figure.

Here's how you put in the few interior walls on the first floor of this house:

1. **With the Tape Measure tool, drag a parallel guide 5 feet, 3½ inches from the inside of my entryway. (See Figure 4-14, left.)**

   To do this, just click the edge from which you want to draw the guide, move your cursor to the right (to tell SketchUp which way to go), type **5'3.5**, and press Enter.

2. **Draw a few more guides the same way you drew the first one.**

   Working from my pencil drawing, figure out the location of each interior wall and create guides to measure the space. (See Figure 4-14, right.)

3. **Switching to the Line tool, draw edges to represent the interior walls.**

   By using the guides as, er, guides, it's easy to draw your edges correctly. Figure 4-15 shows what you have so far.

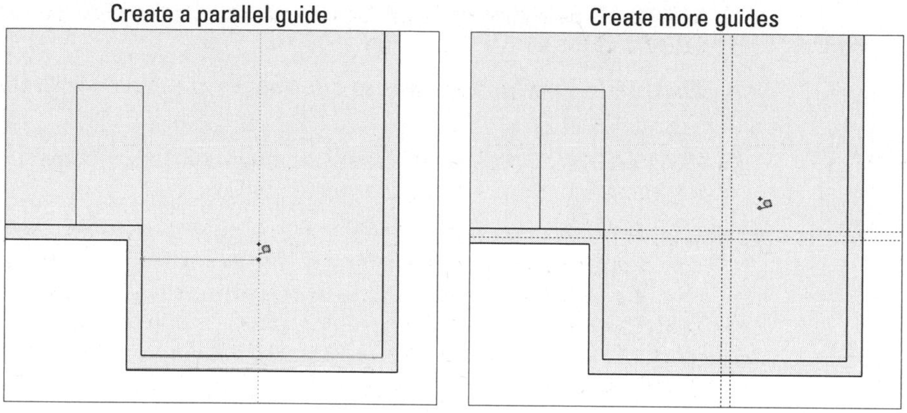

Create a parallel guide   Create more guides

Figure 4-14:
Draw a
guide to
help you
locate your
first interior
wall, and
then draw a
bunch more.

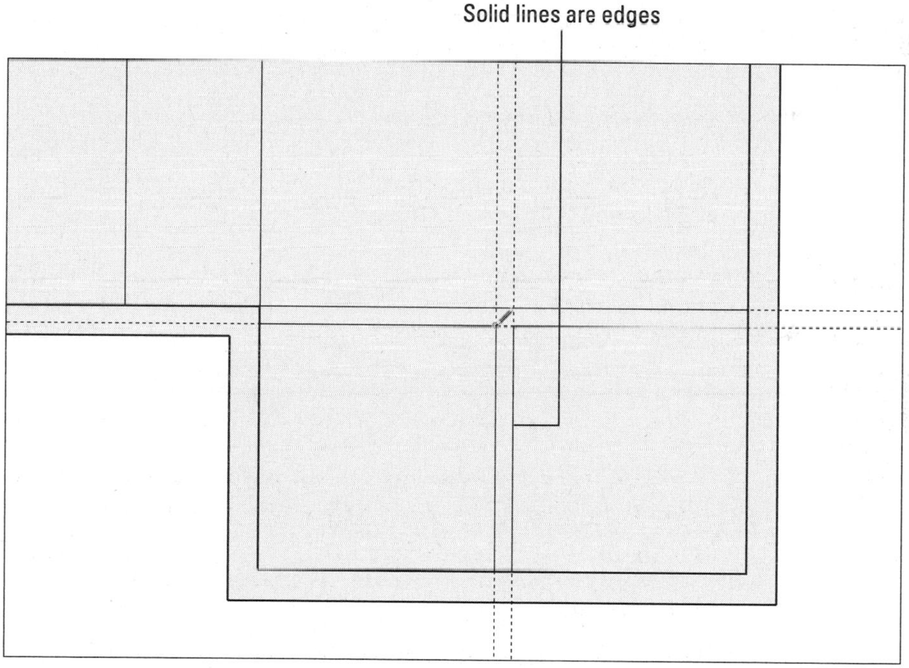

Solid lines are edges

Figure 4-15:
Use
the Line
tool to
create
edges
where
guides
come
together.

Don't forget to zoom! When you have a jumble of edges and guides
and you can't see what you're doing, just zoom in. Many folks forget to
change their point of view while they work, and zooming makes all the
difference.

4. Use the Eraser to delete your guides.

5. Use the Eraser to get rid of any extra edge segments. (See Figure 4-16.)

The goal is to have the smallest-possible number of 2D faces to extrude into 3D walls, a little later on.

Because the exterior-wall face — and the edges that define it — is part of a separate group, accidentally nicking it with the Eraser deletes the whole thing at once. If this happens, just use Undo to go back a step, zoom in a little bit, and try again.

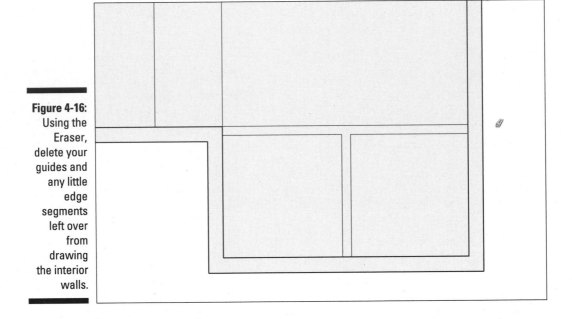

Figure 4-16:
Using the Eraser, delete your guides and any little edge segments left over from drawing the interior walls.

Going from 2D to 3D

With a 2D plan in hand, the next step is to extrude it into a 3D model. This is an enormously enjoyable process, and it involves the tool that made SketchUp famous: Push/Pull. In the following sections, you take a simple floorplan (the one I draw earlier in this chapter) and turn it into 3D walls.

Getting a good view

Before you pop up your plan into the third dimension, change your point of view to get a better view of what you're doing. (See Figure 4-17.) Follow these steps:

Switch to Perspective view

Switch to Iso view

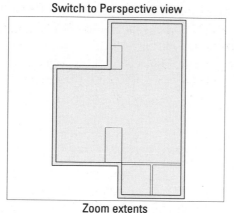

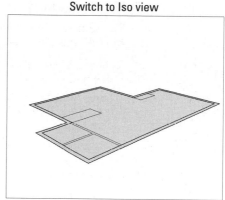

Zoom extents

Figure 4-17:
Before you
start work in
3D, switch
over to a 3D
view.

1. **Choose Camera➪Perspective.**

   This turns on SketchUp's perspective engine, meaning that now you can see things more realistically — the way people really see things in 3D.

2. **Choose Camera➪Standard➪Iso.**

   This switches you from a top view to an *isometric* (three-quarter) one. You can do this with the Orbit tool, too — you always have more than one way to do everything in SketchUp.

3. **Choose Camera➪Zoom Extents.**

   Zoom Extents has its own button on the basic toolbar, but I want to stick with the Camera menu theme, just for consistency.

4. **Choose Camera➪Field of View, type 45, and press Enter.**

   You've changed the field of view from 35 to 45 degrees. By default, SketchUp's field of view is set to 35 degrees. (For more information on what this means, check out Chapter 10.)

Pushing/pulling your way to happiness

The Push/Pull tool is a simple creature; use it to extrude flat faces into 3D shapes. It works (like everything else in SketchUp) by clicking — you click a face once to start pushing/pulling it, move your cursor until you like what you see, and then click again to stop push/pulling. That's it. I doubt that any software tool has ever been so satisfyingly easy to use and understand. For more detail on Push/Pull, see the nearby sidebar, "More fun with Push/Pull."

Push/Pull works only on flat faces; if you need to do something to a curved face, you have to use something else. Read about the Intersect Faces feature in the section "Getting to know Intersect Faces," later in this chapter — it may be what you're looking for.

The following steps outline what to do to use Push/Pull to extrude my house's first floorplan into a 3D model, as shown in Figure 4-18:

1. Push/pull one interior wall

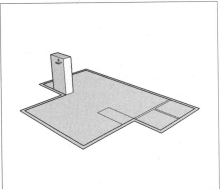

2. Push/pull remaining interior walls

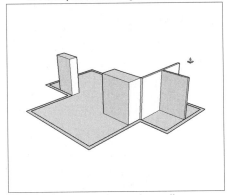

3. Double-click to select exterior wall group

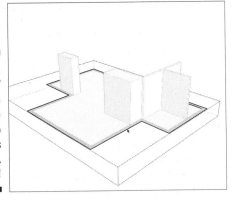

4. Push/pull exterior wall

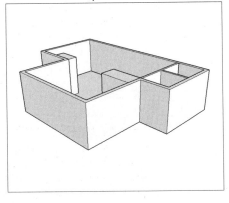

Figure 4-18: Use Push/Pull to extrude faces into all the walls in my house. Presto!

1. **Select the Push/Pull tool from the toolbar.**

   The tool looks like a little box with a red arrow coming out the top.

2. **Click an interior wall's face once to start extruding it.**

   If you click the "floor" face, you'd extrude that, instead. If you choose the wrong face by accident, press Esc to cancel the operation and try again.

3. **Move up your cursor to pull up the wall; click to stop extruding.**

   How much you extrude the face doesn't matter, because you add precision in the next step.

4. **Type 8' and press Enter.**

   When you do this, the push/pull distance is revised to be exactly 8 feet — the height of the ceilings in this house.

5. **Repeat Steps 2–4 for all the interior walls in the house.**

   Using Orbit helps you view what you're doing as you work around the model.

6. **Push/pull the exterior wall to match the height of these interior walls.**

   Because the exterior wall face is part of a group (I made it that way on purpose), you need to edit the group before you can do anything to it. Right-click the exterior wall face and choose Edit Group from the context menu to get "inside," where you can follow Steps 2–4 in the preceding steps, to make the exterior wall group 3D. Clicking anywhere in space exits the group when you're done.

Adding floors to your building

Adding a second (and third, and fourth) floor to your model isn't as hard as it may seem. The key is to think of each level as a separate "tray" consisting of interior walls, a floor surface, and the ceiling of the level below. You model each floor as an individual group, making it easier to hide, edit, and move. For the same reasons, you also make the exterior walls a separate group; they act kind of like a "box" into which your floor levels stack. Take a look at Figure 4-19 for a visual representation of what I mean.

Making groups to keep things separate

If you've been following along since the beginning of this chapter, the edges and faces that make up your exterior walls are already enclosed in a group by themselves. If they're not, seriously consider going back a few steps — taking the time to set things up now will save you hours of headache later. Trust me.

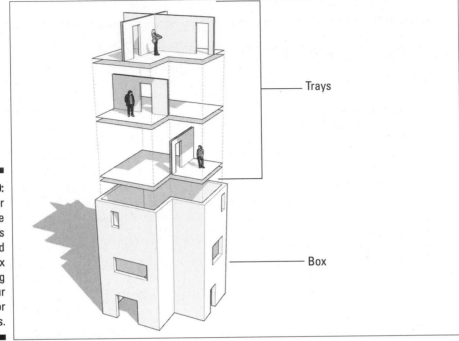

Trays

Box

Figure 4-19:
Floor
levels are
like trays
stacked
inside a box
consisting
of your
exterior
walls.

Otherwise well-meaning people who have worked with other CAD or 3D modeling programs often take this opportunity to bring layers into the discussion. Yes, SketchUp has a Layers feature. And yes, floor "trays" are a lot like layers, at least conceptually. But you should *not* use Layers when modeling multiple levels of the same building. Layers in SketchUp simply don't work the way you might think they do — skip ahead to Chapter 7 if you want to read all about it.

Provided your exterior walls are already a group, the next step is to turn the rest of your first floor's geometry into *another* group. This is how you do just that:

1. **Select the floor and interior walls of the first level.**

   You can accomplish this efficiently (with the Select tool): Just triple-click a face on any interior wall to select everything that's attached to it. Take a look at Chapter 2 for plenty of tips on selecting things.

2. **Make a group by choosing Edit⇨Make Group from the menu bar.**

   Chapter 5 is all about groups and components; peruse the first few pages if you're utterly confused about what just happened.

More fun with Push/Pull

Because Push/Pull is the tool that most people think of when they think of SketchUp, I thought you might appreciate knowing more about what it can do. The people who invented this software (back in the last millennium) *started* with the idea for Push/Pull — that's how closely linked SketchUp and Push/Pull are. Here are five things about Push/Pull that aren't immediately obvious when you start using it:

✔ **Double-click with the Push/Pull tool to extrude a face by the last distance you pushed/pulled.**

✔ **Press the Ctrl key (Option on a Mac) to push/pull a *copy* of your face.** As shown in the first graphic in the following figure, instead of using Push/Pull the regular way, you can use a modifier key to extrude a copy of the face you're pushing/pulling. This comes in super-handy for modeling things like multistory buildings quickly.

✔ **While pushing/pulling, hover over other parts of your geometry to tell SketchUp**

how far to extrude. Take a look at the second graphic. Perhaps you want to use Push/Pull to extrude a cylinder that's exactly the same height as this box. Before you click the second time to stop pushing/pulling, hover over a point on the top of the box; now the cylinder is exactly that tall. To complete the operation, click while you're still hovering over the box. It's pretty simple and saves you hours of time after you're used to doing it.

✔ **Pushing/pulling a face into another, coplanar face automatically cuts a hole.** In fact, this is how you make openings (like doors and windows) in double-face walls. The last graphic shows this in action.

✔ **You can push/pull preselected faces.** New for SketchUp 8, Push/Pull works just like Move, Rotate, Offset, and Scale — you can preselect a face before you start using the tool. This comes in handy when you need to extrude a face you can't see. A rare case, but handy nonetheless.

Hit Control
(Option on Mac)
to copy your face

Click while
you're hovering

Push/Pull a face all the
way into another one
to make both disappear

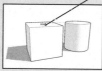

Drawing the next floor

Modeling each new floor directly on top of the one underneath guarantees that everything in your building lines up. Some folks advocate for working "off to the side" and putting things together later, but I think that's a recipe for trouble. Here's how you add a second floor to the house model (check out Figure 4-20 to see the steps as pictures):

1. Trace the inside perimeter
of the exterior wall

2. Push/pull into a thick slab

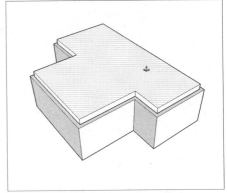

3. Draw interior walls

4. Push/pull interior walls

Figure 4-20:
Draw right
on top of the
lower floor;
then push/
pull the
interior
walls to
ceiling
height.

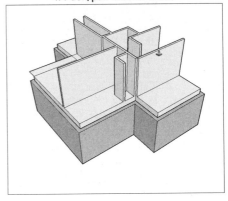

1. **Trace the inside perimeter of the exterior wall to create a new face.**

   I like to use the Line tool to do this. Keep in mind that this works only if everything you touch is already part of another group; if it isn't, your new edges stick to your existing ones, and your model becomes very, very messy.

2. **Push/Pull your new face into a thick slab.**

   How thick? It depends on your building, but a reasonable ceiling-to-floor distance between levels for houses is about a foot. You can figure yours out with a tape measure and a calculator.

   The underside of the new slab is the ceiling of the first floor. I prefer to model buildings this way because it improves visibility when I hide a floor group to see the one below it.

3. **Draw the interior walls of the new floor.**

   This is just like drawing the first floor. Switch to the Top view (Camera⇨ Standard Views⇨Top) and then use the Tape Measure, Eraser, and Line tools to draft your floorplan. Just start at the very beginning of this chapter for a refresher.

   If the floor you're drawing is bigger than the one below it, its outline overlaps the exterior walls. That's okay — just pay special attention to where your edges and faces end up as you draw. Orbit every once in a while to check that everything's copacetic.

   In the event that your new floor is *smaller* than the one underneath, represent the inside boundary of the new exterior walls with a single edge. The next section deals with what to do when your first and second floorplans don't match up exactly.

4. **Push/Pull your interior walls to the correct height.**

   That's 8 feet, in this example.

5. **Group together your interior walls, your floor, and the ceiling of the level below.**

   If you're unsure of how to do this, take a look at the steps in "Making groups to keep things separate," a few pages back.

6. **If your upper floor isn't bigger or smaller than your lower floor, pull up your exterior walls to match your interior ones.**

   Here, you're extending the box that holds your floor trays up another level. Follow these steps:

   a. *Edit your exterior wall group by double-clicking it with the Select tool.*

   b. *Use Push/Pull to extrude it up.*

   c. *Exit (stop editing) the group by clicking somewhere off to the side of your model.*

Chances are your newest floor doesn't line up exactly with the one below it. Keep reading to find out what to do.

Creating additional exterior walls

Most buildings aren't simple extrusions; they bump in and out as they rise. Second-floor decks sit atop first-floor garages; bedrooms cantilever over gardens; intermediate roofs shelter new room additions. Buildings — especially multilevel houses — are complicated assemblies. Figuring out where walls, floors, and ceilings come together takes time, trial and error, and a good dose of spatial reasoning. It's best not to attempt the steps in this section when you're tired or distracted.

TIP

If your building does happen to be one of the few with perfectly aligned floorplans, you can skip this section entirely. Congrats; you're a lucky devil.

I'm not so lucky — in the house I model for this chapter, the second floor both overhangs and, um, underhangs (hooray for neologisms) the first floor. Wherever this happens, you need to add a new section of exterior wall. Take a look at the photograph in Figure 4-21 to see what I mean.

Follow along to watch how to solve this tricky problem:

1. **Draw faces to define any new exterior walls (see Figure 4-22):**

   a. *Use the Line tool to trace the inside perimeter of your new exterior walls.*

   b. *Hide the group that includes your second-floor interior walls by right-clicking it and choosing Hide.*

   c. *Select the face that you created when you traced the inside perimeter in Step a. Don't see a face? Maybe you forgot to draw an edge somewhere.*

   d. *Use the Offset tool to offset the edges of your selected face by the thickness of your exterior walls.*

   In this case, 8 inches.

   e. *Delete the face in the center, leaving only a face that represents your new exterior wall thickness.*

   f. *Unhide the group you hid in Step b by choosing Edit⇨Unhide⇨Last from the menu bar.*

2. **Make a group out of your new exterior wall face by selecting it and then choosing Edit⇨Make Group.**

3. **Delete any floor geometry that doesn't belong. (See Figure 4-23, top.)**

   In this example, part of the floor extends past the exterior wall on the left side of the figure. Double-click the group with the Select tool to edit it, and then use the Eraser to take away only what you need to, being careful to leave the ceiling that covers the first floor, below.

4. **Push/pull down any wall faces to meet the top of the lower floor's exterior wall. (See Figure 4-23, bottom.)**

   Double-click a group with the Select tool to edit it; you need to do this before you can push/pull any of the faces you created in Step 1.

5. Make all your exterior walls part of the same group:

    a. Select the group that contains your new exterior walls and then choose Edit⇨Cut.

    b. With the Select tool, double-click the group containing your lower exterior walls.

    You're "inside" that group.

    c. Choose Edit⇨Paste in Place.

    d. Choose Edit⇨Group⇨Explode to ungroup the edges and faces in the selected group, sticking them to those in the lower group.

    Whew.

Second floor bumps out

Figure 4-21: The outline of the second floor doesn't exactly match that of the first.

First floor bumps out

1. Trace inside perimeter of new exterior walls

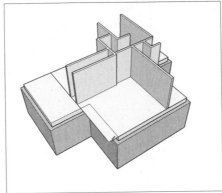

2. Hide second floor group

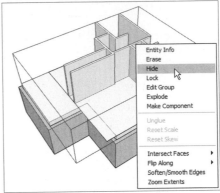

3. Select face

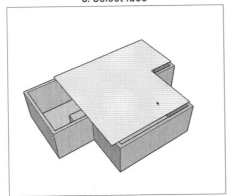

4. Offset exterior walls

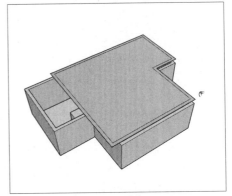

5. Delete inside face

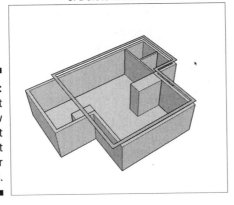

6. Unhide second floor group

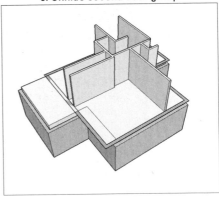

Figure 4-22:
Use Offset
to draw
faces that
represent
new exterior
walls.

1. Delete unwanted floor faces

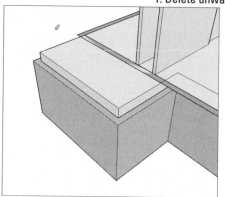
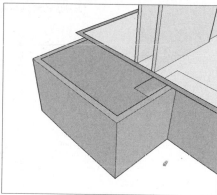

2. Push/pull exterior wall face down

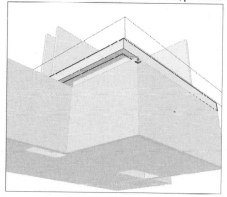
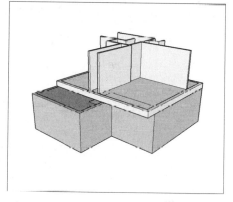

Figure 4-23:
Delete extra
floor faces;
then push/
pull down
the walls.

6. **Use Line, Erase, and Push/Pull to extrude your exterior walls up to the
height of your interior walls (see Figure 4-24).**

After everything's in the same group, adding necessary edges, deleting
extraneous ones, and pushing/pulling faces all at once is easier. Using
your SketchUp virtuosity, watch the colors as you draw, use the Shift
key to lock inferences, and remember to zoom in on what you're doing.
Skimming Chapter 2 provides useful pointers on these actions.

1. Make all exterior walls part
of the same group

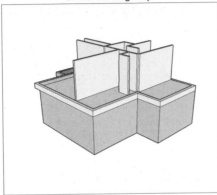

2. Delete edges between faces

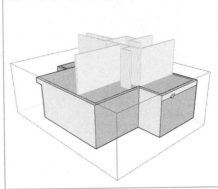

3. Push/pull exterior walls

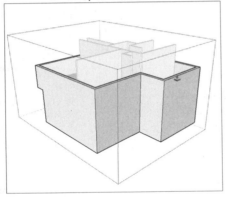

4. Orbit to make sure everything looks right

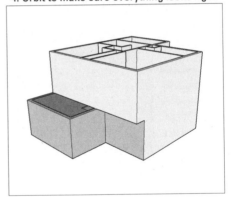

Figure 4-24:
Do what
you need to
do to make
your exte-
rior walls
look right.

Up, up, and away

Now that you're privy to my favorite technique for modeling multilevel buildings, you can build up as high as you like. As you proceed, the following tidbits may be helpful:

✔ **See the results in living color.** To see what a finished building model looks like, check out "Anatomy of a Completed House Model," in the color section somewhere toward the middle of this book.

✔ **Hide things to get a clearer view for your current task.** Right-clicking any entity and choosing Hide often makes it easier to see what you're doing. This is particularly true of groups, which is why I go to so much trouble to create them in the first place. To see stuff that's hidden, choose View➪Hidden Geometry. To unhide something that's hidden, right-click and choose Unhide.

✔ **Better yet, use the Outliner.** Chapter 7 is all about making your SketchUp life easier by using certain tools to work more efficiently. If you're up for it, skip ahead and read the stuff about the Outliner — it's hyper-relevant to what you do here.

✔ **There's gold in Model Info.** Choose Window➪Model Info and then click the Components tab on the left. Clicking the Hide check box next to Fade Rest of Model automatically hides everything outside the group you're editing currently. Smart modelers (such as yourself) make liberal use of this gem when cutting doors and windows in interior walls, which is the topic of the next section. . . .

Inserting doors and windows

You can make openings in your walls in a couple ways. The best option depends on what kind of building you're modeling, whether you're using single-face or double-face walls, and how much detail you plan to include in your model. You have two options:

✔ **Use SketchUp components that cut openings.** The Google 3D Warehouse (read all about it in Chapter 5) contains scores of doors and windows that you can download and use in your models. Some of them cut their own openings when you insert them in a face. Here's the catch, though: SketchUp's cut-opening components work only on single-face walls, which means that they're only really useful for exterior building models. If you're building an interior model, you have to cut your own openings.

✔ **Cut openings yourself.** For double-face walls, this is your only option; luckily, it's easy to do. Basically, draw an outline for the opening you want to create and then use Push/Pull to create the opening — it works the same way for doors and windows.

Using SketchUp's handy-dandy components

As long as you're making an exterior model, you can use some of the doors and windows stored online on Google's 3D Warehouse. These are components, which you can read more about in Chapter 5. Without going into a ton of detail, here's what you need to know about them:

✔ **Components are accessible from the Components dialog box.** Choose Window➪Components to open the dialog box and then choose the Architecture collection from the Navigation drop-down list (it looks like an upside-down triangle). The Doors, Windows, and DC Doors and Windows collections are in there somewhere. Components that can cut their own openings generally contain *gluing* or *cutting* in their descriptions. Keep in mind that you need to be online to access the Google 3D Warehouse.

✔ **You can find hundreds more online.** If you're connected to the Internet, you can type any search query (such as **revolving door**) into the little search area at the top of the Components dialog box. This scours the 3D Warehouse for whatever you're looking for and shows the results below. Some advice: The 3D Warehouse holds so much stuff, making your query specific helps you sort through the results.

✔ **Components are editable.** You find details in Chapter 5, but here's the gist: If you don't like something about a component you find online, you can change it.

✔ **Some components are dynamic.** Dynamic Components have special abilities that make them easier to resize and otherwise reconfigure. You can read all about Dynamic Components in Chapter 5.

✔ **When components cut their own openings, the openings aren't permanent.** When you move or delete a hole-cutting door or window component you've placed in a model, the opening goes with the component.

Follow these steps to adding a hole-cutting component to your model (see Figure 4-25):

Figure 4-25: Placing window and door components in your model is a breeze.

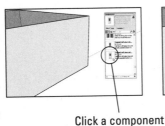 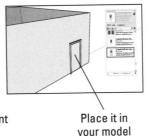 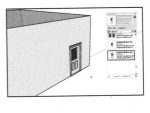

Click a component   Place it in your model

1. **In the Components dialog box, click the component that you want to place in your model.**

2. **Place the component where you want it to be.**

3. **If you don't like where your component is, use the Move tool (read all about it in Chapter 2) to reposition your component.**

Figure 4-26 shows a simple building to which I added a door and a couple window components. Notice how I use guides to line up things — doing so is the best way to ensure that everything's in the right spot.

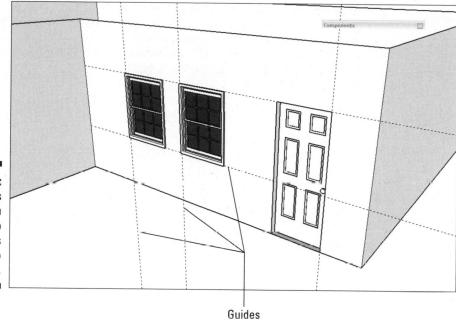

Figure 4-26:
Use guides
to help you
line up
components
you add to
your model.

Guides

Making your own openings

Most of the time, you can't get away with using SketchUp's built-in door and window components — the fact that they can't cut through two-faced walls means that they're limited to external use only. That's okay though; cutting your own holes in walls is quick and easy, and you end up with exactly what you want.

To cut a precise opening in a double-face wall, here's what you need to do; Figure 4-27 shows the basic steps:

1. **Mark where you want your opening to be with guides.**

   For a refresher on using guides, have a look at Chapter 2.

   If you're drawing on a wall that's part of a group, you need to edit that group in order to punch holes in the wall. To edit a group, double-click it with the Select tool. To stop editing, click somewhere off to the side of your model. Check out the first part of Chapter 5 for more info about working with groups.

2. **Draw the outline of the opening you want to create, making sure to create a new face in the process.**

You can use any of the drawing tools to do this, though I recommend sticking with the Line tool when you're starting. Remember to pay close attention to what you're drawing; keep an eye out for the colored inferences, which let you know where you are.

3. **Use Push/Pull to extrude your new face back into the thickness of the wall until it touches the face behind it.**

If everything goes well, your face disappears, taking with it the corresponding area of the face behind it. Now you have an opening in your wall. If your face doesn't disappear, and no opening is created, it's probably for one of the following reasons:

- *Your faces aren't parallel to each other.* This technique works only if both faces are parallel. Keep in mind that just because two faces *look* parallel doesn't mean that they are.

- *You hit an edge.* If you push/pull your face into a face with an edge crossing it, SketchUp gets confused and doesn't cut an opening. Use Undo, get rid of the pesky edge (if you can), and try again.

Figure 4-27:
Use guides
to plan
where you
want an
opening and
then push/
pull all the
way through
both faces.

Create guides   Draw edges   Push/Pull all the way through

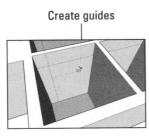 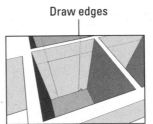 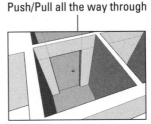

Don't forget to orbit! If you can't quite push/pull what you mean to push/pull, orbit around until you can see what you're doing.

Staring Down Stairs

You can make stairs probably a million different ways in SketchUp, but (naturally) I have my favorites. In the following sections, you find two methods that work equally well; take a look at them both and then decide which work best for your situation. In the last part of Chapter 5, I describe a third, slightly trickier (but way more powerful) way of making stairs using *components;* feel free to take a look if you're feeling more advanced.

SketchUp 7 introduced Dynamic Components, which has some pretty neat implications for people who need stairs to use in their models. So-called *dynamic stair components* automatically add or subtract individual steps as you make them bigger or smaller with the Scale tool. Depending on what you want to accomplish, a pre-made dynamic stair component may save you a bunch of time. Find out more about them in Chapter 5.

Before I dive in, here's some simple stairway vocabulary, just in case you need it; take a look at Figure 4-28 for a visual reference:

- **Rise and run:** The *rise* is the total distance your staircase needs to climb. If the vertical distance from your first floor to your second (your *floor-to-floor* distance) is 10 feet, that's your rise. The *run* is the total *horizontal* distance of your staircase. A set of stairs with a big rise and a small run would be really steep.

- **Tread:** A *tread* is an individual step — the part of the staircase you step on. When someone refers to the size of a tread, he's talking about the *depth* — the distance from the front to the back of the tread. Typically, this is anywhere from 9 to 24 inches, but treads of 10 to 12 inches are most comfortable to walk on.

- **Riser:** The *riser* is the part of the step that connects each tread in the vertical direction. Risers are usually about 5 to 7 inches high, but that depends on your building. Not all staircases have actual risers (think of steps with gaps between treads), but they all have a riser *height*.

- **Landing:** A *landing* is a platform somewhere around the middle of a set of stairs. Landings are necessary in real life, but modeling them can be a pain; figuring out staircases with landings is definitely more complicated. Sometimes, modeling a landing is easier if you think of it as a really big step.

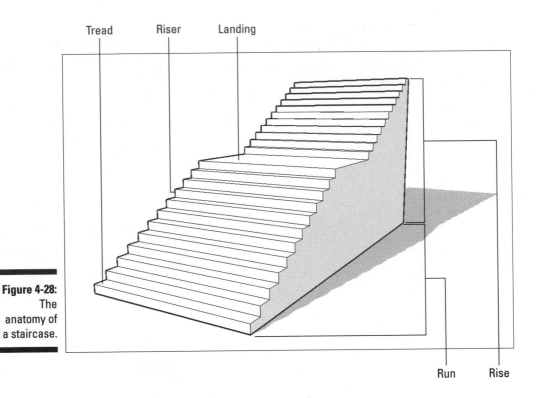

Tread   Riser   Landing

Run   Rise

Figure 4-28:
The
anatomy of
a staircase.

The Subdivided Rectangles method

The Subdivided Rectangles method is how most people think to draw their first set of stairs; it's intuitive and simple, but it's also a bit more time-consuming than the other methods I describe in this book.

The key to the Subdivided Rectangles method is to use a special trick you can do with edges: Called *Divide,* it lets you pick any edge and divide it into as many segments as you want. If you know how many steps you need to draw but not how deep each individual tread needs to be, this comes in really handy.

Here's how the Subdivided Rectangles method works (see Figure 4-29):

Divide edge into smaller edges,
marking off treads

Connect new endpoints

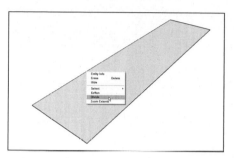

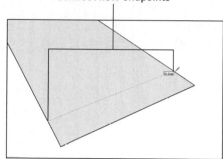

Divide vertical edge marking off vertical risers

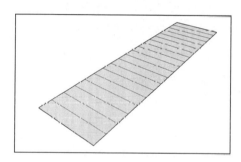

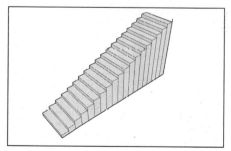

Infer to the endpoints on this divided edge

Figure 4-29:
The
Subdivided
Rectangles
method of
building
stairs.

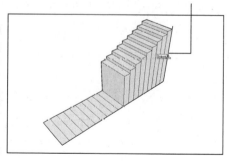

1. **Draw a rectangle the size of the staircase you want to build.**

   I strongly recommend modeling steps as a group, separate from the rest of your building, and moving them into position when they're done. You can read all about groups in Chapter 5.

2. **With the Select tool, right-click one of the long edges of your rectangle and choose Divide.**

   If your staircase is wider than it is long, right-click one of the short edges, instead.

3. **Before you do anything else, type the number of treads you want to create and press Enter.**

   This command automatically divides your edge into many more edges, eliminating the need to calculate how deep each of your treads needs to be. Essentially, each new edge becomes a side of one of your treads.

4. **Draw a line from the endpoint of each new edge, dividing your original rectangle into many smaller rectangles.**

   You can use the Line or the Rectangle tool to do this; pick whichever one you're most comfortable with.

5. **From one of the corners of your original rectangle, draw a vertical edge the height of your staircase's total rise.**

6. **Use the Divide command to split your new edge into however many risers you need in your staircase (generally your number of treads, plus one).**

   Repeat Steps 2 and 3 to do this. The endpoints of your new, little edges tell you how high to make each step.

7. **Push/pull the rectangle that represents your last step to the correct height.**

   Here's where you need to use the hover-click technique that I describe in the sidebar "More fun with Push/Pull," earlier in this chapter. Just click once to push/pull, hover over the endpoint that corresponds to the height of that tread, and click again. Your step is automatically extruded to the right height.

   Extrude your highest step first, but remember that it doesn't go all the way to the top. You always have a riser between your last step and your upper floor.

8. **Repeat Step 7 for each remaining step.**

9. **Use the Eraser to eliminate extra edges you don't need.**

   Don't accidentally erase geometry on the part of your staircase you can't see.

The Copied Profile method

This method for modeling a staircase relies, like the last one, on using Push/Pull to create a 3D form from a 2D face, but I think you'll agree this method is more elegant. In a nutshell, draw the *profile* — the side view, sort of — of a single step and then copy as many steps as you need, create a single face, and extrude the whole thing into shape. The first time you do this is breathtakingly satisfying — one of those "guaranteed to make you smile" SketchUp operations you'll want to repeat for friends (assuming you have nerdy friends like me).

Follow these steps to make a staircase using the Copied Profile method (see Figure 4-30):

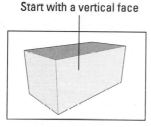

Start with a vertical face

Draw the profile of a single step

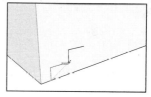

Copy it up

Type the number of copies, then **x**, and press Enter

Push/Pull the stair into 3D

Figure 4-30: The Copied Profile method, in glorious grayscale.

1. **Start with a large, vertical face; make sure that it's big enough for the flight of stairs you want to build.**

   You're going to end up pushing/pulling the whole shebang out of the side of this face, just so you know.

2. **In the bottom corner of the face, draw the profile of a single step.**

   I usually use the Line tool to do this, though you may want to use an arc or two, depending on the level of detail you need. For a refresher on drawing lines accurately, check out Chapter 2.

3. **Select all the edges that make up your step profile.**

You can hold down the Shift key while clicking with the Select tool to add multiple objects to your selection. Chapter 2 has lots of selection tips.

4. **Make a copy of your step profile and place it above your first one.**

   If you're unfamiliar with how to make copies using the Move tool, see Chapter 2.

5. **Type the number of steps you want to make, type x, and then press Enter.**

   For example, if you wanted ten steps, you'd type **10x**. This technique repeats the copy operation you just did by however many times you tell it to; adding an *x* at the end of the number tells SketchUp you want to make copies.

6. **If you need to, draw an edge to make sure that all your step profiles are part of a single face.**

7. **Push/pull the staircase face out to be the width you need it to be.**

   This is the part that seems like magic to most folks; I don't think it ever gets old.

This method of stairway building also works great in combination with the Follow Me tool, which I talk about in Chapter 6. Figure 4-31 whets your appetite — Follow Me is cool beans, all the way around.

Figure 4-31: Using Follow Me with the Copied Profile method produces some impressive geometry, indeed.

Profile   Extrusion path for Follow Me

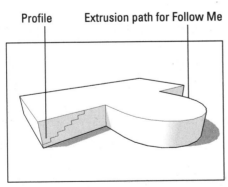
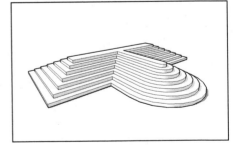

Raising the Roof

If you're lucky, the roof you want to build is fairly simple. Unfortunately, home builders sometimes go a little crazy, creating roofs with dozens of different *pitches* (slopes), dormers, and other doodads that make modeling them a nightmare. For this reason, I keep things pretty simple: The following sections show you how to identify and model basic roof forms. After that, I tell you about a great tool — *Intersect Face* — that you can use to assemble complicated roofs from less-complicated pieces; I think you'll get a kick out of it.

The tricky thing about roofs is that they're hard to see. If you want to make a model of something that already exists, it helps to get a good look at it — that's not always possible with roofs. One neat way to get a better view of a roof you're trying to build is to find it in Google Earth. For more information, check out Chapter 11.

Always, *always* make a group out of your whole building before you work on your roof.

Before I dive in, what follows is a brief guide to general roof types and terminology; this may come in handy for the explanations I give later in this chapter. Figure 4-32 provides a visual accompaniment to my written descriptions:

- **Flat roof:** *Flat roofs* are just that, except they aren't — if a roof were really flat, it would collect water and leak. That's why even roofs that look flat are sloped very slightly.

- **Pitched roof:** Any roof that isn't flat is technically a *pitched roof.*

- **Shed roof:** A *shed roof* is one that slopes from one side to the other.

- **Gabled roof:** *Gabled roofs* have two planes that slope away from a central *ridge.*

- **Hip roof:** A *hip roof* is one where the sides and ends all slope in different directions.

- **Pitch:** The angle of a roof surface.

- **Gable:** A *gable* is the pointy section of wall that sits under the peak of a pitched roof.

- **Eave:** *Eaves* are the parts of a roof that overhang the building.

- **Fascia:** *Fascia* is the trim around the edge of a roof's eaves where gutters are sometimes attached.

- **Soffit:** A *soffit* is the underside of an overhanging eave.

- **Rake:** The *rake* is the part of a gabled roof that overhangs the gable.

- **Valley:** A *valley* is formed when two roof slopes come together; this is where water flows when it rains.

- **Dormer:** *Dormers* are the little things that pop up above roof surfaces. They often have windows and make attic spaces more usable.

- **Parapet:** Flat roofs that don't have eaves have *parapets* — extensions of the building's walls that go up a few feet past the roof itself.

Gabled roof   Dormer   Valley   Hip roof   Flat roof   Parapet   Shed roof

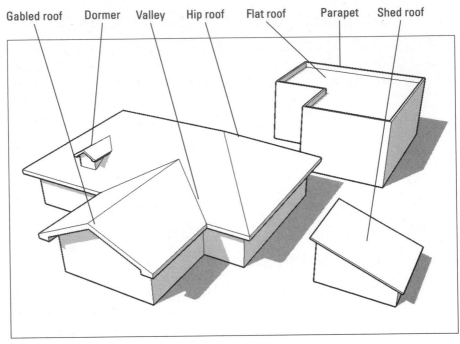

Fascia   Soffit   Gable Rake   Eave

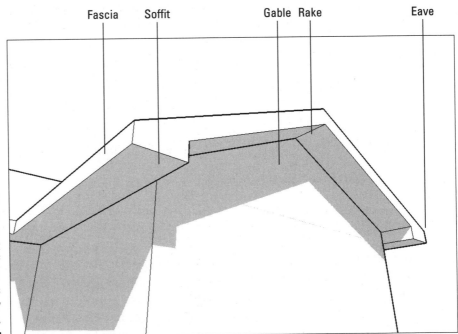

Figure 4-32:
Some
different
kinds of
roofs, and
their various
and sundry
parts.

Building flat roofs with parapets

Good news — SketchUp was practically made for modeling these kinds of roofs. By using a combination of the Offset tool and Push/Pull, you can make a parapet in less than a minute. Follow these steps (see Figure 4-33):

Offset to the inside   Push/pull your parapet up

Figure 4-33:
Modeling parapets on flat-roofed buildings is easy.

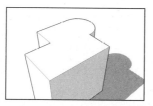 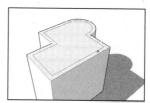 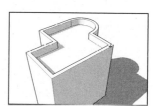

1. **With the Offset tool, click the top face of your building.**

2. **Click again somewhere inside the same face to create another face.**

3. **Type the thickness of your parapet and then press Enter.**

   This redraws your offset edges to be a precise distance from the edges of your original face. How thick should your parapet be? It all depends on your building, but most parapets are between 6 and 12 inches thick.

4. **Push/pull your outside face (the one around the perimeter of your roof) into a parapet.**

5. **Type the height of your parapet and then press Enter.**

Creating eaves for buildings with pitched roofs

My favorite way to create *eaves* (roof overhangs) is to use the Offset tool. Follow these steps to get the general idea (see Figure 4-34):

Offset an overhang   Delete the inside face   Push/Pull a fascia thickness

Figure 4-34:
Eaves are the parts of the roof that overhang a building's walls.

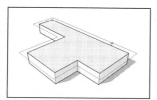 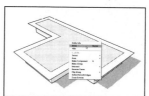 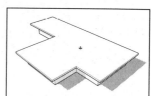

TIP

Pitched roofs can make you crazy

That fact notwithstanding, a few tips might make building your next one a little easier:

✔ **Start by making the rest of your building a group.** Always make a group out of your whole building before you start working on your roof. If you don't, your geometry starts sticking together, you end up erasing walls by accident, and eventually, you lose your mind. On top of that, the ability to separate your roof from the rest of your building whenever you want is handy. You can also group your roof, if that makes sense for what you're doing. Check out Chapter 5 for a full rundown on making and using groups.

✔ **Draw a top view of your roof on paper first.** I find this really helps me figure out things.

Adding measurements and angles is even better — anything so that you know what you need to do when you get around to using SketchUp.

✔ **Figure out how to use the Protractor tool.** This tool (which is on the Tools menu) is for measuring angles and, more importantly, creating angled guides. Because sloped roofs are all about angles, you probably need to use the Protractor sooner or later. One way to find out how this tool works is to open the Instructor dialog box by choosing Window➪Instructor and then activating the Protractor tool. Another way is to read "Rotating the right way", in Chapter 2; the Protractor tool behaves just like the Rotate tool in many ways.

1. **Make a group out of your whole building before you start modeling the roof.**

   This keeps your roof separate, which in turn makes your model easier to work with.

2. **Use the Line tool to create an outline of the parts of your roof that will have eaves of the same height.**

   The goal is a single face that you can offset. A lot of buildings have complex roofs with eaves of all different heights; for the sake of this step, just create a face which, when offset, will create roof overhangs in the right places.

3. **Use the Offset tool to create an overhanging face.**

   For instructions on how to use Offset, see the section "Dusting off SketchUp's drafting tools," earlier in this chapter.

4. **Erase the edges of your original face.**

   A quick way to do this (with the Select tool) is to

   a. Double-click inside your first face.

   This selects both it and the edges that define it.

   b. Press Delete to erase everything that's selected.

5. **Push/pull your overhanging roof face to create a thick fascia.**

   Different roofs have fasciae of different thicknesses; if you don't know yours, just take your best guess.

Constructing gabled roofs

You can approach the construction of a gabled roof in a bunch of ways (every SketchUp expert has her favorite), but I find one method in particular that works well consistently.

Follow these steps to build a gabled roof, which is shown in Figure 4-35:

Create an angled guide with the Protractor

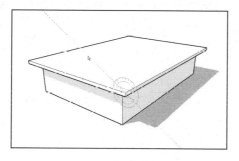

Draw a vertical edge

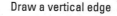
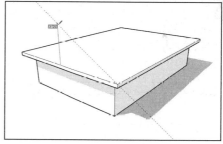

Complete the roof profile

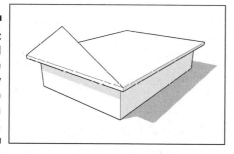

Push/pull it back

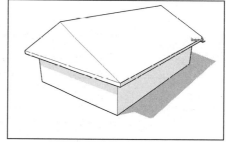

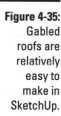

Figure 4-35: Gabled roofs are relatively easy to make in SketchUp.

1. **Create a roof overhang, following the steps in the preceding section.**

   Most gabled roofs have eaves, so you probably need to do this for your building.

2. **Use the Protractor tool to create an angled guide at the corner of your roof.**

See the nearby sidebar, "Pitched roofs can make you crazy," for more information about drawing angled guides with the Protractor.

Architects and builders often express angles as *rise over run ratios*. For example, a 4:12 (pronounced 4 in 12) roof slope rises 4 feet for every 12 feet it runs — a 1:12 slope is very shallow, and a 12:12 slope is very steep. When using the Protractor tool, SketchUp's Measurements box understands angles expressed as ratios as well as those expressed in degrees. Typing **6:12** yields a slope of 6 in 12.

3. **Use the Line tool to draw a vertical edge from the midpoint of your roof to the angled guide you created in Step 2.**

   The point at which your edge and your guide meet is the height of your roof ridge.

4. **Draw two edges from the top of your vertical line to the corners of your roof.**

   This creates two triangular faces.

5. **Erase the vertical edge you drew in Step 3 and the guide you drew in Step 2.**

6. **Push/pull back your triangular gable.**

   If your gabled roof extends all the way to the other end of your building, push/pull it back that far. If your roof runs into another section of roof (as shown in Figure 4-36), extrude it back until it's completely "buried." The section "Sticking your roof together," later in this chapter, has more information on what to do when you make a complex roof.

Push/pull it all the way into the other roof pitch

Figure 4-36:
If your gabled roof is part of a larger roof structure, it may just run into another roof pitch. Let it.

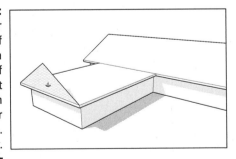
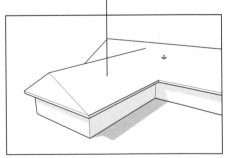

7. **Finish your eaves, fascia, soffit, and rake(s) however you want.**

   You find lots of kinds of gabled roof details, so I can't cover them all, but Figure 4-37 shows a few common ones. Instead of writing about them (which would get confusing anyway), I let the pictures do the talking.

Figure 4-37:
Some
common
gabled roof
details.

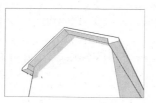
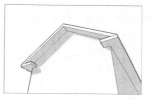
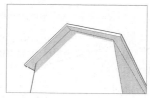

Making hip roofs

Believe it or not, building a hip roof is easier than building a gabled one. *Hip roofs* don't have rakes, which makes them a lot less complicated to model. Follow these steps to find out what I mean (see Figure 4-38):

Measure half-width of your gable

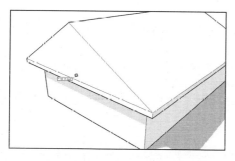

Create a guide that distance
from end of gable

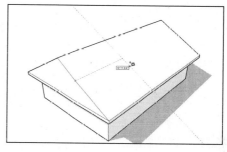

Draw edges connecting ridge and corners
and erase 3 edges that form gable

Now you have a hip

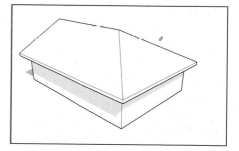

Figure 4-38:
To make
a hip roof,
start with a
gabled one.

1. **Follow Steps 1–5 in the preceding section "Constructing gabled roofs."**

2. **Measure the distance from the midpoint of the gable to the corner of the roof.**

Because hip roofs have pitches that are the same on all sides, you can use a simple trick to figure out where to locate the hip in your roof. It's a lot easier than using the Protractor.

3. **With the Tape Measure, create a guide the distance you just measured from the end of the gable.**

4. **Draw edges from the point on the ridge you just located to the corners of your roof.**

   This does two things: It splits the sides of your roof into two faces each and creates a new face (which you can't see yet) under the gabled end of your roof.

5. **Erase the three edges that form the gabled end of your roof, revealing the "hipped" pitch underneath.**

   Neat, huh? Now all three faces of your roof are the same pitch — just the way they should be.

6. **If appropriate, repeat the process on the other end of your roof.**

Sticking your roof together

In general, the newer and more expensive a house is, the more roof slopes it has. Who knows why this is the case; it probably has something to do with folks thinking complex-roofed houses look more like French chateaus. Whether crazy roofs (there's my bias showing again) are a good thing isn't relevant to this book, but I know one thing for sure: They're a pain in the, um, gutters to model.

Getting to know Intersect Faces

Luckily, SketchUp has a relatively little-known feature that often helps when it comes to making roofs with lots of pitches: *Intersect Faces*. Here's what you need to know about this terrific little tool:

- ✓ **Intersect Faces makes new geometry from existing geometry.** It takes faces you've selected and creates edges wherever they intersect. Figure 4-39 shows what I mean: Perhaps you want to make a model that's a cube with a cylinder-shaped chunk taken out of it. You'd model the cube and model the cylinder. After positioning them carefully, you can then use Intersect Faces to create edges where the two shapes' faces come together. After that, you'd use the Eraser to get rid of the edges you didn't want — the rest of the cylinder, in this case.

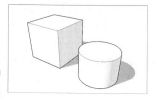
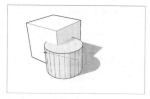
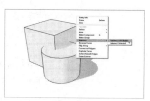

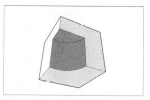

Figure 4-39:
Using
Intersect
Faces to
cut a partial
cylinder out
of a cube.

✔ **Intersect Faces and the Eraser tool go hand in hand.** Anytime you use Intersect Faces, you need to follow up by deleting the geometry you don't want. This isn't a bad thing, but it does mean that you need to be good at orbiting, zooming, and panning around your model. You also need to be handy with the Eraser.

✔ **Most of the time, choose to Intersect Faces with Model.** This tool has three modes, but the majority of the time, you use the basic one. Here's what all three modes do:

- *Intersect Faces with Model:* Creates edges everywhere your selected faces intersect with other faces in your model — whether the other faces are selected or not.

- *Intersect Faces with Selection:* Only creates edges where *selected* faces intersect with other *selected* faces. This is handy if you're trying to be a little bit more precise.

- *Intersect Faces with Context:* This one's a little trickier: Choosing this option creates edges where faces *within the same group or component* intersect; that's why it's available only when you edit a group or component.

✔ **Intersect Faces doesn't have a button.** To use it, you have to either

- *Right-click and choose Intersect Faces.*

- *Choose Edit⇨Intersect Faces.*

Until SketchUp 8, Intersect Faces was called simply *Intersect.* Why the name change? One of the most interesting new features in the Pro version of SketchUp 8 is a set of tools for doing *Boolean* (additive and subtractive) modeling operations on your geometry. One of these new tools is Intersect; the existing tool was renamed to avoid confusion. Collectively, the new additions to SketchUp's Pro tool set are the Solid Tools — read all about them in Chapter 6.

Using Intersect Faces to make roofs

When creating roofs, you can use Intersect Faces to combine a whole bunch of gables, hips, dormers, sheds, and so on into a single roof. Doing so is no cakewalk, and it requires a fair amount of planning, but it works great when nothing else will.

Figure 4-40 shows a complicated roof with several elements. Gabled roofs have been pushed/pulled into the main hip roof at all different heights, but edges don't exist where all the different faces meet. In the steps that follow, use Intersect Faces to create the edges you want and then use the Eraser to clean up the mess:

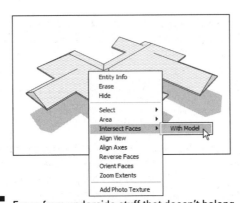
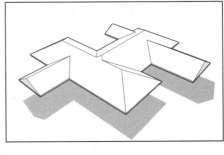

Erase from underside stuff that doesn't belong

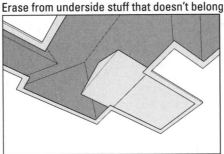

Figure 4-40: Here's a typically complex roof that could use Intersect Faces to unify.

1. **Select the whole roof.**

   You can select the whole roof a number of ways, but the one that I find works the best is to first hide the group that contains the rest of your building and then draw a big selection box around the whole roof with the Select tool.

2. **Choose Edit⇨Intersect Faces⇨With Selected.**

   This tells SketchUp to go through and create edges everywhere you have faces that *intersect* — everywhere they pass through each other without an edge.

3. **Get out your Eraser and *carefully* delete all the extra geometry on the inside of your roof.**

   I won't lie; this can be a lot of work, but it's a whole lot easier than using the Line tool and SketchUp's inference engine to figure out where everything should go.

When all else fails, use the Line tool

Fancy tools like Follow Me and Intersect Faces are useful most of the time, but for some roofs, you just have to resort to drawing good old edges. If that's the case, you'd better get familiar with most of the stuff at the beginning of Chapter 2 because you're going to be inferencing like there's no tomorrow. SketchUp users who really know what they're doing can draw *anything* with the Line and Eraser tools; it's a beautiful thing to watch. Unfortunately, it's not a beautiful thing to write (or read) about in a black-and-white book, so I can't show you as much "modeling from first principles" stuff as I want.

All the same, check out the following figure. In it, I use the Line tool and SketchUp's venerable inference engine to add a gabled dormer to a sloped roof surface. With practice, you can, too.

(continued)

(continued)

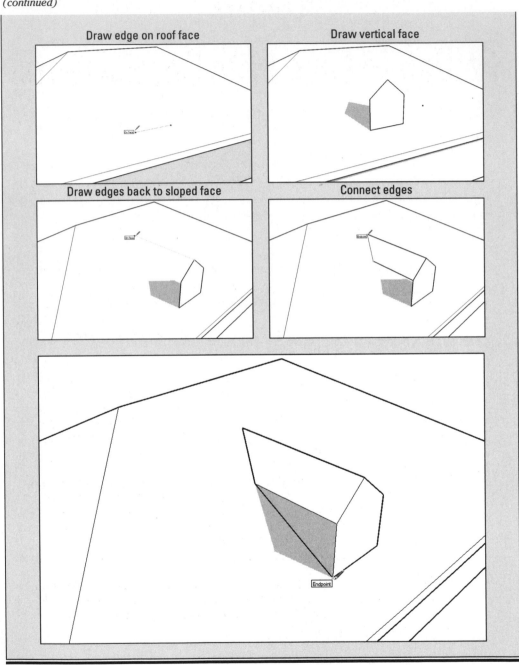

Chapter 5

Falling in Love with Components

I wish there was a way to use the typography in this book to convey the relative importance of certain topics; if there was, the word *COMPONENTS* would be printed 4 inches high, and it would be colored neon green. Components are *that* important.

Making a *component* (or a group) is like gluing together geometry in your model. Edges and faces that are grouped together act like mini-models inside your main model; you use components and groups to more easily select, move, hide, and otherwise work with parts of your model that need to be kept separate. Getting used to using groups and components is the single biggest thing you can do to get better at SketchUp.

This chapter is about creating and using SketchUp components to make your life a whole lot simpler. I begin by talking about groups (which are a little bit like lobotomized components). After that, I jump into components — finding them, managing them, and making your own. Then I talk about Dynamic Components, which are the best thing to happen to SketchUp since the invention of the scroll-wheel mouse.

In the last section of this chapter, I show you a couple modeling techniques that take advantage of component behavior. They're guaranteed to save you time and effort, and using them will make you feel like a rock star — one who makes 3D models, at least.

Grouping Things Together

Anyone who's worked with SketchUp for even a short time has probably noticed something: SketchUp geometry (the edges and faces that make up your model) is *sticky*. In other words, stuff in your model wants to stick to other stuff. The people who invented SketchUp built it this way on purpose; the reasons why would take awhile to explain. Suffice it to say, making and using groups are the keys to keeping the stuff in your model from sticking together.

You have many reasons to make groups; here are a few of them:

✔ **Grouped geometry doesn't stick to anything.** Perhaps you've modeled a building, and you want to add a roof. You want to be able to remove the roof by moving it out of the way with the Move tool, but every time you try, you end up pulling the whole top part of the house along with it (like the middle image in Figure 5-1). Making the roof a separate group allows you to let it sit on top of your house without sticking there, making it easier to deal with, as shown in the right image in Figure 5-1.

The house is being stretched

Figure 5-1:
Making the roof into a group means that it won't stick to the rest of your building.

 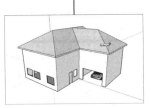 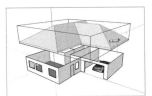

✔ **Using groups makes working with your model easier.** You can select all the geometry in a group by clicking it once with the Select tool. You can move groups and make copies with the Move tool.

✔ **You can name groups.** If you turn a selection of geometry in your model into a group, you can give it a name. In the Outliner (which I talk about in Chapter 7) you can see a list of the groups (and components) in your model, and if you've given them names, you can see what you have.

✔ **Groups can be solids.** Basically, a *solid* is any group (or component) whose geometry can be thought of as *watertight* — continuous, with no holes. Solids are important for a couple reasons:

- *If an object is a solid, SketchUp can calculate its volume.* You can see any solid's volume by looking in the Entity Info dialog box.

- *The Solid Tools let you perform nifty modeling tricks using two or more solids.* You can read all about the Solid Tools toward the end of Chapter 6.

Follow these steps to create a group:

1. **Select the geometry (edges and faces) you want to turn into a group.**

   The simplest way to select multiple *entities* (edges and faces) is to click them one at a time with the Select tool while holding down the Shift key. You can also use the Select tool to drag a box around the entities you want to select, but this can be tough, depending on where they are. For more information on making selections, check out Chapter 2.

2. **Choose Edit⇨Make Group.**

   You can also right-click and choose Make Group from the context menu that pops up.

If you want to ungroup the geometry in a group, you need to explode it. Right-click the group and choose Explode from the context menu. The edges and faces that were grouped together aren't grouped together anymore.

To edit the geometry inside a group, double-click it with the Select tool. You know you're in edit mode when the rest of your model appears to fade back, leaving only your grouped geometry clearly visible. To stop editing a group, click outside it, somewhere else in your modeling window.

Working with Components

Even though components are incredibly important, there's nothing too magical about them. They're just groupings of geometry (edges and faces) that make working in SketchUp faster, easier, and more fun. In a lot of ways, components are really just fancy groups — they do a lot of the same things. In the following sections, I talk about what makes components special and give some examples of what you can do with them. Next, I give a quick tour of the Components dialog box, pointing out where components live and how you can organize them. The last part of this section is devoted to making your own components; it's not hard, and after you can make components, you're on your way to SketchUp stardom. (Check out Chapter 11 for more on sharing your SketchUp models with the world.)

What makes components so great?

By now, you've probably figured out that I'm a big fan of using components whenever you can. Here's why:

- ✔ **Everything that's true about groups is true about components.** That's right: Components are just like groups, only better (in some ways, at least). Components don't stick to the rest of your model, you can give them meaningful names, and you can select them, move them, copy them, and edit them easily — just like you can with groups.

- ✔ **Components update automatically.** When you use multiple copies (called *instances*) of the same component in your model, they're all spookily linked. Changing one makes them all change, which saves loads of time. Consider a window component that I created and made two copies of, as shown in Figure 5-2. When I add something (in this case, some shutters) to one instance of that component, *all* the instances are updated. Now I have three windows, and they all have shutters.

Figure 5-2:
Changing one instance of a component changes all the other instances, too.

These windows are instances of the same component

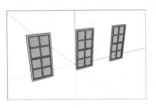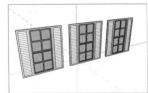

- ✔ **Using components can help you keep track of quantities.** You can use the Components dialog box to count, select, substitute, and otherwise manage all the component instances in your model. Figure 5-3 shows a great big (and ugly) building I designed to go with the window component I made. I have a lot more control than I would have otherwise because the windows are component instances. To illustrate what I mean, I changed all the windows to helicopters in a few clicks.

- ✔ **You can make a component cut an opening automatically.** Perhaps you've made a window (which I have) and you want that window to poke a hole through whatever surface you stick it to (which I do). You can set up SketchUp components to cut their own openings in faces. These openings are even temporary; when you delete the component, the hole disappears.

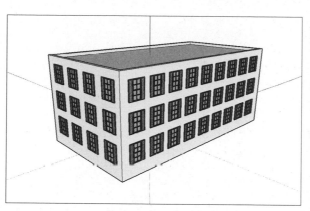
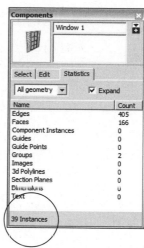

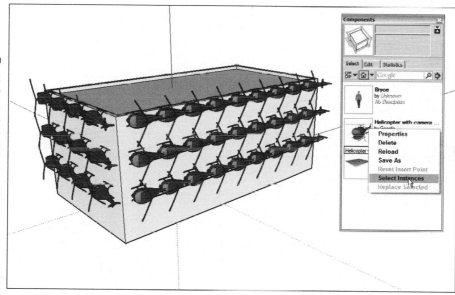

Figure 5-3:
Quickly count all the window instances in your model (top), or even swap them out for another component. (I like helicopters, don't you?)

Components that are set up to automatically cut openings can do so only through a single face. Even if your wall is two faces thick, your components will cut through only one of them.

✔ **You can use your components in other models.** It's a simple operation to make any component you build available for use whenever you work in SketchUp, no matter what model you're working on. If you have a group of parts or other things you always use, making your own component collection can save you a lot of time and effort. There's more information about creating your own component collections later in this section.

✔ **Components are great for making symmetrical models.** Because you can flip a component instance and keep working on it, and because component instances automatically update when you change one of them, using components is a great way to model anything that's symmetrical. And if you look around, you'll notice that most things people use are symmetrical. The second-to-last part of this chapter dives headlong into modeling symmetrical things like couches and hatchbacks; Figure 5-4 shows examples.

Figure 5-4: What do all these things have in common? They're symmetrical.

Exploring the Components dialog box

It's all fine and well that SketchUp lets you turn bits of your models into components, I suppose, but wouldn't it be nice if you had someplace to *keep* them? And wouldn't it be great if you could use components that other people made to spiff up your model, instead of building everything yourself? As you've probably already guessed, both of these things are possible, and both involve the Components dialog box, which you can find on the Window menu.

You can bring any SketchUp model on your computer into your current file as a component. That's because components are really just SketchUp files embedded in other SketchUp files. When you create a component in your model, you're effectively creating a new, nested SketchUp file. Neat, huh?

The Components dialog box is made up of four major areas, which I describe in the following sections.

The Google 3D Warehouse

Imagine a place online where everyone in the world can share SketchUp models for free. That's the *3D Warehouse* in a nutshell. It's hosted by Google, it's available in more than 40 languages, and it's searchable — just like you'd expect from the world's most popular search engine.

You can get to the 3D Warehouse in a couple ways:

✔ **On the Web:** Just type `http://sketch up.google.com/3dwarehouse` into your Web browser.

✔ **Through SketchUp:** The Components dialog box is hooked up directly to the 3D Warehouse, as long as you're online. You can also open the 3D Warehouse in a separate window by choosing File⇨3D Warehouse⇨Get Models.

Anything you find on the 3D Warehouse, you can download and use in your own models. You can also upload anything you make so that other people can use it. Find out more about sharing your work on the 3D Warehouse in Chapter 11.

Info and buttons

I don't really know what to call this part of the Components dialog box, so I call it like it is: It's for information and buttons. Figure 5-5 points out its elements, and here's what everything does:

✔ **Name:** The name of the component you select appears here. If your component is in your model, it's editable. If the component is in one of the default collections, it's not. A component is considered to be in your model if it appears in your In Model collection, which you can read about in the section "The Select tab," later in this chapter.

✔ **Description:** Some, but not all, components have descriptions associated with them. You can write one when you create a new component, or you can add one to an existing component in your model. Just like the name, you can edit descriptions for models only in your In Model library.

✔ **Display Secondary Selection Pane button:** Clicking this button opens a second view of your collections at the bottom of the Components dialog box. Use this to manage the components on your computer.

The Select tab

This is where your components live (if they can be said to live anywhere). Use the Select tab to view, organize, and choose components. Refer to Figure 5-5 to see the Select tab in all its glory.

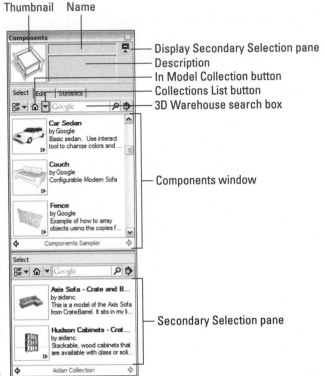

Thumbnail   Name

— Display Secondary Selection pane
— Description
— In Model Collection button
— Collections List button
— 3D Warehouse search box

— Components window

— Secondary Selection pane

Figure 5-5:
The
Components
dialog box is
chock full o'
goodness.

✔ **In Model Collection button:** SketchUp automatically keeps track of the components you've used in your model and puts a copy of each of them in your In Model collection. Each SketchUp file you create has its own In Model collection, which contains the components that exist in that model. Clicking the In Model Collection button displays the components in your In Model collection, if you have any.

✔ **Collections List button:** The components listed under the Favorites heading are a mix of two collection types:

• *Local* collections are folders of components that live on your hard drive. You can access them anytime because they refer to files on your computer.

• *Online* collections are groupings of components that live in the Google 3D Warehouse (which you can read lots more about in this book). Unlike local collections, you can only access online collections when you're — you guessed it — online.

Unfortunately, there's no way to tell just by looking at them in the list which collections are local and which are online. If you click the name of a collection and see a Searching Google 3D Warehouse progress bar before you see any models, that collection is online.

TECHNICAL STUFF

Search the 3D Warehouse like a pro

Simply typing **coffee table** into the 3D Warehouse search bar gets you a bunch of coffee tables — that much is certain. If you want to be more precise, you can use so-called *advanced search operators* to improve your results by a mile. All you have to do is add one or more of them to your search request. These are some of my favorites:

✔ **author:** Sometimes you want to find only models uploaded by a specific user. Example: Typing **table author:aidanc** returns only models created by me with the word *table* somewhere in the title, description, or tags.

✔ **min-rating:** I find it useful to specify a minimum level of quality when I look for

decent stuff to use in my models. Use a number from 1 to 5. Example: Typing **sofa min-rating:4** returns only sofas with a minimum star rating of 4.

✔ **is:dynamic:** Later in this chapter, I go on and on about Dynamic Components (DCs). They're the bee's knees. Use this operator to specify that you want only DCs to show up in your search results. Example: Typing **door is:dynamic** returns only doors that are DCs. Highly recommended.

There are plenty more; you can find a complete list by searching *3dwarehouse advanced search operators* on your favorite search engine.

Google 3D warehouse

| coffee table modern min-rating:4 | (Search) | Advanced Search |

TIP

✔ **3D Warehouse search bar:** It works just like regular Google search: Type what you're looking for and press Enter. Models in the Google 3D Warehouse that match your search terms appear in the Components window below. Naturally, you need to be online for this to work.

✔ **Components window:** This window displays the components in the currently selected component collection, or the results of a 3D Warehouse search you've just performed. Click a component to use it in your model.

Components that have a little green arrow icon next to them are special; they're Dynamic Components. They're relatively new and they have special abilities. You can read about DCs later in this chapter.

✔ **View Options button:** Pretty simple, really. This is where you decide how to view the components (or subcollections) in the Components window.

✔ **Collection Details menu:** Here's where you manage your component collections. A bunch of options exist, so I'd better explain what most of them mean:

- *Open a Local Collection:* Lets you choose a folder on your computer system to use as a component collection. Any SketchUp models in that folder show up in the Components window, ready to be used as components in your models.

- *Create a New Collection:* Allows you to create a folder somewhere on your computer system that you can use as a component collection. A collection is handy if you have a number of components that you use all the time; putting them all in one place makes them easier to find.

- *Save as a Local Collection:* When you choose this option, SketchUp lets you save the components that currently appear in your Components window as a brand-new local collection. If the components you're viewing are online, copies of them get downloaded to your computer. If you're viewing your In Model collection, the contents are copied and included in a new folder. If you're already viewing a local collection, this option isn't available.

- *View in Google 3D Warehouse:* If you're viewing an online collection, this option opens that collection in a separate window that displays the 3D Warehouse in much more detail.

- *3D Warehouse Terms of Service:* Choose this option if you're having trouble sleeping. If you're wondering who owns the stuff on the 3D Warehouse, this is where it's at.

- *Add to Favorites:* Choosing this option adds whatever you're viewing in the Components window to the Favorites section of the Collections list. That goes for local collections (folders on your computer); online collections (from the 3D Warehouse); and 3D Warehouse searches. That's right — you can save a search as a favorite collection. The models in a Favorite Search collection are always different, depending on what's in the 3D Warehouse.

The next two options appear only when you're viewing your In Model collection:

- *Expand:* Because components can be made up of other, nested components, a component you use in your model may really be *lots* of components. Choosing Expand displays all the components in your model, whether or not they're nested inside other components. Most of the time, you probably want to leave Expand deselected.

- *Purge Unused:* Choose this to get rid of any components in your In Model collection that aren't in your model anymore. Be sure to use this before you send your SketchUp file to someone else; it seriously reduces your file size and makes things a whole lot neater.

Select and replace all your troubles away

On top of all the buttons, menus, and windows you can immediately see in the Select tab of the Components dialog box, hidden options that most people don't find until they look for them are on a context menu. The menu pops up when you right-click an In Model collection component:

✔ **Select Instances:** Perhaps you have 15 *instances* (copies) of the same component in your model, and you want to select them all. Just make sure that you're viewing your In Model collection and then right-click the component (in the Components dialog box) whose instances you want to select all. Choose Select Instances, and your work's done. This can save you tons of time, particularly if you have component instances all over the place.

✔ **Replace Selected:** Now you may want to swap in a different component for one that's in your model. Simply select the component instances (in your modeling window) that you want to replace and then right-click the component (in the Components dialog box) that you want to use instead. Choose Replace Selected from the context menu to perform the swap.

Ready for an even better tip? Use Select Instances and Replace Selected together to help you work more efficiently. Instead of placing 20 big, heavy tree components in your model (which can seriously slow down things), use a smaller, simpler component instead (such as a stick). When you're finished modeling, use Select Instances to select all the stand-in components at once and then use Replace Selected to swap in the real component. Figure 5-5 (earlier in this chapter) shows the mechanics of this operation, albeit using windows and helicopters.

The Edit tab

Because the options in this part of the Components dialog box are similar to the ones you get when you make a new component, check out the section "Creating your own components," later in this chapter, for the whole scoop.

You can use only the options in the Edit tab on components in your In Model collection — everything is grayed out for components that live in any other place.

The Statistics tab

Can you remember who won the 1975 Super Bowl? How many home runs did Hank Aaron hit in his career? Do you always check the nutrition information panel on food packaging? You may be a sucker for statistics, and if so, welcome home. . . .

Even if you're not, the Statistics tab is a useful place to spend some time. Use this tab to keep track of all the details related to whatever component you have selected in the Components dialog box. (See Figure 5-6.) This is especially useful for doing the following things:

Figure 5-6:
The
Statistics
tab of the
Components
dialog box:
Geek out on
numbers.

✔ **Checking the size of your components:** The information in the Edges and Faces areas of this tab lets you know how much geometry is in a component. If you're worried about file size or your computer's performance, try to use small components — ones with low numbers of faces and edges.

✔ **Seeing what components are inside your components:** The Component Instances line lists how many component instances are in your selected component. If you switch from All Geometry to Components in the drop-down list at the top of the tab, you can see a list of all the constituent components: subcomponents within your main component.

The Statistics tab *doesn't* show details for components you have selected in your actual model; it only shows information about the component that's selected in the Select tab of the Components dialog box. To see information about whatever component (or other kind of object) you have selected in your modeling window, use the Entity Info dialog box (located in the Window menu).

Save time — go shopping

Why spend hours modeling an oak tree when you can buy a fantastic one for a reasonable price? If you can't find what you need among the zillions of components that you can download for free from the 3D Warehouse, here are a couple great, paid options online:

Form Fonts: Form Fonts (www.formfonts.com) is a Web site that sells components "all you can eat, buffet style." You pay a (surprisingly low) monthly fee, and you have access to *thousands* of high-quality models of just about anything. Form Fonts' international team of modelers even takes requests — if you need

something that they don't have, they can probably make it if you ask nicely. Even if you're not interested in signing up, it's worth checking out the Web site just to see the beautiful models Form Fonts makes.

SketchUpModels.com: Unlike Form Fonts, this site (http://sketchupmodels.com) isn't a buffet; you buy only what you need, *à la carte.* Some of its models may seem a little expensive, but when you consider how much time it'd take you to make them, it may be worth it to get out your credit card — especially if you use SketchUp for work.

Creating your own components

Now that I have you all jazzed up about the wonder and mystery of using components in your models, I bet you can't wait to start making your own. At least I hope so — using components is probably the single best SketchUp habit you can develop. Here's why:

- ✔ **Components keep file sizes down.** When you use several instances of a single component, SketchUp has to remember the information for only one of them. This means that your files are smaller, which in turn means you have an easier time e-mailing, uploading, and opening them on your computer.

- ✔ **Components show in the Outliner.** If you're a person who's at all interested in not wasting time hunting for things you've misplaced, create lots of components. Doing so means that you can see, hide, unhide, and rearrange them in the Outliner, which I cover in Chapter 7.

- ✔ **Components can save your sanity.** Hooray! You've finished a model of the new airport — and it took only three weeks! Too bad the daylighting consultant wants you to add a sunshade detail to every one of the 1,300 windows in the project. If you made that window a component, you're golden. If, on the other hand, that window *isn't* a component, you're going to spend a very long night holding hands with your computer mouse.

✔ **Components can be dynamic.** Dynamic Components are components with special abilities. They can be set up with multiple configurations, taught to scale intelligently, programmed to perform simple animations, and more. Anyone can use existing DCs, but only people with SketchUp Pro can create new ones. Check out "Discovering Dynamic Components" later in this chapter, for the whole story.

Making a new component

Creating simple components is a pretty easy process, but making more complicated ones — components that automatically cut openings, stick to surfaces, and always face the viewer — can be a little trickier. Follow these steps, no matter what kind of component you're trying to make:

1. **Select at least two edges and faces you want to turn into a component.**

   For more information on making selections, see Chapter 2.

2. **Choose Edit⇨Create Component.**

   The Create Component dialog box opens. (See Figure 5-7.)

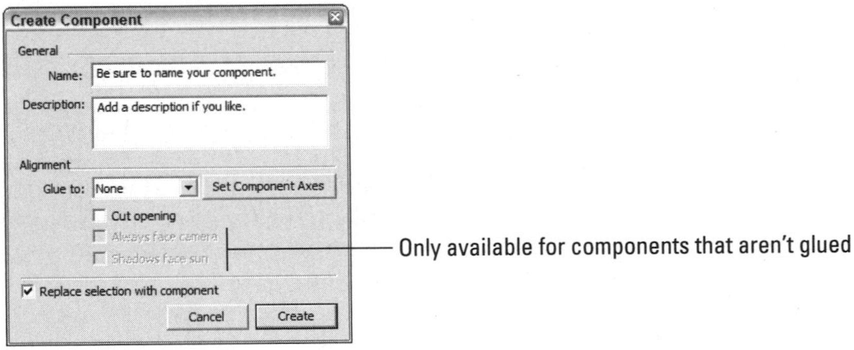

Figure 5-7:
The Create
Component
dialog box.
So many
options. . . .

— Only available for components that aren't glued

3. **Give your new component a name and description.**

   Of these two, the name is by far the most important. Choose a name that's descriptive enough that you'll understand it when you open your model a year from now.

4. **Set the alignment options for your new component.**

   Wondering what the heck all this stuff means? I don't blame you — it can be a bit confusing the first time. For a quick introduction to each option and tips for using it, check out Table 5-1.

5. **Select the Replace Selection with Component check box, if it isn't already selected.**

   This drops your new component into your model right where your selected geometry was, saving you from inserting it from the Components dialog box.

6. **Click the Create button to create your new component.**

Table 5-1	Component Alignment Options	
Option1	*What It Does*	*Tips and Tricks*
Glue To	Makes a component automatically stick to a specific plane. For example, a chair will almost always sit on a floor. It will almost *never* be stuck to a wall, turned sideways. When a component is glued to a surface, using the Move tool moves it only on that surface — never perpendicular to it (up and down, if the surface is a floor).	Use this feature for objects that you want to remain on the surface you put them on, especially objects you want to rearrange: Furniture, windows, and doors are prime examples. If you want to unstick a glued component from a particular surface, right-click it and choose Unglue from the context menu.
Set Component Axes	Sets a component's *axis origin* and *orientation*. This is important primarily if you have SketchUp Pro and plan to make this into a Dynamic Component. If you aren't, you can safely leave this alone.	Click the Set Component Axes button to choose where you want your component's axis origin to be (where the red, green, and blue axes meet). Click once to center your axes, again to establish the red direction, and again to establish the green and blue directions. If you're creating a Dynamic Component, this is something you absolutely must know how to do.
Cut Opening	For components "on" a surface, select this check box to automatically cut an opening in surfaces you stick the component to.	As with pre-made components, this opening is temporary: If you delete the component instance, the opening disappears. If you move the component instance, the opening moves, too.

(continued)

Table 5-1	*(continued)*	
Option1	*What It Does*	*Tips and Tricks*
Always Face Camera	Makes a component *always* face you, no matter how you orbit around. To make your 2D Face-Me components (that's what they're called) work right, rotate your component-to-be so that it's perpendicular to your model's green axis before you choose Make Component.	Using flat, lightweight components instead of 3D heavy ones is a great way to have lots of people and trees in your model without bogging down your computer.
Shadows Face Sun	Only available when the Always Face Camera check box is selected, and is selected by default.	Leave this check box selected unless your Face-Me component meets the ground in two or more separate places, as shown in Figure 5-8.

Components can cut through only one face at a time. If your model's walls are two faces thick, you have to cut your window and door openings manually.

Skip ahead to Chapter 17 to read about Windowizer, a neato Ruby script by Rick Wilson that can help make windows — and a whole lot more.

Editing, exploding, and locking component instances

Right-clicking a component instance in your modeling window opens a context menu that offers lots of useful choices; here's what some of them let you do:

- ✔ **Edit Component:** To edit all instances of a component at once, right-click any instance and choose Edit Component from the context menu. The rest of your model fades back, and you see a dashed bounding box around your component. When you're done, click somewhere outside the bounding box to finish editing; your changes have been made in every instance of that component in your model.

- ✔ **Make Unique:** Sometimes you want to make changes to only one or a few of the instances of a component in your model. In this case, select the instance(s) you want to edit, right-click one of them, and choose Make Unique from the context menu. This turns the instances you selected into a separate component. Now edit any of them; only those instances you made unique reflect your changes.

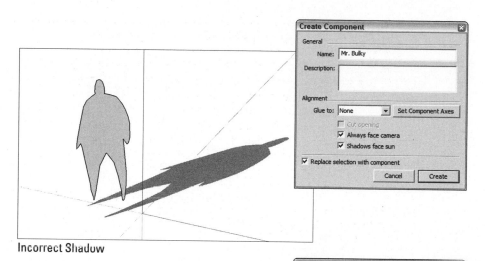

Incorrect Shadow

Figure 5-8:
Deselect the
Shadows
Face Sun
check box
if your
component
touches the
ground in
more than
one place.

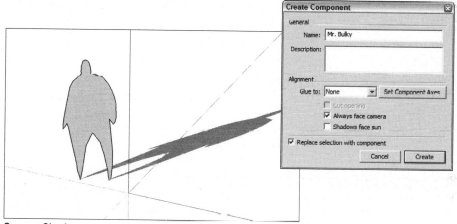

Correct Shadow

✓ **Explode:** When you explode a component instance, you're effectively
turning it back into regular ol' geometry. Explode is a lot like Ungroup in
other software programs (in SketchUp, you use Explode to disassemble
both components and groups).

✓ **Lock:** Locking a group or a component instance means that nobody —
including you — can mess with it until it's unlocked. You should use this
on parts of your model you don't want to change accidentally. To unlock
something, right-click it and choose Unlock.

Discovering Dynamic Components

Once upon a time, the smartest thing a component could do was cut its own hole in a surface. "Wow!" all SketchUp aficionados thought, "Components are *geniuses*!" And so they were — until SketchUp 7 came along. With that release, the folks at Google introduced an entirely new dimension to modeling with SketchUp: Dynamic Components are components with special powers.

Until version 7, SketchUp components were basically dumb. If you wanted to make a staircase longer, you had to make copies of the steps and place them in the right spot. If you needed to change the color of a car, you had to dig out the Paint Bucket and dive in to the geometry. The problem was that components didn't know what they were supposed to represent; they were just groupings of faces and edges in the shape of an object.

Making your own doors and windows

If you're kind of nerdy like I am, nothing beats making your own window and door components. Here's what you need to know (check out the illustration that follows this sidebar for visual instructions):

1. **Draw a rectangle on a vertical surface, such as a wall.**

2. **Delete the face you just created to make a hole in your vertical surface.**

3. **Select all four edges of the hole you just created; then right-click one of the edges and choose Make Component from the context menu.**

4. **Make sure that Glue to Any, Cut Opening, and Replace Selection with Component are all selected; then click the Create button to create your new component.**

5. **With the Select tool, double-click your new component (in the modeling window) to edit it.**

The rest of your model appears to fade back a bit.

6. **Use the modeling tools just like you always would, keep building your door or window how you want.**

7. **When you're done, click outside your component to stop editing it.**

If the opening you create ever closes, one of two things probably happened:

✔ **A new surface was created.** Try deleting the offending surface to see whether that fixes things; it usually does.

✔ **The cutting boundary was messed up.** The cutting boundary consists of the edges that define the hole your component is cutting. If you take away those edges, SketchUp doesn't know where to cut the hole anymore. Drawing them back in usually sets things straight.

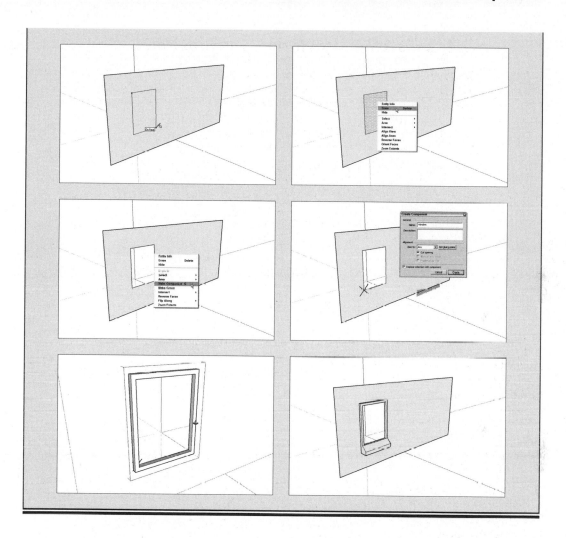

Dynamic Components (DCs) are models that have an idea of what they are; they know what to do when you interact with them. This section outlines what DCs represent for SketchUp modelers and how to use them.

The previous edition of this book included no fewer than 15 pages on authoring your own DCs; I removed that content from this edition to squeeze in new stuff about Solid Tools, Ruby scripts, and LayOut, among other things. The good news: Everything I excised is available in Bonus Chapter 2 on this book's Web site — see the Introduction for the URL.

Getting acquainted with DCs

I have a lot to cover, so dive right in. Here's what you need to know about Dynamic Components:

- ✔ **DCs are just like regular components, but with extra information added.** That extra information makes them easier to deal with than other components because they know how they're supposed to *behave* when you need to use them. More on that later.

- ✔ **They can do all sorts of things.** Describing what DCs *do* is tricky because they're all different. The simple (but totally unsatisfying) answer is that they do what they've been programmed to do. I think some examples are in order (see Figure 5-9):

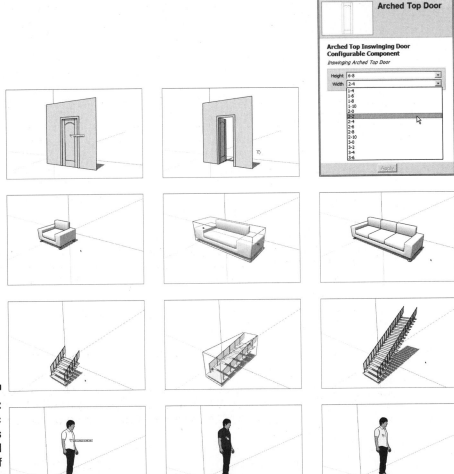

Figure 5-9: Dynamic Components can do all kinds of things.

- A dynamic door component may be set up to swing open when you click it with the Interact tool.

- The same dynamic door may also be configured into different sizes, styles, and finishes by using simple drop-down lists in the Component Options dialog box.

- A dynamic chair may be scaled into a sofa, but without stretching the arms — it would also add cushions as you make it longer.

- A dynamic stair component may automatically add or remove steps as you use the Scale tool to make it taller or shorter.

- Susan (the little person who appears by default when you start a new SketchUp file) is also dynamic: Click her shirt with the Interact tool to cycle through various colors. You can replace Susan with another character, too, and his or her shirt also changes color.

✔ **Anyone can use DCs.** Both the free and Pro versions of SketchUp can read and use Dynamic Components. The SketchUp team invented them (at least partially) to make SketchUp easier for new modelers to pick up.

✔ **You need Pro to make your own DCs.** If you need to build your own Dynamic Components (or modify ones that other folks have made), you need a copy of SketchUp Pro. If you want, you can download a free trial of Pro from the SketchUp Web site: `http://sketchup.google.com`.

✔ **DCs are free.** People are adding new DCs to the Google 3D Warehouse every day. As you can imagine, companies that make things like furniture and building products (windows, kitchen cabinets, and flooring) are really excited about the possibilities that DCs offer. Many of them are in the process of producing DCs of everything in their catalogues and posting them to the 3D Warehouse. That's good news for you; soon you can download and use a configurable model of almost anything you need.

✔ **They're in the 3D Warehouse.** When you download SketchUp, you find a few sample DCs in the Components dialog box. They're the ones with the little, green dynamic icon next to them (that looks kind of like an arrow). The best way to get more is to visit the 3D Warehouse and do a special search:

   1. *Choose File⇨3D Warehouse⇨Get Models to open a window into the 3D Warehouse from inside SketchUp.*

   2. *Add the following advanced search operator to any search for models you do:* `is:dynamic`.

   For example, if you were looking for a dynamic door, you'd search for *door is:dynamic*. See the sidebar "Search the 3D Warehouse like a pro" (earlier in this chapter) for more about advanced search operators.

Using Dynamic Components

In SketchUp, you can interact with Dynamic Components in three basic ways. Depending on what a particular DC has been set up to do, it may respond to one, two, or all three of the following *interactions*.

Smart scaling

DCs designed to react intelligently to the Scale tool are the closest things to true magic that SketchUp offers. Instead of stretching and getting all distorted when you scale them, the parts that are supposed to change dimensions, do; the other parts don't.

Take a look at Figure 5-10. The first image shows what happens when I scale a non-dynamic window component to make it wider. See how the frame stretches? Yuck. The image on the bottom shows the dynamic version of the same window. It gets wider when I scale it, but the frame stays the same thickness. It's smart enough to know that only some parts of it should get wider when I scale it.

Figure 5-10:
Scaling a non-dynamic window (middle) stretches the whole thing. The DC version scales properly.

Original

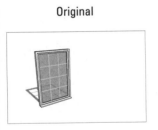

Non-dynamic component stretches

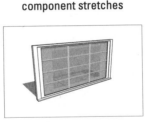

Dynamic component resizes correctly

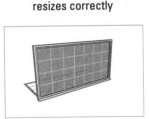

There's another way that DCs can scale smartly: by adding or subtracting pieces as they get bigger or smaller. Dynamic stairs are a perfect example of this, as shown in Figure 5-11. When I use the Scale tool to make the staircase taller, the staircase adds steps instead of stretching.

You can turn on the Dynamic Component toolbar, which is a quicker way to work with DCs than constantly using the menu bar. Just choose View⇨Toolbars⇨Dynamic Components, and you're all set.

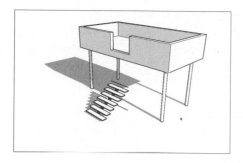

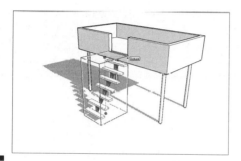

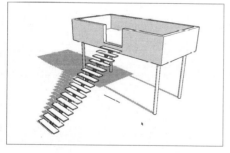

Figure 5-11:
When you make the staircase taller, this dynamic staircase adds steps instead of stretching.

Component Options

SketchUp 7 added the Component Options dialog box, which is on the Window menu. You can configure DCs that have been hooked up to this dialog box by choosing options from drop-down lists, typing dimensions, and performing other simple tasks. When you change a setting in Component Options, the DC you've selected updates to reflect the change, kind of like modeling by remote control.

The Component Options dialog box looks different for every DC.

The first image in Figure 5-12 shows the Component Options dialog box for a simple, straight staircase I built. I set it up so you can choose a riser height and a tread depth from preprogrammed lists. The dialog box also displays the total height *(rise),* total length *(run),* and number of steps in the staircase as it currently appears.

The second image in Figure 5-12 shows the Component Options for a circular-stair DC. I wanted to provide a lot of configuration options, so it looks a lot different. The dialog box lets you enter a size, structure type, and other information and then redraws the staircase based on your specifications.

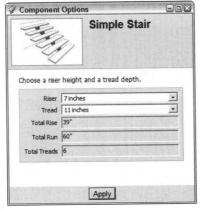

Figure 5-12:
The
Component
Options
dialog box
looks differ-
ent for every
Dynamic
Component.

The Interact tool

Activate the Interact tool by choosing it from the Tools menu. Using this tool couldn't be simpler: When a DC is set up to react to the Interact tool, it does stuff when you click it. Its actions depend on what you've programmed it to do.

Check out the truck in Figure 5-13; it's been designed to react to the Interact tool in a few ways:

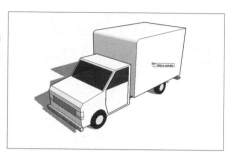
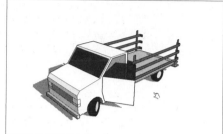

Figure 5-13:
Clicking stuff
with the
Interact tool
makes things
happen.

✔ Clicking the back of the truck cycles through the following options: box, flatbed, or flatbed with rails.

✔ Clicking the front wheels turns them from side to side.

✔ Clicking the doors makes them open and close.

When you're hovering over a DC that's been connected to the Interact tool, your cursor (it was originally called the Magic Finger) glows a little yellow at the end.

Poking around to see what happens

You can't know which interactions you can use with any particular DC just by looking at it. If you know you're dealing with a DC, the best way to figure out what it does is to experiment:

✔ Select it and open Component Options to see whether anything's there.

✔ Hover over it with the Interact tool to see whether a glow appears at the end of your cursor.

✔ Click it with the Select tool to show its scale *grips* (little green boxes). If any show up, grab one and scale to see what happens. If none show up, your DC can't be scaled with the Scale tool.

Groups can be dynamic, too. Deep down in the dark recesses of SketchUp's programming, groups and components are pretty much the same thing — groups are just components that behave differently. This means that a group can be assigned dynamic abilities. What does this matter to you? Not much, but I thought I'd point it out. It's good to know, especially if you plan to build your own DCs with SketchUp Pro. You can find more details about creating DCs on this book's companion Web site. DC-creation is tricky, and the extra room that cyberspace affords means more images, *color* images, and direct links to working examples in the 3D Warehouse. If the site isn't already bookmarked in your browser, check the Introduction for the address of this book's companion Web site.

Taking Advantage of Components to Build Better Models

The fact is a huge amount of the stuff in the galaxy is made of some kind of *repeated element*. In the case of bilaterally symmetrical objects (like most furniture), that element is a mirrored half; for things like staircases, it's a step or tread. The *whole* is composed of two or more instances of a single *part*. This makes modeling a heck of a lot easier because you don't often have to model things in their entirety — especially if you use components.

The following is a list of reasons why you need to work with components whenever you build an object that's made up of repeated elements:

✔ **It's faster.** This one's obvious. Not having to model the same things twice provides you with more time to play golf or answer e-mail, depending on what you prefer to do.

✔ **It's smarter.** Everybody knows that things change, and when they do, it's nice not to have to make the same changes more than once. Using component instances means only doing things once.

✔ **It's sexy.** Modeling something and then watching it repeat in a bunch of other places are fun to do, and the overall effect impresses the heck out of a crowd. Somehow, people will think you're smarter if they see things appearing "out of nowhere."

In this section, I describe two methods for modeling with components. The first involves symmetrical objects, and it covers about 50 percent of the things you might ever want to model. The second technique applies to things like stairs and fences, which are both perfect examples of why components were invented in the first place.

Modeling symmetrically: Good news for lazy people

And smart people, I suppose. First off, take a hard look at the shape of the things you may want to model. I want you to think about all the objects in the universe. I'll wait a couple of minutes while you do that. Done so soon? Good. Everything in the world (as I'm sure you realized) can be categorized as either of the following formal types:

✔ **Symmetrical:** Objects that exhibit *bilateral symmetry* are made of mirrored halves. You're (more or less) bilaterally symmetrical, and so is your car. Another kind of symmetry is *radial symmetry;* starfish are good examples of this, as are umbrellas and apple pies. If you were going to build a model of something that exhibits some form of symmetry, building one part and making copies would be a smarter way to do it.

✔ **Asymmetrical:** Some things — puddles, oak trees, and many houses — aren't symmetrical. There's no real trick to making these things; you just have to make some coffee, settle in, and get to work.

You can take advantage of both bilateral and radial symmetry with SketchUp components. To do so, assemble those components as follows, depending on what type of symmetry your object has (also take a look at Figure 5-14):

✔ **Bilateral symmetry:** To make a model of something that's bilaterally symmetrical, build half, make it into a component, and flip over a copy.

✔ **Radial symmetry:** Radially symmetrical objects can be (conceptually, anyway) cut into identical wedges that all radiate from a central axis. You can use components to model things like car wheels and turrets by building a single wedge and rotating a bunch of copies around a central point.

Axis of symmetry

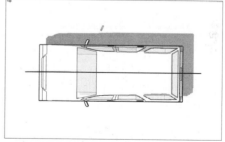

Figure 5-14:
Bilateral
symmetry
(top) and
radial
symmetry
(bottom)
make your
SketchUp
life a lot
easier.

Multiple axes of symmetry

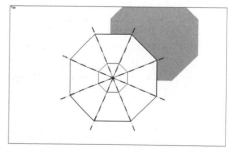

Working smarter by only building half

Bilaterally symmetrical forms are everywhere. Most animals you can name, the majority of the furniture in your house, and your personal helicopter — they can all be modeled by building half, creating a component, and flipping over a copy.

Follow these steps to get the general idea of how to build a bilaterally symmetrical model in SketchUp (see Figure 5-15):

Make a box    Turn it into a component    Move a copy over

Flip the copy   Stick the two halves together

Figure 5-15:
Getting set
up to build
a bilaterally
symmetrical
model.

1. **Make a simple box.**

   You can do this however you want, but I think the easiest way is to draw a rectangle and push/pull it into 3D.

2. **Draw a diagonal edge on the corner of your box.**

   The point of this step is to mark one side of your box so that when you flip it over, you don't get confused about which side is which.

3. **Turn your box into a component.**

   See "Creating your own components," earlier in this chapter, if you wonder how to do this.

4. **Make a copy of your new component instance.**

   The last part of Chapter 2 has information about moving and copying objects in SketchUp, but here's a simple version:

   a. *Choose the Move tool and then press the Ctrl key (Option on a Mac) to toggle from Move to Copy mode.*

A little plus sign (+) appears next to your cursor.

    b. Click your component instance, move your copy beside the original, and click again to drop it.

Make sure that you move in either the red or the green direction; it makes things easier in the next step.

5. Flip over the copy.

To do this, right-click the copy and choose Flip Along from the context menu. If you moved your copy in the red direction in the previous step, choose Flip Along⇨Component's Red. Choose Component's Green if you moved in the green direction.

6. Stick the two halves back together.

Using the Move tool (this time without Copy toggled on), pick up your copy *from the corner* and move it over, dropping it *on the corresponding corner* of the original. Take a look at the last image in Figure 5-15 to see what I mean. Doing this precisely is important, if you want your model to look right.

Now you're set up to start building symmetrically. If you want, you can do a test to make sure things went smoothly (see Figure 5-16). Follow these steps:

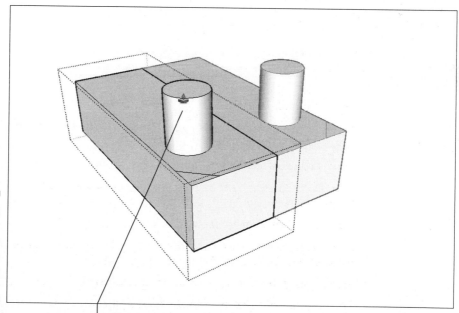

Figure 5-16:
Test your setup to make sure that everything works.

Whatever you do on this
side should happen on the
other side, too

1. **With the Select tool, double-click one of the halves of your model to edit it.**

2. **Draw a circle on the top surface and push/pull it into a cylinder.**

If the same thing happens on the other side, you're good to go. If the same thing *doesn't* happen on the other side, it's possible that:

✔ **You're not really editing one of your component instances.** If you aren't, you're drawing *on top of* your component instead of *in* it. You know you're in edit mode if the rest of your model looks grayed out.

✔ **You never made a component in the first place.** If your halves don't have blue boxes around them when you select them, they're not component instances. Start a new file and try again, paying particular attention to Step 3 in the previous steps.

The coolest things since radially sliced bread

You can model objects that exhibit radial symmetry just as easily as those with bilateral symmetry; you just start slightly differently. The only thing you have to decide before you start is how many wedges — how many identical parts you need to make the whole object.

To model something with radial symmetry, start with one wedge, make it into a component, and then rotate copies around the center. Follow these steps to get the hang of it:

1. **Draw a polygon with as many sides as the number of segments you need for the object you're modeling.**

   Here's the easiest way to draw a polygon in SketchUp, as shown in Figure 5-17:

   a. *Choose Tools⇨Polygon to select the Polygon tool.*

   b. *Click once to establish the center (I like to do this on the axis origin), move your cursor, and then click again to establish the radius.*

   Don't worry about being accurate right now.

   c. *Before you do anything else, type the number of sides you want your polygon to have and press Enter.*

2. **Draw edges from the center of your polygon to two adjacent vertices (endpoints) on the perimeter, creating a wedge.**

   To find the center of a polygon (or a circle), hover your cursor over the outline for a couple seconds and move the cursor toward the middle; a center inference point appears.

3. **Erase the rest of your polygon, leaving only the wedge.**

4. **Turn your wedge into a component.**

   Check out "Creating your own components," earlier in this chapter, if you're unsure of how to do this.

5. **Make copies of your wedge component instance with the Rotate tool (see Figure 5-18).**

Make a polygon

Define a wedge

Erase the rest

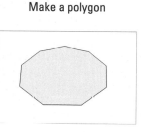 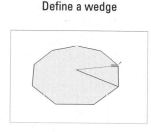 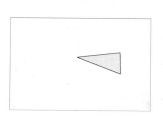

Click to define center of rotation

Click to start rotating

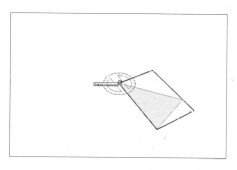 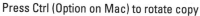 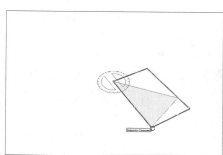

Press Ctrl (Option on Mac) to rotate copy

Make more copies

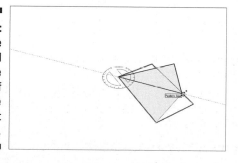 

Just like with the Move tool, you can use the Rotate tool to make copies. You can even make an *array* (more than one copy at a time). Here's how:

    a. *Select your wedge's edges (sorry — I just wanted to say that) and select the face, too.*

    b. *Choose Tools⇨Rotate to select the Rotate tool.*

    c. *Press the Ctrl key (Option on a Mac) to tell SketchUp you want to make a copy.*

       A + appears next to your cursor.

    d. *Click the pointy end of your wedge to set your center of rotation.*

    e. *Click one of the opposite corners of your wedge to set your rotation start point.*

    f. *Click the other corner to make a rotated copy of your wedge.*

    g. *Type the number of additional wedges you want, followed by the letter x, and then press Enter.*

  6. (Optional) Test your setup.

    Follow the steps associated with Figure 5-16 to test whether updates to a single component in your new object updates all instances of the component.

Hiding the edges in your component instances makes your finished model look a whole lot better. Take a look at the sidebar "Making two halves look like one whole," earlier in this chapter, to read how.

Modeling with repeated elements

A staircase is a perfect example of an object that's composed of several identical elements. If, when you hear the phrase "several identical elements," a big, flashing neon sign that screams "COMPONENTS!" doesn't appear in your head, you're not using SketchUp enough. On the other hand, maybe there's something wrong with *me*. . . .

In the following example, I kill two birds with one stone: I use it to demonstrate how you might use components to model more efficiently and to show readers of Chapter 4 the smartest way to build a set of stairs.

The Treads Are Components method involves (you guessed it) making each *tread* (step) in your staircase into an instance of the same component. Basically, you build one simple tread that's the right depth, make it into a component, and copy a bunch of instances into a full flight of stairs. Because every step is linked, anything you do to one automatically happens to them all. If you don't know the first thing about components, now would be a terrific time to start from the beginning of this very chapter.

Go through these steps to build a staircase using the Treads Are Components method:

1. **Model a single step, including the tread and the riser.**

    You can make this very simple at this stage, if you want to; all that matters is that the tread depth and the riser height are correct. You can fiddle with everything else later. Figure 5-19 shows a simple example of this.

Figure 5-19:
Model a single step, making sure that the depth and height are accurate.

  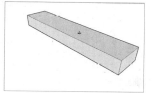

2. **Make a component out of the step you just built.**

    Take a look at "Creating your own components," earlier in this chapter, if you need help.

3. **Move a copy of your step into position, above the first one (see Figure 5-20).**

4. **Type the total number of steps you want, type an x, and then press Enter.**

    You're creating a *linear array,* meaning that you're making several copies at regular intervals, in the same direction you moved the first one. Typing **12x** generates 12 steps the same distance apart as the first step and its copy. The last image on the right in Figure 5-20 shows what I mean.

5. **With the Select tool, double-click any one of your steps to edit all instances of your component.**

    Everything besides the component instance you're editing fades out a little.

6. **Go nuts.**

    This really is the fun part. Having your staircase made up of multiple component instances means that you have all the flexibility to make drastic changes to the whole thing without ever having to repeat yourself. Add a *nosing* (a bump at the leading edge of each tread), a *stringer* (a diagonal piece of structure that supports all your steps), or even a handrail by getting creative with how you modify a single component instance. Figure 5-21 shows some of what you can do. The color insert in this book shows the Treads Are Components method applied to building a spiral stair.

1. Create a component

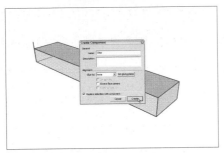

2. Move up a copy

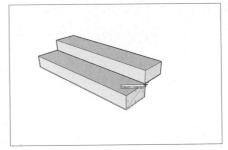

3. Type the number you want, then **x**, and press Enter

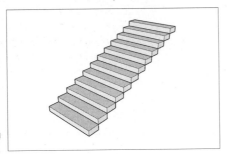

4. Edit one instance

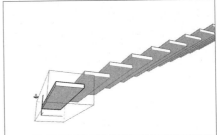

Figure 5-20: Make your step into a component instance, move a copy into position above the original, and then create an array.

5. All components change

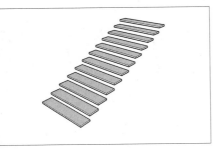

Figure 5-21: A flight of stairs with side stringers and a handrail. On the right, a single component instance.

Series of component instances

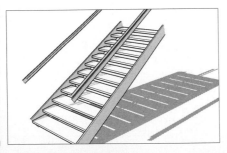

A single component instance

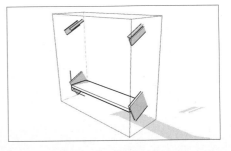

Making two halves look like one whole

Looking carefully at the little boat in the figure that follows, notice how the edges in the middle clearly show that it's made out of two halves? If I were to erase those edges, my whole model would disappear, because those edges are defining faces, and without edges, faces can't exist.

Instead of erasing those unwanted edges, I can hide them by using the Eraser while pressing the Shift key. See the second and third images of the boat? When I hold down Shift as I drag over the edges I want to hide with the Eraser, they disappear. Two things are important to know about hidden edges:

✔ **Hidden edges aren't gone forever.** Actually, this applies to any hidden geometry in your model. To see what's hidden, choose View➪Hidden Geometry. To hide it again, just choose thve same thing.

✔ **To edit hidden edges, you have to make them visible.** If you need to make changes to your model that involve edges you've already hidden, you can either view your hidden geometry (see the previous point) or unhide them altogether. Just show your hidden geometry, select the edges you want to unhide, and choose Edit➪Unhide➪Selected.

Distracting edges

Use Eraser to hide

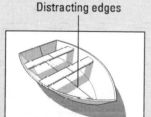
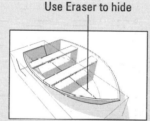

Chapter 6

Going Beyond Buildings

Here's something you already know: There's more to life than modeling buildings. Even though SketchUp is *really good* at letting you make models of built structures, you can use it to build just about anything you can think of — all it takes is time, ingenuity, and the ability to take a step back and break down things into their basic parts. SketchUp provides fantastic tools for creating forms that aren't the least bit boxy, but they're not as obvious as Push/Pull and Rectangle, so most people never find them. This chapter is devoted to helping you discover SketchUp's "rounder" side.

In this chapter, I present tools, techniques, and other tips for creating forms that are distinctly unbuilding-like — my hope is that you'll use them to push the limits of what you think SketchUp can do.

Extruding with Purpose: Follow Me

Follow Me is probably the best example of a powerful SketchUp tool with kind of an underwhelming name. The problem that faced the software designers when they were trying to figure out what to call their new baby was this: It does what other 3D modeling programs dedicate two or three other tools to doing. They chose an unconventional name because it's a wholly unconventional tool.

In the following sections, I talk about how to use Follow Me to create a number of different types of shapes; examples of these are shown in Figure 6-1 and are as follows:

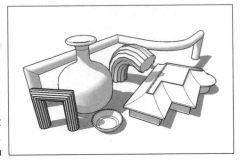

Figure 6-1:
Follow Me
lets you cre-
ate all kinds
of different
shapes.

✔ **Bottles, spindles, and spheres:** These are all examples of *lathed* forms. You can create these by spinning a 2D *profile* (shape) around a central axis to create a 3D model.

✔ **Pipes, gutters, and moldings:** If you look closely, all three of these things are basically created by extruding a 2D face along a 3D path; the result is a complex 3D form.

✔ **Chamfers, fillets, and dados:** Without explaining what all these things are (that's what Internet search engines are for), know this: You can use Follow Me to *cut away* profiles, too.

Using Follow Me

At its core, Follow Me lets you create forms that are extrusions. It's a little bit like Push/Pull, except that it doesn't just work in one direction. You tell Follow Me to follow a path, and it extrudes a face all along that path. So, you need three things to use Follow Me:

✔ **A path:** In SketchUp, you can use any edge, or series of edges, as a path. All you have to do is make sure that they're drawn before you use Follow Me.

✔ **A face:** Just like with Push/Pull, Follow Me needs a face to extrude. You can use any face in your model, but it needs to be created before you start using Follow Me.

✔ **Undo:** Imagining what a 2D face will look like as a 3D shape isn't easy — it usually takes a couple tries to get a Follow Me operation right. That's what Undo is for, after all.

Follow these steps to use Follow Me; Figure 6-2 shows a basic example of how it works:

Figure 6-2:
Using
Follow Me
to create
a simple
extruded
shape.

Select the whole path

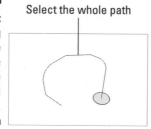

Click the face with Follow Me

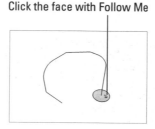

1. **Draw a face to use as an extrusion profile.**

   In this example, you create a pipe, so the extrusion profile is a circular face.

2. **Draw an edge (or edges) to use as an extrusion path.**

   Although the edge (or edges) is touching the face in this case, it doesn't have to for Follow Me to work.

3. **Select the complete extrusion path you want to use.**

   Check out the section on making selections in Chapter 2 for pointers on using the Select tool to best advantage.

4. **Activate the Follow Me tool by choosing Tools⇨Follow Me.**

5. **Click the face you want to extrude.**

   Magic! Your face (extrusion profile) is extruded along the path you chose in Step 3, creating a 3D form (in this case, a section of pipe).

If you want to use Follow Me all the way around the perimeter of a face, you don't need to spend time selecting all the individual edges. Just select the face and then use Follow Me; the tool automatically runs all the way around any face you have selected.

You can use Follow Me another way, too: Instead of preselecting a path (as in Step 3 of the preceding list), you can click any face with Follow Me and attempt to drag it along the edges in your model. Although this works on simple things, I find that preselecting a path works a lot better — it's really the only option for using Follow Me in a predictable way.

Making lathed forms like spheres and bottles

And nuclear power plant chimneys. A surprising number of things can be modeled by using Follow Me to perform a lathe operation. A *lathe* is a tool that carpenters (and machinists) use to spin a block of raw material while they carve into it — that's how baseball bats are made (the good ones, anyway).

A simple example of a lathed object is a sphere. Here's how you might make one with Follow Me:

1. **Draw a circle on the ground.**

2. **Rotate a copy of your circle up by 90 degrees, as shown in Figure 6-3.**

Click and hold down
mouse button

Drag here

Figure 6-3:
Using the
Rotate tool
to make a
rotated copy
of a circle.

If you're wondering how to do this, follow these steps:

a. *Select the face of your circle with the Select tool and then choose Tools⇨Rotate to activate the Rotate tool.*

b. *Press the Ctrl key (Option on a Mac) to tell SketchUp you want to make a copy.*

c. *Click a green endpoint inference along the edge of your circle and hold down your mouse button to drag. Don't let go just yet.*

d. *Still dragging, move your cursor over to the endpoint on the exact opposite side of your circle; then release your mouse button.*

Your axis of rotation is a line right through the center of your circle.

e. *Click anywhere on the edge of your circle and then move your mouse over a little bit.*

f. *Type **90** and press Enter.*

You can read all about the Rotate tool in Chapter 2.

3. **Make sure that one of your circles is selected.**

4. **With the Follow Me tool, click the circle that's not selected (see Figure 6-4).**

Now you have a sphere. The Follow Me tool lathed your circular face around the path you selected — the other circle.

Figure 6-4:
Clicking one
circle with
Follow Me
while the
other one
is selected
produces a
sphere.

Select one circle   Click the other with Follow Me

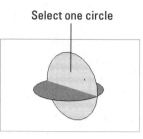
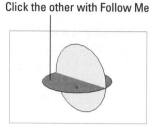
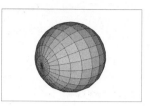

If you really need a sphere, the easiest way to get one is in the Components dialog box. The Shapes library that comes installed with SketchUp has a selection of spheres (and cones and other things) you can choose from.

If you want to make your curved surfaces look *smooth* (hiding the edges between them), check out the sidebar "Smoothing those unsightly edges," later in this chapter.

Under normal circumstances, you only have to model half a profile to use Follow Me to make it three-dimensional. Figure 6-5 shows a few examples of 3D objects.

Figure 6-5:
A few
examples
of lathed
objects cre-
ated with
Follow Me.

Creating extruded shapes like gutters and handrails

A lot of the time, you want to use Follow Me to create geometry (edges and faces) that's attached to another part of your model. An example of this may be modeling a gutter that runs all the way around the roof of your house. In this case, you already have the path along which you want to extrude a profile (the edge of the roof).

When you use Follow Me to extrude a face along a path that consists of edges that already exist as part of your model, *always* do two things:

- **Before using Follow Me, make the rest of your model a separate group.** Take my word for it — Follow Me can sometimes mess up your model, so keep the geometry Follow Me creates separate, just in case.

- **Make a copy of your extrusion path outside your group.** There's a consequence to working with Follow Me on top of a group: The edge (or edges) you want to use as an extrusion path aren't available because you can't use Follow Me with a path that's in a separate group or component.

  What to do? You need to make a copy of the path *outside* the group and then use the *copy* to do the Follow Me operation. Here's the best way to make a copy of the path:

  a. *With the Select tool, double-click your group to edit it.*

  b. *Select the path you want to use for Follow Me and then choose Edit⇨Copy.*

  c. *Exit (stop editing) your group by clicking somewhere else in your modeling window.*

  d. *Choose Edit⇨Paste in Place.*

     You have a copy of the path you want to use, and it's outside your group.

Take a look at Chapter 17. You find the Weld Ruby script (don't worry — I explain what that means) that's super-useful for creating extrusion paths for Follow Me.

When you use an existing edge (or series of edges) as an extrusion path, the hard part is getting your profile in the right place. You can proceed in two ways; which one you choose depends on what you need to model:

- **Draw the profile in place.** Do this only if the extrusion path is parallel to one of the colored drawing axes.

- **Draw the profile on the ground and then move it into position.** If your extrusion path doesn't start out parallel to a colored drawing axis, you should probably draw your profile somewhere else and move it into place later.

Drawing your profile in place

Consider that you have a model of a house. You want to use Follow Me to add a gutter that goes all the way around the perimeter of the roof. You decide to draw the profile in place (right on the roof itself) because the edges of the roof are drawn parallel to the colored drawing axes. This means that you'll have an easier time using the Line tool to draw in midair.

Why your computer is so slow

When you use Follow Me with an extrusion profile that's a circle or an arc, you create a piece of 3D geometry that's very big. By *big,* I mean that it has lots of faces, and faces are what slow down your computer. Without going into detail about how SketchUp works (I don't really know that anyway), keep this in mind: The more faces you have in your model, the worse your computer's performance will be. At a certain point, you'll stop being able to orbit, your scenes (which I talk about in Chapter 10) will stutter, and you'll be tempted to do something terrible out of frustration.

The first pipe in the figure that follows has been extruded using Follow Me; it was made with a 24-sided circle as an extrusion profile, and it has 338 faces. Hidden Geometry is turned on (in the View menu) so that you can see how many faces you have.

The second pipe uses a 10-sided circle as an extrusion profile. As a result, it has only 116 faces. What an improvement!

The third pipe also uses a 10-sided circle as an extrusion profile, but the arc in its extrusion path is made up of only 4 segments, instead of the usual 12. This pipe has a total of 52 faces. Even better.

The second image in the figure shows all three pipes with Hidden Geometry turned off. Is the difference in detail worth the exponential increase in the number of faces? Most of the time, the answer is no.

To change the number of sides in a circle or an arc, just before or just after you create it, follow these steps:

1. Type the number of sides you want to have.

2. Type an **s** to tell SketchUp that you mean "sides."

3. Press Enter.

338 faces   116 faces   52 faces

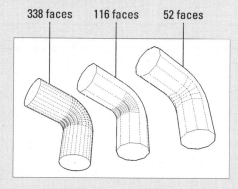 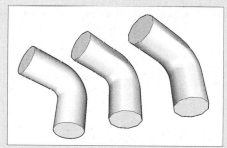

The trick to drawing an extrusion profile that isn't on the ground is to start by drawing a rectangular face. You then draw the profile on the face and erase the rest of the rectangle. Figure 6-6 shows how you'd draw the profile of a gutter directly on the corner of a roof; the steps that follow explain the same things in words:

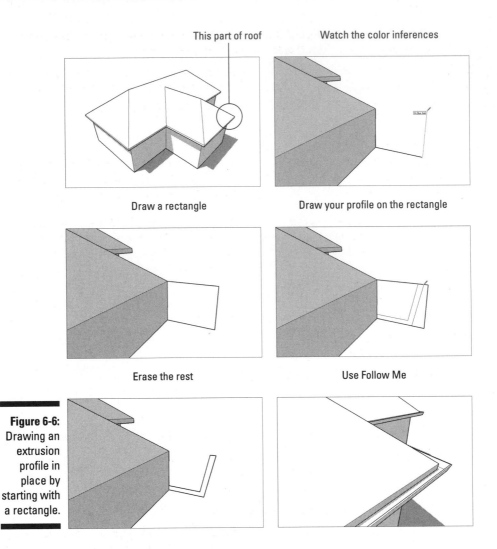

Figure 6-6: Drawing an extrusion profile in place by starting with a rectangle.

1. **Zoom in on what you're doing.**

   I can't tell you how many people try to work without filling their modeling windows with the subject at hand. Not doing so is like trying to do a crossword puzzle while looking the wrong way through a pair of binoculars. Get close — SketchUp models don't bite!

2. **Using the Line tool, draw a rectangle whose face is perpendicular to the edge you want to use for Follow Me.**

   Pay careful attention to SketchUp's inference engine; watch the colors to make sure that you're drawing in the right direction.

3. **Use the Line tool (and SketchUp's other drawing tools) to draw your profile directly on the rectangle you just drew.**

   The important thing here is to make sure that your extrusion profile is a single face; if it's not, Follow Me won't work the way you want it to.

4. **Erase the rest of your rectangle, leaving only the profile.**

Drawing your profile somewhere else

The awful thing about handrails is that they're almost always at funny angles, not parallel to a colored axis. When drawing your extrusion profile in place isn't convenient, draw it on the ground and move it into position after.

Here's the trick: Draw a *tail* — a short edge — perpendicular to your extrusion profile. You can use this tail to help line up your profile with the edge you want to use as an extrusion path for Follow Me. The following steps and Figure 6-7 describe how you'd draw and position a profile for a handrail:

1. **Draw your extrusion profile flat on the ground.**

2. **Draw a short edge perpendicular to the face you just drew.**

   This tail should come from the point where you want your profile to attach to the extrusion path.

3. **Make your profile and its tail into a group.**

   This makes it easier to move and rotate around all at once. See Chapter 5 for information on creating and using groups, if you need it.

4. **Using the Move tool, place your profile at the end of the extrusion path.**

   To make sure that you position your profile accurately, pick it up by clicking the point where the tail meets the face and then drop it by clicking the end of the extrusion path.

5. **With the Rotate tool, rotate your profile into position.**

   Here's where you need to use a bit of skill. (See Chapter 2 for guidance.) The Rotate tool is easy to use — after you get the hang of it.

6. **Right-click the group you made in Step 3 and choose Explode; delete your tail.**

Subtracting from a model with Follow Me

What if you want to model a bar of soap? Or a sofa cushion? Or anything that doesn't have a sharp edge? The best way to round off edges in SketchUp is to use Follow Me. In addition to using Follow Me to *add* to your model, you can also *subtract* from your model.

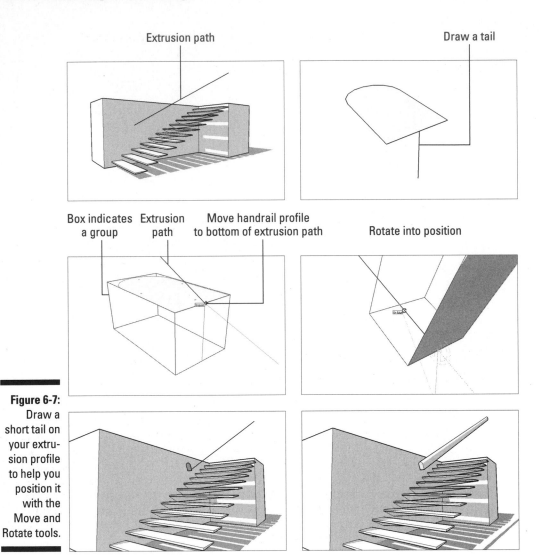

Figure 6-7:
Draw a short tail on your extrusion profile to help you position it with the Move and Rotate tools.

Here's how it works: If you draw an extrusion profile on the end face of a long-ish form, you can use Follow Me to remove a strip of material along whatever path you specify. Figure 6-8 demonstrates the concept on the top of a box.

If the extrusion path you want to use for a Follow Me operation consists of the entire perimeter of a face (as is the case in Figure 6-8), you can save time by just selecting the face instead of all the edges that define it.

Draw an arc

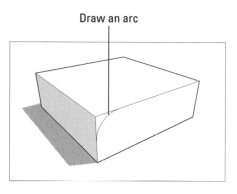

Select a path

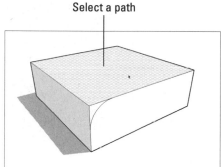

Click the face with Follow Me

Figure 6-8:
Creating
a rounded
edge with
Follow Me.

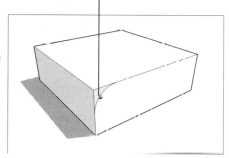

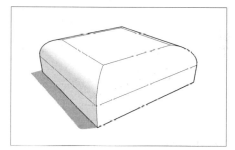

But what if you want to create a corner that's rounded in *both* directions, as so many corners are? That one's a little trickier to do in SketchUp, but because it's such a common problem, I thought I'd devote a few hundred words to explaining how to do it. The basic technique involves using Follow Me on a corner you've already rounded with the Push/Pull tool. After you have a corner that's rounded with an arc of the correct radius, you can use copies (or component instances, if you're clever) of that corner several times, wherever you need them. Although I wouldn't call this solution elegant, it works when you need it to.

There's a beautiful RoundCorner (by Fredo6) Ruby script that mostly automates the process I'm about to describe. If you're so inclined, check out its description in Chapter 17.

Figure 6-9 gives a step-by-step, visual account of the process, while I explain it in words, as follows:

Draw an arc

Push/Pull away the corner

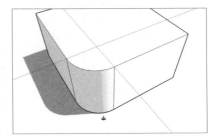

Draw identical arc

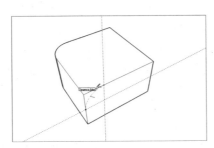

Select the whole path

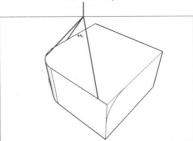

Click with Follow Me

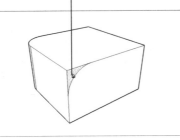

Figure 6-9:
Making
a corner
that's
rounded
in both
directions.

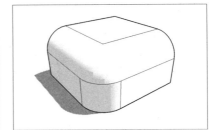

1. **Draw a box.**

   It doesn't really matter how big, as long as it's big enough for the round you want to apply.

2. **With the Arc tool, draw an arc on the corner of the box.**

   When you're drawing an arc on a corner, keep an eye out for the inferences that help you draw properly:

   • After clicking to place one endpoint of your arc, as you cut across the corner, the point at which your line turns magenta is where your endpoints are *equidistant* (the same distance) from the corner across which you're cutting.

   • After clicking to place your second endpoint, you see a point at which the arc you're drawing turns magenta — this means your arc is *tangent to* (continuous with) both edges it's connected to. You want this to be the case, so you should click when you see magenta.

I strongly recommend reducing the number of sides on your arc before you start rounding away. See the sidebar "Why your computer is so slow," earlier in this chapter, to find out why.

3. **Push/pull down the new face to round off the corner.**

4. **Draw another *identical* arc on one of the corners directly adjacent to the corner you just rounded.**

   This is where you refer to Figure 6-9. Pictures are better than words when explaining things like which corners are adjacent to which.

5. **Select the edges shown in Figure 6-9.**

6. **Activate the Follow Me tool.**

7. **Click the arc corner face to extrude it along the path you selected in Step 4.**

8. **Hide or smooth any edges that need it.**

   For information about hiding edges, see Chapter 5. Check out this chapter's "Smoothing those unsightly edges" sidebar for the whole scoop on how to smooth edges.

After you have a fully rounded corner, you can use a bunch of them to make anything you want; it just takes a little planning. Figure 6-10 shows a simple bar of soap I created out of eight rounded corners, copied, and flipped accordingly. The text (in case you're wondering) was created with SketchUp's 3D Text tool, which you can find on the Tools menu.

Copy and flip   Copy and flip

Copy and flip Hide and smooth edges; then add text

Figure 6-10: Assembling a bunch of rounded corners to make objects is relatively easy.

Smoothing those unsightly edges

If you're wondering how to get rid of all the ugly lines that appear when you use Follow Me, the answer is pretty simple: You can *smooth* edges, just like you can hide them. (See Chapter 5 for more information about hiding edges.) The difference between hiding and smoothing is illustrated by the images of the cylinders in the figure that follows:

- ✔ **When you *hide* an edge between two faces,** SketchUp still treats those faces as though your edge is still there — it just doesn't show the edge. Materials you've applied to each face stay separate, and each face is lit separately by SketchUp's sun. The latter fact is the reason why simply hiding the edges between faces that are supposed to represent a smooth curve doesn't make things look smooth — you still end up with a faceted look.

- ✔ **When you *smooth* an edge between two faces,** you're telling SketchUp to treat them as a single face — with a single material and smooth-looking shading. The difference is pretty huge, as you can see in the second cylinder in the figure.

You can smooth edges in two ways:

- ✔ **Use the Eraser.** To smooth edges with the Eraser tool, hold down the Ctrl key (Option on the Mac) while you click or drag over the edges you want to smooth.

- ✔ **Use the Soften Edges dialog box.** Located on the Window menu, this dialog box lets you smooth a bunch of selected edges all at once, according to the angle of their adjacent faces. It's a little complicated at first, but here's what you need to know to get started: Select the edges you want to smooth and then move the slider to the right until you like the way your model looks.

To unsmooth edges, follow these steps:

1. **Turn on Hidden Geometry to make edges visible.**

2. **Select the edges you want to unsmooth.**

3. **In the Soften Edges dialog box, move the slider all the way to the left.**

Visible edges	Hidden edges	Smoothed edges

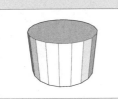  

Modeling with the Scale tool

Real heroes are rarely obvious. The Scale tool is, in my opinion, the single most misunderstood member of SketchUp's mercifully limited toolkit. New modelers assume that Scale is for resizing things in your model. That's technically true, but most folks only use it to resize *whole* objects; the real power of Scale happens when you use it on *parts* of objects to change their shape. Take a look at Figure 6-11 to see what I mean.

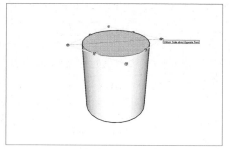

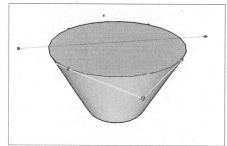

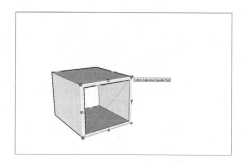

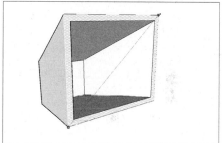

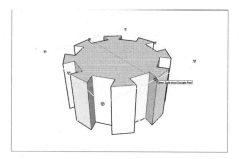

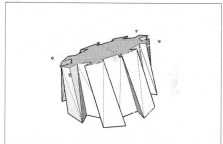

Figure 6-11:
Using the
Scale tool
on parts
of objects
changes
their shape.

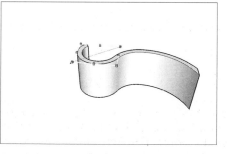

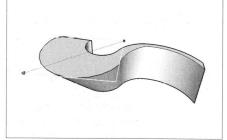

Getting the hang of Scale

The basic principle of this technique is pretty simple: You select the geometry (edges and faces) in your model that you want to resize, activate the Scale tool, and go to town.

Here's a list of steps, just so it's crystal clear (Figure 6-12 tells the story in pictures):

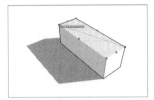

Figure 6-12:
The Scale
tool is a
cinch
to use.

1. **Select the part of your model that you want to scale.**

   Use the Select tool to do this; check out the latter part of Chapter 2 if you need a refresher.

2. **Activate the Scale tool by choosing Tools⇨Scale from the menu bar.**

   You can also make Scale active by clicking its button on the toolbar or by pressing the S key on your keyboard. After you activate Scale, the geometry you selected in Step 1 should be enclosed in a box of little green cubes, or *grips*.

3. **Click a grip and then move your mouse to start scaling your selected geometry.**

   Take a look at the next part of this section for the lowdown on all the different grips.

4. **When you're finished scaling, click again to stop.**

While I'm on the subject of Scale, here are a few more things you should know:

✔ **Use different grips to scale different ways.** Which grip (the little green boxes that appear when you activate the Scale tool) you use determines how your geometry scales:

   • *Corner* grips scale proportionally — nothing gets distorted when you use them.

   • *Edge* and *side* grips distort your geometry as you scale — use them to squeeze what you're scaling.

✔ **Hold down the Shift key to scale proportionally.** This happens automatically if you're using one of the corner grips, but not if you're using any others. If you don't want what you're scaling to be distorted, hold down Shift.

✔ **Hold down the Ctrl key (Option on a Mac) to scale about the center of your selection.** I find myself doing this more often than not.

✔ **Type a scaling factor to scale accurately.** To scale by 50 percent, type 0.5. Typing 3.57 scales your geometry by 357 percent, and typing 1.0 doesn't scale it at all. Take a look at Chapter 2 to read more about using numbers while you work.

✔ **Which grips appear depend on what you're scaling.** Have a look at Figure 6-13 to see what I mean.

- Most of the time, you see a scaling box enclosed by 26 green grips.

- If you're scaling flat, *coplanar* geometry (faces and edges that all lie on the same plane) and that plane is perfectly aligned with one of the major planes in your model, you get a rectangle consisting of 8 grips instead of a box comprised of 26.

- If what you're scaling is a Dynamic Component, you may see anywhere from 0 to all 26 grips; it depends on how the builder set up the component. Take a look at Chapter 5 for more information about Dynamic Components.

✔ **You can't make a copy while you scale.** Both the Move and Rotate tools let you make copies by holding down a button on your keyboard while you're using them, but Scale doesn't work this way, unfortunately. If you need to make a scaled copy, try this instead:

   a. *Select the geometry that you want to scale and copy, and then make it into a group.*

   See Chapter 5 for more information on making groups.

   b. *Choose Edit⇨Copy from the menu bar and then choose Edit⇨Paste in Place from the menu bar.*

   c. *Scale the copied group as you would anything else.*

Figure 6-13:
Grips
depend on
what you're
trying to
scale.

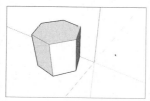
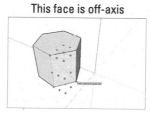
This face is off-axis

This face is perpendicular
to blue axis

Scaling profiles to make organic forms

Here's where it gets really interesting. I need to thank über-SketchUpper Justin Chin (who goes by the handle monsterzero online) for demonstrating the power of scaling profiles to make organic forms; it's great because it's easy to understand *and* powerful enough to be applied all over the place. That's why I'm so excited to show it to you in this book.

So what is this method? It involves using the Scale tool in combination with a series of 2D profiles to create curvy, lumpy, distinctly un-boxy 3D shapes. An awful lot of the stuff in the universe fits squarely in this category: me, you, slugs, intergalactic alien fighter vessels, bananas — just about everything that wasn't made by a machine can be modeled using the scaled profiles method of 3D modeling.

Read about the Ruby script FredoScale in Chapter 17 — it's hyper-relevant to the material in this section.

Combining Scale and Push/Pull

The simplest way to use this method is in association with Push/Pull. Here's a very simple example of how it works (check out Figure 6-14 for an illustrated view):

1. Create a 2D shape.

This shape may be something simple (such as a circle) or something more complex; it all depends on what you're trying to model. The shape may also be a half-shape if what you're trying to make exhibits bilateral symmetry. Take a look at the last section in Chapter 5 for more information on using components to build symmetrical models.

2. Push/pull your 2D shape into a 3D form.

3. Scale the new face you created so it's slightly bigger (or slightly smaller) than the original 2D shape from Step 1.

See the previous section in this chapter for more specifics about using the Scale tool. Pay special attention to the points about using *modifier keys* (keyboard buttons) to scale proportionally or about the center of what you're working on.

4. Push/pull the face you scaled in the preceding step.

Try to make this extrusion about the same as the one you made in Step 2.

You can usually double-click a face with the Push/Pull tool to repeat the last Push/Pull operation you did.

5. Repeat Steps 3 and 4 until you're done.

You can add skillful use of the Rotate tool into the mix if you like; doing so allows you to curve and bend your form as you shape it.

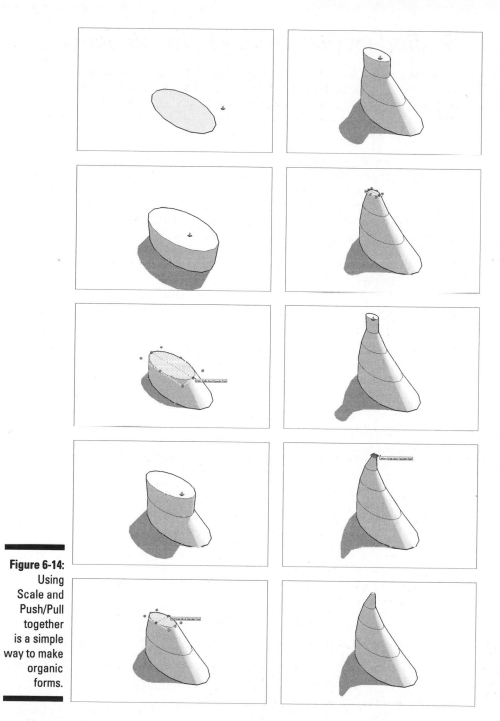

Figure 6-14:
Using
Scale and
Push/Pull
together
is a simple
way to make
organic
forms.

Keep the following tidbits in mind as you explore this technique:

- ✔ **Watch your polygon count.** *Polygons* are faces, basically — the more you have, the "heavier" your model becomes, and the worse it performs on your computer. Try to minimize the number of faces you're working with by reducing the number of edges in your original 2D shape. Have a look at the sidebar "Why your computer is so slow," earlier in this chapter, for the whole scoop.

- ✔ **Don't be afraid to go back and tweak.** The beauty of this method is its flexibility. While you're working, you can select any of the 2D *profiles* (shapes) in your model and use the Scale tool to tweak them. Just select the loop of edges along the perimeter of the profile you want to scale and take it from there. Check out Figure 6-15 to see what I mean.

Figure 6-15:
You can go back and scale any profile at any time while you work.

  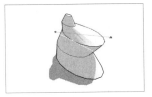

Combining Scale and Follow Me

Another way to create extruded forms is to use Follow Me. (See the first part of this chapter if you need a refresher.) This technique is ideally suited to making long, curvy, tapered things like tentacles and antlers; it's a little time-consuming but works like a charm.

Modeling a simplified bull's horn is a good, straightforward illustration of how the Follow Me variation of this method works. Here's how to go about it; take a look at Figure 6-16 to see the story in pictures:

1. **Draw a circle.**

   This is the extrusion *profile* for Follow Me. Strongly consider reducing the number of sides in your circle from the standard 24 to something more like 10 or 12. See the sidebar "Why your computer is so slow" (earlier in this chapter) to find out how and why you should do this.

2. **Draw a 10-sided arc that starts perpendicular to the center of the circle you drew in Step 1.**

   Type **10s** and press Enter right after you click to finish drawing your arc.

This tells SketchUp to make sure your arc has 10 sides (instead of the default 12). Why 10 sides? It makes the math easier a few steps from now.

The easiest way to create a halfway-accurate arc in 3D space is to start by drawing a rectangle. When you're sure this rectangle is properly situated, use the Arc tool to draw on top of it and then delete everything but the arc.

3. **Select the arc you just drew.**

   This is the extrusion *path* for Follow Me.

4. **Activate the Follow Me tool by choosing Tools⇨Follow Me from the menu bar.**

5. **Click the circle you drew in Step 1 to extrude it along the path you drew in Step 2.**

6. **Choose View⇨Hidden Geometry from the menu bar.**

   Showing the hidden geometry in your model lets you select the edges that were automatically *smoothed* (made hidden) when you used Follow Me in Step 4.

7. **Scale the face at the end of your new extrusion by a factor of 0.1.**

   See "Getting the hang of Scale," earlier in this chapter, for instructions on how to do this. Use any of the four corner grips on the scaling box, and don't forget to hold down the Ctrl key (Option on a Mac) while you're scaling — this forces SketchUp to scale about the center of the face you're resizing.

8. **Select the edges that define the next-to-last profile in your extruded form.**

   Depending on the angle of your arc, making this selection can get tricky. Here are some considerations that may help:

   - See Chapter 2 for tips on making selections.

   - Choose View⇨Face Style⇨X-Ray from the menu bar to make it easier to see what you've selected.

   - Hold down the Ctrl key (Option on a Mac) while you orbit to turn off SketchUp's "blue is up/down gravity bias." While orbiting this way, try drawing lots of tight, little circles with your mouse to get your view to tilt in the direction your want. This is by no means simple stuff, but getting the hang of temporarily disabling the Orbit tool's tendency to keep the blue axis straight up and down is a very nifty way to work. Doing so makes it infinitely easier to get just the right angle for making a window selection. This in turn makes selecting the edges that define profiles a whole lot easier, and that's what becoming a Zen master of the Orbit tool is all about.

9. **Scale the edges you selected in the preceding step by a factor of 0.2.**

   Starting to see what's happening?

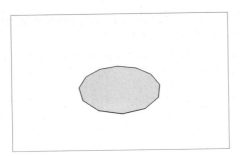

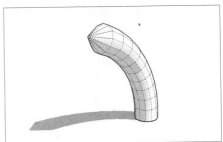

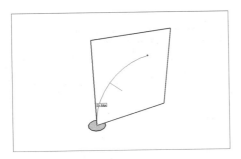

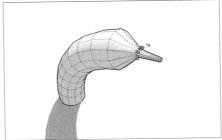

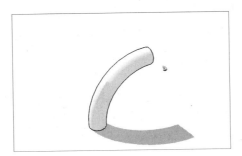

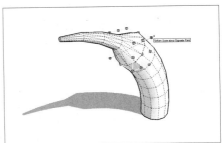

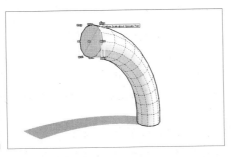

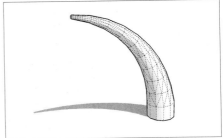

Figure 6-16:
Use Scale
with Follow
Me to
create long,
tapered
forms like
this bull's
horn.

10. **Repeat Steps 8 and 9 for each of the remaining profiles in your form, increasing the scaling factor by 0.1 each time.**

   Of course, you can absolutely choose to sculpt your form however you like, but this method (counting up by tenths) yields a smooth taper.

Have a look at the Santa and reindeer project in the color insert (in the center of this book) to get an idea of the kind of fancy, not-a-box models you can build after you master the Scale tool. It's not beginner-level material, but it's worth the time when you're ready for it.

Making and Modifying Terrain

Continuing in the grand tradition of building extremely powerful tools and then hiding them so you'll never find them, the people at SketchUp introduced the *Sandbox* in version 5 of the software. I introduce the Sandbox here because it helps people to model *terrain* — the stuff your buildings sit on (or in, if what you're making is underground).

The Sandbox isn't new, but owing to it's less-than-obvious location, most SketchUp users have never used it. Here are the facts:

✔ **The Sandbox is a collection of tools.** Each tool serves a fairly specific purpose and is meant to be used at a particular stage of the terrain-modeling process. That said, like all SketchUp's tools, they're incredibly flexible. You can use them to model anything you want.

✔ **The Sandbox is in both free and Pro:** Despite what many people think, the Sandbox tools aren't just for Pro users; people who use the free version of SketchUp can use them, too. They're just hidden, which brings me to my next point.

✔ **The Sandbox is hidden.** The reasons for this are complicated, but the tools in the Sandbox are a little bit special; they're *extensions* — you have to find them and turn them on before you can use them. If you're using SketchUp Pro, you can skip the first two steps in the following list — they're already turned on.

   Follow these steps to switch on the Sandbox tools:

   a. *Choose Window⇨Preferences from the menu bar to open the Preferences dialog box.*

   Choose SketchUp⇨Preferences if you're on a Mac.

   b. *In the Extensions panel, make sure the Sandbox Tools check box is selected and then close the Preferences dialog box.*

   c. *Choose View⇨Toolbars⇨Sandbox from the menu bar to show the Sandbox toolbar.*

Rather than doggedly describe what each element of the Sandbox does, I mention each tool as it becomes necessary. Don't worry about figuring out everything all at once — pick up new tools as you need them.

Creating a new terrain model

Whether you're modeling a patch of ground for a building or redesigning Central Park, you need one of two terrain-modeling methods:

- **Starting from existing data:** This existing data usually arrives in the form of *contour* or *topo* lines; see the next section to read more about them.

- **Starting from scratch;** If you don't have any data to start or if you're beginning with a perfectly flat site, you can use SketchUp's From Scratch tool to draw a grid that's easy to form into rolling hills, berms, and valleys. Skip ahead to "Modeling terrain from scratch" for more information.

There's a neat trick I learned for modeling small (yard-sized) amounts of terrain — the piece of land immediately surrounding a building, for example. You *could* use the From Scratch tool to start with a flat site, but there's a better way: See "Roughing out a site" a little later in this chapter to see what I mean.

Modeling terrain from contour lines

You know the squiggly lines on topographical maps that show you where the hills and valleys are? They're *contour lines* (or *contours*) because they represent the contours of the terrain; every point on a single line is the same height above sea level as every other point on that line. Where the lines are close together, the ground between them is steep. Where the lines are far apart, the slope is less steep. Cartographers, surveyors, engineers, and architects use contour lines to represent 3D terrain in flat formats like maps and site drawings.

Sometimes, you have contour lines for a building site that you want to model in 3D. You can use the From Contours tool in the Sandbox to automatically generate a three-dimensional surface from a set of contour lines. Have a look at Figure 6-17 to see what I mean.

Here are some things to keep in mind about the From Contours tool:

- **It's a two-step tool.** Using From Contours is simple after you get the hang of it:

    a. *Select all the Contour lines you want to use to create a surface.*

    b. *Choose Draw⇨Sandbox⇨From Contours from the menu bar (or click the From Contours tool button, if the Sandbox toolbar is visible).*

Select your lines

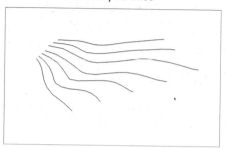

Choose From Contours

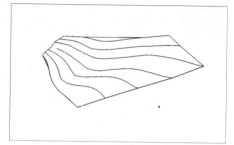

Show Hidden Geometry

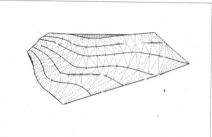

Separate your lines from your surface

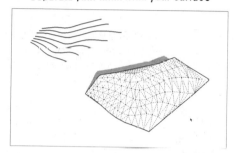

Figure 6-17:
Use the
From
Contours
tool to turn
a set of con-
tour lines
into a 3D
surface.

If you can't see the Sandbox tools in your menus, you haven't turned them on yet. See the beginning of this section, "Making and Modifying Terrain," to rectify the situation.

✔ **Your contour lines need to be lifted up.** The From Contours tool creates a surface from contour lines that are already positioned at their proper heights in 3D space. Most of the time you work with contours that were part of a 2D drawing, and that means you probably have to lift them up yourself using the Move tool — one at a time. It's tedious but necessary. Just oil up the Select tool, put on some music, and get to work. For a refresher on selecting things, take a look at the last part of Chapter 2.

✔ **Download and install Weld.** The Weld Ruby script (which you can read about in Chapter 17) turns selections of individual line segments into *polylines* — this makes them much, much easier to work with. If you work with contour lines imported from a computer-aided drawing (CAD) file, using Weld makes your life a little easier.

✔ **You end up with a group.** When you use From Contours, SketchUp automatically makes your new surface (the one you generated from your contour lines) into a group. It leaves the original lines themselves completely alone; you can move them away, hide them, or delete them if you want. I recommend making another group out of them, putting them on a separate layer (see Chapter 7 for more on this), and hiding that layer until you need it again.

To edit the faces and edges inside a group, double-click it with the Select tool. Chapter 5 has all the details on groups and components.

✔ **To edit your new surface, turn on Hidden Geometry.** The flowing, organic surface you just created is actually just a bunch of little triangles. The From Contours tool smoothes the edges that define them, but they're there. To see them, choose View⇨Hidden Geometry from the menu bar.

✔ **Try to keep your geometry reasonable.** The From Contours tool is super useful, but it has its limits. The trouble is that it's too easy to use it to create enormous amounts of geometry (faces and edges) that can really bog down your system. If it takes forever for your contours to turn into a surface, or if that surface is so big that your computer turns blue and curls up into a fetal position (so to speak), you need to go back a few steps and do one (or perhaps all) of the following:

• *Work on a smaller area.* As nice as it'd be to have the whole neighborhood in your SketchUp model, you may have to narrow your scope. Creating only what you need is good modeling policy.

• *Use only every other contour line.* Doing this effectively halves the amount of geometry in your resulting surface.

• *Dumb down the contour lines.* This is a little bit hard to explain, but here goes: The From Contours tool works by connecting adjacent contour lines together with edges that form triangles. How many triangles it creates depends on how many individual edge segments are in each contour line; Figure 6-18 provides an illustration. Unless you created the contour lines to begin with — there's a good chance you imported them as part of a CAD — you have no control over how detailed they are. Redrawing each contour line is a major bummer, but luckily, you can download a great Simplify Contours Ruby script that makes the process much simpler. Take a look at Chapter 17 for more information on using Ruby scripts.

✔ **You don't have to start with existing contour lines.** In fact, drawing your own edges and using From Contours to generate a surface from them is one of the most powerful ways to create organic, non-boxy forms in SketchUp. Take a look at the next part of this chapter to see what I mean.

✔ **Get ready to do some cleanup.** The surfaces that From Contours creates usually need to be cleaned up to some extent. Use the Eraser to delete extra geometry (you'll find lots along the top and bottom edges of your surface). Use the Flip Edge tool to correct the orientation of your triangular faces. See the nearby sidebar "Don't flip out — Flip Edge" for the lowdown.

Don't flip out — Flip Edge

The Sandbox's Flip Edge tool is a simple beast, but it's indispensable if you're working with the From Contours tool. Basically, you use Flip Edge to clean up the surfaces that From Contours creates. When you turn contour lines into a surface, lots and lots of triangular faces appear. Sometimes, the From Contours tool decides to draw an edge between the wrong two line segments, creating two triangular faces that form a "flat spot" in your surface. The following image shows what I mean.

You get rid of these flat spots manually by flipping the edges that create them. Doing so changes the resulting triangular faces, usually making them end up side-by-side (instead of one-above-the-other).

To use the Flip Edge tool (choose Tools⇨Sandbox⇨Flip Edge), just click the edge you want to flip. If you're not sure about an edge, go ahead and flip it; then see if things look better. If they don't, you can always undo or flip it back.

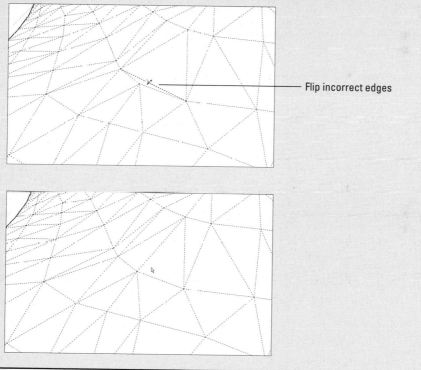

Flip incorrect edges

Modeling terrain from scratch

Without contour lines that define the shape of the terrain you want to model, you have to start with a level surface. Use the From Scratch tool to create a big, flat rectangle that represents a chunk of ground. Because the rectangle is already divided into triangular faces, it's easy to use the Smoove tool (which I talk about next in this chapter) to shape the rectangle into hills, valleys, sand traps, and whatever else you have in mind.

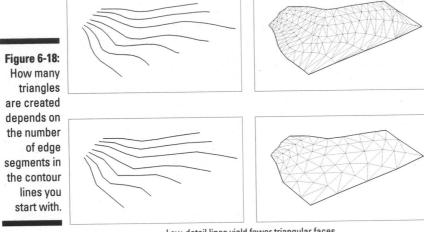

Figure 6-18:
How many
triangles
are created
depends on
the number
of edge
segments in
the contour
lines you
start with.

Low-detail lines yield fewer triangular faces

Here's the thing, though: It's a very rare occasion that you have *carte blanche* with a piece of land. Unless you design something like a golf course in the middle of a dry lake bed or terraform a new planet for colonization, you probably have pre-existing terrain conditions to contend with. And if that's the case, you're probably better starting off with a set of contour lines that describe those conditions — I talk all about the From Contours tool earlier in this chapter.

So although the From Scratch Tool works great, I doubt you'll need to use it much. All the same, here's how to do so, just in case.

Follow these steps to create a new terrain surface with the From Scratch tool and take a look at Figure 6-19 while you're at it:

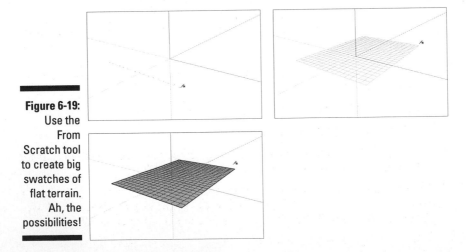

Figure 6-19:
Use the
From
Scratch tool
to create big
swatches of
flat terrain.
Ah, the
possibilities!

1. **Choose Draw⇨Sandbox⇨From Scratch from the menu bar to activate the From Scratch tool.**

2. **Type a grid spacing amount and press Enter.**

   The default grid spacing amount is 10 feet, which means the tool draws a rectangle made up of squares that are 10 feet across. The grid spacing you choose depends on how big an area you're planning to model and how detailed you plan to make the terrain for that model.

   If I were modeling a single-family house on a reasonably sized lot, I'd probably use a grid spacing of 2 feet — that'd provide enough detail for elements like walkways and small berms without creating too much geometry for my computer to handle. If I were laying out an 18-hole golf course, on the other hand, I'd choose a grid spacing closer to 50 feet and then add detail to certain areas later.

3. **Click to position one corner of your new terrain surface where you want it.**

4. **Click to determine the width of the surface you're drawing.**

5. **Click to establish the length of your new terrain surface.**

   When you're done, the great big rectangle you've created will automatically be a group. Double-click with the Select tool to edit it and good luck. You'll probably decide to use the Smoove tool next; jump ahead to "Making freeform hills and valleys with Smoove" (later in this chapter) to find out how.

Roughing out a site

Perhaps you want to model a smallish chunk of non-flat terrain that surrounds a building. Maybe you're trying to reproduce existing site conditions, or maybe you're in the process of designing the landscape for a project. There's a neat technique for cases like this one: You can use From Contours to quickly generate a surface from just a few simple outlines.

Follow these steps to model a simple terrain surface with the From Contours tool (see Figure 6-20):

1. **Extend the bottom of your building down so the exterior walls drop below ground level.**

2. **Make your building into a group.**

   See Chapter 5 if you need help.

3. **Use the Tape Measure and Line tools to draw the outline of the chunk of terrain you want to model around the building.**

   Keep in mind that the resulting horizontal face is flat; just pretend you're drawing in 2D space. It doesn't matter if the outline you draw is below, above, or in line with the building, as you see in the next step.

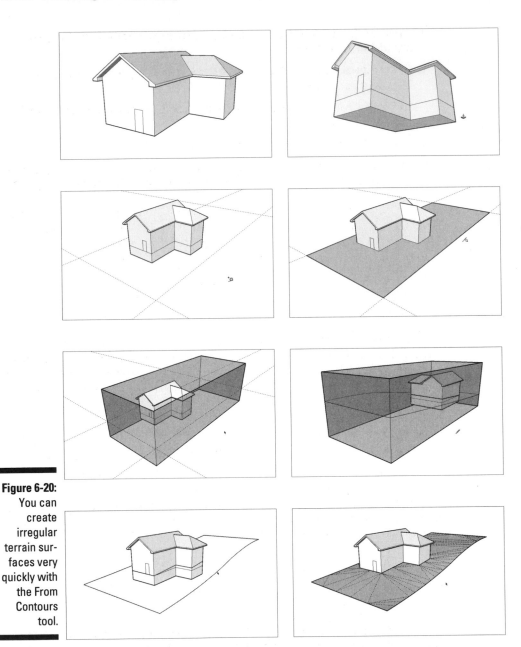

Figure 6-20:
You can create irregular terrain surfaces very quickly with the From Contours tool.

4. **Use the Push/Pull tool to extrude the face you drew in Step 3 into a box that extends above and below your building, and then delete the top and bottom faces of the box you just drew.**

5. **Paint the walls of your box with a translucent material.**

   You can find some in the Translucent library, in the Materials dialog box.

6. Draw edges on the sides of the box that represent where the ground should intersect them.

7. Draw edges on the sides of the building that represent where the ground meets the building.

8. Delete the box you created in Step 4, leaving only the edges you drew in Step 6.

9. Select all the edges you drew in Steps 6 and 7.

10. Choose Draw⇨Sandbox⇨From Contours from the menu bar to generate a surface based on the edges you selected in the previous step.

Take a look at the section "Modeling terrain from scratch" for tips on using From Contours; at this point, you need to use the Flip Edge tool and the Eraser to clean up your terrain model — particularly where your building is supposed to go.

Editing an existing terrain model

No matter how you make a terrain model, there's a 99-percent chance that it consists of lots and lots of triangles. Switch on Hidden Geometry (choose View⇨Hidden Geometry) to see them. As long as you have triangles, you can use the Sandbox's terrain editing tools. This section shows you how to do the following:

- Shape (or re-shape) your terrain with the Smoove tool.
- Create a flat spot for a building with the Stamp tool.
- Draw paths and roads with the Drape tool.

Keep in mind that both From Contours and From Scratch create terrain objects that are groups. To edit a group, double-click it with the Select tool. When you're done, click somewhere else in your modeling window.

Making freeform hills and valleys with Smoove

Smoove is a tool *for moving smoothly* — get it? Smooth + Move = Smoove. I'll wait while you compose yourself.

Smoove is actually one of the coolest tools in SketchUp; it lets you shape terrain (or any horizontal surface that's made up of smaller, triangular faces) by pushing and pulling (sort of) bumps and depressions of any size. Smoove is fun to use and yields results that you'd be hard-pressed to produce with any other tool in SketchUp. Figure 6-21 shows what Smoove can do.

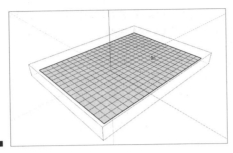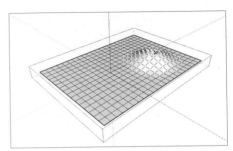
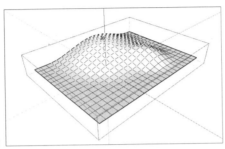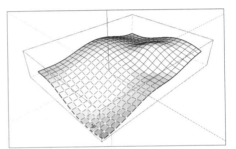

Figure 6-21:
Smoove
creates
shapes that
are unlike
anything
else you can
make with
SketchUp.

Follow these steps to shape a surface with Smoove:

1. **Double-click the group containing your terrain to edit it.**

   If your terrain isn't part of a group, forget I said that.

2. **Choose Tools➪Sandbox➪Smoove from the menu bar to activate the Smoove tool.**

3. **Type a radius and press Enter.**

   Smoove creates lumps, bumps, and dimples that are circular. The radius you enter here determines how big those lumps, bumps, and dimples should be.

4. **Click somewhere on your terrain surface to start smooving.**

5. **Move your mouse up or down (to create a bump or a depression, respectively), and then click again to stop smooving.**

Fun, huh? Here are some more things to keep in mind when you use Smoove:

- ✔ **Use the From Scratch tool beforehand.** You don't have to, but creating a surface with the From Scratch tool (which I describe earlier in this chapter) is by far the easiest way to end up with terrain that you can smoove easily.

- ✔ **Try smooving to edit other terrain surfaces.** You can also use Smoove after you create a terrain surface with the From Contours tool.

✔ **Double-click to repeat your previous Smoove.** As with Push/Pull, double-clicking tells SketchUp to carry out the same operation as you did the last time you used the tool.

✔ **Preselect to smoove shapes other than circles.** Any faces and edges you select before you use the Smoove tool will move up (or down) by a constant amount. This means you can use Smoove to create things like ridges and ditches by selecting the right geometry beforehand. Figure 6-22 provides a much-needed picture of what I mean.

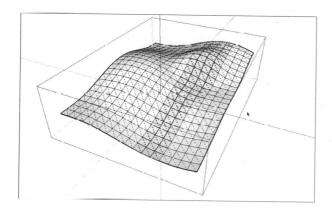

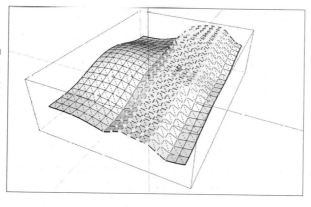

Figure 6-22: Preselect faces and edges to smoove shapes other than circles.

Placing a building on your terrain with Stamp

Eventually, you may need to plunk down a building (or some other structure) on the terrain you've lovingly crafted. The Stamp tool provides an easy way to — you guessed it — stamp a building footprint into a terrain surface, creating a flat "pad" for something to sit on. This tool also provides a way to create a gently sloping offset around the perimeter of your stamped form. This creates a smoother transition between the new, flat pad and the existing terrain.

Need more triangles? Add Detail

Like the Flip Edge tool, Add Detail is kind of a one-trick pony. Use it to add triangles to areas of your terrain surface that need more detail. That way, you can save geometry (and file size, and waiting) by having lots of faces only in the areas of your terrain that require it. If I were designing a golf course, I'd use very big triangles for the vast majority of it. I'd use the Add Detail tool to add triangles to areas where I planned to have smallish things like sand traps.

You can use the Add Detail tool in two ways:

✔ **Add detail to faces one at a time.** To be honest, I've never used the tool this way,

but here goes: You can activate the tool (see the next bullet) *without* having any geometry selected. Then click faces or edges on your terrain to divide them into more faces. I suppose this comes in handy when you model something very precisely.

✔ **Add detail to an area all at once.** This is actually my favorite way to use this tool; it's quick and easy to understand. Simply select the faces on your terrain you want to subdivide and choose Tools⇨Sandbox⇨Add Detail from the menu bar. Take a look at the figure to see what happens when you do.

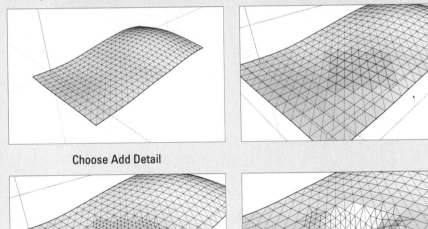

Choose Add Detail

Follow these steps to use the Stamp tool; check out Figure 6-23 to see the corresponding pictures:

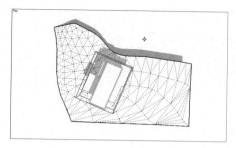
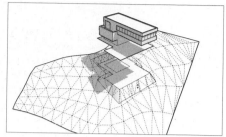
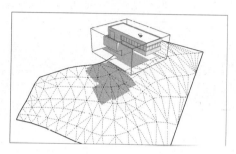
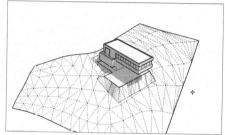
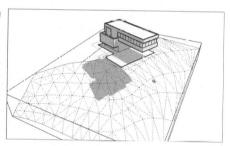
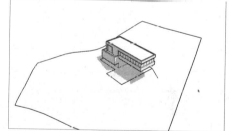

Figure 6-23:
Use the
Stamp tool
to create
a nice, flat
spot for your
building.

1. **Move the building you want to stamp into position above your terrain surface.**

   The building shouldn't touch the terrain but float in space directly above it. Also, turn the building into a group before you start moving anything; take a look at Chapter 5 to find out all about groups and components.

   If you're having trouble moving your building into position accurately, move it to the correct height first and then switching to a top, no-perspective view to finish the job. Look in the Camera menu for both these commands.

2. **Choose Tools⇨Sandbox⇨Stamp from the menu bar to activate the Stamp tool.**

3. **Click the floating object to tell SketchUp what you want to use as the stamp.**

4. **Type an offset distance and press Enter.**

   The *offset distance* is the amount of space around the perimeter of whatever you're stamping that SketchUp uses to smooth the transition between the flat spot it's creating and the existing terrain. The offset amount you choose depends entirely on what you're stamping. Go nuts, and thank your lucky stars for Undo.

5. **Move your cursor over your terrain surface and click again.**

6. **Move (but don't drag) your mouse up and down to position the flat pad in space. Click again to finish the operation.**

Here are a couple things that are handy to know when you use Stamp:

✔ SketchUp uses the bottommost face in your stamp object as the template for the flat pad it creates in your terrain.

✔ Read the "Don't flip out — Flip Edge" sidebar, earlier in this chapter; Stamp creates triangular faces that sometimes need cleaning.

Creating paths and roads with Drape

The Drape tool works a little like a cookie cutter; use it to transfer edges from an object down onto another surface, which is directly beneath it.

Perhaps you have a gently-sloping terrain and you want to draw a meandering path on it. The path has to follow the contours of the terrain, but because you want to paint it with a different material, it needs to be a separate face. In this case, you'd draw the path on a separate face and use the Drape tool to transfer it to your terrain surface.

Taking the preceding example, follow these steps to use the Drape tool to draw a path on a non-flat terrain surface (Figure 6-24 illustrates the steps):

1. **Use the Line tool (see Chapter 2) to draw a flat face somewhere directly above your terrain surface.**

   If you can, make your flat face exactly the same size as your terrain. Just make sure it's big enough for whatever you plan to draw next (in this example, a path).

2. **Paint the face you just created with a translucent material.**

   I find that a light gray works well; there's a good one in the Translucent library, inside the Materials dialog box.

3. **Use the Line tool to carry up any important points on your terrain surface.**

   In this case, make sure the path begins precisely at the door of the building, so draw vertical lines from the sides of the door to the flat face directly above. That way, you have something to inference to in Step 6.

4. **Choose Camera⇨Standard Views⇨Top from the menu bar to switch to a top view.**

5. **Choose Camera⇨Parallel Projection from the menu bar to turn off perspective.**

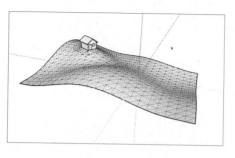
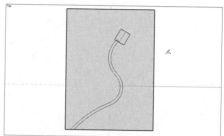
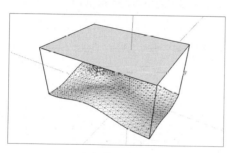
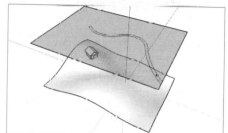
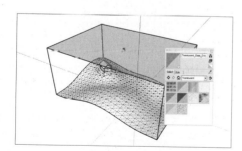
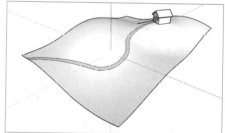
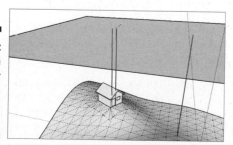

Figure 6-24:
Use Drape to transfer edges onto your terrain surface.

6. **On the upper face, draw the edges you want to drape.**

   Make sure that your edges form closed loops to create faces. If they don't, you'll have a miserable time trying to paint the path (in this case) after it's draped onto your terrain surface.

7. **Orbit your model so you can see both the upper and lower surfaces.**

8. **Soften/smooth the edges of the triangles in your terrain surface (if they aren't already).**

   To do this, follow these steps:

   a. *Select all the edges and faces in your terrain, and then choose Window⇨Soften Edges from the menu bar.*

   b. *In the Soften/Smooth Edges dialog box, move the slider to the far right and make sure that both the Smooth Normals and Soften Coplanar check boxes are selected.*

9. **Select the edges you want to drape.**

   If your edges define closed faces, you can select those faces instead; sometimes that's easier than selecting a bunch of individual edges. Take a look at Chapter 2 for tips on selecting things.

10. **Choose Draw⇨Sandbox⇨Drape from the menu bar to activate the Drape tool.**

11. **Click once on your terrain surface to drape the edges you selected in Step 9.**

    It doesn't matter if your terrain is inside a group — the Drape tool works anyway.

My friend Daniel Tal (a landscape architect and SketchUpper extraordinaire who regularly builds models that defy explanation) has written *Google SketchUp for Site Design: A Guide to Modeling Site Plans, Terrain and Architecture* (published by Wiley), which is available online and at your local bookstore. I *highly* recommend checking it out.

Building a Solid Tools Foundation

Brand new for SketchUp 8, the Solid Tools provide a completely new way for SketchUp modelers to work. So-called *solid modeling operations* (fancy people refer to them as *Boolean operations*) give you the ability create the shapes you need by adding or subtracting other shapes to or from each other. This type of modeling is actually pretty common in other 3D apps; now SketchUp can do it, too. In the next few pages, I show you how to use all six of SketchUp 8's new Solid Tools, giving detailed examples for the three that I think are the most useful.

I think it's important to mention right away that five of the six Solid Tools are only in the Pro version of SketchUp 8. Take a look at Table 6-1 (later in this chapter) to see what's available to you.

Understanding solids

Before you can use the new Solid Tools, you need *solids.* Here are six things you need to know about solids; you can think of them as the Solid Rules:

✔ **A solid is nothing more than an object that's completely enclosed.** It has no holes or other gaps; if you filled it with water, none would leak out. For this reason, solids are sometimes referred to as being *watertight.* Here's another way to think about it: Every edge in a solid must be bordered by two faces.

✔ **No extra edges or faces allowed.** You wouldn't think that one or two edges or faces would make much of a difference, but it does — solids can't contain *any* extra geometry, period. Figure 6-25 shows some examples of things that can disqualify otherwise completely enclosed shapes from being solids.

✔ **Only groups and components can be solids.** This one's a biggie. For SketchUp to *realize* an object is a solid, you have to make it into either a group or a component first. Another thing: Solid groups and components can't have other groups and/or components nested inside them.

✔ **Making a solid doesn't require any special tools.** You don't have to pick from a special list of objects to create solids; you make them with the same SketchUp tools you use all the time. Case in point: Every time you've push/pulled a rectangle into a box, you've created a solid.

✔ **Solids have volumes.** The easiest way to tell whether a group or component is a solid is to select it and choose Window⟹Entity Info. If the dialog box includes a value for Volume, you have a solid on your hands. Have a look at Figure 6-26 to see what I mean.

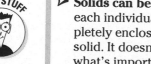

✔ **Solids can be multiple objects.** This one confused me at first. As long as each individual cluster of geometry within a group or component is completely enclosed, SketchUp considers that group or component to be a solid. It doesn't matter that they're not connected or touching in any way; what's important is that an area of space is fully surrounded by faces.

Solid

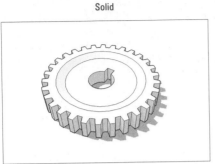

Missing face

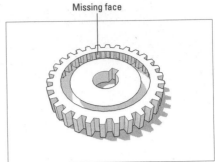

Loose face

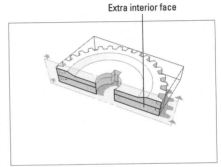

Extra interior face

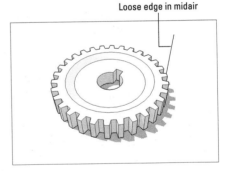

Loose edge on face

Loose edge in midair

Figure 6-25:
Solids can't
contain any
extra edges
or faces.

Figure 6-26:
Check
the Entity
Info dialog
box to see
whether
your selec-
tion is a
solid.

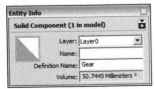

Checking out the Solid Tools

When you have a solid object or objects, you can use SketchUp 8's Solid Tools in powerful ways to create shapes that'd otherwise be very complicated and time-consuming to make. For example:

✔ Add two solids together to create a new one.

✔ Use one solid to cut away part of another one.

With the SketchUp Intersect Faces tool (formerly Intersect with Model), you can achieve many of the same things that the Solid Tools do. Intersect Faces takes longer because it requires an awful lot of cleanup; however, it's still useful for two very important reasons: It's available in both the free and Pro versions of SketchUp, and it works on any face in your model — not just on solids. You can read about Intersect Faces in Chapter 4.

Two things you need to know before you start using the Solid Tools:

✔ **Open the dedicated toolbar.** Choose View➪Toolbars➪Solid Tools to open the toolbar that contains all six tools. You can also find them on the Tools menu. Keep in mind that five of them — all but the Outer Shell tool — are available only if you have SketchUp Pro 8.

✔ **To use the Solid Tools, preselect — or don't.** Pick the tool you want to use either *before* or *after* you've told SketchUp which solid objects you want to affect. Like most "order of operations" issues (are you listening, Follow Me tool?), this can be confusing for some folks.

I find the easiest way to use the Solid Tools is to preselect the solids I want to use and *then* choose the tool to carry out the operation. The glaring exceptions to this rule are the Subtract and Trim tools; both of these depend heavily on the *order* in which you pick your solids. Take a peek at Table 6-1 for more specifics.

Without further ado, here they are (check out Figure 6-27 for a visual):

Table 6-1		The Solid Tools			
Tool	*Free or Pro?*	*What It Does*	*How to Use It*	*Start With*	*End With*
Union	Pro only	Combines two or more solids into a single solid. Deletes overlapping geometry. Preserves internal pockets.*	Select the solids you want to use and then activate the tool.	Two+ solids	One solid

(continued)

Table 6-1 *(continued)*

Tool	Free or Pro?	What It Does	How to Use It	Start With	End With
Outer Shell	Free and Pro	Combines two or more solids into a single solid. Deletes overlapping geometry, including internal pockets.*	Same as Union tool.	Two+ solids	One solid
Intersect	Pro only	Makes a single solid where two or more solids overlap. Deletes everything else.	Same as Union tool.	Two+ solids	One solid
Subtract	Pro only	Uses one solid to cut away part of another solid. Deletes the first solid when it's done.	Activate the tool, click "cutting" solid, and then click solid to be cut.	Two solids	One solid
Trim	Pro only	Uses one solid to cut away part of another solid. Keeps what's left of both solids.	Same as Subtract tool.	Two solids	Two solids
Split	Pro only	Cuts two solids where they overlap and creates a new solid from the overlap. Doesn't delete anything.	Same as Union tool.	Two solids	Three solids

*An internal pocket is like a solid within a solid — it's a completely enclosed volume that happens to be located inside the main volume of a solid. Picture a SketchUp model of a tennis ball. Because tennis balls have a thickness, you'd need two surfaces to model one: one for the inside, and one for the outside. If you selected both and made a group, you'd have a solid with an internal pocket inside.

Note that the Split tool actually does three operations every time you use it: It yields two subtractions and an intersection. That is to say, using Split is like using both Subtract *and* Intersect on your solids. For this reason, I've taken to replacing both of these tools with Split full-time. It's easier to keep track of what's going to happen, and the only downside is that I have to delete a couple extra objects when I'm done.

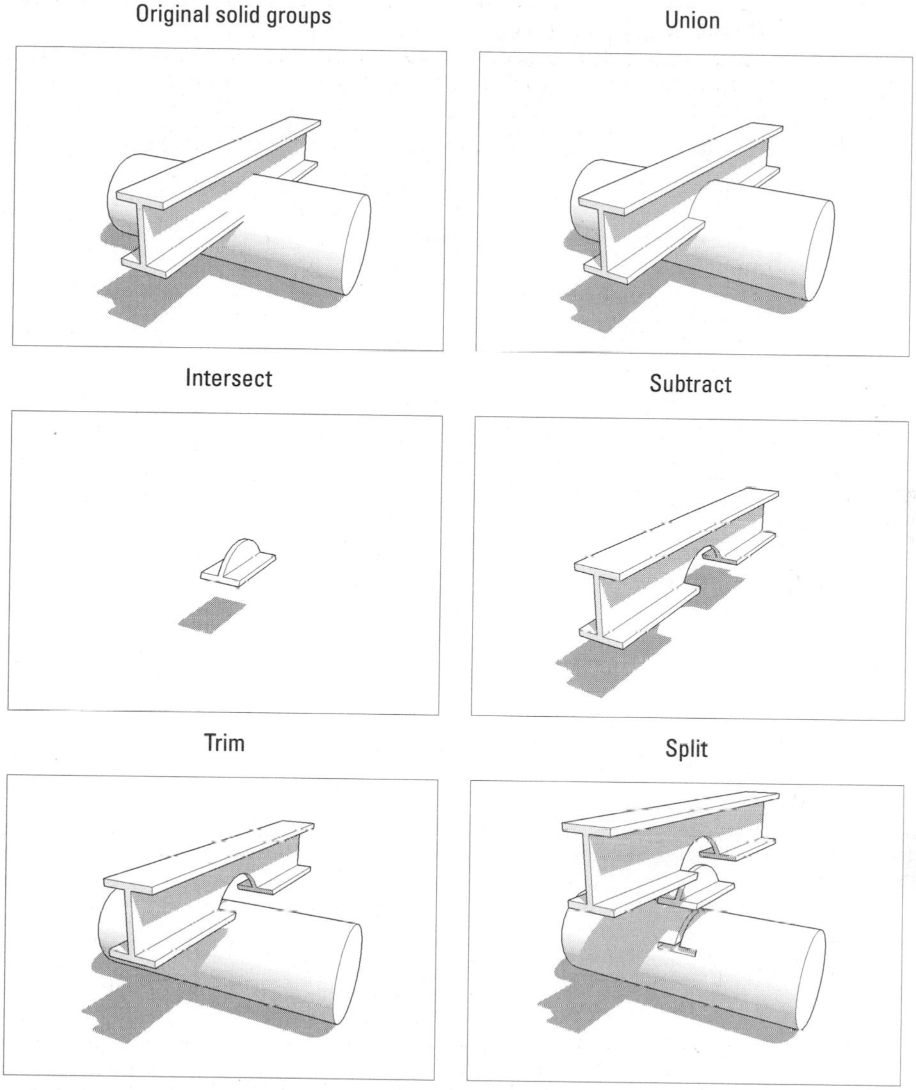

Original solid groups

Union

Intersect

Subtract

Trim

Split

Figure 6-27:
The Solid
Tools lets
you do addi-
tive and
subtractive
modeling
operations.

Putting the Solid Tools to work

In this section, I give a few examples of everyday modeling challenges that the Solid Tools can help make less challenging. You're almost certain to encounter these tricky situations while you climb the ladder toward ultimate SketchUp ninjahood.

Assembling complex objects with Union or Outer Shell

Chapter 4 has a section about using the Intersect Faces tool to combine multiple roof pitches into a single, solitary roof. If all those gables, hips, dormers, and other roof elements are solids, you can absolutely use SketchUp's Union or Outer Shell tools to make quick work of the problem.

The same goes for anything that's composed of several disparate elements that you've assembled by moving them together until they overlap. In the spacecraft in Figure 6-28, the *hull* (or body) of the craft is a combination of different pieces I modeled separately. Notice the lack of edges where the components intersect? I don't like that — I think edges add detail and definition, especially when my model is displayed using a lines-only style (as it is here). There's also the issue of all the geometry hidden inside the hull. Combining everything together into a single solid helps it shed weight and look better, all at the same time.

Figure 6-28:
Using Union or Outer Shell to combine several solids into one produces edges where their faces intersect and gets rid of excess geometry.

Start with several solids

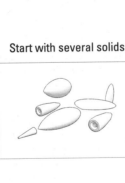
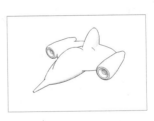

Use Union to put them together

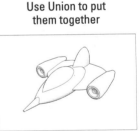

Using Intersect in combination with front, top, and side views

Anyone who's ever tried to model a car with SketchUp knows it's a tricky undertaking. The problem is that cars (and most other vehicles) are kind of curvy; worse yet, they're curvy in several directions.

One trick lots of modelers use to block out a basic shape for things like cars is to start with *orthographic* — straight-on top, front, and side — views of the thing they're trying to model. Here's how the method works:

1. **Position each 2D view where it belongs in 3D space.**
2. **Push/pull them all so their extrusions overlap.**

3. **Use the Intersect tool (Tools➪Solid Tools➪Intersect) to find the object the extrusions all have in common.**

This method doesn't always produce perfect results, but it's a lot better than guessing. Plus, it's fun. Figure 6-29 shows the technique in action.

1. Create solids from front, top, and side views

2. Position them precisely

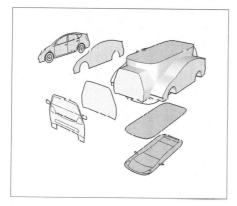
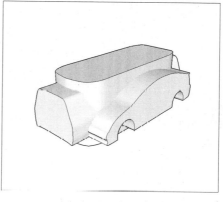

3. Use Intersect to find shape they have in common

4. Smooth edges and use Intersect Faces with Model to transfer details

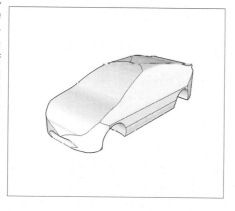

Modeling close-fitting parts with Trim

Woodworkers and industrial designers, take heed: SketchUp Pro 8's Trim tool saves you literally hours of work. Any time you need to build a model with parts that interlock or otherwise fit together closely, Trim is where you should look first.

Trim basically tells one part to "take a bite" out of another, which is perfect for joinery (dovetails, finger joints, dadoes, and so on), machine parts, ball-and-socket joints, and any other positive/negative conditions where two parts meet.

In Figure 6-30, I build a small wooden box with dovetailed sides and a dadoed bottom.

The only tricky thing about using the Trim tool is remembering which solid to pick first. Remember that the first thing you pick (or click) is the one you want to use to cut with. In the case of the box in Figure 6-30, that would be side with the dovetails. When I select the dovetails and then select the blank side, the Trim tool cuts the dovetails into the second piece. You get the hang of it after a few tries.

The Trim tool has a neat trick up its sleeve: You can keep using your cutting solid on multiple other solids. To cut the *dado* (or groove) into the sides of the box in Figure 6-30, follow these steps:

1. **Choose Tools⇨Solid Tools⇨Trim to activate the Trim tool.**

   Your cursor has the number 1 on it.

2. **Select the box bottom.**

   Your cursor changes to show the number 2.

3. **Select one side on the box.**

   You just cut a dado using the box bottom you picked in Step 2. Your cursor still says 2.

4. **Select another of the box's sides to create another dado.**

5. **Select the remaining two sides to cut dadoes in them, too.**

   Fun!

A question that comes up pretty frequently concerns what happens when you use one of the Solid Tools on a component instance. Why doesn't the effect of what you just did affect all the other instances of that component? It should, shouldn't it? Anyone who's read Chapter 5 of this book should know that . . .

Here's the thing: As soon as you use a Solid Tool on a component instance, SketchUp makes that instance unique; it's still a component — it just isn't connected to the other instances anymore.

1. Start with sides as solid components

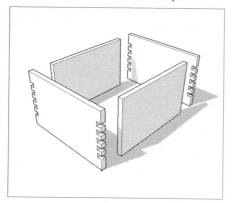

2. Fit everything together

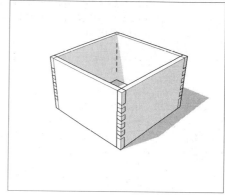

3. Use Trim to cut dovetails into other two sides

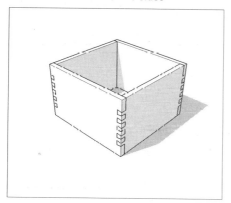

4. Create bottom to fit

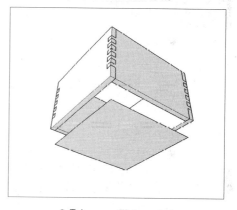

5. Position bottom and use Trim to cut dadoes in sides

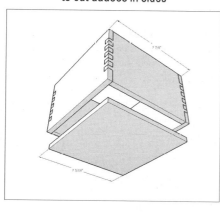

6. Take everything apart to make sure it looks right

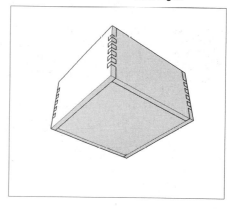

Figure 6-30:
The Trim tool is perfect for modeling joinery and other close-fitting parts.

Chapter 7

Keeping Your Model Organized

tarting with this chapter, I may sound like your mom: "Clean up your room! Don't leave your toys in the driveway! Put your dishes in the sink!" As everybody knows, living life can be a messy ordeal, and modeling in SketchUp is no exception. As you crank away at whatever it is you're building, you'll reach a time when you stop, orbit around, and wonder how your model got to be such a pigsty. It's inevitable.

Luckily, SketchUp includes a bunch of different ways to keep your *geometry* (edges and faces) from getting out of control. Because big, unwieldy, disorganized models are a pain to work with — they can slow your computer, or even cause SketchUp to crash — you should definitely get in the habit of *working clean* (as cooking shows like to call it). As I say earlier, I don't mean to nag; I just want you to be familiar with the techniques experienced SketchUp modelers use to keep their sanity.

In this chapter, I present the two main tools that SketchUp provides for organizing your model. In the first section, I outline both tools and talk about what they're for. Then I dive in to the details about each one, describing how to use them and how *not* to use them (are you listening, layers?). This chapter ends with a detailed example of how you can use both tools together to make your life easier; I show you how I organize a model of my house.

Taking Stock of Your Organization Options

When sorting out the thousands of edges and faces in your model, it's all about lumping things together into useful sets. After you separate things into sets, you can name them, hide them, and even lock them so that you (or somebody else) can't mess them up.

If you haven't read about groups and components yet, now would be a good time to take a look at Chapter 5 — the stuff in this chapter is best understood if you have a firm grasp on the stuff in that one.

You have two organizational methods at your disposal in SketchUp. The best modelers use both all the time:

- ✔ **Outliner:** The Outliner is a dialog box that's basically a fancy list of all the groups and components in your SketchUp model. It shows you which groups and components are nested inside other ones, lets you assign names for them, and gives you an easy way to hide parts of your model that you don't want to see. If you use a lot of components (and you should), the Outliner may well become your new best friend.

- ✔ **Layers:** This is where a lot of people reading this book let out a big sigh of relief. "Thank goodness," they're thinking, "I was beginning to think SketchUp doesn't have layers." For people who are used to organizing content in other software programs, layers are usually where it's at — you put different kinds of things on different layers, name the layers, and then turn them on and off when you need to. It's a pretty simple concept. In SketchUp, layers are similar — but the ways in which SketchUp layers work differently are important for modelers to know.

In SketchUp, using layers the wrong way can seriously mess up your model. I'm not kidding. If you plan to use them, read the section "Discovering the Ins and Outs of Layers," later in this chapter. Not doing so can result in serious injury or even death (depending on how upset you get when your 50-hour model gets ruined).

Seeing the Big Picture: The Outliner

I'm a person who really likes to make lists. Not only that, but I love to *look at* lists — information arranged neatly into collapsible rows is the kind of thing that brings a tear to my eye.

Now, before you decide that I ought to be locked in a small room with cushions on the walls, consider this: Most halfway-complicated SketchUp models consist of dozens, if not hundreds, of groups and components. These groups and components are nested inside each other like Russian dolls, and many are heavy, computer-killing behemoths like three-dimensional trees and shrubs.

Without a list, how are you going to manage all your groups and components? How are you going to keep track of what you have, hide what you don't want to see, and (more importantly) *unhide* what you *do* want to see? I thought so — I guess it turns out I'm not so crazy after all.

Taking a good look at the Outliner

You can open the Outliner dialog box by choosing Window⇨Outliner. Figure 7-1 shows what it looks like when a model consists of a simple room with some furniture in it. Each piece of furniture is a separate component that I downloaded from the Google 3D Warehouse. (Check out Chapter 5 for the whole story.)

The Outliner dialog box has the following features:

- **Search filter box:** If you type a word or phrase into this box, the Outliner shows only the items in your model that include that word or phrase in their names. If you were to type *coffee,* only the coffee table component would be visible.

- **Outliner Options flyout menu:** This handy little menu contains three options:

  - *Expand All:* Choose this option to have the Outliner show *all* the nested groups and components in your model — every last one of them (provided they're on visible layers).

    The Outliner shows only groups and components that exist on layers that are visible in your model. In other words, anything on a hidden layer doesn't appear in the Outliner, so be extra careful if you're using both the Outliner and layers to organize your model. You can read all about layers in the "Discovering the Ins and Outs of Layers" section, later in this chapter.

  - *Collapse All:* This option collapses your Outliner view so that you see only *top-level* groups and components — ones that aren't nested inside other groups and components.

  - *Sort by Name:* Select this option to make the Outliner list the groups and components in your model alphabetically.

- **Outliner List window:** All the groups and components in your model are listed here. Groups and components that have nested groups and components inside them have an Expand/Collapse toggle arrow next to their names. When they're expanded, the constituent groups and components appear as an indented list below them.

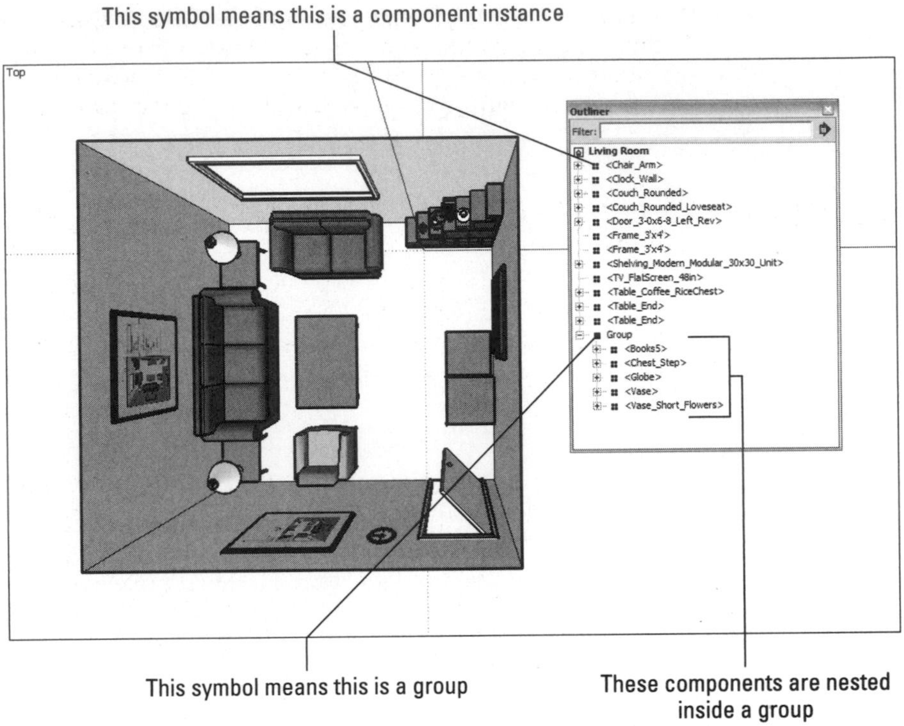

This symbol means this is a component instance

Top

Outliner

Filter:

Living Room
- <Chair_Arm>
- <Clock_Wall>
- <Couch_Rounded>
- <Couch_Rounded_Loveseat>
- <Door_3-0x6-8_Left_Rev>
- <Frame_3'x4'>
- <Frame_3'x4'>
- <Shelving_Modern_Modular_30x30_Unit>
- <TV_FlatScreen_48in>
- <Table_Coffee_RiceChest>
- <Table_End>
- <Table_End>
- Group
  - <Books5>
  - <Chest_Step>
  - <Globe>
  - <Vase>
  - <Vase_Short_Flowers>

Figure 7-1:
The Outliner, when I have a few components in my model.

This symbol means this is a group

These components are nested inside a group

Making good use of the Outliner

If you use lots of groups and components (and you should), having the Outliner open onscreen is one of the best things you can do to model efficiently.

Here's why:

- ✔ **Use the Outliner to control visibility.** Instead of right-clicking groups and components in your model to hide them, use the Outliner instead. Just right-click the name of any element in the Outliner and choose Hide. When you do, the element is hidden in your modeling window, and its name is grayed out and italicized in the Outliner. To unhide it, just right-click its name in the Outliner and choose Unhide.

- ✔ **Drag and drop elements in the Outliner to change their nesting order.** Don't like having the component you just created nested inside another component? Simply drag its name in the Outliner to the top of the list. This moves the component to the top level, meaning that it's not embedded in anything. You can also use the Outliner to drag groups and components into other ones, too.

✔ **Find and select things using the Outliner.** Selecting something in the Outliner highlights that something's name and selects it in your modeling window. This is a much easier way to select nested groups and components, especially if you're working with a complex model.

Discovering the Ins and Outs of Layers

I'm gonna give it to you straight: Layers are a very useful part of SketchUp, and they can make your life a lot easier. Layers can also be a major source of heartache because they can *really* mess up your model if you're not careful. In this section, I try to set you on the right track.

What layers are — and what they're not

In a 2D program like Photoshop or Illustrator, the concept of layers makes a lot of sense: You can have content on any number of layers, sort of like a stack of transparencies. You find a distinct order to your layers, so anything on the top layer is visually in front of everything on all the other layers. Figure 7-2 shows what I mean.

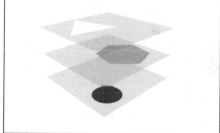

But hold on a second — SketchUp isn't a 2D program; it's a 3D program. So how can it have layers? How can objects in three-dimensional space be layered on top of each other so that things on higher layers appear in front of things on lower ones? In short, they can't — it's impossible. Layers in SketchUp are different from layers in most other graphics programs, and that's confusing for lots of people.

SketchUp has a layers system because some of the very first SketchUp users were architects, and many, *many* architects use AutoCAD drawing software. Because AutoCAD uses layers extensively, layers were incorporated into SketchUp to maximize compatibility between the two products. When you import a layered AutoCAD file into SketchUp, its layers show up as SketchUp layers, which is pretty convenient.

So what are SketchUp layers for? Layers control visibility. Use them to gather particular kinds of geometry so that you can easily turn it on (make it visible) and turn it off (make it invisible) when you need to. That said, layers *don't* work the same way as groups and components; your edges and faces aren't isolated from other parts of your model, which can cause major confusion if you're not careful. Take a look at the section "Staying out of trouble," later in this chapter, to find out more.

Using layers in SketchUp

You can find the Layers dialog box on the Window menu. It's a pretty simple piece of machinery, as shown in Figure 7-3. Here's what everything does:

Add Layer   Layer Options flyout menu

Delete Layer

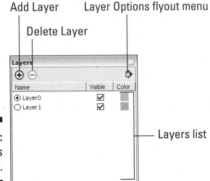

Figure 7-3:
The Layers
dialog box.

Layers list

✔ **Add Layer:** Clicking this button adds a new layer to your SketchUp file.

✔ **Delete Layer:** Click this button to delete the currently selected layer. If anything is on the layer you're trying to delete, SketchUp asks what you want to do with it; choose an option and select Delete.

✔ **Layer Options flyout menu:** This contains the following useful options:

• *Purge:* When you choose Purge, SketchUp deletes all the layers that don't contain geometry. This is a handy way to keep your file neat and tidy.

• *Color by Layer:* Notice how each layer in the list has a little material swatch next to it? Choosing Color by Layer temporarily changes all the colors in your SketchUp model to match the colors (or textures) assigned to each layer. To see what's on each layer, this is the way to go.

✔ **Layers list:** This is a list of all the layers in your SketchUp file. You need to know about these three columns:

- *Name:* Double-click a layer's name to edit it. Giving your layers meaningful names is a good way to quickly find what you want.

- *Visible:* This check box is the heart and soul of the Layers dialog box. When it's selected, the geometry on that layer is visible; when the check box isn't selected, the layer's geometry isn't visible.

- *Color:* You can choose to view your model using Color by Layer, which I describe earlier in the list. You can choose which material (color or texture) to assign to each layer by clicking the Color swatch.

Adding a new layer

Follow these steps to add a layer to your SketchUp file:

1. **Choose Window➪Layers.**

   The Layers dialog box opens.

2. **Click the Add Layer button to add a new layer to the Layers list.**

   If you want, you can double-click your new layer to rename it.

Moving entities to a different layer

Moving things from one layer to another involves using the Entity Info dialog box. Follow these steps to move an *entity* (an edge, face, group, or component) to a different layer:

1. **Select the entity or entities you want to move to another layer.**

   Move only groups and components to other layers; have a look at the next section in this chapter to find out why.

2. **Choose Window➪Entity Info.**

   The Entity Info dialog box opens. You can also open it by right-clicking your selected entities and choosing Entity Info from the context menu.

3. **In the Entity Info dialog box, choose a layer from the Layer drop-down list.**

   Your selected entities are now on the layer you chose from the list.

Staying out of trouble

As I said before, layers can be really helpful, but you need to know how to use them; if you don't, bad things can happen. Check out the following do's and don'ts before you start working with layers:

✔ **Do all your modeling on Layer0.** Always make sure that Layer0 is your current layer when you're working. Keeping all your loose geometry (that's not part of a group or component) together in one place is the *only* way to make sure that you don't end up with edges and faces all over the place. SketchUp, unfortunately, lets you put geometry on whatever layer you want, which means that you can end up with a face on one layer, and one or more of the edges that define it on another. When that happens, it's next to impossible to work out where everything belongs; you'll spend literally hours trying to straighten out your model. This property of SketchUp's layers system is a major stumbling point for new SketchUp users; knowing to keep everything on Layer0 can save you a lot of anguish.

✔ **Don't move anything but groups and components to other layers.** If you're going to use layers, follow this rule: *Never* put anything on a layer other than Layer0 unless it's a group or a component. Doing so ensures that you don't end up with stray edges and faces on separate layers.

✔ **Use layers to organize big groups of similar things.** More complicated SketchUp models often include things like trees, furniture, cars, and people. These kinds of things are almost always already components, so they're perfect candidates for being kept on separate layers. I often make a Trees layer and put all my tree components on it. This makes it easy to hide and show all my trees all at once. This speeds my workflow by improving my computer's performance. (Trees are usually big, complicated components with lots of faces.)

✔ **Don't use layers to organize interconnected geometry; use the Outliner instead.** By *interconnected geometry,* I mean things like building floor levels and staircases. These model parts aren't meant to be physically separate from other parts like vehicles and people are. When you put Level 1 on one layer and Level 2 on another, more often than not, you become confused about what belongs where: Is the staircase part of Level 1 or Level 2? Instead, make a group for Level 1, a group for Level 2, and a group for the staircase — you'll need less headache medicine at the end of the day.

✔ **Feel free to use layers to iterate.** *Iteration* is the process of doing multiple versions of the same thing. Lots of designers work this way to figure out problems and present different options to their clients. Using layers is a great way to iterate: You can move each version of the thing you're working on to a different layer, and then turn them on and off to show each in turn. Just remember to follow the rule about using groups and components only on separate layers (mentioned previously), and you'll be fine.

Check out the sidebar "Using Scenes to control layers" (later in this chapter) for a nifty way to quickly flip through layers that represent design iterations in your model.

Putting It All Together

In this chapter (and in Chapter 5), I talk about each of SketchUp's organizational methods in isolation: discussing how they work, why they're special, and when to use them. When you're actually working in SketchUp, you probably use a combination of them all, so I thought you'd find an example of all the organization tools in action especially helpful.

Figure 7-4 (along with a couple pages in this book's color insert) shows a model of a small house I'm building in SketchUp. I'm using all of SketchUp's organizational tools to help me manage my model's complexity while I'm working:

- ✔ **Each floor level is a group.** By working with each floor level as a separate group, I can use the Outliner to hide whichever one I'm not working on. This makes it easier to see what I'm doing. I'm including the house's only staircase in the first floor group because that turns out to be the easiest thing to do.

  I've decided to include the interior walls on each level of my house in that level's group. I don't think I'll ever have to hide them, so it wasn't worth making them a separate group. For what it's worth, I think the same thing probably applies to most buildings, unless you plan to study different floor plans with different interior wall arrangements.

- ✔ **The roof and exterior walls are groups inside of another group.** I want to be able to "remove" the roof and the exterior walls separately, so I've made each of them a group. I also want to be able to hide and unhide them both at the same time, so I made a Shell group that includes them both. Using the Outliner, I can selectively show or hide just the geometry I want. (See Figure 7-5.)

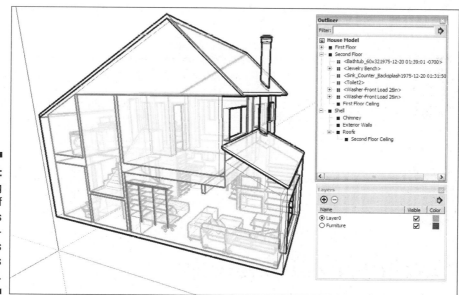

Figure 7-4:
I'm using all of SketchUp's organizational tools to build this model.

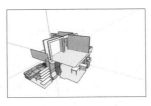
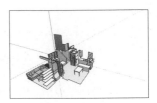

Figure 7-5:
Each floor of my house, as well as the roof and the exterior walls, is a group.

The floor levels, roof, and exterior walls of my house are groups instead of components because they're *unique* — I only have one First Floor, so it doesn't need to be a component.

✔ **All the furniture and plumbing fixtures are components.** All the components I use to furnish my house are ones I built myself, took from the Components dialog box, or found in the 3D Warehouse.

But I have only one couch: Why make it a component instead of a group? By making every piece of furniture in my model a component, I can see a list of my furniture in the In Model collection of the Components dialog box. I can also save that as a separate component collection on my computer. The next time I move, I'll have all my furniture in a single place, ready to drop into a model of my new house.

✔ **All my furniture is on a separate layer.** Because furniture components can be a little *heavy* (taxing my computer system) and because I want the ability to see my house without furniture, I created a new Furniture layer and moved all my furniture onto it. Using the Layers dialog box, I can control the visibility of that layer with a single mouse click.

But why not just create a group from all my furniture components and use the Outliner to hide and unhide them all, instead of bothering with layers? Good question. Because changing a component's layer is easier than adding a component to an existing group. To add something to a group, I'd need to use the Outliner to drag and drop that something in the proper place; with complex models, this can be a hassle. Changing a component's layer is just a matter of using the Entity Info dialog box to choose from a list.

Using Scenes to control layers

If you're reading this book from front to back, you haven't yet encountered any mention of SketchUp's Scenes feature — Chapter 10 is where you can go to read all about it. Without diving into too much redundant detail, *scenes* are basically saved views of your model. Instead of fiddling with navigation tools and dialog boxes every time you want to return to an important view, you can click a scene tab.

Scenes are relevant in this chapter because scenes don't just save different camera positions; you can also use them to control layer visibility. Being able to click a scene tab to instantly change which layers are showing is a crazy-powerful way to do *iterative design*: creating and presenting different options within the same design.

A very simple example: You've modeled a living room and want to try three different furniture configurations:

1. **Make three layers — Option 1, Option 2, and Option 3.**

2. **Do three separate furniture arrangements, one per layer.**

   Of course, this means that you have three copies of each object you move.

3. **Use the Layers dialog box to show Option 1, and hide Option 2 and Option 3.**

4. **Create a new scene and name it Option 1 using the Scenes dialog box.**

5. **Repeat Steps 3 and 4 for the other two configurations.**

Now all you have to do is click a scene tab to switch between the three options; this is much more elegant than having to fiddle with the Layers dialog box during a presentation. See the image below to get an idea of the setup.

The key to making this technique really sing is a working knowledge of how to use the Properties to Save check boxes in the Scenes dialog box. I should warn you: This isn't beginner-level stuff. Hooking up scenes and layers takes practice, but after you get the hang of it, it's an elegant way to work. Pick your way through Chapter 10, when you're ready.

One more useful tidbit: The Layers Ruby script plugin lets you (among other things) create a new layer that isn't visible in any of the scenes you've made previously. This plugin comes in handy when you need to add a new iteration *after* you've already made a bunch of scenes; without the plugin, your new layer is visible in every scene, forcing you to manually go through and hide it in each one. Take a look at Chapter 17 for more information about the Layers Ruby script.

(continued)

(continued)

Chapter 8

Modeling with Photographs

. . . .

In This Chapter

▶ Painting faces in your model with photographs

▶ Photo-texturing curved surfaces

▶ Building a model from scratch with SketchUp's photo-matching tools

▶ Using photo-matching to match your model to a photograph

▶ Modeling on top of photo-textured faces

. . . .

*T*hese days, it's next to impossible to meet someone who doesn't take pictures. Aside from the millions of digital cameras out there, lots of mobile phones have cameras in them, too. I expect that by the time I work on the next edition of this book, I'll be writing about digital cameras in sunglasses — just wink to take a snapshot and then blink three times to e-mail it to your grandma.

You can use all these photos you take in SketchUp in a couple ways:

▶ **If you have a model you want to paint with photographs,** you can do that in SketchUp. You can apply photos to faces and then use the information in the pictures to help you model; building windows is a lot easier when they're painted right on the wall. That's what I talk about in the first part of this chapter.

▶ **If you want to use a photo to help you model something from scratch,** you can do that in SketchUp, too. Photo-matching makes it (relatively) simple to bring in a picture, set things up so that your modeling window view matches the perspective in the photo, and then build what you see by tracing with SketchUp's modeling tools. Sound like fun? It is — and that's why I devote the whole second half of this chapter to it.

One great application for *photo-textured* (painted with photos) models is Google Earth. You can make buildings and see them in Earth — you can even contribute models to Google Earth's default 3D Buildings layer where *everyone* can see them. This chapter talks about the techniques to use if that's where your models are headed. Take a look at Chapter 11 for details about actually putting your models in Google Earth.

Painting Faces with Photos

Technically, painting surfaces with pictures using 3D software is called *mapping,* as in "I *mapped* a photo of your face to the underside of the pile-driver model I'm building." Different software programs have different methods for mapping pictures to faces, and luckily, SketchUp's are pretty straightforward.

This section deals with mapping photos to two different kinds of faces: flat ones and curved ones. The tools are similar, but the methods aren't. I thought I'd show both — you never know what you're going to run into.

SketchUp uses lots of different terms to refer to the stuff you can paint faces with; generically, they're all *materials.* Materials can be colors or textures; *textures* are image-based, and *colors* are a single, solid hue. When you import an image to map it to a face, it becomes a texture — just like any of the other textures in your Materials dialog box. Read more about using materials in SketchUp in Chapter 2.

Adding photos to flat faces

When mapping photos onto flat faces, you can choose the easy way or the hard way. Unfortunately, the hard way is the method you end up using the vast majority of the time, so I describe it first. Importing images using the File menu lets you take any image and map it to any flat face in your model.

The easy way, which I get to in a few pages, is designed for one particular case: It gives you access to Google's vast collection of Street View imagery, letting you paint your models with building facades photographed by Google's roving fleet of specialized vehicles. The feature is cool, but also very specific.

Importing images: Use your own photos

Follow these steps to map an image to a face (and find additional help on this book's companion Web site; see the Introduction for details):

Before you follow these steps, have at least one face in your model because you map your texture to a face.

1. **Choose File⇨Import.**

   The Open dialog box opens.

2. **Select the image file you want to use as a texture.**

   You can use JPEGs, TIFFs, and PNGs as textures in SketchUp; all these are common image-file formats.

3. **Select the Use as Texture option, as shown in Figure 8-1.**

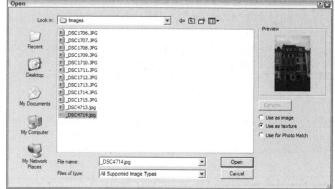

Figure 8-1:
Make sure
to pick Use
as Texture.

4. **Click the Open button.**

   The Open dialog box closes, and Paint Bucket becomes your active tool, with the cursor loaded with the image you chose to import.

5. **Click once in the lower-left corner of the face you want to "paint" (see Figure 8-2).**

   Where you click tells SketchUp where to position the lower-left corner of the image you're using as a texture. You can click anywhere on the face you're trying to paint, but I recommend the lower-left corner — it keeps things simple.

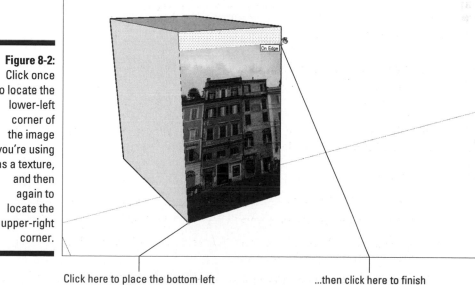

Figure 8-2:
Click once
to locate the
lower-left
corner of
the image
you're using
as a texture,
and then
again to
locate the
upper-right
corner.

Click here to place the bottom left
corner of your image...

...then click here to finish
placing your image

6. Click somewhere else on the face you're painting; see Figure 8-2.

Time for a little bit of theory: Image textures in SketchUp are made up of *tiles*. To make a large area of texture, such as a brick wall, SketchUp uses a bunch of tiles right next to each other. In the case of a brick wall, it may look like there are thousands of bricks, but it's really just the same tile of about 50 bricks repeated over and over again.

Because SketchUp treats imported image textures just like any other texture, what you're really doing when you click to locate the upper-right corner of your image is this: You're telling SketchUp how big to make the tile for your new photo texture. Don't worry too much about getting it right the first time, though — you can always tweak things later.

Unless the proportions of your image perfectly match the face onto which it was mapped, you should see your image repeating. Don't worry — that's normal. SketchUp automatically *tiles* your image to fill the whole face. If you want to edit your new texture so that it doesn't look tiled (and you probably do), skip to the later section, "Editing your textures." You can scale, rotate, skew, or even stretch your texture to make it look however you want.

Get Photo Texture: Use online imagery

A few years ago, Google undertook a Street View project to enhance Google Maps. The company built special photography units, strapped them onto the roofs of vehicles, and drove them down every public highway, street, and lane it could, snapping away. The result is an immersive and spookily cool way to experience the outside world from the lazy comfort of your computer screen.

Google recently wired together Street View and SketchUp, making it possible to grab imagery from the former and use it in the latter. If your goal is to build photo-textured models of real-world buildings, you're in luck.

Building Maker, which Google debuted around the middle of 2009, is an incredibly useful tool for creating photo-textured models based on aerial imagery which it provides. See the nearby sidebar "Introducing Building Maker" to find out more.

To use this feature, you must meet two important prerequisites:

- ✔ **Your model must be *geo-located.*** You have to have already told SketchUp precisely where it is by adding a geo-location snapshot to your file. Consult Chapter 11 if the preceding sentence makes no sense to you.

- ✔ **Street View data must exist for the thing you're trying to texture.** Google's photographed an awful lot of places, but it's always possible that wherever you're working isn't one of them.

Follow these steps to paint a flat face in your model with Google Street View imagery (Figure 8-3):

1. **Select the face you want to paint with Street View imagery.**

   Selecting a rectangle-shaped face helps. You see why in a couple steps.

2. **Choose Edit⇨Face⇨Get Photo Texture.**

   The Photo Textures window pops up. If Street View data isn't available for the location where you're modeling, this is when you find out.

3. **Frame the imagery you want to use in the window:**

   a. Click and drag to swivel the "camera."

   b. Click the arrows superimposed on the photo to move up and down the street.

   c. Zoom in and out using the + and – buttons.

   If you need to, try resizing the whole window to get a better view.

4. **Click the Select Region button in the upper-right corner of the window.**

   A rectangle with blue pins at the corners appears.

5. **Drag the blue pins to define an area to paint on the face you selected in Step 1.**

   This is the fun part.

6. **Click the Grab button to paint the face you selected in Step 1 with the imagery you defined in Step 5.**

7. **Close the Photo Textures window.**

The photo textures you apply using Get Photo Texture are just like any other photo textures in your model; you can edit them exactly the same way, as I explain in the next section.

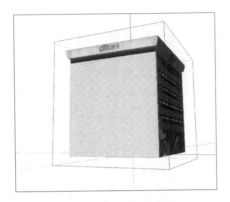

Figure 8-3:
You can use
Google's
Street View
imagery
to photo-
texture your
model.

Introducing Building Maker

Sometime between the release of SketchUp 7 and SketchUp 8, Google launched a brand-new application — Building Maker; it's free, runs inside a Web browser (such as Firefox, Chrome, Safari, or Internet Explorer), and is hyper-specialized. Building Maker's sole *raison d'être* is to make it easier for people to create photo-textured building models that will be displayed in Google Earth (and the new Earth view in Google Maps).

In areas where Google's gathered the right kind of aerial imagery, all you have to do is pick a building and start modeling. Type **Building Maker** into your favorite search engine to give it a whirl. I don't describe how to use it in this book for two main reasons:

✔ **It's not SketchUp.** Building Maker works absolutely nothing like SketchUp. To build a model, line up *primitives* (basic shapes like boxes and pitched roofs) with bird's-eye images of the building you're working on. Outline the shape, and Building Maker takes care of the rest: It automatically geo-locates, photo-textures, and adds your

building to the Google 3D Warehouse. Too cool.

✔ **It's a Web app.** And Web apps change weekly. Anything I write now will be obsolete by the time you read it. So-called *cloud computing* is great for users but a little bit lousy for books.

SketchUp 8 is tightly integrated with Building Maker. There's even a brand-new Add New Building button on the Getting Started toolbar. Clicking that button opens Building Maker in a dedicated browser window and lets you use it right away. If you've already added a *geo-location* (see Chapter 11), you can plunk anything you make right into your model — perfect for adding context to your design.

If *geo-modeling* (modeling for Google Earth) is your objective, the ability to start buildings in Building Maker and touch them up in SketchUp is really nice. The first app provides free, easy imagery; the second gives you the freedom to model anything you like.

Editing your textures

After you successfully map an image to a face, you probably want to change the image somehow: Make it bigger, flip it over, rotate it — you get the idea. This is where the Position Texture tool comes in.

The Position Texture tool is actually more of a mode; I call it Texture Edit mode. Within this mode, you can be in either of two *submodes*. Their names are less important than what they do, so that's how I describe them:

✔ **Move/Scale/Rotate/Shear/Distort Texture mode:** Use this mode to move, scale, rotate, shear, or distort your texture (surprised?); it's technical name is *Fixed Pin mode* — you see why in a little bit.

✔ **Stretch Texture mode:** Stretch Texture mode lets you edit your texture by *stretching* it to fit the face it's painted on. If you want to map a photograph of a building façade to your model, this is the mode you want to use. In SketchUp's Help documentation, Stretch Texture mode is called *Free Pin mode,* just in case you're interested.

You can edit textures only on flat faces; the Position Texture tool doesn't work on curved faces. To find out more about working with textures and curved faces, see the section, "Adding photo textures to curved surfaces," later in this chapter.

Moving, scaling, rotating, shearing, and distorting your texture

The title of this section pretty much says it all — doing the aforementioned things to your texture involves Texture Edit mode, which is a little bit hidden, unfortunately.

Follow these steps to move, scale, rotate, or skew your texture:

1. **With the Select tool, click the face with the texture you want to edit.**

2. **Choose Edit➪Face➪Texture➪Position.**

   This enables (deep breath) the Move/Scale/Rotate/Shear/Distort Texture mode. You see a transparent version of your image, along with four pins, each a different color. Have a look at Color Plate 9 to see what I mean. If all your pins are yellow, you're in Stretch Texture mode. Right-click your textured face and select Fixed Pins to switch into the correct mode.

   A quicker way to get to Texture Edit mode is to right-click the textured face and then choose Texture➪Position from the context menu.

3. **Edit your texture.**

   At this point, the things you can do to edit your texture are located in two places.

   Right-clicking your texture opens a context menu with the following options:

   • *Done:* Tells SketchUp you're finished editing your texture.

   • *Reset:* Undoes all the changes you've made to your texture and makes things look like they did before you started messing around.

   • *Flip:* Flips your texture left to right or up and down, depending on which suboption you choose.

   • *Rotate:* Rotates your texture 90, 180, or 270 degrees, depending on which suboption you choose.

- *Fixed Pins:* When this option is selected, you're in Move/Scale/ Rotate/Shear/Distort Texture mode (Fixed Pin mode). Deselecting it switches you over to Stretch Texture mode, which I talk about in the section "Stretching a photo over a face," later in this chapter.

- *Undo/Redo:* Goes back or forward a step in your working process.

Dragging each of the colored pins has a different effect (see Figure 8-4):

- *Scale/Shear (Blue) pin:* Scales and shears your texture while you drag it. *Shearing* keeps the top and bottom edges parallel while making the image "lean" to the left or right.

- *Distort (Yellow) pin:* Distorts your texture while you drag it; in this case, the distortion looks like kind of a perspective effect.

- *Scale/Rotate (Green) pin:* Scales and rotates your texture while you drag it.

- *Move (Red) pin:* Moves your texture around while you drag it. Of all four colored pins, I think this one's the most useful. I use it all the time to precisely reposition brick, shingle, and other building material textures in my model.

Blue (Scale/Shear) pin

Yellow (Distort) pin

Figure 8-4: Dragging each of the colored pins does something different.

Green (Scale/Rotate) pin

Red (Move) pin

Instead of just dragging around the colored pins, try single-clicking one of them to pick it up; this lets you place it wherever you want (just click again to drop it). This comes in handy especially when you're using the Move and Rotate pins.

4. **Click anywhere outside your texture in your modeling window to exit Texture Edit mode.**

   You can also right-click and choose Done from the context menu, or press Enter.

Stretching a photo over a face

The basic metaphor here is one of a photograph printed on a piece of really stretchy fabric. Stretch the fabric until the photo looks the way you want and then hold it in place with pins.

Follow these steps to stretch your texture using the Position Texture tool's Stretch Texture mode:

1. **With the Select tool, click the face with the texture you want to edit.**

2. **Choose Edit⇨Face⇨Texture⇨Position.**

   A quicker way to get to Texture Edit mode is to right-click the textured face and choose Texture⇨Position from the context menu.

3. **Right-click your texture and *deselect* the Fixed Pins option (make sure that no check mark is next to it).**

   Deselecting Fixed Pins switches you to Stretch Texture mode (or Free Pin mode, if you're reading SketchUp's online Help). Instead of four differently colored pins with little symbols next to them, you see four, identical yellow pins — Figure 8-5 shows you what to expect.

4. **Click a pin to pick it up.**

   Your cursor clenches into a fist, and the pin follows it as you move your mouse.

   Press the Esc key to drop the pin you're carrying without moving it; pressing Esct cancels any operation in SketchUp.

5. **Place the pin at the corner of the building in your photograph by clicking once.**

   If the pin you're "carrying" is the upper-left one, drop it on the upper-left corner of the building in your photograph, as shown in Figure 8-6.

6. **Click and drag the pin you just moved to the corresponding corner of the face you're working on.**

   If the pin you just moved is the upper-left one, drag it over to the upper-left corner of the face whose texture you're editing. Check out Figure 8-7 to see this in action.

Figure 8-5:
You know you're in Stretch Texture mode when all the pins are yellow.

Place the pin here

Figure 8-6:
Place the pin at the corresponding corner (upper left to upper left, for instance) of the building in your photo.

Move pin here

Figure 8-7:
Drag the pin you just placed to the corresponding corner of the face you're working on.

7. **Repeat Steps 4–6 for each of the three remaining pins (see Figure 8-8).**

   If you need to, feel free to orbit, zoom, and pan around your model to get the best view of what you're doing; just use the scroll wheel on your mouse to navigate without switching tools.

   A good way to work is to pick up and drop each yellow pin in the general vicinity of the precise spot you want to place it. Then zoom in and use your better point of view to do a more accurate job.

8. **Press Enter to exit Texture Edit mode.**

If you don't like what you see, go back and edit the texture again; there's no limit to the number of times you can muck around.

Scaling your model until the photo looks right

When you're happy with the way your texture is stretched to fit the face, one of two things will be true:

- ✔ **The proportions are correct.** By this, I mean that the photo doesn't look stretched or squashed. This is the case only if the face to which you applied the photo texture was already exactly the right size.

- ✔ **The proportions aren't correct.** If the photo texture you just "tweaked" looks stretched or squashed, the face it's on is the wrong size. No worries — you just need to stretch the whole face until the texture looks right. Better yet, if you know how big the face is *supposed* to be (in real life), you can stretch it until it's correct.

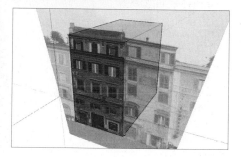

Figure 8-8:
Repeat
Steps 4–6
for each of
the other
three yellow
pins.

Follow these steps to stretch a face until the texture looks right:

1. **Use the Tape Measure tool to create guides that you can use to accurately stretch your face.**

   In this case, I know the building I'm modeling is supposed to be 50 feet wide. I talk about using the Tape Measure tool and guides in Chapter 2, just in case you need a refresher.

2. **Select the face you want to stretch.**

   If your model is at a fairly early stage, just select the whole kit and caboodle. Triple-click the face with the Select tool to select it and everything attached to it. Figure 8-9 shows my whole model selected because I'm just starting out.

3. **Choose Tools⇨Scale to activate the Scale tool.**

   When the Scale tool's active, everything that's selected in your model should be surrounded by SketchUp's scaling box — its 27 little green cubes (or *grips*) and thick, yellow lines are hard to miss.

4. **Scale your selection to the right size (see Figure 8-10).**

   Use the Scale tool by clicking the grips and moving your cursor to stretch whatever's selected (including your texture). Click again to stop scaling.

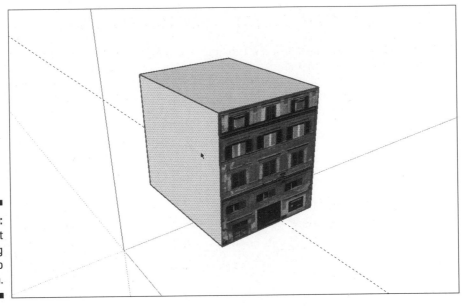

Figure 8-9:
Select
everything
you want to
stretch.

To scale something precisely using a guide, click a scale grip to grab it and then hover over the relevant guide to tell SketchUp that's where you want to scale *to*. Click again to finish the scale operation.

Click here to start stretching   Click here to stretch as far as this guide

Figure 8-10:
Use the
Scale tool's
grips to
stretch your
selection
(texture and
all).

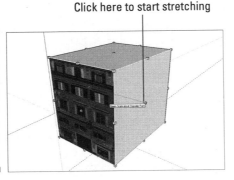

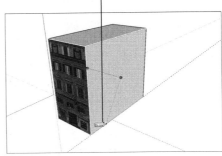

It's perfectly normal to want to keep modeling with your photo-textured faces; tracing a window and pushing it in a bit with the Push/Pull tool is one of the most satisfying things you can do in SketchUp. Flip to the end of this chapter and take a look at "Modeling on Top of Photo Textures" to discover everything you need to know.

Optimizing your photo textures

If your goal is to build models that will eventually show up in Google Earth, one of your primary concerns has to be file size. Big models give Google Earth conniptions. In fact, anything over 10 megabytes can't even be uploaded to the 3D Warehouse, which is the first step in getting your models accepted into Earth's default 3D Buildings layer.

Optimizing your photo textures goes a long toward reducing your file size. Back in SketchUp 7, the folks at Google added two super-useful new features that make it a whole lot easier to build efficient photo-textured models.

Make Unique Texture

Right-clicking any face in your model and choosing Make Unique Texture do two things: These actions create a copy of the texture you've selected and *crop* (trim away everything that isn't visible) that copy according to the face it's on. Why is this important? Just because you can't see part of an image doesn't mean it's not there; SketchUp saves the whole photo with the model, even if you use only a little bit of it. In a complex model with dozens of photo textures, all that invisible, extra photo data adds up. Making your textures unique can make your models much, much smaller.

Combine Textures

Take two or more textures in your model and combine them into a single texture. Why? The fewer unique textures in your model, the smaller its file size. Follow these steps to use this feature:

1. **Select two or more *coplanar* (on the same plane) faces with different textures applied to them.**

   Obviously, the faces you select must all be adjacent to each other.

2. **Right-click any of the faces you selected in Step 1 and choose Combine Textures.**

   This creates a new texture in the In Model library of your Materials dialog box. Letting SketchUp delete the *interior edges* (the ones between the faces whose textures you combined) further reduces your file size because it eliminates faces.

Edit Texture Image

This feature isn't about reducing file size; it's for editing the pixels in your photo textures themselves. Perhaps there's something *in* a photograph you're using, and you don't want it to be there. You can use Edit Texture

Image to open the texture you've selected in an image-editing program, where you can edit the texture directly.

Follow these steps to use Edit Texture Image:

1. **Right-click the texture in your model you want to edit and choose Texture➪Edit Texture Image.**

2. **In the program that opens, make whatever changes you need to make.**

3. **Save (don't Save As and change the filename) the image you're editing and close it if you like.**

4. **Back in SketchUp, check to make sure your edits have been applied.**

Which image-editing program actually opens depends on what you have installed on your computer; you specify which one to use in the Applications panel of the Preferences dialog box. For what it's worth, most designers use Adobe Photoshop, but you can use whatever you have.

Take a look at Figure 8-11. In it, I use Edit Texture Image to remove a pesky element from a photograph I'm using as a photo texture.

Adding photo textures to curved surfaces

Notice how the title of this section ends with "surfaces" and not with "faces?" That's because (as you know by now) individual faces in SketchUp are always flat — no exceptions. When you see a non-flat surface, it's actually made up of multiple faces. You can't see the edges between them because they've been *smoothed*. Choosing View➪Hidden Geometry exposes all curved surfaces for what they really are. Check out Figures 2-3 and 2-5 (in Chapter 2) for a visual reminder.

How you go about mapping an image to a curved surface in SketchUp depends on what type you have. With that in mind, curved surfaces fall into two general categories (see Figure 8-12):

✔ **Single-direction curves:** A cylinder is a classic example of a surface that curves only in one direction. In SketchUp, a cylinder is basically a series of rectangles set side-by-side. Most curved walls you see on buildings are the same way; they don't taper in or out as they rise.

Another way to think about single-direction curves is to consider how they might have been made. If the curved surface you're staring at could be the result of a single push/pull operation (such as turning a circle into a cylinder), there's an excellent chance it's single-direction.

For mapping an image to a single-curve surface, you can use the Adjacent Faces method; it works well and doesn't stretch your image.

✔ **Multi-direction curves:** Terrain objects, saddles, and curtains are all prime examples of surfaces that curve in more than one direction at a time. They're always composed of triangles — never basic rectangles.

To map an image to this type of curved surface, you must use the Projected Texture method. Skip ahead a couple pages to read all about it.

Please keep in mind that I totally made up names for the Adjacent Faces and Projected Texture methods of mapping images to non-flat surfaces. I had to call them *something*, and these sounded descriptive without seeming too technical.

I want to remove this traffic light

Removing the light in Photoshop

Gone!

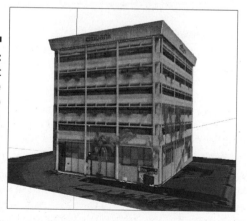

Figure 8-11: Use Edit Texture Image to open an image in a photo-editing app like Photoshop.

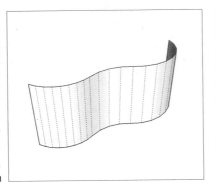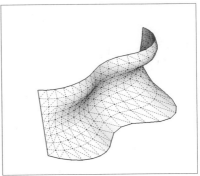

Figure 8-12:
All curved surfaces are either single-direction (left) or multi-direction.

The Adjacent Faces method

If you need to paint an image onto a surface that curves only in a single direction (such as a cylinder), you can use this technique. Follow these steps to see how and see Figure 8-13 to see the process in action:

1. **Choose View⇨Hidden Geometry to turn on Hidden Geometry so you can see the individual faces in your model.**

2. **"Load" your cursor with an imported image.**

   Follow Steps 1–4 in "Importing Images: Use your own photos" (earlier in this chapter) to import an image as a texture.

3. **Paint the leftmost sub-face entirely with the image.**

   Your curved surface is composed of sub-faces. Here's how to paint the right one:

   a. *Hover your loaded cursor over the lower-left corner of the sub-face farthest to the left. Don't click yet.*

   b. *When the image is oriented in the right direction, click once.*

   c. *Click again on the upper-right corner of the same sub-face.*

      This places the image; it should be cropped on the right.

4. **Use the Paint Bucket tool with the Alt key (Command on a Mac) held down to sample the texture (image) you just placed.**

   This "loads" your Paint Bucket tool with the texture.

5. **With the Paint Bucket tool, click once on the face immediately to the right of the face you painted in Step 3.**

   If everything's working correctly, the image you placed appears on the face you just clicked.

6. **Keep painting sub-faces until you're done.**

   Remember to work your way from left to right; skipping a sub-face messes up things. To fix a problem, just Undo and keep going.

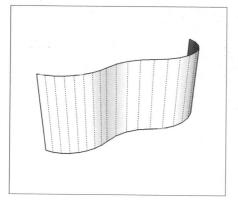
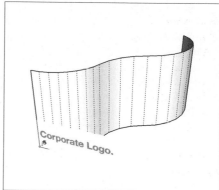

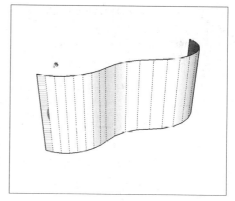
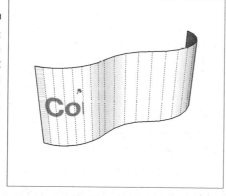

Figure 8-13: The Adjacent Faces method lets you map images to simple curved surfaces.

The Projected Texture method

For painting an image onto a complex curved surface, there's literally no substitute for this method. Chunks of terrain are good examples of complex curved surfaces — bumpy, twisted, rippled, and multi-directional. If the curve you're dealing with is more complicated than a simple extrusion, you need to use this image-mapping technique.

The key is to line up a flat surface with the curved surface to which you want to apply the photo texture. You then "paint" the flat surface with the texture, make it projected, sample it, and finally, paint the curved surface with the projected, sampled texture. Whew.

Follow these steps to get the basic idea (see Figure 8-14):

Hidden Geometry off

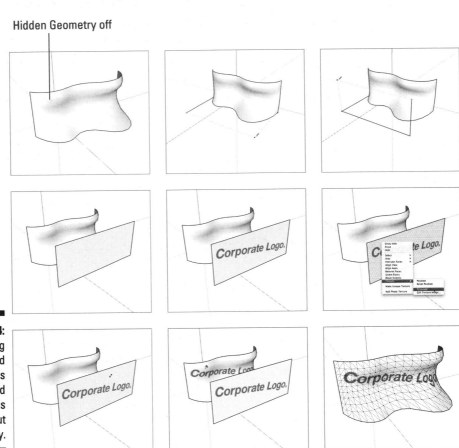

Figure 8-14:
Mapping
projected
textures
to curved
surfaces is
possible, but
it ain't easy.

1. **Create a flat surface that lines up with your curved surface.**

   I use the Line tool and SketchUp's inferencing system to draw a flat face that lines up with (and is the same size as) my curved surface.

2. **Apply a photo texture to your flat surface and make sure that it's positioned correctly.**

   You can refer to the earlier parts of this chapter for detailed instructions on how to do this.

3. **Right-click the textured face and choose Texture⇨Projected.**

   This ensures that the texture is projected, which is the key to this whole operation.

4. **Hold down the Alt key (Command on a Mac) while using the Paint Bucket tool to sample the projected texture.**

   This "loads" your Paint Bucket tool with the projected texture.

5. **Use the Paint Bucket tool *without* pressing anything on your keyboard to paint the curved surface with the projected texture.**

   The photo texture is painted on your curved surface, although the pixels in the image look stretched in some places.

6. **Delete the flat surface that you originally mapped the image to; you don't need it anymore.**

If you're trying to do this on your own curved surface and things don't seem to be working, your curved surface is probably part of a group or component. Either explode or double-click to edit the group or component before you do Step 5 and see whether that helps.

Modeling Directly from a Photo: Introducing Photo-Matching

The first time I saw SketchUp's photo-matching feature in action, I giggled and clapped my hands like a 2-year-old at a petting zoo. I'm not ashamed of it, either. Sometimes technology that's so useful, so *unexpectedly satisfying,* comes along, and you just can't help yourself. Besides — people think I'm a little strange, anyway.

So what does photo-matching do? You can use this feature to do a couple things:

✔ **Build a model based on a photograph:** If you have a good photograph (or multiple photographs) of the thing you want to model, SketchUp's photo-matching feature can help you set up things up so that building your model is much easier.

✔ **Match your model view to a photograph:** Perhaps you have a model of a building and a photograph of the spot where the building will be constructed. You can use photo-matching to position your "camera" in SketchUp to be exactly where the real-life camera was when the photograph was taken. Then, you can create a composite image that shows what your building will look like in context.

Photo-matching works only on photographs of objects with at least one pair of surfaces that are at right angles to each other. Luckily, this includes millions of things you may want to build, but still, if the thing you want to photo-match is entirely round, or wavy, or even triangular, this method won't work.

Looking at all the pretty colors

Like some of SketchUp's other features, photo-matching is more of a *method* than a tool: You use it to set up things, you model a bit, you use the Match Photo dialog box a bit, and so on. If you don't know the basics of modeling in SketchUp yet, you won't have any luck with photo-matching — it's really more of an intermediate-level feature, if such a thing exists.

Color Plate 10 shows what your screen may look like when you're in the throes of photo-matching. I admit it's daunting, but after you use it once or twice, it's not so bad. I include the image in the color section of this book because SketchUp's photo-matching method (at least at the beginning of the process) uses color as a critical part of its user interface.

The following elements of the photo-matching interface show up in your modeling window:

- **Photograph:** Your photograph shows up as a kind of background in your modeling window; it stays there as long as you don't use Orbit to change your view. To bring your photo back, click the Scene tab (at the top of your modeling window) labeled with the photograph's name.

- **Perspective bars:** These come in two pairs: one green and one red. Use them when you're setting up a new matched photo by dragging their ends (grips) to line them up with *perpendicular* pairs of *parallel* edges in your photograph. For a clearer explanation of how this works, see the next section in this chapter.

- **Horizon line:** This is a yellow, horizontal bar that, in most cases, you won't have to use. It represents the horizon line in your model view, and as long as you placed the perspective bars correctly, it takes care of itself.

- **Vanishing point grips:** These live at both ends of the horizon line, and once again, as long as you did a good job of setting up the perspective bars, you shouldn't have to touch them.

- **Axis origin:** This is the spot where the red, green, and blue axes meet. You position it to tell SketchUp where the ground surface is.

- **Scale line/vertical axis:** Clicking and dragging this blue line lets you roughly scale your photograph by using the colored photo-matching grid lines. After you're done, you can always scale your model more accurately using the Tape Measure tool (check out Chapter 2 for more information on how to do this).

You also need to work with a few things that appear outside your modeling window:

- ✔ **Matched photo scene tab:** When you create a new matched photo, you create a new scene, too (you can read all about scenes in Chapter 10). Clicking a matched photo scene tab returns your view to the one you set up when you created (or edited) that matched photo. It also makes the associated photograph reappear — handy if you've orbited into another view.

- ✔ **Match Photo dialog box:** This is photo-matching Mission Control; it's where you can find almost all the controls you need for creating, editing, and working with your matched photo.

- ✔ **Photo visibility settings in the Styles dialog box:** Deep, deep down in the bowels of the Styles dialog box, in the Modeling Settings section of the Edit tab, you can control the visibility of your matched photo. Chapter 9 is where to find out all about Styles.

Getting set up for photo-matching

Modeling with SketchUp's photo-matching feature is generally a step-by-step procedure. Whether you're building a new model or lining up an existing model with a photograph, start by getting your modeling window ready. How you do this depends on which one you're trying to do:

- ✔ **Line up a model you've built already with a photograph:** This case requires you to re-orient your view and then reposition your drawing axes before you're ready to begin photo-matching. To do this, follow these steps:

  1. Orbit around until your model view more or less matches the camera position in your photograph.

  2. Choose Tools⇨Axes and then click to place your axis origin somewhere on your model.

  The *axis origin* is where your colored axes meet. Try to choose a spot that's also visible in your photograph, if there is one.

  3. Click somewhere in the lower-left quadrant of your modeling window.

  This ensures that the red axis runs from the upper-left to the lower-right corner of your screen.

  4. Watch your linear inferences to be sure that your repositioned red axis is parallel to some of the edges in your model.

  Chapter 2 has more about linear inferences.

  5. Click somewhere in the upper-right quadrant of your modeling window to make sure that the blue axis is pointing up.

- ✔ **Use a photograph to build a model:** Open a fresh, new SketchUp file, and you're good to go.

After your modeling window is set up, follow these steps to create a new matched photo in your SketchUp file:

1. **Choose Camera⇨Match New Photo.**

   A dialog box opens.

2. **Select the image on your computer that you want to use and click the Open button.**

   The dialog box closes, and you see the image you chose in your modeling window. You also see a jumble of colorful techno-spaghetti all over the place. Don't worry — it's all part of the photo-matching interface. Figure 8-15 gives you an idea of what I mean; Color Plate 10 shows the same image in color.

   SketchUp's photo-matching feature requires that you use certain kinds of photographs for it to work properly. See the sidebar, "Taking the right kind of picture," later in this chapter, for pointers on what kinds of photos you can — and can't — use.

3. **In the Match Photo dialog box (Window⇨Match Photo), choose the style that matches your photograph.**

   The style buttons in the Match Photo dialog box correspond to three types of photographs you may use:

Perspective Bars

Scale Line/Vertical Axis   Photograph   Match Photo dialog box

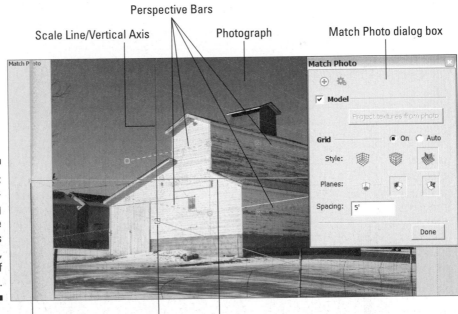

Figure 8-15:
The photo-matching interface includes your picture, plus lots of other things.

Vanishing Point Grip   Axis Origin   Horizon Line

- *Inside* if your photo is an interior view.

- *Above* if it's an aerial shot.

- *Outside* if your photo is an exterior view taken from a human vantage point.

Figure 8-16 shows examples of each of these scenarios.

4. **Begin positioning the perspective bars, starting with the two green ones, by lining them up with any two parallel edges.**

   The tops and bottoms of windows are good candidates, as are rooflines, tabletops, and ceiling tiles. Take a deep breath — this is easier than it looks. Move each perspective bar one at a time, dragging each end into position separately. Color Plate 11 shows what I mean in color.

   The following tips can help you position the bars correctly:

   - Zoom in and out (using the scroll wheel on your mouse) to better view your photograph while you place your perspective bars. The more accurately you place the bars, the better things will turn out.

   - Match your perspective bars to nice, long edges in your photograph; you get better results that way.

   - If you're working with an existing model, hiding it while you place your perspective bars may help; sometimes a model gets in the way. Just deselect the Model check box in the Match Photo dialog box to temporarily hide it.

5. **Line up the two red perspective bars with a different set of parallel edges — just be sure that these parallel edges are *perpendicular* (at right angles) to the first pair.**

Inside   Above   Outside

Figure 8-16: Choose the style that best describes your photograph's camera position.

If the parallel edges aren't perpendicular to the first set of edges, photo-matching doesn't work. Color Plate 12 shows what it looks like when all four perspective bars have been positioned properly.

6. **Drag the *axis origin* (the little square where the axes come together) to a place where your building touches the ground.**

   This is how you tell SketchUp where the ground plane is. Try to make sure your axis origin is right at the intersection of two perpendicular edges. Color Plate 13 shows what this looks like.

   If you're photo-matching an existing model, dragging the axis origin moves your model, too. Line up your model with the photograph so that the spot where you placed the axis origin is right on top of the corresponding spot in your photo. Don't worry about size right now; you deal with that in a moment.

7. **Roughly set the scale of your photograph by clicking and dragging anywhere on the blue scale/vertical axis line to zoom in or out until your photograph looks to be at about the right scale.**

   Do this by first setting your grid spacing in the Match Photo dialog box and then using the grid lines in your modeling window to "eyeball" the size of your photo until it looks about right.

   Color Plate 14 shows an example where my grid spacing is set at 5 feet (the default setting). Because I know the barn in my photo is about 20 feet tall, I zoom in or out until it's about 4 grid lines high because 4 times 5 feet is 20 feet.

   If you're trying to match an existing model to your photo, just zoom in or out until your model looks like it's the right size. You don't have to be very exact at this stage of the game. You can always scale your model later by using the Tape Measure tool (Chapter 2 talks about how to do that).

8. **Click the Done button in the Match Photo dialog box.**

   When you click the Done button, you stop editing your matched photo. All the colorful lines and grips disappear, and you're left with the photo you brought in, your model axes, and your thoughts. It may have seemed like a lot of magic, but what you did was pretty simple: You used photo-matching to create a scene (which I talk about extensively in Chapter 10) with a camera position and lens settings that match the ones used to take the picture that's on your screen. In effect, you're now "standing" exactly where the photographer was standing when the photograph was taken.

Taking the right kind of picture

Your level of success with photo-matching depends to some extent on the photograph you use. Here are tips for choosing a photo for this process:

- **Make sure that the edges of two perpendicular surfaces are visible in the shot.** You need to see planes that are at right angles to each other in order to use photo-matching properly.

- **Shoot at a 45-degree angle if you can.** Because of the way perspective works, your results are more accurate if you use a photograph in which you can see both perpendicular surfaces clearly; if one of them is sharply distorted, you have a harder time. The images in the following figure show what I mean.

- **Watch out for lens distortion.** When you take a picture with a wide-angle lens, some straight lines in the image bow a little bit, depending on where they are in the frame. Try to use photos taken with a normal or telephoto lens: 50mm to 100mm is a good bet.

Bad Match Photo candidate: bad angle

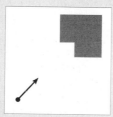

Good Match Photo candidate: you can see both sides clearly

Modeling by photo-matching

Setting up a new matched photo was just the first step. Now it's time to use SketchUp's modeling tools (with a little help from the Match Photo dialog box) to build a model based on the photograph you matched. Here are a couple basic concepts:

- ✔ **The process is iterative, not linear.** Building a model using a matched photo entails going between drawing edges, orbiting around, drawing more edges, going back to your matched photo scene, and drawing yet more edges. Every photo is different, so the ones you work with will present unique challenges that you'll (hopefully) have fun figuring out.

- ✔ **Don't forget the photo textures.** By far one of the coolest features of photo-matching is the ability to automatically photo-texture your model's faces using your photograph as "paint." It's a one-button operation, and it's guaranteed to make you smile.

Follow these steps to start building a model with a matched photo:

1. **Click the matched photo scene tab to make sure that you're lined up properly.**

   If you orbit away from the vantage point you set up, you'll know it; your photograph will disappear. You can easily get back by clicking the scene tab for your matched photo. The tab is labeled with the name of your photo at the top of your modeling window (see Figure 8-17).

2. **Trace one of the edges in your photograph with the Line tool.**

   Make sure that you're drawing in one of the three main directions: red, green, or blue. Color Plate 15 shows this in action.

   It's a good idea to start drawing at the axis origin; it'll help to keep you from getting confused.

3. **Keep tracing with the Line tool until you have a rectangular face, watching the color of your edges as you draw.**

   You always want your lines to turn red, green, or blue when you're starting. Have a look at Color Plate 16 to see what this looks like.

   Be careful not to orbit while you draw — if you do, repeat Step 1 and keep going. You *can* zoom and pan all you want, though.

4. **Use SketchUp's modeling tools to continue to "trace" the photograph in three dimensions.**

Here are pointers for doing this successfully:

- *Always start an edge at the end of an edge you've already drawn.* Doing so helps to assure that your results are what you expect.

- *Never draw an edge in "midair."* Okay — this is the same as the last one, but it bears repeating: When you draw edges based on other edges, you get the best results.

- *Orbit frequently to see what's going on.* You'll be surprised what you have sometimes — tracing a 2D image in 3D is tricky business. Get in the habit of orbiting around to check on things and draw certain edges. Click the matched photo scene tab to return to the proper view.

- *Use other tools (such as Push/Pull and Offset) when appropriate.* Nothing prevents you from using the full complement of SketchUp's modeling tools. I just prefer to stick to Line and Eraser while I draw the basic skeleton of my model with SketchUp's photo-matching tools. I think it's simpler.

- *Pay attention to the colors.* With a color photograph as an overlay, seeing what you're doing can be tricky. Watching to make sure that you're drawing the edge you intend to draw is critical.

- *Draw angles by "connecting the dots."* If you need to trace an edge in your photo that doesn't line up with any of the colored axes (an angled roofline, for example), figure out where the endpoints are by drawing perpendicular edges and connecting them with an angled line. Color Plate 18 shows this in glorious, full-spectrum detail.

- *Show or hide your photograph.* You can fiddle with the visibility of the picture you're using — doing so sometimes helps you see what you're working on. You can find the controls in the Modeling Settings section of the Styles dialog box's Edit tab. Have a look at Chapter 9, for more detail.

If you have more than one photo of your modeling subject, you can have multiple matched photos in the same SketchUp file. Just get as far as you can with the first photo and then start again with the next using the geometry you created as an "existing building." See "Getting set up for photo-matching" earlier in this chapter and follow the steps to line up an existing model with a new photograph.

Color Plate 19 shows a model I started to build of Habitat 67, in Montreal. I used two pictures to create two matches in the same SketchUp file, which let me build more of the model than I could see in a single picture.

You can edit any texture in your model — including ones produced by photo-matching — by opening them in image-editing software (such as Photoshop) directly from SketchUp. This is handy for taking out stuff you might not want in your photos, such as trees, cars, and ex-husbands. Take a look at "Optimizing your photo textures," earlier in this chapter, for all the juicy details.

Scene tab for this matched photo

Figure 8-17:
Clicking the scene tab for your matched photo zings you back to that vantage point (and brings back your photograph).

Modeling on Top of Photo Textures

After you place a photo texture on the right face and in the right place on that face (I'm turning into Dr. Seuss), I wouldn't blame you a bit for wanting to use the information in your photograph to help you add geometry to your model. It's a great way to be more or less accurate without having to measure much, and the combination of photo textures and a few simple push/pull operations can be very convincing.

Making a texture projected

Modeling with photo-textured faces isn't hard, but you *have* to know one critical step before you can do it: You have to make sure that your texture is *projected*.

Figure 8-18 shows what happens when you try to push/pull an opening in a photo-textured face: On the left, when the texture *isn't* projected, the inside faces are painted with random parts of the texture, making your model look like a sticker-laden eye puzzle. On the right, when it *is* projected, note how the "inside" faces that are produced by the push/pull operation are a plain, easy-to-discern gray. I call this painting with *stretched* pixels, and the result is typically more appropriate for what you're doing.

Figure 8-18:
Pushing/
pulling an
opening in
a textured
face when
the texture
isn't pro-
jected (left),
and when it
is projected.

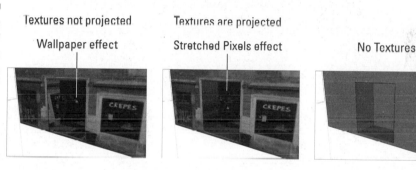

Textures not projected — Wallpaper effect

Textures are projected — Stretched Pixels effect

No Textures

It's a good idea to make sure that your face's texture is projected *before* you start drawing on top of it. Happily, telling SketchUp to make a photo texture projected is just a matter of flipping a switch. Right-click the face with the photo texture and choose Texture⇨Projected from the context menu. If you see a check mark next to Projected, your texture is already projected; don't choose anything.

Modeling with projected textures: A basic workflow

Follow these steps to get the hang of working with projected textures (and see the steps in action in Figure 8-19):

1. **Make a basic rectangular box and then apply a photo texture to one of the side faces.**

   Check out the section, "Adding photos to flat faces," earlier in this chapter.

2. **Right-click the textured face and choose Texture⇨Projected from the context menu.**

   Make sure that Projected has a check mark next to it.

3. **Draw a rectangle on the textured face and push/pull it inward.**

   Notice the "stretched pixels" effect?

4. **(Optional) Add other angles or features to your model.**

   In Figure 8-19, I create an angled face.

5. **Switch to the Paint Bucket tool, hold down the Alt key (Command on a Mac), and click somewhere on the textured face to sample the texture. (Your cursor looks like an eyedropper when you do this.)**

   This "loads" your Paint Bucket with the projected texture.

6. **Release the Alt (Command) key to switch back to the Paint Bucket cursor and then click the angled face once to paint it with the projected texture.**

   You see the "stretched pixels" effect here, too.

Stretched pixels

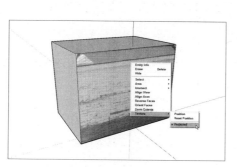
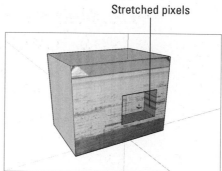

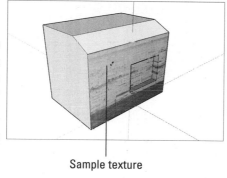
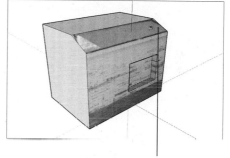

Sample texture

Paint texture on sloped surface

Part III

Viewing Your Model in Different Ways

The 5th Wave   By Rich Tennant

"Oddly enough he spent nine hours organizing the layout of this room in SketchUp."

In this part . . .

Building models is actually only half of what Google SketchUp is all about. After you actually build something, you can do a whole bunch of things with your geometry. Chapter 9 describes Styles, a unique feature that lets you change the way your model looks. Want to make it look hand-drawn? One click. How about something more realistic? Another click. Using Styles is like having a tiny artist strapped to your clicking finger — but in a good way.

Also in Chapter 9, I talk about using Shadows to make your model look more realistic, and (in cases where it's relevant) to study how the sun will affect your design. Just like Styles, applying Shadows to your model is laughably easy; it's just a matter of clicking a box and moving a couple sliders.

Chapter 10 covers three important aspects of exploring your model: walking around, Scenes, and Sections. When seeing (and showing off) your model from inside SketchUp, this is pretty much where it begins and ends.

Chapter 9

Working with Styles and Shadows

It's all fine and well to build elegant and efficient models, but that's only part of what this software's all about. SketchUp is also a very capable tool for presenting the stuff you build. Deciding how your models should look — loose and sketchy, quasi-photorealistic, or anything in between — can be lots of fun, and making the right decisions can help your models communicate what they're supposed to.

The first half of this chapter is about Styles. If you're the sort of person who likes to draw, you're in for a treat. If you can't draw a straight line with a ruler, you're in for an even bigger treat. SketchUp Styles is all about deciding how your geometry   all your faces and edges — will actually *look*. Take a peek at Color Plate 21 for an idea of what styles can do.

I've dedicated the second half of this chapter to SketchUp's Shadows feature. Displaying shadows is an easy operation; it's a matter of clicking a button. Adding shadows to your model views offers lots of ways to make them look more realistic, more accurate, and more readable. And, well, more *delicious*. You'll see what I mean.

Changing Your Model's Appearance with Styles

This section provides a complete rundown of how to use styles in SketchUp 8. First off, I talk about *why* you'd want to use styles in the first place. With so many options, I go into how you can avoid *stylesitis* — an inflammation of your styles related to getting stuck trying to decide how to make your model look.

Choosing how and where to apply styles

Styles are endless. With a million permutations of dozens of settings, you can spend all day fiddling with the way your model looks. But you don't have all day, so keep one question in mind: Does this setting help your model say what you want it to say? Focus on what's important. Styles are cool, no doubt, but making them *useful* is the key to keeping them under control.

To help you make smart decisions about using SketchUp styles, consider at least two factors when you're styling your model:

- ✔ **The subject of your model's "level of completeness:"** I like to reserve sketchy styles for models that are still evolving. The message that a sketchy style sends is "this isn't permanent/I'm open to suggestions/all this can change if it has to." As my design gets closer to its final form, the appearance of my model generally gets less rough and more polished. I use styles to communicate how much input my audience can have and what decisions still need to be made.

- ✔ **How much your audience knows about design:** An architecture-school jury and a nondesigner client who's building a house for the first time perceive styles differently. Design professionals are more experienced at understanding 3D objects from 2D representations, so they don't need as many visual clues to help them along. Styles' essential purpose is to provide these clues, so here's a rule of thumb: The more your audience knows about design, the simpler you should keep your styles.

Before you dive in to styles, remember also that a little style goes a long way. No matter how tempting it is to go hog-wild with the styles settings, please resist the urge. Remember that the purpose of styles is to help your model communicate and *not* to make it look "pretty" or "cool." If the *style* of your work overpowers its content, tone down the styles. Figure 9-1 shows an example of going overboard with styles and then reining them in.

Figure 9-1: Abusing styles is altogether too easy.

Applying styles to your models

The easiest way to get started with styles is to apply the pre-made styles that come with SketchUp. You find scads of them, which is great, because seeing what's been done is the best way to see what's possible. As you go through this section, you'll no doubt get ideas for your own styles, and that's where the fun begins.

Applying a SketchUp style to your model is a four-step process that goes like this:

1. **Choose Window⇨Styles to open the Styles dialog box.**

2. **Click the Select tab and then choose a styles collection from the Styles Collections drop-down list.**

   I introduce you to the collections that come preinstalled with SketchUp 8 in a moment.

3. **Click a style in the Styles window to apply it to your model.**

This may come as a surprise, but it's not possible to view your model without any style at all because styles are really just combinations of display settings. Some styles are fancier than others, but no matter what you do, you always have to have a style applied. If you want a relatively neutral view of your model, I suggest choosing a style in the Default Styles collection.

Wonderfully, SketchUp doesn't leave you out in the cold when it comes to content. Whether styles, components, or materials, SketchUp comes with plenty of examples to get you started. Figure 9-2 is a shot of the Styles Collections drop-down list you see when SketchUp 8 is new out of the box.

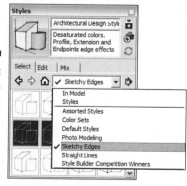

Figure 9-2:
The Styles
Collections
drop-down
list is where
you find all
your styles.

Here's a quick introduction to the most interesting options in the Styles Collections drop-down list:

✔ **In Model:** The In Model collection shows you all the styles you've applied to your model. It keeps track of every style you've *ever* applied to your model, whether or not that style is still applied. To see a current list of styles in your SketchUp file:

1. Choose the In Model styles collection to show a list of styles you've applied to your model.

2. Click the Details flyout menu and choose Purge Unused to get rid of any styles you aren't currently using.

✔ **Default Styles:** Think basic. With the exception of the first one (which is the default style for all new SketchUp files you create), these styles are as minimal as it gets: white background, black edges, white-and-gray front-and-back faces, and no fancy edge effects. I use these styles to get a clean starting point for all my models; I like to start simple and build from there.

✔ **Photo Modeling:** These styles make it easier to work when you're building models that are *photo-textured* — completely covered in photographs. Use them when you model for Google Earth. Chapter 8 covers modeling with photos in detail.

✔ **Sketchy Edges:** The Sketchy Edges styles in SketchUp 8 are the result of more than a year's work on *nonphotorealistic rendering* (see the nearby sidebar, "Running from realism: NPR styles," for the whole story). Basically, the miracle (okay, technological innovation) involves using real hand-drawn lines instead of digital ones to render edges, making your models look more like manual sketches than ever before. Before SketchUp 6, this effect has always looked unbelievably cheesy on the computer, like an anxious robot trying too hard to seem human. Not anymore, though. You can safely use the Sketchy Edges styles to convey any of the following:

• That your design is in process

• That your model is a proposal and not a finished product

• That you welcome feedback in any and all forms

Editing your styles

If you're handy in the kitchen, you've probably heard that cooking is an art and baking is a science. Cooking allows you to experiment — adding a little of this and a dash of that while you're making a sauce won't wreck anything. Taking liberties with a cake recipe, however, can easily turn the cake into a doorstop. I found this out when I made a lovely chocolate doorstop for my wife's birthday not so long ago. . . .

Running from realism: NPR styles

In the world of 3D modeling software, the trend has been toward *photorealism*. Rays of digital light are bounced around a billion times inside your computer until you can see every glint of sunlight in every dewdrop on every blade of grass on the lawn. The standard of perfection is how close the model comes to looking like a photograph, and in a lot of cases, that standard has been met — I've seen computer renderings that look more lifelike than life itself.

But what about models of buildings or other things that aren't completely finished? Perhaps you're an architect who's designing a house for a client. If you aren't sure what kind of tile you'll use on your roof, how are you supposed to make a photorealistic rendering of it? You *could* just go ahead and throw any old tile up there as a placeholder, but that could backfire. Your client could hate the tile and decide not to hire you without ever telling you why, and all because of something you didn't even choose.

What you need is a way to show only the decisions you've made so far, and *that* is exactly why architects and other designers make sketches instead of photorealistic renderings. When you're designing, decisions don't all happen at once, so you need to be able to add detail as your design evolves. Sketching allows you to do that because it offers a *continuum* from "cartoony" to photographic, with everything in between. The following figure is an illustration of this.

Programs like SketchUp offer what's *NPR*, or *nonphotorealistic rendering*, as a way to solve this problem for people who design in 3D. Instead of spending processor power on making representations that look like photographs, the people who make SketchUp went in the opposite direction; they've made a tool that lets you make drawings that are useful throughout the design process. And because SketchUp's NPR engine works in real time, you can make changes on the fly, in front of your audience.

Luckily, making your own styles has a lot more in common with cooking than it does with baking. Go ahead and fiddle around; you can't do any irreversible harm. Playing with styles doesn't affect the geometry in your model in any way, and because styles are just combinations of settings, you can always go back to the way things were before you started.

Of the three tabs in the Styles dialog box, Edit is definitely the blue whale of the group. Because you find so many controls and settings here, SketchUp's designers broke the Edit tab into the following five sections:

- ✔ **Edge:** The Edge section contains all the controls that affect the appearance of edges in your model. This includes their visibility, their color, and other special effects you can apply.

- ✔ **Face:** This section controls the appearance of faces in your model, including their default colors, their visibility, and their transparency.

- ✔ **Background:** The Background section has controls for setting the color and visibility of the background, the sky, and the ground plane in your model.

- ✔ **Watermark:** These are images that you can use as backgrounds or as overlays. The Watermark section gives you control over these.

- ✔ **Modeling:** The Modeling section provides controls for setting the color and visibility of a bunch of elements in your model, including section planes and guides.

The following sections explain each part of the Edit tab in detail; I also provide suggestions for using some of the settings.

Tweaking edge settings

The Edge section is tricky because it changes a little bit depending on what kind of style you currently have applied to your model. NPR styles have different settings than regular, non-NPR styles. Figure 9-3 shows both versions of the Edge section, which you open by choosing Window➪Styles, selecting the Edit tab, and then clicking the box icon on the far left.

Introducing Style Builder

If you're using the Pro version of SketchUp 8, you have access to a relatively new Style Builder tool. It's a completely separate application (just like LayOut) that's put on your computer when you install SketchUp Pro 8.

Style Builder lets you create NPR styles based on edges *you* draw. Yep, that's right — you can make your SketchUp models look like you drew them by hand with *your* medium of choice (finger paint, Sharpie, bloody knife . . .). All you need is a scanner and a piece of software like Photoshop,

and you're good to go. The best thing about the styles you create with Style Builder is that they're completely unique. Unless you share them with someone else, no one can ever make SketchUp models that look like yours.

Because Style Builder is a whole other program and because it's only included in the Pro version of SketchUp, this is all I'll say about it in this book. Take a look at this book's Web site for lots more information, though — if you have it, Style Builder is too cool to ignore.

Figure 9-3:
The Edge section comes in two flavors: regular and NPR.

SketchUp 8 comes with two kinds of styles: regular and NPR. In NPR, SketchUp uses digitized, hand-drawn lines to render the edges in your model. All the styles in the Sketchy Edges collection, as well as all the ones in the Assorted Styles collection, are NPR styles. Because you can create your own styles based on existing ones, all the styles you create using edge settings from one of these NPR styles is an NPR style, too.

Here's the lowdown on some of the less-obvious settings in the Edge section; check out Figure 9-4 for a visual reference:

- ✔ **Back Edges:** Switching this on tells SketchUp to draw all your model's *obscured* (hidden behind a face) edges as dashed lines. This comes in surprisingly handy. For instance, I've discovered the ability to inference to edges and points I couldn't see before. Also, there's nothing like a bunch of dashed lines to make a technical drawing look impressive and complex.

- ✔ **Profiles:** Selecting the Profiles check box tells SketchUp to use a thicker line for edges that outline shapes in your model. Using profile lines is a pretty standard drawing convention that's been around for a long time. I think SketchUp looks better with Profiles on, but it comes at a price; Profiles take more computer horsepower to draw, which can seriously affect your model's performance. If your model's big, think twice before you turn on Profiles.

- ✔ **Depth Cue:** Using different line thicknesses to convey depth is another popular drawing convention. Objects closest to the viewer are drawn with the thickest lines, whereas the most distant things in the scene are drawn with the thinnest ones.

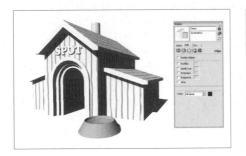

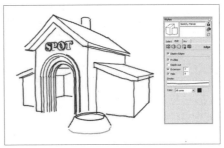

Figure 9-4:
Choose among the edge settings to give your model the desired look, from realistic to sketchy.

Depth Cue automatically applies this effect to your models. When its check box is selected, Depth Cue dynamically assigns line thicknesses (draftspersons call them *line weights*) according to how far away from you things are in your model. The number you type is both your desired number of line weights *and* the thickness of the fattest line SketchUp will use. I like to use a maximum line weight of 5 or 6 pixels.

One more thing: When I'm using Depth Cue, I turn off Profiles. I don't think these two drawing conventions work well together, so I always choose to use one or the other.

- **Halo:** I *really* wish Halo were available for non-NPR styles because it's just that great. Halo simply ends certain lines before they run into other ones, creating a halo of empty space around objects in the foreground. This keeps your model looking neat and easy to read. In fact, this is a drawing trick that pencil-and-paper users have been using forever to convey depth; look closely at most cartoons, and you'll see what I mean.

  The number you type into the Halo box represents the amount of breathing room SketchUp gives your edges. The unit of measure is pixels, but there's no real science to it; just play with the number until things look right to you. For what it's worth, I like to crank it up.

- **Level of Detail:** When you slide the Level of Detail controller (which appears only when you've applied an NPR style) back and forth, you're effectively telling SketchUp how *busy* you want your model to look. The farther to the right you slide it, the more of your edges SketchUp displays. Experiment with this setting to see what looks best for your model. The last two images in Figure 9-4 show what happens when I slide the Level of Detail controller from left to right.

- **Color:** Use the Color drop-down list to tell SketchUp what color to use for all the edges in your model. Here's what each option does:

  - *All Same:* Tells SketchUp to use the same color for all the edges in your model. Select a color by clicking the color well on the right and choosing a color.

  - *By Material:* Turns your model's edges the color of whatever material they're painted with. Because most people don't know that you can paint edges different colors, this doesn't get used very often.

  - *By Axis:* Now *here's* a useful, but hidden, gem. Tells SketchUp to make everything that's parallel to one of the colored axes the color of that axis. Edges that aren't parallel to any axis stay black. Why is this so important? When something is screwy with your model — faces won't extrude, or lines won't sink in — switching your edge colors to By Axis is the first thing you should do. You'll be surprised how many of your edges aren't what they seem. Have a look at Chapter 16 for more about this.

Changing the way faces look

The Face section of the Styles dialog box is very simple — at least compared to the Edge section (what isn't, really?). This area of the SketchUp user interface controls the appearance of faces, or surfaces, in your model. From here, you can affect their color, visibility, and translucency. Figure 9-5 shows the Face section in vivid grayscale, and you can open it by choosing Window➪Styles, selecting the Edit tab, and clicking the box icon that's second from the left. The following sections describe each element in detail.

In a fog?

If you're looking for something to provide a sense of depth in your model views, look no further than the Fog feature. Fog does exactly what it says — it makes your model look like it's enshrouded in fog (see the accompanying figure). You'd think that a feature this neat would be a little complicated, but it's the opposite. Follow these three steps to let the fog roll into your model:

1. **Choose Window⇨Fog to open the Fog dialog box.**

2. **Select the Display Fog check box to turn on the fog effect.**

3. **Fool around with the controls until you like what you see.**

I wish the process of controlling how Fog looks was more scientific, but I'm afraid it's not. You just play around with the sliders until you have the amount of fog you want. But just in case you absolutely need to know, here's what the sliders do:

✔ **Top slider (0%):** This controls the point in space at which fog begins to appear in your model. When it's all the way to the right (toward infinity), you can't see any fog.

✔ **Bottom slider (100%):** This controls the point in space at which the fog is completely opaque. As you move the slider from left to right, you're moving the "completely invisible" point farther away.

Figure 9-5:
The Face section controls the appearance of your model's faces.

Front color/Back color

In SketchUp, every face you create has a back and a front. To choose the default colors for all new faces you create, click the Front and Back color wells and then pick a color. I recommend sticking with neutral tones for your defaults; you can always paint individual faces later.

Sometimes when you model in SketchUp, a face is turned inside out. Follow these steps to flip a face so that the right side shows:

1. **Select the face you want to flip.**

2. **Right-click and choose Reverse Faces.**

Knowing which face is the front and which is the back is especially important if you plan to export your model to another program. Some of these, such as Autodesk 3ds Max, use the distinction between front and back to determine what to display. In these cases, showing the wrong side of a face can produce unexpected results.

Style

Face styles have nothing to do with *Styles,* the SketchUp feature that half of this chapter is about. *Face styles* may as well be called Face modes because that's what they are: different modes for viewing the faces in your model. You can flip among them as much as you like without affecting your geometry. Each Face style has its purpose, and all are shown in Figure 9-6:

- ✔ **Wireframe:** In Wireframe mode, your faces are invisible. Because you can't see them, you can't affect them. Only your edges are visible, which makes this mode handy for doing two things:

- • When you select edges, switch to Wireframe mode to make sure that you've selected what you meant to select. Because no faces block your view, this is the best way to make sure that you select only what you want. The new Back Edges setting is handy for this, too.

- • After you use Intersect Faces, you usually have stray edges lying around. Wireframe is the quickest way to erase them because you can see what you're doing. See Chapter 4 for details on Intersect Faces.

- ✔ **Hidden Line:** Hidden Line mode displays all your faces using whatever color you're using for the background; it's really as simple as that. If you're trying to make a clean, black-and-white line drawing that looks like a technical illustration, make your background white. (I talk about how later in this chapter.)

- ✔ **Shaded:** This Face style displays colors on your faces. Faces painted with a solid color appear that color. Faces to which you've added textures are shown with a color that best approximates their *overall color.* If your texture has a lot of brown in it, SketchUp picks a brown and uses that. For models with a lot of these textures, switching to Shaded mode can really speed up orbiting, zooming, and otherwise navigating around. Unless I absolutely need to see textures I've applied to my faces, I tend to stay in Shaded mode whenever I work on my model.

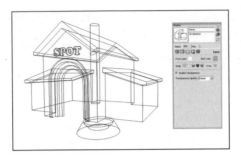

Figure 9-6:
Use Face
styles to
change
the way
your faces
appear.

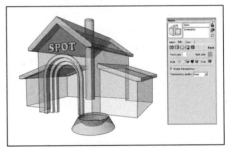

- **Shaded with Textures:** Use Shaded with Textures when you want to see your model with textures visible. Because this mode puts a lot of strain on your computer, it can also be the slowest mode to work in. I turn it on only when I work on a small model, or when I need to see the textures I've applied to my faces. Obviously, if you're going for a photorealistic effect, this is the mode to choose. This mode also best approximates what your model looks like when (and if) you export it to Google Earth.

- **Display Shaded Using All Same:** When you want to quickly give your model a simplified color scheme, use this Face style; it uses your default front and back face colors to paint your model. You can also use this setting to check the orientation of your faces if you're exporting your model to another piece of 3D software.

✔ **X-Ray:** Unlike using translucent materials on only *some* of your faces (such as glass and water), flipping on X-Ray lets you see through *all* your faces. I tend to use it when I want to see through a wall or a floor to show what's behind it. If you're in a plan (overhead) view, it's a great way to demonstrate how a floor level relates to the one below it.

Transparency

Displaying *transparency* (as in translucent materials) is an especially taxing operation for SketchUp and your computer to handle, so you can decide how to display translucent materials:

✔ **Enable transparency:** Deselect this check box to display translucent materials as opaque. Turn off transparency to speed SketchUp's performance if you find that it's slowed down.

✔ **Transparency quality:** If you decide to display transparency, you can further fine-tune your system's performance by telling SketchUp how to render that transparency: You have the choice of better performance, nicer graphics, or an average of the two.

Setting up the background

In the Background section of the Styles dialog box, you choose colors and decide whether you want to see a sky and a ground plane. Check out Figure 9-7 to get a view of the Background section, along with an idea of how it works. To open these options in your own copy of SketchUp, choose Window⇪Styles, select the Edit tab, and click the middle icon, at the top of the tab. You have the following options in the Background section:

✔ **Background:** For most models, I set the background to white — I guess I'm a traditionalist.

✔ **Sky:** Displaying a sky in your modeling window makes things slightly more realistic, but the real purpose of this feature is to provide a point of reference for your model. In 3D views of big things like architecture, it's nice to be able to see the horizon. Another reason for turning on the sky is to set the mood — keep in mind that the sky isn't always blue. I've seen some beautiful SketchUp renderings wherein the sky was sunset (or maybe nuclear winter) orange.

✔ **Ground:** I have to admit that I'm not a big fan of turning on the Ground feature, and here's why: It's *very* hard to find a ground color that looks halfway good, no matter what you're building. I also don't like that you can't dig into the earth to make sunken spaces (such as courtyards) with the Ground turned on. Instead of turning on this feature, I prefer to make my own ground planes with faces and edges. It's more flexible, and I think it looks better.

Figure 9-7:
Use the Background section to turn on the sky and the ground, and to choose colors.

Working with watermarks

Watermarks are much easier to understand if you don't think about them as actual watermarks. They're not anything like watermarks, in fact — they're much more useful. If I had to define them (and because I'm writing this book, I guess I do), I'd put it this way: *Watermarks* are graphics that you can apply either *behind* or *in front of* your model to produce certain effects. Here are a few of the things you can do with SketchUp watermarks:

- ✔ Simulate a paper texture, just like some of the styles in the Assorted Styles collection.

- ✔ Apply a permanent logo or other graphic to your model view.

- ✔ Layer a translucent or cutout image in the foreground to simulate looking through a frosted window or binoculars.

- ✔ Add a photographic background like Outer Space or Inside My Colon to create a unique model setting.

Eyeing the watermark controls

Figure 9-8 shows the Watermark section of the Styles dialog box. Here's a brief introduction to what some of the less-obvious controls do:

- ✔ **Add, Remove, and Edit Watermark buttons:** The +, –, and gears icons allow you to add, remove, and edit (respectively) watermarks in the style you're editing.

- ✔ **Watermark list:** This list shows all your watermarks in relation to *Model Space,* which is the space your model occupies. All watermarks are either in front of or behind your model, making them overlays or underlays, respectively.

- ✔ **Move Up or Down arrows:** Use these buttons to change the stacking order of the watermarks in your model view. Select the watermark you want to move in the list and then click one of these buttons to move it up or down in the order.

Edit Watermark button

Adding a watermark

Watermarks are by no means simple, but working with them, miraculously enough, is. Follow these steps to add a watermark to your model view:

1. **Click the Add Watermark button to begin the process of adding a watermark.**

   The Open dialog box appears.

2. **Find the image you want to use as a watermark and then click the Open button to open the first Create Watermark dialog box (see Figure 9-9).**

   You can use any of these graphics file formats: TIFF, JPEG, PNG, and GIF.

   This is *way* beyond the scope of this book, but I think it's worth mentioning because you're bound to need this sooner or later: If you want to make a watermark out of an image that isn't a solid rectangle (such as a logo), you need to use a graphics file format that supports alpha channels (such as PNG). An *alpha channel* is an extra layer of information in a graphics file that describes which areas of your image are supposed to be transparent. It sounds complicated, but it's really a straightforward concept. To make an image with an alpha channel, you need a piece of software like Photoshop or GIMP. Try searching for *alpha channels* on Google for more information.

3. **Type a name for your watermark in the Name box.**

4. **Choose whether you want your new watermark to be in the background or in the foreground as an overlay and click the Next button.**

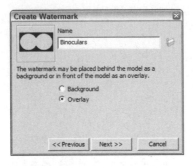

Figure 9-9:
The Create
Watermark
series of
dialog
boxes.

5. **Decide whether to use your watermark as a mask.**

   Selecting this check box tells SketchUp to make your watermark transparent, which kind of simulates a real watermark. *How* transparent each
   part becomes is based on how bright it is. White is the brightest color,
   so anything white in your watermark becomes completely transparent.
   Things that are black turn your background color, and everything in
   between turns a shade of your background color. The possibilities for
   this feature are interesting, but I haven't found any good uses for it yet.

6. **Adjust the amount that your watermark blends with what's behind it
   and then click the Next button.**

   In this case, Blend is really just a synonym for Transparency. By sliding
   the Blend slider back and forth, you can adjust the transparency of your
   watermark.

Blend comes in handy for making paper textures because that process involves using the same watermark twice: once as an overlay and once as an underlay. The overlay version gets blended in so that your model appears to be drawn on top of it. To see how this works, apply one of the Paper Texture styles to your model and then edit each of the watermarks to check out its settings.

7. **Decide how you want your watermark to be displayed and then click the Finish button.**

   You have three choices for how SketchUp can display your watermark: stretched to fit the entire window, tiled across the window, and positioned in the window. If you select Stretched to Fit the Screen, be sure to select the Lock Aspect Ratio check box if your watermark is a logo that you don't want to appear distorted.

Editing a watermark

You can edit any watermark in your SketchUp file at any time. Follow these simple steps to edit a watermark:

1. **Select the watermark you want to edit in the Watermark list.**

   You can find the Watermark list in the Watermark section of the Edit tab of the Styles dialog box.

2. **Click the Edit Watermark button (it looks like a couple of tiny gears) to open the Edit Watermark dialog box.**

3. **Use the controls in the Edit Watermark dialog box and then click OK when you're done.**

   For a complete description of the controls in this dialog box, see "Adding a watermark" earlier in this chapter.

Tweaking modeling settings

All you need to know about the controls in the Modeling section (see Figure 9-10) of the Styles dialog box is that there's not much to know. Use the controls to adjust the color and visibility of all the elements of your model that aren't geometry. To open these options, choose Window⇨Styles, click the Edit tab, and then click the box icon on the far right, at the top of the tab. The controls are described as follows:

- **Controls with color wells:** Click the wells to change the color of that type of element.

- **Section Cut Width:** This refers to the thickness of the lines, in pixels, that make up the section cut when you use a section plane. For more about this, have a look at the information on cutting sections in Chapter 10.

- **Controls with check boxes:** Use these to control the visibility of that type of element in your model. Three of them are a little confusing:

- *Color by Layer:* Tells SketchUp to color your geometry according to the colors you've set up in the Layers dialog box. Check out Chapter 7 for more on this.

- *Section Planes:* This refers to the section plane objects that you use to cut sections. They're gray with four arrows on their corners.

- *Section Cuts:* Unlike section planes, this setting controls the visibility of the section cut effect itself. With this deselected, your section planes don't appear to cut anything.

✔ **Match Photo settings:** When you photo-match (which you can read all about in Chapter 8), adjusting the visibility of your photograph is sometimes helpful. Use these controls to hide, show, and adjust the photo's opacity in both the background and the foreground.

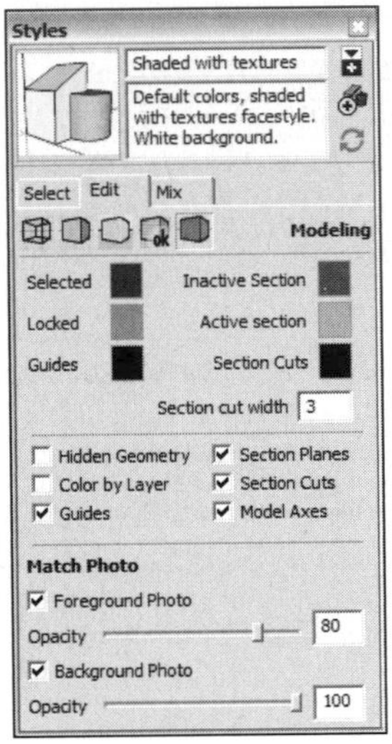

Figure 9-10: The controls in the Modeling section are every bit as simple as they look.

Mixing styles to create new ones

You can use the Mix tab to combine features of multiple styles to make new ones. Instead of working through the sections of the Edit tab, flipping controls on and off, sliding sliders, and picking colors, the Mix tab lets you build new styles by dropping existing ones onto special "category" wells. In addition to being a nifty way to work, this is the only way you can switch a style's edge settings between NPR and non-NPR lines.

NPR refers to the styles in the Assorted Styles, Sketchy Edges, and Competition Winners collections. These nonphotorealistic rendering styles use scanned, hand-drawn lines to draw the edges in your model. If you have SketchUp Pro, you can use Style Builder to make your own NPR styles from lines you draw and scan in. Take a look at the sidebar "Introducing Style Builder," earlier in this chapter, for more information.

Follow these steps to change a style using the Mix tab (see Figure 9-11):

1. **Choose Window⇨Styles and click the Mix tab in the Styles dialog box.**

   As part of the Mix tab, the secondary section opens at the bottom of the dialog box. This provides you with a way to view your styles without having to switch from the Mix to Select sections.

2. **Find the style you want to sample *from* in the Select section.**

   You can call this your *source* style. Say that you're working on a new style and you want your edges to look just like those in the Marker Loose style that came with SketchUp. In this example, choose the Sketchy Edges collection from the Styles Collections drop-down list, where you'll find the Marker Loose style.

3a. **(Windows) Click the source style from the Styles list in the Select section to sample it and then click the category well that corresponds to the style setting you want to apply.**

3b. **(Mac) Drag your source style from the Styles list in the Select section to the category well that corresponds to the style setting you want to apply.**

   In this case, sample the Marker Loose style from the Select section and drop it on the Edge Settings Category well because you want the edge settings from that style to be applied to the style you're working on.

4. **To save your style after you're done adding all the bits and pieces, see the following section.**

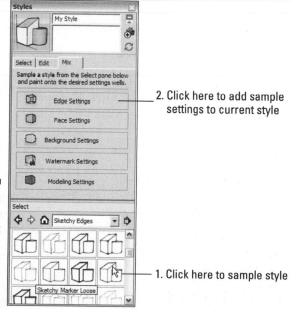

Figure 9-11: Sample from different styles to update the style you're working on.

2. Click here to add sample settings to current style

1. Click here to sample style

Creating a new style

Creating a new style adds it to your In Model collection of styles, so you can come back and apply it to your model anytime you like. Follow these steps to create a new style:

1. **Click the Create New Style button in the Styles dialog box.**

    This duplicates the style that was applied to your model before you clicked the Create New Style button. Your new style appears in your In Model collection as *[name of the original style]*1.

2. **Use the controls in the Edit tab to set up your style the way you want.**

    Frequently, you want to make a new style *after* you already make changes to an existing one. If you want to create a new style that reflects modifications you've made already, just switch Steps 1 and 2.

3. **Use the Name box (at the top of the Styles dialog box) to give your new style a name and press Enter.**

    If you want, you can also give your new style a description in the Description box, though you may want to wait until later.

4. **Click the Update button.**

    This updates your new style with all the changes you made in Steps 2 and 3.

5. **Check the In Model collection in the Select tab to make sure that your new style is there.**

6. **Click the In Model button (which looks like a little house) to see your In Model Styles collection.**

    Your new style appears alphabetically in the list.

If a bunch of styles exist in your In Model collection that you don't use anymore and you want to clean up things, right-click the Details flyout menu and choose Purge Unused. This gets rid of any styles that aren't currently applied to any scenes in your model. Have a look at Chapter 10 to find out more about scenes.

Creating a new style *doesn't* automatically make it available for use in other SketchUp files. To find out how to do this, keep reading.

Saving and sharing styles you make

As you work along in SketchUp, you'll want to create your own styles. You'll also want to save those styles so that you can use them in other models. If you're part of a team, everyone will likely want to access to the same styles so that all your models look consistent.

Saving the styles you make

When creating your own styles, you can approach things in two ways. Each of these ways gets its own button (see Figure 9-12):

✔ **Create New Style:** Clicking this button creates a new style with the settings you currently have active. When you create a new style, it shows in your In Model collection of styles and is saved with your model. The Create New Style button can be found in the upper-right corner of the dialog box and looks like a couple objects with a + sign on it.

✔ **Update Style with Changes:** This button updates the current style with any settings changes you've made in the Edit or Mix tabs. If you want to modify an existing style without creating a new one, this is the way to go. You can find the update button right below the create button in the upper-right corner of the dialog box; it looks like two arrows chasing each other in a circle.

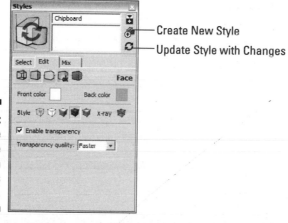

Create New Style

Update Style with Changes

Figure 9-12:
The update and create buttons in the Styles dialog box.

Updating an existing style

To make adjustments to a style in your model, you need to update it. Follow these steps to update a style:

1. **Apply the style you want to update to your model.**

   If you need help with this, follow the steps in the section, "Applying styles to your models," earlier in this chapter.

2. **Use the controls in the Edit tab to make changes to the style.**

3. **Click the Update Style with Changes button in the Styles dialog box to update the style with your changes.**

Use the Update Style with Changes button to rename existing styles, too. Just type the new name into the Name box (at the top of the Styles dialog box), press Enter, and then click the update button.

When you update a style, only the copy of the style that's saved with your model is updated. You aren't altering the copy of the style that shows in every new SketchUp file you create.

Using your styles in other models

After you update or create a style, you probably want to make that style available in other SketchUp models. To make this happen, you need to be able to create your own styles collections. *Collections* are folders on your computer that contain the styles that appear in the Styles dialog box. You can create your own collections to keep the styles you invent neat and tidy.

Follow these steps to create a collection to contain your styles:

1. **Choose Window⇨Styles to open the Styles dialog box.**

2. **Click the Select tab, click the Details flyout menu, and choose Create A New Collection.**

   The Add New Collection dialog box opens.

3. **Navigate to the folder on your computer or network where you want to create your collection.**

   You can locate your new collection anywhere you like, but I recommend putting it in the same folder as the other styles collections on your computer:

   • *Windows:* C:/Program Files/Google/Google SketchUp 8/Styles

   • *Mac:* Hard Drive/Library/Application Support/Google SketchUp 8/ SketchUp/Styles

4. **Click the Make New Folder button (Windows) or the New Folder button (Mac).**

   The new folder you create becomes your new collection.

5. **Type a name for your new collection.**

   Call your new collection Josephine's Collection. You can call it something else if your name isn't Josephine.

6. **(Mac) Make sure that the Add to Favorites check box is selected.**

7. **Click the Save button.**

   The Add New Collection dialog box closes, and your collection is added to the Favorites section of the Collections drop-down list. It will be there in every SketchUp model you open on this computer.

After you create a new collection, you can add styles to it to make them available from any model you work on.

Follow these steps to make a style available for use in other SketchUp files:

1. **Choose Window⇨Styles.**

   The Style dialog box appears.

2. **Click the Select tab and then click the In Model button to display your In Model collection.**

   The In Model button looks like a little house. The In Model collection contains all the styles you've used in your model, including the ones you've created.

3. **Click the Show Secondary Selection Pane button.**

   When you click this button, which looks like a black-and-white rectangle and is in the upper-right corner of the Styles dialog box, a second copy of the Select section pops out of the bottom of the Styles dialog box (see Figure 9-13). Use this section to drag and drop styles between folders on your computer, which makes it easier to keep them organized.

4. **In the Select section, choose the collection to which you want to add your style.**

   If you've created a collection specifically for the styles you make, choose that one, or you can pick any collection in the Collections drop-down list.

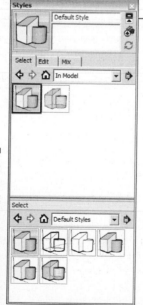

Show/Hide Secondary Selection Pane

Figure 9-13:
Use the Select section to manage your styles without leaving SketchUp.

5. **Drag your style *from* the In Model styles list *to* the Styles list in the Select section.**

   By dragging and dropping your style from the upper list to the lower one, you make the style available to anyone who has access to that collection. This means that you can use the style in other SketchUp models you build on your computer. To share it with other members of your team, copy your style to a collection somewhere where other people can get to it, such as on a network.

Working with Shadows

Typically, you add shadows to a SketchUp drawing for two key reasons:

- ✔ **To display or print a model in a more realistic way:** Turning on shadows adds depth and realism, and gives your model an added level of complexity that makes it look like you worked harder than you really did.

- ✔ **To study the effect of the sun on what you've built (or plan to build) in a specific geographic location:** Shadow studies are an integral part of the design of any built object. If you're making a sunroom, you need to know that the sun is actually going to hit it, no? You can use SketchUp to show exactly how the sun will affect your creation, at every time of day, on every day of the year.

In this section, I start with a brief, nuts-and-bolts description of how all the controls work, without diving too much into why you'd want to pick one setting instead of another. The second part of this section is devoted to running through each of the preceding scenarios and using the controls to make SketchUp do exactly what you want it to.

Discovering SketchUp's Shadow Settings

The basic thing to understand about shadows in SketchUp is that, just like in real life, they're controlled by changing the position of the sun. Because the sun moves exactly the same way every year, you just pick a date and time, and SketchUp automatically displays the correct shadows by figuring out where the sun should be. Hooray for math!

You do all these simple maneuvers in the Shadow Settings dialog box, as shown in Figure 9-14. The sections that follow introduce how the controls work so you can apply to them to your model.

Figure 9-14:
Dial up the
sun in the
Shadow
Settings
dialog box.

Turning on the sun

Shadows aren't turned on by default, so the first thing you need to know about applying shadows is how to turn them on. Follow these simple steps:

1. **Choose Window⇨Shadows to display the Shadow Settings dialog box.**

2. **In the upper-left corner of the dialog box, click the Show/Hide Shadows button.**

   Clicking it turns on the sun in SketchUp, casting shadows throughout your model and, generally speaking, making everything much more exciting.

Setting a shadow's time and date

The Shadow Settings dialog box has time and date controls, which you use to change the position of the SketchUp sun. The time and date you choose, in turn, controls the appearance of shadows in your model:

- ✔ **Setting the time:** You don't have to be Copernicus to figure out how to set the time of day; move the Time slider back and forth, or type a time into the little box on the right. Notice the little times at each end of the slider? These represent sunrise and sunset for the day of the year you've set in the Date control, described in the next point.

- ✔ **Setting the date:** Just like the time of day, you set the day of the year by moving the Date slider back and forth, or by typing in a date in the little box on the right. If you slide the Date control back and forth, notice that the sunrise and sunset times change in the Time control, in the preceding point.

To toggle open or closed the extra shadow controls, click the triangular Expand button in the upper-right corner of the Shadow Settings dialog box.

Choosing where shadows display

The Display check boxes in the Shadow Settings dialog box enable you to control *where* shadows are cast. Depending on your model, you may want to toggle these on or off.

✔ **On Faces:** Deselecting the On Faces check box means that shadows aren't cast on faces in your model. This is on by default, and should probably be left on, unless you want to cast shadows only on the ground. For what it's worth, I always have it selected.

✔ **On Ground:** Deselecting the On Ground check box causes shadows not to be cast on the ground plane. Again, this is on by default, but sometimes you want to turn it off. A prime example of this is when something you build extends underground.

✔ **From Edges:** Selecting the From Edges check box tells SketchUp to allow edges to cast shadows. This applies to single edges that aren't associated with faces — things like ropes, poles, and sticks are often modeled with edges like these.

Using shadows to add depth and realism

The neat thing about shadows in SketchUp is how easily you can apply them — and how easy they are to adjust. In the previous sections, I give a dry rundown of the basic controls in the Shadow Settings dialog box. In the following sections, I show you how to use those controls to add depth, realism, and delicious nuance to your models. If only Caravaggio had had it so good. . . .

You often need shadows to make your drawings read better, especially in the following instances:

✔ **Indoor scenes:** The sun is the only source of lighting that SketchUp has, so any shadows you use in interior views have to come from it.

✔ **Objects that aren't in any particular location:** For things like cars and furniture, it doesn't matter that the shadows are *geographically accurate;* all that matters it that they help make your model look good.

✔ **2D views:** Without shadows, reading depth in 2D views of 3D space is next to impossible.

Lighting indoor spaces

Adding shadows to interior views presents an interesting problem: Because SketchUp has no lights besides the sun, how are you supposed to make anything that looks halfway realistic? With a ceiling in your room, everything's dark. If you leave off the ceiling, your model looks ridiculous. Don't despair — here are some tricks I've learned:

✔ **Decrease the darkness of the shadows.** Sliding the Dark slider to the right brightens your view considerably. You can still see the shadows cast by the sun coming through windows and other openings, but the whole room won't look like something bad is about to happen. Check out Figure 9-15 to see what I mean.

✔ **Make an impossible ceiling.** As long as you haven't modeled anything on top of the interior you're planning to show, you can tell the ceiling not to cast a shadow. That way, sunlight shines directly onto your furniture, casting gloriously complex shadows all over everything.

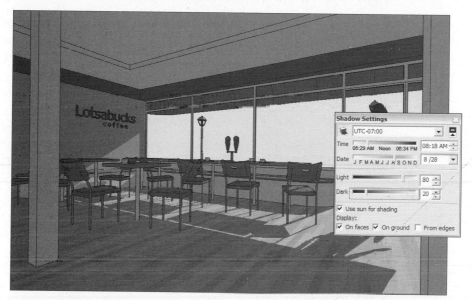

Figure 9-15: Brighten the room by decreasing the Dark slider.

Figure 9-16 shows this ceiling method in action; follow these steps:

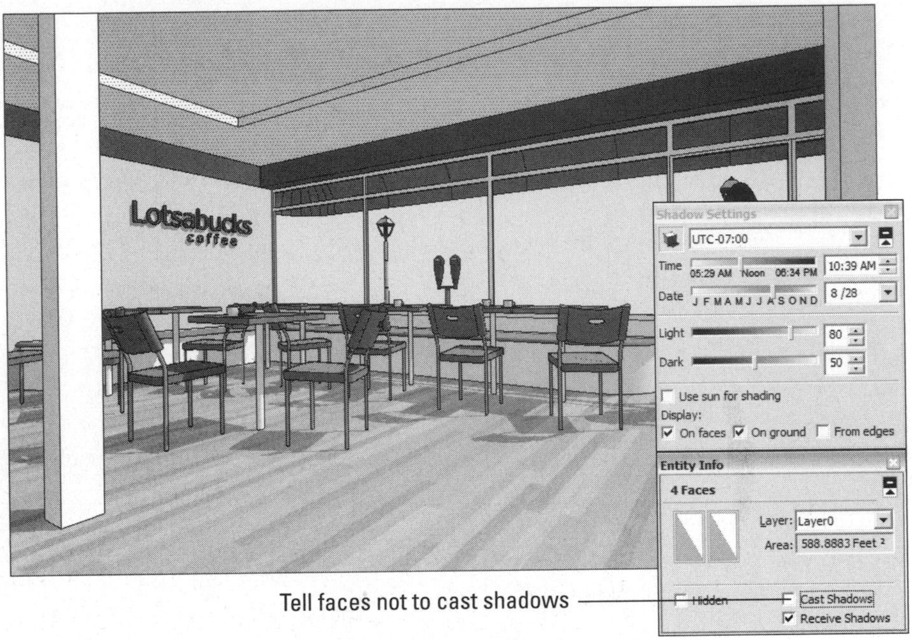

Figure 9-16:
Tell the
ceiling not
to cast a
shadow.

Tell faces not to cast shadows

1. **Adjust the settings in the Shadow Settings dialog box until the sun shines through one or more windows in your view.**

   This ensures that shadows cast by objects in your room look like they're caused by light from the windows.

   To make it seem like overhead lighting is in your space, set the time of day to about noon. The shadows cast by furniture and similar objects will be directly below the objects themselves. One more thing: If you have lighting fixtures on the ceiling, remember to set them not to cast shadows in the Entity Info dialog box (read on).

2. **Choose Window⇨Entity Info.**

   This opens the Entity Info dialog box.

3. **Select any faces that make up the ceiling.**

   Hold down the Shift key to select more than one thing at a time.

4. **In the Entity Info dialog box, deselect the Cast Shadows check box.**

   The ceiling now no longer casts a shadow, brightening your space considerably.

5. **Repeat Steps 3 and 4 for the following faces and objects:**

   - The wall with the windows in it

   - The windows themselves

   - Any walls in your view that cast shadows on the floor of your space

6. **Move the Dark slider to about 50.**

   This brightens things even more and makes your shadows more believable.

Making 3D objects pop

Adding shadows to freestanding things like tables, lamps, and pineapples is a mostly aesthetic undertaking; just fiddle with the controls until things look good to you, and you'll be okay. Keep the following tips (which I illustrate in Figure 9-17) in mind:

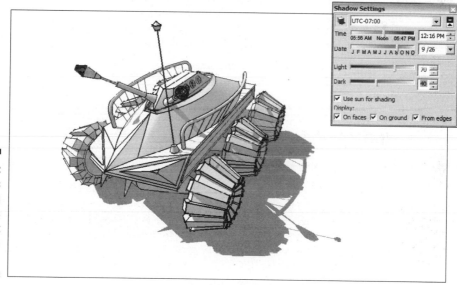

Figure 9-17: Some tips for making objects stand out with shadows.

✔ **Take it easy on the contrast** — especially when it comes to very complex shapes or faces with photos mapped to them. When your model is too contrasty and dramatic, it can be hard to figure out what's going on. To decrease the contrast:

   1. Move the Dark slider over to about 55.

   2. Move the Light slider down to 60 or 70.

✔ **Shorten your shadows.** It's strange to see objects lit as though the light source is very far away; overhead lighting looks more natural. To make your shadows look better, follow these steps:

1. *Set the Date slider to a day in the early autumn.*

2. *Set the Time slider to a time between 10 a.m. and 2 p.m.*

✔ **Don't be afraid to rotate your model.** Remember that you can't get every possible shadow position by using only the controls in the Shadow Settings dialog box; to get the effect you want, you may have to rotate your model by selecting it and using the Rotate tool.

✔ **Select the From Edges check box.** Lots of times, modelers use free edges to add fine detail to models (think of a harp or a loom). Selecting the From Edges check box tells SketchUp to allow those edges to cast shadows, which makes complex objects look about 900-percent cooler.

✔ **Pay attention to the transparency of faces.** When you have a face painted with a transparent material, you can decide whether that face should cast a shadow — chances are that it shouldn't. In SketchUp, the rule is that materials that are more than 50-percent transparent cast shadows. So, if you don't want one of your transparent-looking faces to cast a shadow, do one of the following:

• *Select the face and then deselect the Cast Shadows check box in the Entity Info dialog box.*

• *Adjust the opacity of the face's material to be less than 50 percent in the Materials dialog box.* For more information on how to do this, have a look at Chapter 2.

Creating accurate shadow studies

SketchUp can display accurate shadows, one of its most useful features. To do this, three pieces of information are necessary:

✔ The time of day

✔ The day of the year

✔ The latitude of the building site

The sun's position (and thus the position of shadows) depends on geographic location — that is to say, *latitude*. The shadow cast by a building at 3:00 on March 5 in Minsk is very different from that cast by a similar building, at the same time of day, on the same date in Nairobi.

If you display shadows on a model of a toaster oven, geographic location probably doesn't matter to you; the shadows are just there for effect. But if you try to see how much time your pool deck will spend in the sun during the summer months, you need to tell SketchUp where you are.

Telling SketchUp where you are

Do you know the precise latitude of where you live? I sure don't. It's a good thing SketchUp helps you figure out where in the world your model is supposed to be. You can *geo-reference* your model (give it a geographic location) in two ways; which one you choose probably depends on whether you have an Internet connection handy:

- ✓ **Using a geo-location snapshot:** This is by far the simplest approach, but it requires that you have a precise idea of where your model is supposed to be on the globe. It also requires that you be connected to the Internet for the operation. If you know exactly where your model is supposed to go, and you're online, use this method. Take a look at Chapter 11 for a complete set of instructions.

- ✓ **Using the Model Info dialog box:** This method is a little more complicated, but it's your only option if you're not online. Read on for all the gory details.

To give your model a geographic location when you're offline, follow these steps (see Figure 9-18):

1. **Choose Window➪Model Info to open the Model Info dialog box.**

2. **On the left side of the Model Info dialog box, choose Geo-Location.**

   If you see anything other than `This model is not geo-located`, stop here. Your model has already been geographically located and you don't need to go through any of the following steps. Close the Model Info dialog box, make yourself some coffee, and waste the time you just saved avoiding the next steps.

3. **Click the Set Manual Location button to open another dialog box.**

4. **Enter the required information and click OK.**

   What you type in the Country and Location fields is entirely up to you; it doesn't affect your model's geo-location one bit. The Latitude and Longitude fields are the important parts of this dialog box.

Whether you imported a geo-location snapshot or entered a set of coordinates manually, the next step is to make sure your model is rotated correctly relative to north. If your model faces the wrong way, your shadow studies are completely inaccurate.

All you really need to know is this: By default, the green axis runs north-south, with the solid part pointing north. If north-for-your-building doesn't line up with the green axis, just select everything and use the Rotate tool to spin the building into place.

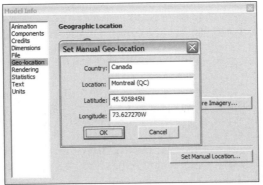

Figure 9-18:
Giving your
model a
geographic
location
when you're
not online.

Here's a method I find works well, which I illustrate in Figure 9-19:

1. **On the ground somewhere, draw an edge that points to where north *should* be.**

2. **Starting at the southern endpoint of the edge you just drew, draw another edge that's parallel to the green axis.**

   You have a V shape.

3. **Select everything in your model *except* the edge you drew in Step 2.**

   Your geo-location snapshot (if you have one) should have a red border around it; that's because it's locked. If for some reason it isn't, right-click it and choose Lock — you don't want to rotate it accidentally.

4. **Activate the Rotate tool.**

5. **Click the *vertex* (pointy end) of the V to establish your center of rotation.**

6. **Click the north end of the edge you drew in Step 1.**

7. **Click the north end of the edge you drew in Step 2.**

   Now everything's lined up properly.

Displaying accurate shadows for a given time and place

Now that you've told SketchUp where your model is, it's a pretty simple process to study how the sun will affect your project, as shown in Figure 9-20. This is the fun part; all you have to do is move some sliders. If you have an audience, get ready for completely undeserved praise.

1. Draw two lines

2. Select all except line parallel to green axis

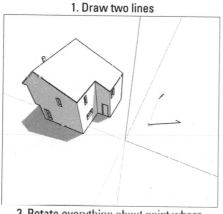

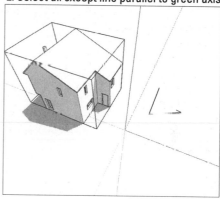

3. Rotate everything about point where lines meet

4. Rotate until lines are parallel

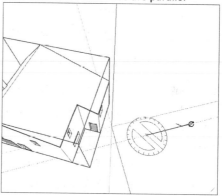

Figure 9-19:
Make sure
your model
is correctly
oriented
relative to
north.

To study how the sun affects your project, follow these steps:

1. **Orbit, zoom, and pan around until you have a good view of the part of your project you want to study.**

2. **Choose Window⇨Shadows to open the Shadow Settings dialog box.**

3. **Select the Show/Hide Shadows button to turn on SketchUp's sun.**

4. **Make sure the time zone setting is correct for your location.**

   SketchUp doesn't always get the time zone right for every location in the world; time zones don't always map directly to coordinates. If the time zone you see in the Time Zone drop-down list (at the top of the Shadow Settings dialog box) isn't correct, choose another one.

   Wondering what your time zone is in UTC? Try searching Google for "UTC time zones" to find a list to which you can refer.

5. **Type a month and day into the box to the right of the Date slider and then press Enter.**

6. **Move the Time slider back and forth to see how the shadows will move over the course of that day.**

7. **Pick a time of day using the Time controls.**

8. **Move the Date slider back and forth to see how the sun will affect your project at that time of day over the course of the year.**

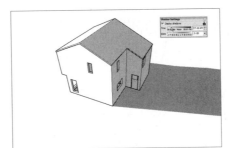

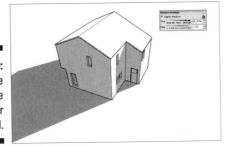

Figure 9-20:
Studying the effect of the sun on your model.

Uses for shadows

Even if you're not an architect, you may want to study shadows accurately for these reasons:

- ✔ To figure out where to locate the plants in your garden that need the most light (or the most shade)

- ✔ To see when sunlight will come straight through the skylight you're thinking of installing

- ✔ To make sure that the overhang behind your house will provide enough shade at lunchtime in the summer

- ✔ To plan and build a 50-foot stone sundial as a birthday gift for your Druidic neighbor

Chapter 10

Presenting Your Model Inside SketchUp

After you make a model, you probably want to show it to someone. How you present your work depends on the idea you want to convey. The tricky part about using SketchUp to present a model isn't actually using the tools; it's choosing the *right* tools to get your idea across without a bunch of extra information distracting your audience. Most 3D models have so much to look at that the real challenge is finding a presentation method that helps you focus on the stuff you want to talk about.

In this chapter, I talk about three ways to show off your models without ever leaving SketchUp. If you've made a building, you can walk around inside it. You can even walk up and down stairs and ramps — just like in a video game. You can create animated slide shows by setting up scenes with different camera views, times of day, and even visual styles. If you want to talk about what's *inside* your model, you can cut sections through it without taking it apart.

As you read this chapter, keep in mind what you want your model to communicate. Think about how you might use each method to make a different kind of point and think about the order in which you want those points to be made. As with everything else in SketchUp (and in life, I suppose), a little bit of planning goes a long way. That said, presenting a model live in SketchUp is undeniably sexy; you can't really go wrong, so have fun.

Exploring Your Creation on Foot

Few experiences in life are as satisfying as running around inside your model. After you've made a space, you can drop down into it and explore by walking around, going up and down stairs, bumping into walls, and even falling off ledges. You can check to make sure that the television is visible from the kitchen, say, or experience what it'd be like to wander down the hall. In a potentially confusing building, such as an airport or a train station, you can figure out where to put the signs by allowing someone who's never seen your model to explore the space "on foot."

These tools were made for walking

A couple tools in SketchUp are dedicated to moving around your model as if you were actually inside it. The first step (no pun intended) is to position yourself so that you seem to stand inside your model. This can be tricky with just the Orbit, Pan, and Zoom tools, so SketchUp provides a tool just for this: Position Camera. After you're standing in the right spot (and at the right height), you use the Walk tool to move around. It's as simple as that.

The Position Camera and Walk tools enable you to walk around inside your model.

Standing in the right spot: The Position Camera tool

The Position Camera tool precisely places your viewpoint in SketchUp in a particular spot. That's really all it does, but it works in two ways. (See this book's Web site, which I explain in detail in the Introduction, for more details.)

✔ **You want to stand right here.** Choose Camera➪Position Camera from the menu bar and then click anywhere in the modeling window to automatically position your viewpoint 5 feet, 6 inches above wherever you clicked. Because this is the average *eye-height* of an adult, the result is that you are, for all intents and purposes, standing on the spot where you clicked; see Figure 10-1. After using Position Camera, SketchUp automatically switches to the Look Around tool, assuming that you may want to have a look around. I talk about Look Around in the "Stopping to look around" section of this chapter.

You're not stuck being five-and-a-half-feet tall forever. After you use Position Camera, type the height you'd rather be and press Enter. Type **18"** to see a golden retriever's view of the world, or type **7'** to pretend you play for the L.A. Lakers. Keep in mind that the Measurements box (the spot in the lower-right corner where numbers appear) displays your eye height as a distance from the ground, and not from whatever surface you're "standing on." To set your eye height to be 5 feet above a platform that's 10 feet high, you'd type **15'**.

✔ **You want your eyes to be right here, and you want to look in this direction.** Select Position Camera, click the mouse button while in the spot where you want your eyes to be, drag over to the thing you want to look at (you see a dashed line connecting the two points), and release the mouse button (see Figure 10-2). Try this technique a couple times; it takes a bit of practice to master. Use Position Camera in this way if you want to stand in a particular spot *and* look in a particular direction. This technique works great with scenes, which I talk about later in this chapter.

Figure 10-1:
Drop your-
self into
your model
with the
Position
Camera tool.

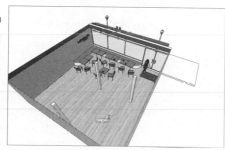

Figure 10-2:
Aim your
view by
using
Position
Camera
in another
way.

Stepping out with the Walk tool

After you use Position Camera to place yourself in your model, use the Walk tool to move through it. (Again, find out more on this book's companion Web site.)

To walk around, click and drag the mouse in the direction you want to move:

✔ Straight up is forward.

✔ Straight down is backward.

✔ Anything to the left or right causes you to turn while you walk.

The farther you move your cursor, the faster you walk. Release the mouse button to stop. If you've ever played video games, you'll get used to it quickly. If Scrabble is more your speed, it'll take a few minutes to get the hang of things.

You can even use the Walk tool to walk up and down stairs and ramps. Keep in mind that the highest step you can climb is 22 inches — anything higher and you get the "bump" cursor, just like you walked into a wall. Also, if you walk off a high surface, you fall to the surface below. It's times like these that I wish SketchUp had cartoon sound effects. . . .

Using modifier keys in combination with the Walk tool makes SketchUp even more like a video game:

✔ Hold down the Ctrl key (Option on a Mac) to run instead of walk. This may be useful if you're trying to simulate what it'd be like if a werewolf were chasing you through your model.

✔ Hold down the Shift key to move straight up like you're growing, straight down like you're shrinking, or sideways like a crab.

✔ Hold down the Alt key (Command on a Mac) to disable collision detection, which allows you to walk through walls instead of bumping into them. Burglars find this handy for entering models without breaking any windows.

Stopping to look around

Look Around is the third tool in SketchUp that's dedicated to exploring your model from the inside. If using Position Camera is like swooping in to stand in a particular spot and Walk is like moving around while maintaining a constant eye-height, Look Around is like turning your head while standing in one spot. It's pretty well named, I think; it does exactly what it says.

Using Look Around is so simple it hardly merits these steps:

1. **Choose Camera⇨Look Around.**

2. **Click and drag around in the modeling window to turn your virtual head.**

   Don't move too fast, or you'll strain your virtual neck, though. Just kidding.

While in any of the navigation tools, right-click to access any other navigation tool; this makes switching between them a little easier.

When you use Look Around with the field of view tool I discuss in the next section, you get a pretty darned realistic simulation of what it'd be like to stand in your model.

Setting your field of view

Field of view is how much of your model you can see in your modeling window at one time. Imagine your eyesight kind of like a cone, with the pointy end pointing at your eyes and the cone getting bigger as it gets farther away from you. Everything that falls inside the cone is visible to you, and everything outside the cone isn't.

If you increase the angle of the cone at the pointy end, the cone gets wider, and you see more of what's in front of you. If you decrease the angle, the cone gets narrower, and you see less; see Figure 10-3.

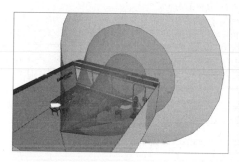 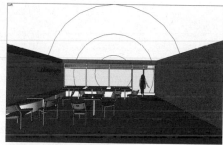

 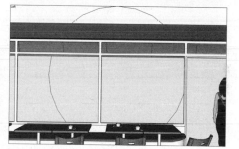

Figure 10-3: The wider your field of view, the more you can see.

Measured in degrees, a *wide field of view* means that you can see more of your model without having to move around. The bigger the angle, the more you can see. A wide field of view comes in handy when you're inside a SketchUp model, because working on a model you can't see is hard.

It's a good idea to fiddle with your field of view while walking around inside your model. Follow these steps to do so:

1. **Choose Camera⇨Field of View.**

   Notice that the Measurements box in the lower-right corner of your modeling window says `Field of View` and that the default value is 35 degrees. This means that you currently have a 35-degree cone of vision, which is kind of narrow.

2. **Type** 60 **and press Enter.**

   Your field of view increases, and you now have a wider view of your model. The trade-off is that you see more distortion at the edges of your modeling window as more information is displayed in the same amount of space.

A good rule of thumb for setting your field of view is to strike a balance between quantity and quality; a wider view always means more distortion. For views of the *outside* of something I've built, I like to use a field of view of 35 to 45 degrees. For interior views, I use 60 or 70 degrees.

If you know something about photography, you can express field of view in millimeters, just like you're using a camera lens. Typing **28mm** gives you a wide-angle view, just like you're looking through a 28mm lens. For people who think about field of view in these terms, this can be a lot more intuitive than trying to imagine cones of vision.

Taking the Scenic Route

Wouldn't it be great if you could save a particular view of your model? And wouldn't it be even greater if that view could also save things like styles and shadow settings? What if you could come back to any of these saved views by clicking a button on your screen? What if this whole paragraph were just a series of questions?

SketchUp *scenes* are (you guessed it) saved views of your model. It's probably easiest to think of scenes as cameras, except that scenes can save much more than just camera positions.

Although they don't get a lot of space in this book (they don't even get their own chapter), scenes are an important feature in SketchUp for three reasons:

✔ **Scenes can save you hours of time.** It's not always easy to get back to exactly the right view by using Orbit, Zoom, and Pan. Sometimes a view involves shadows, styles, sections (you read about those later), and even hidden geometry. Setting up everything the way you need it, every time you need it, can be a pain. It's not that SketchUp's *hard* — it's just that you have a lot of different ways to view your model. Making a scene reduces the process of changing dozens of settings to a single click of your mouse.

✔ **Scenes are *by far* the most effective way to present your model.** Saving a scene for each point that you want to make in a presentation allows you to focus on what you're trying to say. Instead of fumbling around with the navigation tools, turning on shadows, and making the roof visible, you can click a button to transition to the next scene (which you've already set up exactly the way you want it). Figure 10-4 shows a set of scenes I created to present a house I designed for my dog, Savannah.

✔ **Scenes are the key to making animations.** You make animations by creating a series of scenes and telling SketchUp to figure out the transitions between them. The process, which I explain in later sections, is as simple as clicking a button.

 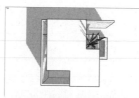 

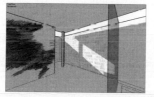 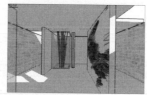

Figure 10-4: To show very specific views, create scenes.

After you get used to scenes, you'll find yourself using them all the time. Here are some of the most common uses for scenes:

✔ Showing shade conditions for the same area at different times of the day

✔ Saving scenes for each floorplan, building section, and other important views of your model

✔ Building a walk-through or flyover animation of your design

✔ Creating scenes that show several views of the same thing with different options (the pointy roof or the flat one, madam?)

✔ Demonstrating change over time by showing or hiding a succession of components

Creating scenes

Time to get one thing straight: Making a scene in SketchUp is *not* like taking a snapshot of your model. If you create a scene to save a view, continue working on your model, and then return to that scene, your model doesn't go back to the way it was when you created the scene. The camera position will be the same, and the settings will be the same, but your geometry won't be. This is a pretty important concept, and one that makes using scenes so powerful.

A *scene* is just a set of view settings, which means that they're automatically updated to reflect your changes every time you edit your model. You can make some scenes and use them all the way through your process, from when you start modeling to when you present your design to the president. Or to your mother.

Creating scenes is a simple process. The basic idea is that you add a scene to your SketchUp file whenever you have a view you want to return to later. You can always delete scenes, so there's no downside to using lots of them. Follow these steps to make a new scene (and check this book's companion Web site for additional help):

1. **Choose Window⇨Scenes to open the Scenes dialog box.**

   When the Scenes dialog box first opens, it doesn't look like there's much to it. Expanding it by clicking the Show Details button in the upper-right corner reveals more options, but don't worry about that right now.

2. **Set up your view however you want.**

   Navigate around until you're happy with your point of view. If you want, use the Shadows and Styles dialog boxes to change the way your model looks.

3. **Click the Add button to make a new scene with your current view settings.**

   A new scene is added to your SketchUp file. If this is the first scene you've created, it's called Scene 1 and appears in two places (see Figure 10-5):

   • As a list item in the Scenes dialog box, right underneath the Add button

   • As a tab at the top of your modeling window, labeled Scene 1

The SketchUp design team added a handy new feature to SketchUp 8: thumbnail images of your scenes in the Scenes dialog box. To see them, just click the View Options button and choose either Small Thumbnails or Large Thumbnails.

Nothing is generated outside of SketchUp when you add a scene; it's not like exporting a JPEG or a TIFF. Scenes are just little bits of programming code that "remember" the view settings in effect when they're created. Scenes also don't add much to your file size, so you don't have to worry about using too many of them.

When scenes and styles collide

Sooner or later, you'll be presented with the Warning — Scenes and Styles dialog box shown here. It pops up whenever you try to create a scene without first saving the changes you've made to the style applied to your model. In other words, SketchUp tries to help by reminding you to keep styles in mind while you work with scenes. (The first part of Chapter 9 is all about styles, just in case you need a refresher.)

This warning dialog box gives you three options; here's some guidance on which one to choose:

✔ **Save as a New Style:** Adds a new style to your In Model styles library. When you come back to this scene, it looks exactly the way it did when you created it. Choosing this option is the safest way to proceed because it can't affect any other scene.

✔ **Update the Selected Style:** Choose this option only if you know what effect this will have on the other scenes in your model —

if the style you're updating is applied to any of them, you'll affect the way they look. In models with lots of scenes and styles, this can have big implications.

✔ **Do Nothing to Save Changes:** Creates a scene with your current style applied, completely ignoring any changes you may have made to that style. When you come back to this scene, it looks different than it did when you created it. Only choose this option if you really know what you're doing, or if you enjoy doing the same thing more than once.

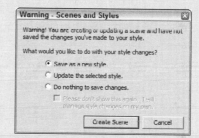

Moving from scene to scene

Activate a scene you've added earlier by doing one of three things:

> ✔ Double-clicking the name (or thumbnail image) of the scene in the Scenes dialog box.
>
> ✔ Clicking the tab for that scene at the top of the modeling window.
>
> ✔ Right-clicking any scene tab and choosing Play Animation to make SketchUp automatically flip through your scenes. (Choose Play Animation again to make the animation stop.)

Notice how the transition from one scene to the next is animated? You don't have to do anything special to make this happen; it's something SketchUp automatically does to make things look better (and ultimately, to make *you* look better).

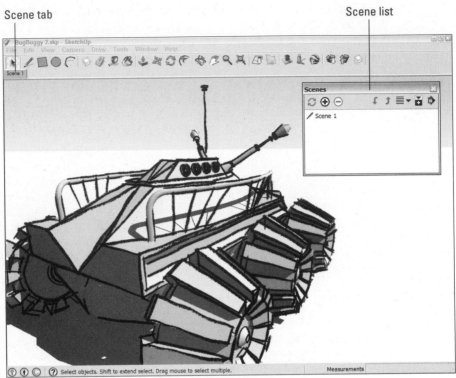

Figure 10-5:
The scene you just added appears in two places.

You can adjust the way SketchUp transitions between scenes, which is handy for customizing your presentations. Follow these steps to access these settings:

1. **Choose Window⇨Model Info.**

2. **On the left side of the Model Info dialog box, choose Animation.**

   The Animation settings panel in the Model Info dialog box (see Figure 10-6) isn't very complicated, but it can make a huge difference in the appearance of your scene-related presentations.

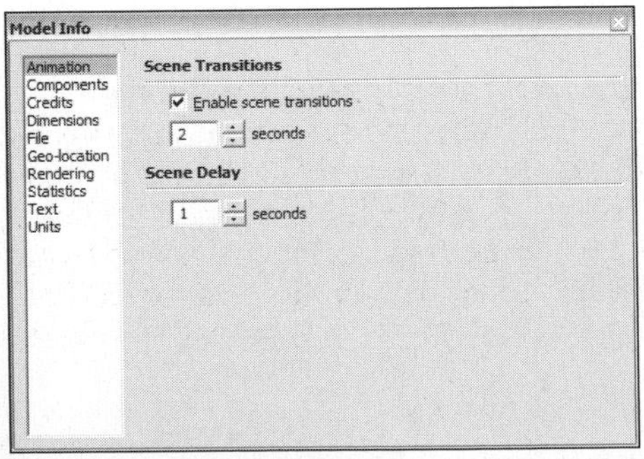

Figure 10-6:
The Animation settings panel is a big help in customizing your presentations.

3. **In the Scene Transitions area, set how SketchUp transitions from one scene to another.**

   These settings apply to both manual (clicking a page tab) and automatic (playing an animation) scene transitions:

   - *Enable Scene Transitions:* Deselect this check box to make SketchUp change scenes without animating the transitions between them. You probably want to do this if your model is so complex (or your computer is so slow) that animated transitions don't look good.

   - *Seconds:* If you've selected the Enable Scene Transitions check box, the number of seconds you enter here indicates the time SketchUp takes to transition from one scene to the next. If you're "moving the camera" very far between scenes, bump up the transition time so that your audience doesn't get sick. I find three seconds to be a good compromise between nausea and boredom.

If you're presenting an incomplete model (perhaps you've thought about the garage and the living room, but nothing in between), it can be helpful to turn off scene transitions. That way, your audience won't see the things you haven't worked on when you click a tab to change scenes. It's sneaky, but effective.

4. **In the Scene Delay area, set the length of time SketchUp pauses on each slide before it moves to the next one.**

   If you want the presentation to seem like you're walking or flying, set this to 0. If you want time to talk about each scene in your presentation, bump this up a few seconds.

Modifying scenes after you make 'em

After you create a whole bunch of scenes, you inevitably need to fiddle with them in some way. After all, modifying something is almost always easier than making it all over again, and the same thing holds true for scenes. Because your SketchUp model will change a million times, understanding how to make changes to your existing scenes can save you a lot of time in the long run.

Certain aspects of the scene-modification process can get a little tricky. This is kind of surprising, given how simple the rest of working with scenes can be. You deal with a lot of complexity when working in SketchUp, and this is just one of the places where that complexity rears its ugly head. The upshot: Pay special attention to the section on updating scenes and don't worry if you take a little while to figure things out. It happens to the best of us.

Making walk-throughs

A really great way to use scenes is to pretend you're walking or flying through your model. By setting up your scenes sequentially, you can give a seamless tour without messing around with the navigation tools. This is especially handy when you need to walk and talk at the same time.

Here are some tips that can help you to simulate a person walking or flying through your model with scenes:

✔ **Adjust your field of view.** For interior animations, make your camera "see" a wider area by setting your field of view to 60 degrees. I like to set my field of view between 30 and 45 degrees for exterior views, but there's no hard-and-fast rule. I talk about how to do this in the section "Setting your field of view," earlier in this chapter.

✔ **Make sure that your scenes aren't too far apart.** Instead of racing through a room like it's on fire, don't be afraid to add more scenes. Your audience will thank you by not throwing up on your conference table

✔ **Add scenes at equal distance intervals.** Because SketchUp only lets you control the scene transition timing for all your scenes at once, it's best to make sure that your scenes are set up about the same distance apart. If you don't, your walk-through animations will be jerky and strange, like my dancing.

✔ **Don't forget the animation settings in the Model Info dialog box.** Set the scene delay to 0 seconds so that your animation doesn't pause at every scene. For a normal walking speed, set your scene transitions so that you move about 5 feet per second. If your scenes are about 20 feet apart, set your scene transition time to 4 seconds. This gives your audience time to look around and notice things. For flying animations, pick a scene transition time that looks good.

✔ **Slide around corners.** When you set up a walking animation, you have an easy, reliable way to turn corners without seeming too robotic. The method is illustrated in the following figure. Basically, the trick is to add a scene just short of where you want to turn — in this case, a few feet ahead of the doorway. The key is to angle your view *into* the turn slightly. Set up your next scene just past the turn, close to the inside and facing the new view. This technique makes it seem like you're turning corners naturally.

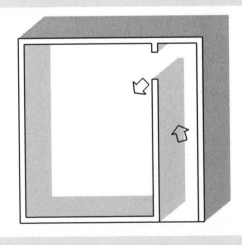

Reordering, renaming, and removing scenes

Making simple modifications to scenes, such as reordering, renaming, and removing them, is easy. You can accomplish each of these in two ways: You either use the Scenes dialog box or you right-click the scene tabs at the top of your modeling window (see Figure 10-7).

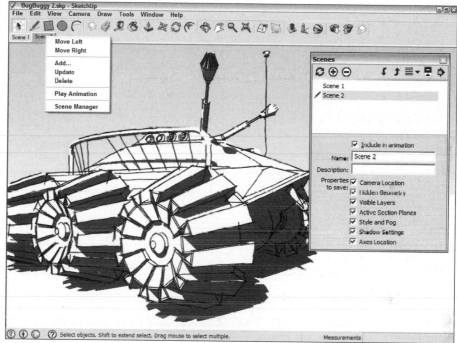

Figure 10-7:
You can modify scenes by right-clicking scene tabs or by using the Scenes dialog box.

To access the modification controls in the Scenes dialog box, click the arrow-shaped expansion button in the upper-right corner.

Here's how to reorder, rename, or remove scenes:

✔ **Reordering scenes:** You can change the order in which scenes play in a slide show. If you're using scenes, you need to do this often — trust me. Use one of the following methods:

• Right-click the tab of the scene you want to move (in the modeling window) and choose Move Right or Move Left.

• In the expanded Scenes dialog box, click the name (or thumbnail image) of the scene you want to move to select it. Then click the up or down arrows to the right of the list to change the scene's position in the scene order.

✔ **Renaming scenes:** It's a good idea to give your scenes meaningful names: Living Room, Top View, and Shadows at 5:00 P.M. are descriptive enough to be useful. Scene 14, I find, lacks a certain *je ne sais quoi.* Use one of the following methods:

- Right-click the scene tab and choose Rename.

- In the Scenes dialog box, select the scene you want to rename and type something into the Name field below the list. If you're feeling really organized, go ahead and give it a description, too — more information never hurts.

✔ **Removing scenes:** If you don't need a scene anymore, feel free to delete it. However, if you have a scene that you don't want to appear in slide shows, you don't have to get rid of it. Use one of the following methods to remove a scene:

- Right-click the scene tab and choose Delete to get rid of it permanently.

- In the Scenes dialog box, select the scene you want to ax and click the Delete button.

To exclude a scene from slide shows without getting rid of it, select its name (or thumbnail) and deselect the Include in Animation check box.

Working with scene properties

Okay. Turn off the television. Send the kids outside to play. Do whatever you need to do to concentrate because wrapping your head around the concept of scene properties isn't altogether straightforward. I do my best to explain it.

Basically, a scene is just a collection of saved viewing *properties.* Each of these properties has something to do with how your model looks:

✔ **Camera Location:** Camera Location properties include the camera position, or *viewpoint,* and the field of view. I discuss field of view earlier in this chapter.

✔ **Hidden Geometry:** Hidden Geometry properties are really just one thing: what elements are hidden and what elements aren't. These properties keep track of the visibility of the lines, faces, groups, and components in your model.

✔ **Visible Layers:** Visible Layer Properties keep track of the visibility of layers in your model.

✔ **Active Section Planes:** Active Section Plane properties include the visibility of section planes and whether they're active. I talk about sections in the last part of this chapter.

✔ **Style and Fog:** Style and Fog properties are all the settings in the Styles and Fog dialog boxes, and there are a lot of them.

✔ **Shadow Settings:** Shadow Settings properties include whether shadows are turned on and the time and date for which the shadows are set. They also include all the other settings in the Shadow Settings dialog box.

✔ **Axes Locations:** Axes Location properties are very specific. They keep track of the visibility of the main red, green, and blue axes in your modeling window. Because you often want to hide the axes when giving a presentation, these elements get their own properties.

Here's the tricky part: Scenes can *save* (remember) any combination of the preceding properties — it's not an all-or-nothing proposition. After the full impact of this information soaks in, you'll realize that this means that scenes are *much* more powerful than they first appear.

By creating scenes that save only one or two properties (instead of all seven), you can use scenes to do some pretty nifty things. Here are three of my favorites:

✔ Create scenes that affect only your camera location, allowing you to return to any point of view without affecting anything else about the way your model looks (such as styles and hidden geometry).

✔ Create scenes that affect only styles and shadows, letting you quickly change between simple and complex (hard on your computer) display settings without affecting your camera location.

✔ Create scenes that have different combinations of Hidden Geometry to look at design alternatives without changing your model's style and camera location.

The key to working with scene properties is the expanded Scenes dialog box, visible in Figure 10-8. Although this dialog box is pretty simple, folks who understand it are few and far between. Prepare to join the informed minority.

Figure 10-8:
Choose which scene properties to save in the expanded Scenes dialog box.

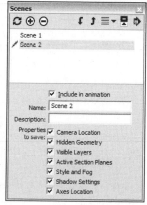

Follow these steps to set which properties a scene saves:

1. **In the Scenes dialog box, select the scene whose properties you want to fiddle with.**

   You don't have to view this scene when you edit it; you can edit properties for any scene at any time.

2. **If not already expanded, click the Show Options button in the upper-right corner of the Scenes dialog box.**

3. **Select the check boxes next to the properties you want to save.**

   That's it. You don't have to click Save anywhere to make your changes stick. A little anticlimactic, no?

One terrific use of scene properties is to create scenes that help you show off different *iterations* (versions) of your design. Take a look at Chapter 7 for more information.

Updating scenes

If you want to *update* (make changes to) an existing scene, you have a couple options:

✔ Update all the scene's properties at once, which is a piece of cake.

✔ Update the scene's properties selectively, which isn't quite as simple. Read on for both sets of instructions.

Updating all the scene properties at once

The simplest way to modify a scene is to not worry about individual properties.

After you update a scene, you can't use Undo to revert things back to the way they were. Save your SketchUp file right before you update a scene and choose File⇨Revert if you don't like the results.

If all you want to do is update a scene after you make an adjustment to the appearance of your model, you're in luck. Follow these steps:

1. **Click the tab of the scene you want to update.**

   The tabs are at the top of the modeling window.

2. **Make whatever styles, shadows, camera, or other display changes you want to your model.**

3. **Right-click the current scene tab and choose Update.**

   Be careful not to accidentally double-click the tab, or you'll reactivate the scene and lose all the changes you made. The old scene properties are replaced by the new ones, and you're home free.

Updating scene properties selectively

Here's where things get complicated. At times in your SketchUp life, you'll want to update a scene without updating all its properties.

When you update scenes selectively, you make changes that you can't see immediately, which means disaster might strike. Copy your SketchUp file before you update more than one scene at a time, just in case something awful happens.

Maybe you've used scenes to create a tour of the sunroom you're designing for a client, and you want to change the shadow settings to make your model look brighter. You have 30 scenes in your presentation, and your meeting's in 5 minutes. You don't have time to change and update all 30 scenes one at a time. What to do? Follow these steps:

1. **Adjust the Shadow Settings properties to where you want them to be for all the scenes you want to update.**

   Although this example deals with shadows, this same method applies to any scene properties changes you want to make.

2. **In the Scenes dialog box, select all the scenes you want to update.**

   Hold down the Shift key to select more than one scene at a time.

3. **Click the Update button in the Scenes dialog box.**

   The Scenes Update dialog box appears, as shown in Figure 10-9.

4. **Select the Shadow Settings check box and click the Update button.**

   If all you want to update are the Shadow Settings, make sure that only that check box is selected. More generally, you'd select the check box next to each of the properties you want to update. All the selected scenes are updated with those new properties, and all the properties left deselected remain unchanged.

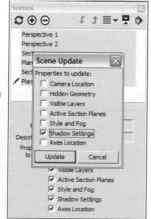

Figure 10-9: Updating only certain scene properties is a little more involved.

Mastering the Sectional Approach

Software like SketchUp has a funny way of providing moments of perfect simplicity, moments when you sit back, scratch your head, and think to yourself, "That's it? That's all there is to it?"

Sections in SketchUp offer one of those moments. To put it simply, *sections* are objects that let you cut away parts of your model to look inside. You place sections wherever you need them, use them to create views you couldn't otherwise get, and then delete them when you're done. When you move a section plane, you get instant feedback; the cut view of your model moves, too. If you want to get fancy, you can embed sections in scenes and even use them in animations. Sections are the icing on the SketchUp cake: easy to use, incredibly important, and impressive as all get out.

People use sections for all kinds of things:

✔ Creating standard orthographic views (such as plans and sections) of buildings and other objects

✔ Making cutaway views of complex models to make them easier to understand

✔ Working on the interiors of buildings without moving or hiding geometry

✔ Generating sectional animations with scenes

Cutting plans and sections

The most common use for sections is to create straight-on, cut-through views of your model. These views often include dimensions and are typical of the drawings that architects make to design and explain space.

Straight-on, cut-through views are useful because

✔ They're easy to read.

✔ You can take measurements from them (if they're printed to scale).

✔ They provide information that no other drawing type can.

The following terms (which I illustrate in Figure 10-10) can help you create different views of your model more easily:

✔ **Plan:** A *planimetric* view, or plan, is a top-down, two-dimensional, non-perspectival view of an object or space. Put simply, it's every drawing of a house floorplan you've ever seen. You generate a plan by cutting an imaginary *horizontal* slice through your model. Everything below the slice is visible, and everything above it isn't.

✔ **Section:** Not to be confused with sections (the SketchUp feature about which this section of the book is written), a *sectional* view, or *section,* is a from-the-side, two-dimensional, nonperspectival view of an object or space. You make a section by cutting an imaginary *vertical* slice through your model. Just like in a plan view, everything on one side of the slice is visible, and everything on the other side is hidden.

Figure 10-10:
A plan is a horizontal cut, whereas a section is a vertical one.

You cut plans and sections by adding section planes to your model. These are a little abstract because nothing like them exists in real life. In SketchUp, *section planes* are objects that affect the visibility of certain parts of your model. When a section plane is active, everything in front of it is visible and everything behind is hidden. Everywhere a section plane cuts your model, a slightly thicker section cut line appears.

TIP

Cutting like an architect

In architecture, the convention is to *cut* plans at a height of 48 inches, meaning that the imaginary horizontal slice is made 4 feet above the floor surface. This ensures that doors and most windows are shown cut through by the slice, whereas counters, tables, and other furniture are below it, and thus are fully visible. You can see what I mean in Figure 10-10. These things are important when you try to explain a space to someone. After all, architectural drawings are two-dimensional abstractions of three-dimensional space, and every little bit of clarity helps.

When it comes to architectural sections (as opposed to sections, the SketchUp feature), there's no convention for where to cut them, but you should follow a couple rules:

✔ **Never cut through columns.** If you show a column in section, it looks like a wall. This is bad because sections are supposed to show the degree to which a space is open or closed. You can walk around a column, but you can't walk through a wall (at least I can't).

✔ **Try your best to cut through stairs, elevators, and other vertical circulation.** Showing how people move up and down through your building makes your drawings a lot more readable, not to mention interesting. See Figure 10-10 for an example.

If you're using Windows, open the Sections toolbar by choosing View⇨ Toolbars⇨Sections. If you're on a Mac, the Section Plane tool is in the Large Tool Set, which you can activate by choosing View⇨Tool Palettes⇨Large Tool Set. On both platforms, Section Plane looks like a white circle with letters and numbers in it.

To add a section plane, follow these steps:

1. **Choose Tools⇨Section Plane to activate the Section Plane tool.**

   You can also activate Section Plane by choosing its icon from the Large Tool Set (Mac) or the Sections toolbar (Windows), if you have it open.

2. **Move the Section Plane tool around your model.**

   Notice how the orientation of the Section Plane cursor (which is quite large) changes to be coplanar to whatever surface you hover over.

3. **After you figure out where you want to cut, click once to add a section plane.**

   To create a plan view, add a horizontal section plane by clicking a horizontal plane like a floor. For a sectional view, add a vertical section plane by clicking a wall or other vertical surface. You can, of course, add section planes wherever you want; they don't have to be aligned to horizontal or vertical planes. Figure 10-11 shows a section plane being added to a model of a house.

4. **Choose the Move tool.**

5. **Move the section plane you just added by clicking it once to pick it up and again to drop it.**

   You can only slide your section plane back and forth in two directions; SketchUp only allows section planes to move perpendicular to their cutting planes. When you're deciding where to locate your cut, the nearby sidebar, "Cutting like an architect," offers helpful pointers.

   After you add a section plane and move it to the desired location, you can rotate and even copy it, just like any other object in your model. The section plane never affects your geometry — just the way you view it.

6. **If you need to rotate your section plane, select it and use the Rotate tool.**

   Why rotate a section plane? In certain circumstances, rotating a section plane (instead of creating a brand-new one) can help explain a complex interior space. Showing a plan view *becoming* a sectional one is a powerful way to explain architectural drawings to an audience that doesn't understand them.

   Read more about the Rotate tool in Chapter 6.

7. **To make a new section plane by copying an existing one, use the Move or Rotate tool to do it the same way you'd make a copy of any other SketchUp object.**

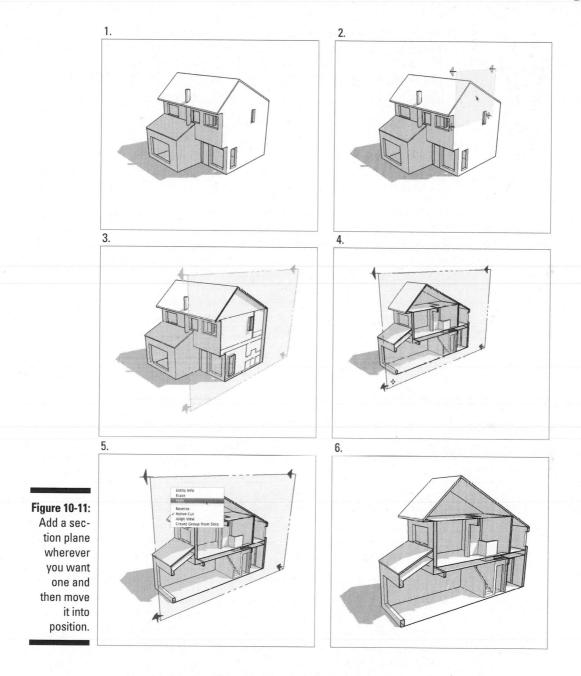

Figure 10-11:
Add a section plane wherever you want one and then move it into position.

Chapter 2 explains these basic actions in detail.

Copying section planes is a great way to space them a known distance apart; this can be trickier if you use the Section Plane tool to keep adding new ones, instead.

Figure 10-12 shows moving, rotating, and copying a section plane.

Figure 10-12:
Moving,
rotating,
and copying
a section
plane.

When the section plane you've added is in position, you're ready to control how it impacts visibility in a number of other ways. See the following sections for details.

Controlling individual section planes

You can control the way section planes behave by right-clicking them to bring up a context menu, as shown in Figure 10-13. I show examples of what the following options do in the same illustration:

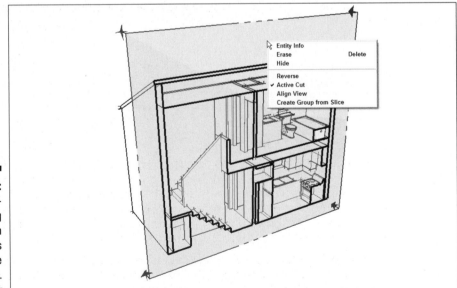

Figure 10-13:
Right-
clicking
a section
plane gives
you some
options.

✔ **Reverse:** This option flips the direction of the section plane, hiding everything that was previously visible, and revealing everything that used to be behind the cut. Use this when you need to see inside the rest of your model.

✔ **Active Cut:** Although you can have multiple section planes in your model, only one plane can be active at a time. The *active cut* is the section plane that is actually cutting through your model; others are considered *inactive*. If you have more than one section plane, use Active Cut to tell SketchUp which one should be active.

You *can* have more than one active section plane in your model at a time, but doing so requires that you nest, or embed, each section plane in a separate group or component. You can achieve spiffy effects with this technique, but I'm afraid I don't have room to include more than this mention of it in this book. You can read all about groups and components in Chapter 5.

✔ **Align View:** When you choose Align View, your view changes so that you look straight on at the section plane. You can use this option to produce views like the ones that I describe in the section "Getting different sectional views," later in this chapter.

✔ **Create Group from Slice:** This option doesn't have much to do with the other choices in this context menu; it's really a modeling tool. You can use this to do exactly what it says: Create a group from the active slice, or section plane. I don't use this very often, but it comes in handy for creating filled-in section cuts for final presentations.

Setting section-plane visibility

If you want to control the visibility of all your section planes at once, a couple menu options can help. Use both of these toggles in combination to control how section cuts appear in your model. These two options, shown on the View menu, are illustrated in Figure 10-14:

✔ **Section Planes:** This choice toggles the visibility of section-plane objects without affecting the section cuts they produce. More simply, deselecting Section Planes hides all the section planes in your model, but doesn't turn off the section cut effect, as shown in the middle image in Figure 10-14. This is how you probably want to show most of your sectional views, so this is a pretty important toggle.

✔ **Section Cut:** Deselecting this option toggles the section cut effect on and off without affecting the visibility of the section-plane objects in your model. This choice is sort of the opposite of Section Planes, in the previous point, but it's every bit as important.

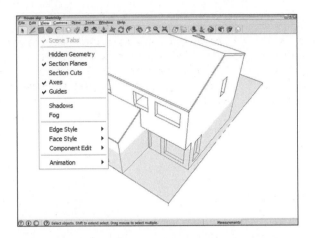

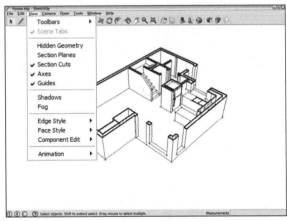

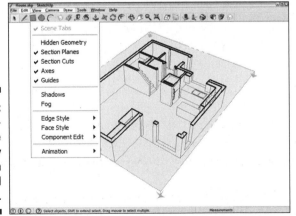

Figure 10-14:
Control sec-
tion plane
visibility
with Section
Planes and
Section Cut.

Getting different sectional views

Using section planes, you can create a couple useful and impressive views of your model without much trouble. The second builds on the first, and both are shown in Figure 10-15. A section perspective (left) is a special view of a three-dimensional space. The second type, an orthographic view (right), is straight on and doesn't use perspective.

Figure 10-15:
Turn on
Perspective
for a section
perspec-
tive; choose
Parallel
Projection
to produce
an ortho-
graphic
view.

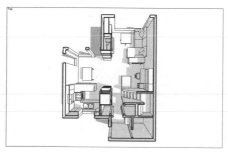

Making a section perspective

If you imagine cutting a building in half and then looking at the cut surface straight on while looking inside, you have a section perspective. The *section* part of the term means that the building has been cut away. The *perspective* part indicates that objects inside the space seem smaller as they get farther away.

Section perspectives are a great (not to mention incredibly cool) way of showing interior space in a way most people can understand. To create a section perspective using the Section Plane tool in SketchUp, follow these steps (and check out this book's companion Web site, explained in the Introduction for additional help):

1. **Select the section plane you want to use to make a section perspective by clicking it with the Select tool.**

   When it's selected, your section plane turns blue, assuming that you haven't changed the default colors in the Styles dialog box.

2. **If the selected section plane isn't active, right-click it and choose Active Cut.**

   Active section planes cut through their surrounding geometry. If your section plane is visible but isn't cutting through anything, it's not active.

3. **Right-click the selected section plane and choose Align View.**

This aligns your view so that it's straight on (perpendicular) to your section plane.

4. **If you can't see your model properly, choose Camera⇨Zoom Extents.**

This zooms your view so that you can see your whole model in the modeling window.

Generating an orthographic section

Ever seen a technical drawing that included top, front, rear, and side views of the same object? Chances are that was an *orthographic projection,* which is a common way for 3D objects to be drawn so that they can be built.

Producing an orthographic section of your model is pretty easy; it's only one extra step beyond making a section perspective. Here's how to do it:

1. **Follow Steps 1–3 in the preceding section, as if you're making a section perspective.**

2. **Choose Camera⇨Parallel Projection.**

This switches off Perspective, turning your view into a true orthographic representation of your model. If you printed it at a specific scale, you could take measurements from the printout.

To print a plan or section view of your model at a particular scale, have a look at Chapter 12, where I explain the whole process. If you have SketchUp Pro, see Chapter 14; printing to scale is what LayOut was created to do.

Creating section animations with scenes

Combining section views with scenes to create an animation is both a useful and impressive way to show off your model. The basic idea is that you can use scenes to create animations where your section planes move inside your model. Here are a few reasons you may want to use this technique:

✔ If you have a building with several levels, you can create an animated presentation that shows a cutaway plan view of each level.

✔ Using an animated section plane to "get inside" your model is a much classier transition than simply hiding certain parts of it.

✔ When you need to show the relationship between the plan and section views for a project, using an animated section plane helps to explain the concept of different architectural views to 3D beginners.

Follow these steps to create a basic section animation; a simple example is illustrated in Figure 10-16 (and check out this book's companion Web site for additional help):

Figure 10-16: Making a section animation is a fairly straight-forward process.

 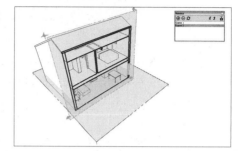

1. **Add a section plane to your model.**

   I explain how to create section planes in the section "Cutting plans and sections," earlier in this chapter.

2. **Add a scene to your model.**

   Check out the section "Creating scenes," earlier in this chapter, for a complete rundown on adding scenes.

3. **Add another section plane to your model.**

   You can add another section plane in one of two ways:

   • *Use the Section Plane tool to create a brand-new one.* This is probably the easiest option, and it's the one I recommend if you're just starting.

   • *Use the Move tool to copy an existing section plane.* I talk about copying section planes in the section "Cutting plans and sections," earlier in this chapter.

   Make sure that your new section plane is active; if it is, it cuts through your model. If it's not active, right-click the section plane and choose Active Cut from the context menu.

4. **Add another scene to your model.**

   This new scene remembers which is the active section plane.

5. **Click through the scenes you added to view your animation.**

   You see an animated section cut as SketchUp transitions from one scene to the next. If you don't, make sure that you have scene transitions enabled: Choose Window➪Model Info and then choose the Animations panel in the Model Info dialog box. Make sure the Scene Transitions check box is selected.

If you don't like seeing the section-plane objects (the boxy things with arrows on their corners) in your animation, switch them off by deselecting Section Planes on the View menu. Then you see the section cuts without any ugly gray rectangles flying around.

The hardest thing to remember about using scenes and section planes to make section animations is this: *You need a separate section plane for each scene that you create.* That is to say, SketchUp animates the transition from one active section plane to another active section plane. If all you do is move the same section plane to another spot and add a scene, this technique won't work. Believe it or not, it took me two years to figure this out, so don't feel dense if you need to come back and read this section a couple times.

Part IV
Sharing What You've Made

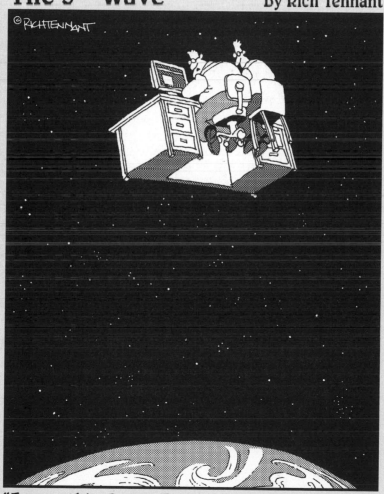

"Jeez – this Google Earth just gets better and better, doesn't it?"

In this part . . .

I suppose for some people in the world, 3D modeling is an intensely private endeavor; they build something in SketchUp, burn the SKP file to a disc, and then hide the disc in the crawlspace under the house.

If you're not one of these people, you're probably looking forward to *doing* something with the models you make — printing them, making animations, and sending them to other software programs. After all, for most folks, SketchUp is just the beginning of a process that includes lots of other steps.

The chapters in this part describe all the things you can do with your models after you build them. Chapter 11 talks about using SketchUp with Google Earth and the 3D Warehouse. Chapter 12 is about printing, and Chapter 13 describes the process of exporting images and animations. Chapters 14 and 15 provide a thorough introduction to *LayOut,* the presentation document design tool that comes with SketchUp Pro 8.

Chapter 11

Working with Google Earth and the 3D Warehouse

*I*f you've ever used Google Earth, you know what it's like to look up from your computer and realize you just have no idea what time it is. What better way to spend several hours than to travel to Paris, Cairo, and the South Pole while checking out the peak of Mount Everest and looking at your old elementary school along the way? I love Google Earth because it does what *Star Trek* said computers are *supposed* to let people do — forget they're using technology and explore information in a way they never could before.

What if you could see 3D models of buildings and other man-made structures in Google Earth the same way that you can see aerial images and 3D topography? You can. What if you could build your own models, in SketchUp, and see them in Google Earth? You can do that, too. What if you could allow *everyone* who uses Google Earth — hundreds of millions of people — to see your models in *their* copies of Google Earth, no matter where they are? Now you're getting the idea. . . .

In this chapter, I talk about making SketchUp models that you and (if you want) anyone else can see on Google Earth. I also talk about the *Google 3D Warehouse:* a great big, online repository of free 3D models that anyone (including you) can contribute to or borrow from. It's a big, friendly 3D world out there, and this chapter is your Getting Started guide.

Getting the Big (3D) Picture

Okay. So there's SketchUp, which (I have to assume) you're pretty familiar with by now. Then there's Google Earth, which you've probably seen and which you probably think is pretty neat. There's Google Building Maker, a relatively new modeling tool that most people still haven't tried. Finally, there's the 3D Warehouse, which you may not know anything about — don't worry about that. Here's the "lay of the land" when it comes to the relationship among these four things and what they're supposed to do:

- ✔ **Google SketchUp:** Because SketchUp is especially good for architecture, you can use it to make buildings that you can look at in Google Earth. If you want, you can also *upload* (send) what you make to the 3D Warehouse, where anyone who finds your model can *download* (borrow) it to use in her copy of SketchUp.

- ✔ **Google Building Maker:** Building Maker is the newest addition to Google's stable of 3D tools. This free, online application makes modeling existing buildings much, much easier — provided they're located in an area for which Google has special, multi-angle aerial imagery. You can use SketchUp to open Building Maker models; doing so lets you improve them by tweaking their geometry and textures. (www.google.com/buildingmaker)

- ✔ **Google Earth:** Earth is a software program that lets you explore the world by "flying" around, zooming in on things that interest you. The more you zoom, the better the detail gets; in some places, you can see things as small as coffee cups. The imagery in Google Earth is anywhere from a couple weeks to four years old, but it gets updated all the time. If you want, you can build models in SketchUp and view them in Google Earth. You can also see models that *other* people have made. (http://earth.google.com)

- ✔ **Google 3D Warehouse:** The 3D Warehouse is a huge collection of 3D models that lives on Google's servers. The models all come from people just like you and me; anyone can contribute models, and anyone can use them in their own SketchUp projects. Some of the best models in the 3D Warehouse are used in a special layer where anyone can see them while they're flying around in Google Earth. (http://sketchup.google.com/3dwarehouse)

If you're the kind of person who likes diagrams (I know I am), Figure 11-1 may help; it shows the SketchUp/Earth/Building Maker/3D Warehouse workflow in a nonparagraphish way.

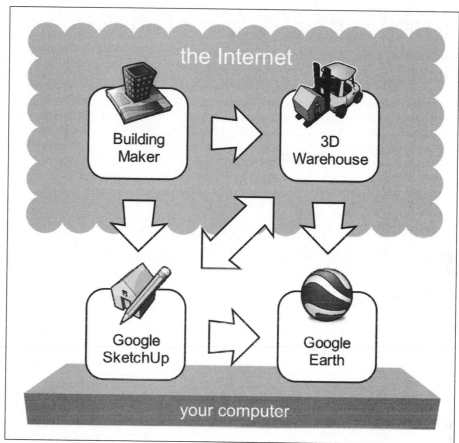

Figure 11-1:
SketchUp,
Google
Earth,
Building
Maker,
and the 3D
Warehouse
are all
related.

Sending Your Models to Google Earth

The kinds of models you might like to view in Google Earth fall into two basic categories:

- ✔ **Existing buildings:** People make models of real-life buildings simply to provide context for a structure they're designing or to display their models on Google Earth's default 3D Buildings layer where everyone in the world can see them.

- ✔ **Unbuilt buildings:** If you're designing a new structure and you want to see (and show other people) how it might look in the context of the rest of the built environment, there's no better way than to view it in Google Earth.

If you're modeling existing buildings specifically so they'll appear in everyone's Google Earth, you're *geo-modeling* — the next section in this book is just for you.

If, on the other hand, you already have a model of something you want preview in Google Earth, please skip ahead to "Geo-locating your model," later in this chapter.

Geo-modeling for Google Earth

The folks at Google are on a mission: To make Google Earth into a hyper-realistic, fully-3D map of the planet, complete with everything from mountains to weather systems. The idea is to create a "mirror world" that can someday be the basis for experimenting, teaching, and shopping as well as tourism and just about anything else you can imagine. It's an exciting project, and plenty of 3D enthusiasts are pitching in to help make Google's mission a reality by modeling as many buildings as they can — one building at a time.

The thing is, *geo-modeling* (building models for Google Earth) is different from other kinds of SketchUp modeling. All Google Earth models are

- ✔ **Geo-located:** They know where on earth they're supposed to sit.

- ✔ **Geometrically simple:** Having lots of edges and faces doesn't cut it; big models plus Google Earth equals sluggish performance (like molasses in the cold), and no one wants that.

- ✔ **Hollow:** Earth models are basically shells; they contain no interior walls or other details at all.

- ✔ **Completely photo-textured:** *Photo-texturing* your model means painting it with photographs of the building it's supposed to represent.

You can approach geo-modeling in a few ways — SketchUp is no longer the only tool at your disposal. The following sections are all about techniques for making models whose sole purpose is to reside in Google Earth.

Starting with Google Building Maker

Building Maker is purpose-built for geo-modeling; making accurate, photo-textured models of existing buildings is literally all it does. Provided your modeling target is in an area where Building Maker data exists, this is definitely where you should start. Why? Because Building Maker gives you two things that are otherwise very, very hard to obtain:

✔ **Aerial imagery:** Being able to use photo-textures that have been taken from above (rather than from street level) automatically takes care of things like trees, cars, people, and anything else that'd otherwise get in the way.

✔ **Building height:** Believe it or not, figuring out the height of an existing building you're trying to model is one of the hardest parts of the geo-modeling process. Because Building Maker makes you "trace" (sort of) oblique photos to build models, you always end up with a building of acceptably accurate height.

To find out if you can use Building Maker for your model, search for *building maker available locations* into your favorite search engine.

Here's another neat thing about Building Maker: You can open the models it creates in SketchUp and refine them there. Here's what the workflow looks like; Figure 11-2 shows the steps along the way:

1. **Open a new SketchUp file and make sure you're online.**

   Building Maker is a *Web application;* it exists only on Google's servers. You need an Internet connection to use it. Welcome to the cloud, *compadre.*

2. **Choose File➪Building Maker➪Add New Building.**

   A Building Maker window appears.

3. **Model a building with Building Maker.**

   Here's the thing: Building Maker is a completely separate program, with all the tools, widgets, and buttons that implies. What's more, its status as a Web application makes it easy to change with a fair amount of frequency. So anything I write today could (and probably will) be obsolete next month. For both these reasons, I don't dive in to how to use Building Maker in this book. What I *can* do is provide the following brief list of Three Things You Should Know about Building Maker:

   • *Building Maker is nothing like SketchUp.* It takes you about 5 seconds to figure this out — there's no Orbit, no Line tool, no Push/Pull, and no faces — the whole modeling *paradigm* is different in Building Maker. All you're doing is matching basic 3D shapes to different views of the same building. After you get used to it, it can be downright Zen.

   • *The Help link is in the upper-right corner of the screen.* There's also plenty of contextual help that pops up while you model.

   • *It saves everything to the 3D Warehouse.* To save a Building Maker model, you need to be logged in to your 3D Warehouse account. Read more about this later in this chapter. If ever you want to see all the Building Maker models you've made, just check the My Models section of the 3D Warehouse.

1. Start in Building Maker

2. Export to SketchUp

3. Improve in SketchUp

4. Upload to 3D Warehouse

Figure 11-2:
Start geo-
modeling
with Building
Maker; then
improve
things with
SketchUp.

4. **When you're ready, click the SketchUp Export button.**

   A bunch of behind-the-scenes stuff happens, and eventually your model pops open in SketchUp.

5. **Work on your model until it looks the way you want it to.**

   The point here is to do two things: Add *geometric* detail that you didn't (or couldn't) in Building Maker and improve photo-textures using all the tools in SketchUp. Some things to think about:

   • *Everything you brought in from Building Maker is just plain ol' edges and faces.* This means you can continue to model the way you always would.

- *Chapter 8 is your friend.* In Chapter 8, I talk about all the ways you can slather images onto your models. You can use your own photos or even Google Street View imagery (if it's available).

- *Use the Match Photo scenes.* See the little scene tabs at the top of your modeling window? They correspond to the aerial imagery from Building Maker. You can use the Match Photo dialog box to re-texture parts of your model as you work on it. Check out Chapter 8 for more information about using Match Photo.

6. **When you're done, choose File⇨3D Warehouse⇨Share Model.**

   Your revised SketchUp model automatically overwrites the original Building Maker model on the 3D Warehouse. Google presumes that it's better than its predecessor.

Doing it all in SketchUp

Of course, Building Maker is only an option for a miniscule percentage of the world's buildings. Google adds coverage all the time, but chances are you still need to use SketchUp — and only SketchUp — for most of the geo-models you want to make.

Geo-modeling with SketchUp involves a whole bunch of operations, most of which I cover elsewhere in this book. Given that, the steps that follow are mostly pointers to other sections.

 It's a happy coincidence that I also wrote most of Google's Help Center content on geo-modeling with SketchUp. There's more room on the Internet than there is between the covers of this book, so I strongly advise you to look there for even more information. A Web search for *SketchUp introduction to geo-modeling* ought to take you right where you need to go.

Follow these steps to build a geo-model with SketchUp, as shown in Figure 11-3:

1. **Open a new SketchUp file.**

2. **Import a geo-location snapshot by geo-locating your model.**

   Take a look at "Geo-locating your model," later in this chapter, for complete instructions. Basically, you start modeling on top of a piece of color imagery and 3D terrain.

3. **Make sure that you look at the flat version of your terrain.**

   Choose File⇨Geo-location from the menu bar; make sure Show Terrain is deselected.

4. **Trace the footprint of the building you want to model directly on the color snapshot (see image A in Figure 11-3).**

   I like to use the Rectangle tool to block out the main shapes and then draw angles and other details with the Line tool.

If the building you're trying to make doesn't line up perfectly with the colored axes, using the Line and Rectangle tools can be tricky. To fix this problem, reposition your main drawing axes by choosing Tools⇨Axes. Click once to set your origin, again to establish the direction of your red axis (parallel to one of the edges in your photo), and a third time to establish your green axis. I usually set my origin at the corner of the building I'm trying to make; I think it makes things easier.

 5. **Use Push/Pull to extrude the footprint to the correct height (see image B in Figure 11-3).**

    If you don't know how tall the building you're modeling is, some tricks help you make an educated guess. Search the Web for *SketchUp estimating building height* to find an article I wrote on the subject.

 6. **Model until you're satisfied with what you have.**

    The brevity of the preceding sentence belies the depth of its meaning; this is by far the most time-consuming part of the whole geo-modeling process. The key — no, the *art* — of building a great Google Earth model is to combine clean photo-textures with simple geometry to produce a model that's both detailed and lightweight.

    Chapter 8 is all about photo-texturing your models; definitely peruse those pages sooner than later. The nearby sidebar "Thinking big by thinking small" offers tips on reducing the amount of geometry (faces, basically) in your work. Finally, the sidebar "Making sure your models get accepted" enumerates Google's acceptance criteria for Google Earth.

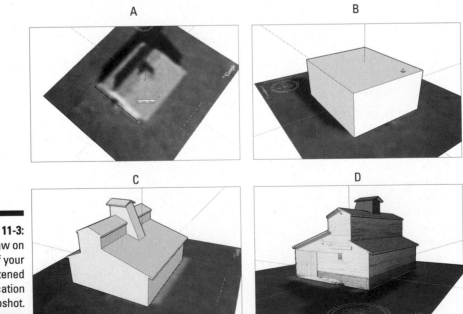

Figure 11-3: Draw on top of your flattened geo-location snapshot.

7. **Flip to the 3D version of your snapshot (choose File⟹Geo-location⟹Show Terrain) and then move your building up or down until it sits properly, poking through the ground just a little bit, as shown in Figure 11-4.**

   Select everything you want to move, and then use the Move tool to move it up or down. You can press the up- or down-arrow key to constrain your move to the blue axis if you want.

8. **Preview your model in Google Earth to make sure it looks right.**

   This is an important step, but you'd be surprised by the number of people who skip it altogether. Jump ahead to "Exporting from SketchUp to Google Earth," in this chapter, for a complete set of instructions. Previewing is easy — I promise.

9. **Upload your model to the Google 3D Warehouse.**

   The 3D Warehouse is the source for every *user-generated* (not modeled by Google) geo-model that's added to the 3D Buildings layer in Google Earth. By selecting the checkbox to indicate that it's Google Earth–ready and then uploading it, you're submitting your model for consideration. Take a look at the steps in "Uploading your models," near the end of this chapter, for everything else you need to know.

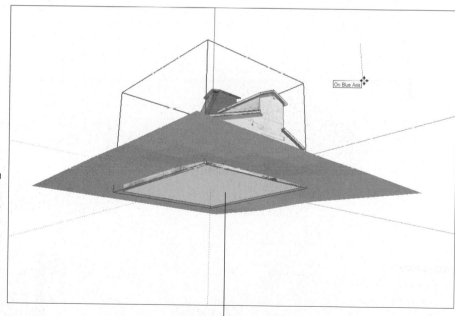

Figure 11-4: Move your model up or down until it sits properly on the terrain.

Make sure your building pokes through the ground

Thinking big by thinking small

When modeling for Google Earth, lightness is next to godliness. By *light,* I mean the file size of your model, and by *file size,* I mean the number of faces and textures you use to build it. The more complicated your model, the slower Google Earth runs, and the more likely you'll be to throw your computer through a window in frustration. Now more than ever, think about how you can do the most with the least — geometry, that is. Follow these tips:

Get rid of extra geometry. When modeling, you often end up with edges (and even faces) that have no purpose. Spend a few minutes deleting any edges separating faces that can be combined.

Reduce the number of sides in your extruded arcs and circles. SketchUp's default number of sides for circles is 24. This means that every time you use Push/Pull to extrude a circle into a cylinder, you end up with 25 faces: 24 around the sides and the original one on top. Instead of using circles with 24 sides, reduce the number of sides by typing a number followed by the letter *s* and pressing Enter right after you draw a circle. For example, to draw a 10-sided circle (plenty for Google Earth), follow these steps:

1. **Draw a circle with the Circle tool.**

2. **Type** 10s **(this appears in the lower-right corner of your modeling window) and then press Enter.**

The same thing goes for arcs; you change the number of sides in them in exactly the same way. I like to use 10-sided circles and 4-sided arcs when I model for Google Earth. The following image shows the same pipe constructed by using Follow Me on two circles: one with 24 sides and one with only 10. Note the difference in the number of faces in each version.

When you can, use photo detail instead of geometry. It's a good idea to make as basic a model as you can and let the detail in the photo "do the talking." Resist the temptation to model windows and doors. Consider using PNG images with transparency to represent columns, fences, and other thin building elements.

Limit the size of your photo-textures. Check out Chapter 8 for a rundown on some new tools that Google introduced for SketchUp 7. Basically, photos that you use to paint your models can be heavy, so make sure that you save only the parts of them that you need — pay special attention to the new Make Unique Texture command.

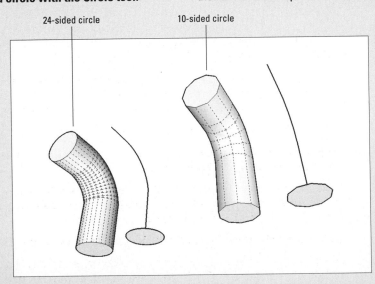

24-sided circle   10-sided circle

Geo-locating your model

No matter what kind of model you build, displaying it in Google Earth — for yourself, for a client, or for everyone in the world — begins with giving it a geographic location, or *geo-location* for short. In SketchUp, geo-locating your model involves placing it where it belongs on a chunk of terrain and aerial imagery (called a *geo-location snapshot*) that you download from the Web.

Adding a geo-location snapshot to your model in SketchUp 8 is about ten times easier than it was in SketchUp 7. The 3D terrain data in SketchUp 8's geo-location snapshots is also more detailed and accurate than it used to be, and the aerial imagery is in full color.

Follow these steps to add a geo-location snapshot to your SketchUp file:

1. **Make sure you're online.**

   All Google's geo-data is stored on its far-flung servers; if you don't have an Internet connection, you can't use the geo-data.

2. **Open the SketchUp file you want to geo-locate.**

   You can add a geo-location snapshot to your model anytime as you work on it. If you haven't started modeling yet, it's perfectly okay to add a geo-location to an empty file.

3. **Choose File⇨Geo-Location⇨Add Location from the menu bar.**

   A new window that you may recognize opens: It's a simplified version of Google Maps.

4. **Find the area where you want your model to be located.**

   You can type an address into the search bar in the upper-left corner if you like. You can also just use your mouse or the controls on the left side of the window to navigate around. Scroll your mouse wheel to zoom; click and drag to pan.

   When you're zoomed in close enough, you see a white, 1 km x 1 km square: This is the largest snapshot you can import all at once. That's still a very big area, so you probably want to keep zooming.

5. **Click the Select Region button to display a cropping rectangle.**

6. **Drag the blue pins to specify the precise corners of your geo-location snapshot, as shown in Figure 11-5.**

   Try to frame an area that's just big enough to provide a base for your model. Importing too much terrain data can bog down your computer. You can always bring in more terrain data later.

7. **Click the Grab button to add a geo-location to your SketchUp file.**

   The separate window closes, and a big, colorful rectangle appears in the middle of your model. That's your new geo-location snapshot.

Making sure your models get accepted

When you take the trouble to build a model for Google Earth, you naturally want it accepted into Google Earth's 3D Buildings layer so that everyone in the world can see it. The following tips help you avoid common problems among rejected models:

✔ **Match your model's terrain to the physical world:** When the 3D terrain you import doesn't cut it, you may have to "build up" the terrain around your building by modeling it in SketchUp. Search the Web for *SketchUp create terrain skirt* to find an article that helps you figure out what to do.

✔ **To replace an existing model, make your model better:** Before you submit your model for consideration, check Google Earth to make sure there isn't already a version of your building on the 3D Buildings layer. If there is, your model needs to be better than what's already there in order to replace it.

✔ **Apply photo-textures that look accurate:** Use good photographs as textures when you model and be sure to position them accurately. Take a look at Chapter 8 for the whole scoop.

✔ **Size and scale your model to match its photo in Google Earth:** This may seem obvious, but it's a common occurrence; if your model isn't the same size as it is in the aerial imagery in Google Earth, it won't be accepted. It also needs to appear in the correct spot — right on top of its own photo in Google Earth.

✔ **Model existing buildings:** If the building you submit doesn't appear in Google Earth's aerial imagery, chances are good that it'll get the big thumbs-down. If it really does exist, include Web links to images of the building in its surroundings in the model description when you upload it to the 3D Warehouse. If it's still under construction, include a link to somewhere on the Web that details when it's due to be completed.

✔ **Sink your model into the ground just a bit so it doesn't float:** This one's simple — make sure your building doesn't float above the ground in Google Earth. It should be sunken into the ground just enough to appear realistic.

✔ **Avoid ads:** You can't include ads or other visual "spam" on your models. If the building has a mural or a billboard on it, that's okay, but the ad has to be part of the original photo-texture on the model — it has to be a part of the structure in real life.

✔ **Model only the building:** Don't include extras like cars, trees, streetlamps, people, or anything else that isn't a part of the building when you upload it.

✔ **Check for and correct Z-fighting:** When two faces are in the plane, they flash when you orbit your model. This is *Z-fighting,* and it's as common as dirt. If you see this phenomenon, there's a good chance you slipped up and chose Use as Image instead of Use as Texture when you imported the image into your model — resulting in two co-planar faces. Check out Chapter 8 for the right way to apply images when you model.

✔ **Keep your model's file size lean:** Take a look at "Thinking big by thinking small," earlier in this chapter, for tips on minimizing the size of what you make. *Remember:* In Google Earth, smaller files are always better.

Keep zooming

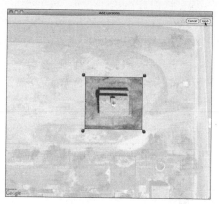

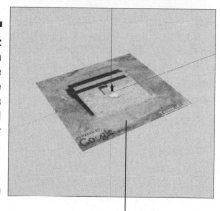

Figure 11-5:
The area you frame with blue pins is imported into your model as a geo-location snapshot.

Snapshot in SketchUp

All about geo-location snapshots

When you import a geo-location snapshot, you access Google's huge repository of geographic data; snapshots are a lot more than just pretty pictures:

✔ **A snapshot *geo-locates* your position automatically.** This means that it sets your model's latitude and longitude, and orients itself in the right cardinal direction. Any shadow studies you do with the Shadows feature are automatically accurate for your model's new geo-location. See Chapter 9 for more information.

✔ **Everything's already the right size.** Perhaps you take a snapshot of a football field; when you measure that football field in SketchUp, it is exactly 100 yards long. That's because

SketchUp scales your snapshot to the correct size as part of the import process.

✔ **Snapshots look flat but contain terrain data, too.** The snapshot that SketchUp imports is more than just a color aerial photo — it also includes a chunk of topography — terrain. The *terrain* is flat when you first import it because it's easier to build on that way, but you can toggle between flat and 3D (not flat) views by choosing File⇨Geo-Location⇨ Show Terrain. Don't fret if you don't see any difference when you flip between the views — you probably just chose a flat site. The image below shows the same snapshot with terrain toggled off (left) and on.

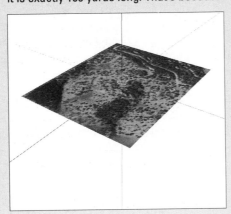 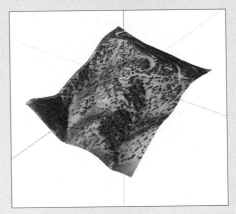

8. **If you're geo-locating a model you've built already, move it into position on the snapshot.**

   Use the Move tool (and maybe the Rotate tool) to pick up your model and place it where it belongs. You're not done yet, though — you still need to make sure your model is *vertically* situated on the terrain. Follow these steps to do just that:

   a. *Choose File⇨Geo-location⇨Show Terrain to switch to the 3D version of your geo-location snapshot.*

b. *Select everything you want to move and use the Move tool to start moving; tap the up- or down-arrow key to constrain your move to the blue axis.*

c. *Sink your model into the terrain until it sits properly — avoid the dreaded floating model syndrome at all costs.*

If you want to import another snapshot into SketchUp, you can. SketchUp automatically tiles all the snapshots you "take" to form a patchwork in your model. This is super-handy if you find that you didn't get everything you needed the first time.

Viewing your model in Google Earth

After you make (or simply position) a model on top of a geo-location snapshot, sending it to your copy of Google Earth is a simple operation. And after you do that, you can save your model as a Google Earth KMZ file and e-mail it to all your friends. If you model for clients instead of friends, you can send the file to them, too.

Taking the five-minute tour of Google Earth

Google Earth is a pretty deep piece of software, not because it's hard to use (it's not) but because you can use it to do an awful lot. In this section, you get a "zooming past it in a speeding car" tour that should be enough to get you started.

Here's a piece of good news for you: Just like Google SketchUp, the basic version of Google Earth is free. Why? My mother always told me not to look a gift horse in the mouth, and Google Earth is the Secretariat of gift horses. All that matters to me is that people with a computer that can run SketchUp can also run Google Earth, and they don't have to pay for it. Here are some more things you need to know:

✔ **You get Google Earth by downloading it.** Just go to http://earth. google.com and click the big Download button. While you're there, check out the other features of the site. You can find answers to any other questions you have, as well as links to online help, user communities, and more. You can even find out what's available in the fancier versions of Google Earth, if that's what floats your boat.

✔ **You need a fast Internet connection.** The magic of Google Earth is its ability to show you detailed imagery of the *whole world* — that's lots and lots of data that Google keeps on its servers until you request it by flying somewhere and zooming in. The faster your Internet connection, the faster you can stream imagery, 3D buildings, and topography into your copy of Google Earth. As you can imagine, Google Earth isn't worth a darn if you're not online.

✔ **It helps to know how to move around.** Check out the upper-right corner of the screen, where the navigation controls for Google Earth are conveniently grouped together. Notice how they appear when you hover over them? Go ahead and play around to figure out what they do. Here's some help:

- *Zoom:* Move this slider back and forth to zoom in and out on whatever's in the center of your screen. As you approach the ground, you automatically "pull up" to end up "standing" on your virtual feet. You can also use the scroll wheel on your mouse to zoom, just like you do in SketchUp.

- *Pan/Move:* You can move around by clicking and holding down the arrow buttons to go forward, backward, left, and right, but the easier way is to use your mouse. Just click and drag to "spin" the world in whatever direction you want.

- *Rotate/Tilt:* Drag the wheel to spin around without moving. Click N on your keyboard to reorient the world so that north is up. Click and drag on the arrows in the center to turn and tilt your view (a lot like the Look Around tool in SketchUp).

  If you're looking at an area with mountains, they should look like a 3D image. (If they don't, make sure that the Terrain layer is enabled in the lower-left corner.) You can also tilt by holding down your scroll wheel button, the same way you do to orbit in SketchUp. (See Chapter 2 for more on orbiting.)

Exporting from SketchUp to Google Earth

This process is so simple you can probably figure it out while you talk on the phone. Follow these steps to send your model from SketchUp to Google Earth on your computer:

1. **Choose File⇨Preview in Google Earth.**

   Doing this sends everything in your modeling window (with the exception of the geo-location snapshot) over to Google Earth. Your computer automatically switches to Google Earth and flies you in so that you look at your model (see Figure 11-6).

2. **If you want to make changes to your model, go back to SketchUp, make your changes, and then choose Preview in Google Earth again.**

   Google Earth pops up a dialog box that asks whether you want to overwrite the old version of the model you placed the first time.

3. **Click the Yes button if you're sure that's what you want to do.**

4. **Continue to go back and forth between SketchUp and Google Earth until your model looks exactly the way you want.**

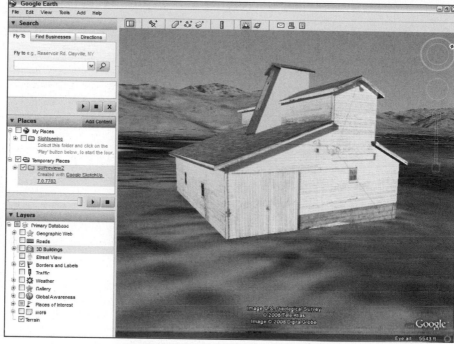

Figure 11-6:
Your
SketchUp
model
(actually, my
SketchUp
model) in
Google
Earth.

When you preview your SketchUp model in Google Earth, it's visible only on your computer — no one else can see it. If you've modeled an existing building and you want to contribute it to Earth's default 3D Buildings layer, you can; take a look at "Geo-modeling for Google Earth," near the beginning of this chapter, for more information.

Saving your model as a Google Earth KMZ file

You can save your SketchUp model as a Google Earth KMZ file that you can send to anyone. When someone opens the KMZ file, Google Earth opens on his computer (if he has Google Earth), and he's "flown in" to look at the model you made. Try sending directions to your next party this way; your friends will think you're related to Albert Einstein. Follow these steps to save your model:

1. **In Google Earth, select your model by clicking it in the Temporary Places list on the left of the screen.**

   Unless you've renamed it, your model is SUPreview1.

2. **Choose File⇨Save⇨Save Place As.**

   The Save File dialog box opens.

3. **Give your file a name and figure out where to put it on your hard drive.**

4. **Click the Save button to save your model as a KMZ file.**

 I prefer to save KMZs from Google Earth because doing so forces me to pre-view my models first. You can skip the Google Earth step altogether if you're in a hurry. Choose File⇨Export⇨3D Model while you're still in SketchUp, then choose Google Earth File (.kmz) from the Format drop-down list.

Becoming a SketchUp All-Star with the 3D Warehouse

Residing wherever Google's other jillions of bits of data do, the *3D Warehouse* is a huge collection of 3D models that is searchable and, most importantly, free for everyone to use. It's basically a Web site; it exists online, and you need an Internet connection to access it.

If you have a SketchUp model you want to share with the world, share with just a few people, or just store on Google's servers for safekeeping, the 3D Warehouse is where you put it.

Getting to the 3D Warehouse

You can get to the 3D Warehouse in two ways:

- ✔ **From SketchUp:** Choose File⇨3D Warehouse⇨Get Models; when you do, a mini Web browser opens right in front of your modeling window. *Voilà!*

- ✔ **From the Web:** Browse to `http://sketchup.google.com/ 3dwarehouse`. This is a great way to hunt for 3D models without opening SketchUp first.

Go ahead and poke around the 3D Warehouse. It's amazing what you find; thousands of people add new content every day. Much of it isn't very useful, but you still find plenty of interesting things to download and look at. Taking apart strangers' models is a great way to figure out how they're built. Refer to Chapter 5 for plenty of information about grabbing what you need from the 3D Warehouse.

Minding your modeling manners

People sometimes ask me if anyone at Google pays attention to what gets uploaded to the 3D Warehouse. The answer to that question is a little bit complicated. For instance, nobody at Google minds if you refer to a Web site or enter tags that don't have anything to do with the model you upload — stuff like that is entirely up to you.

On the other hand, it's very frowned upon to go anywhere near the usual taboo subjects for public, G-rated Web sites: Pornography and/ or foul language sounds an alarm somewhere at Google that will get your model yanked off the 3D Warehouse quicker than you can say "First amendment." Tens of thousands of impressionable, young eyeballs peruse Google's Web sites every day, so it behooves Google to keep those sites clean. If you have kids, I'm sure you understand.

Uploading your models

You can break the models in the 3D Warehouse into two broad categories:

- **Geo-located:** Things like buildings, monuments, bridges, and dams exist in a specific geographic location; they never move around. These models show up on the 3D Buildings layer in Google Earth, and the 3D Warehouse is where they come from. Check out the section "Geo-modeling for Google Earth," earlier in this chapter, for a blow-by-blow account of how to build geo-located models that you can upload to the 3D Warehouse.

- **Not geo-located:** Objects like toasters, SUVs, wheelchairs, and sofas aren't unique, and they don't exist in any one geographic location. No physical address is associated with a model of a Honda Accord because millions of them exist and because they move around. Stuff like this never shows up in Google Earth because the folks at Google wouldn't know where to put it. That doesn't mean it doesn't belong in the 3D Warehouse, though; models of nongeo-located stuff are incredibly valuable for people who make their own SketchUp models. When I modeled my house, I furnished it with couches, beds, and other models I found in the 3D Warehouse.

Follow these steps to upload your model to the Google 3D Warehouse:

1. **Open the model you want to upload in SketchUp and fiddle around with your view until you like what you see.**

   When you upload a model to the 3D Warehouse, SketchUp automatically creates a preview image that's a snapshot of your modeling window.

2. **Choose File⇨3D Warehouse⇨Share Model.**

   A mini-browser window opens, and it shows the logon screen for the 3D Warehouse. If you want to upload models, you need a Google account. They're free; you just need a valid e-mail address to get one. If you don't already have one, follow the onscreen instructions to sign up.

   When you create your Google account, be sure to type something where the system asks for a nickname. If you don't, everything you upload is attributed to Anonymous.

3. **Enter your Google account information, click the Sign In button, and fill out the Upload to 3D Warehouse form as completely as you can:**

   - *Title:* Enter a title for your model. If it's a public building, you may enter its name. Something like Royal West Academy would do nicely.

   - *Description:* Models with complete descriptions are very popular with people who hunt around the Warehouse. Try to use complete sentences here; the more you write, the better.

   - *Tags:* Type a string of words that describe the thing you modeled. The 3D Warehouse search engine uses whatever you enter here to help people find your model. To increase the number of people who see what you made, add lots of tags. If I were uploading a modern coffee table, I'd enter the following tags: coffee table, table, coffee, modern, living room, furniture, glass, chrome, metal, and steel. You get the idea — be exhaustive.

   - *Address:* This field appears only if your model is geo-located, meaning that you started with a geo-location snapshot. If you know the physical address of the thing you made, type it.

   - *Google Earth Ready:* You see this option only if your model is geo-located. If your model is accurate, correctly sized, and in the right location, and if you want it to be considered for inclusion on the default 3D Buildings layer of Google Earth, select this check box. If you do, the folks at Google will consider adding it to Google Earth. Keep your fingers crossed!

   - *Web Site:* If you have a Web site address that you want people who view your model to visit, enter it here. For example, if your model is a historic building, you may include the Web site that provides more information about it.

   - *Viewing:* The check box next to the sentence Allow Anyone to View This Model and See It in Search Results lets you control access to your model on the Web. Checking it gives anyone the right to find, download, and use it however they like. If you deselect it, your model stays hidden (from everyone but you). Flip ahead to "Managing your models online," in this chapter, for more about this topic.

• *Links for Containing Collections:* You (and everyone else) can create collections of models on the 3D Warehouse. Anyone can add any model to one of their collections; checking this box allows Google to display a list of collections that contain your model on your model's unique Web page.

4. **Click the Upload button to add your model to the 3D Warehouse.**

   If everything works properly, you see a page with your model on it, along with all the information you just entered. The words `Model has been uploaded successfully` are highlighted in yellow at the top of your browser window. Congratulations — you're now a member of the worldwide 3D community.

You can't upload just any old model to the 3D Warehouse, unfortunately. At the time I was working on this book, the maximum file size you could upload was 10MB, which is actually pretty big. You can check your model's file size in Explorer (on a Windows machine) or in Finder (on a Mac).

Managing your models online

The 3D Warehouse isn't a free-for-all of individual models floating around in cyberspace; it's actually a pretty organized place. Understanding collections and access settings makes your time as a member of the worldwide modeling community even more productive and enjoyable.

If you want to group together a bunch of models so they're easier to find, make a collection. In the upper-right corner of your screen, choose My Warehouse⇨My Collections to bring up a page that lists all the collections you've made. Somewhere on the page, there's a link to Create a 3D Collection — click it and fill out the information on the form that opens up. Three more things you need to know about collections:

✔ **Collections can contain either models or other collections.** When you create a collection, you decide which kind of collection it should be.

✔ **You can share collections with other people.** On the main page of one of your collections, find the Share link. Clicking it lets you invite other people to collaborate with.

✔ **Your collections can contain other people's models.** And their collections can contain your models — provided you've set them to be publicly viewable. Which brings me to my next point . . .

You actually have quite a lot of control over who gets to do what with the models you upload to the 3D Warehouse. Somewhere near the top of one of your model's pages, click the Access link. A Privacy Settings page opens, where you set who can see, edit, download, or even delete your model. The settings themselves are pretty self-explanatory, but I thought I'd point them out — lots of folks don't even know they're there.

Chapter 12

Printing Your Work

In This Chapter

▶ Printing views of your model

▶ Figuring out the printing dialog boxes

▶ Printing to scale

As much as everyone likes to pretend that we all live in an all-digital world, the ugly truth is that we don't. People use more paper now than they ever have; I have a stack of junk prints on the coffee table in front of me as I write this. It's not that I have anything against trees — it's just that printing is so *satisfying*. I love having something I can fold up and put in my pocket, or stick to the fridge, or mail to my Luddite relatives. Computer screens are nice, but in most people's minds, paper is *real*.

In this chapter, I talk about how to print views of your SketchUp model. Because the Windows and Mac versions of this procedure are so different, I dedicate a whole section to each platform. The last part of this chapter is devoted to scaled printing — a topic that can sometimes make experienced architects nervous. SketchUp makes printing to scale a little harder than it could be, but it's still a whole lot better than drawing things by hand.

If you're using the Pro version of SketchUp, you can always use LayOut to print views of your models. Making both scaled and non-scaled prints is easier in LayOut than in SketchUp; take a look at Chapter 14 for all the juicy details.

Printing from a Windows Computer

Printing from SketchUp is easy, as long as you're not trying to do anything too complicated. By complicated, I mean printing to a particular scale, which can be a harrowing experience the first couple times you attempt it. Fortunately, printing to scale is something most people almost never have to do, so I've included instructions for how to do it at the end of this chapter.

Making a basic print (Windows)

Most of the time, all you need to do is print exactly what you see on your screen. Follow these steps to do that:

1. **Make sure that the view you want to print appears in your modeling window.**

   Unless you're printing to scale (which I cover in the last part of this chapter), SketchUp prints exactly what you see in your modeling window.

2. **Choose File⇨Print Setup.**

   The Print Setup dialog box opens, which is where you choose what printer and paper you want to use.

3. **In the Print Setup dialog box (see Figure 12-1), do the following:**

   a. Choose the printer you want to use.

   b. Choose a paper size for your print.

   c. Choose an orientation for your print; most of the time, you want to use Landscape because your screen is usually wider than it is tall.

Figure 12-1:
The Print Setup dialog box in Windows.

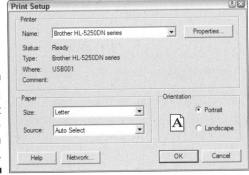

4. **Click OK to close the Print Setup dialog box.**

5. **Choose File⇨Print Preview.**

   The Print Preview dialog box opens. As an exact copy of the Print dialog box, Print Preview lets you see an image of what your print will look like before you send it to a printer. Lots of trees thank you for saving paper by using Print Preview every time you print.

6. **In the Print Preview dialog box, do the following:**

   a. In the Tabbed Scene Print Range area, choose which scenes you want to print, if you have more than one.

   If you need to, you can read all about scenes in Chapter 10.

   b. Tell SketchUp how many copies of each scene you need.

   c. Make sure that the Fit to Page check box is selected.

   d. Make sure that the Use Model Extents check box isn't selected.

   e. Choose a print quality for your printout.

      I recommend High Definition for most jobs.

For a complete description of all the knobs and doohickeys in the Print Preview and Print dialog boxes, have a look at the next section in this chapter.

7. Click OK.

The Print Preview dialog box closes, and you get an onscreen preview of what your print will look like.

8. If you like what you see, click the Print button in the upper-left corner of the Print Preview window to open the Print dialog box.

If you *don't* like what you're about to print, click the Close button (at the top of the screen) and go back to Step 1.

9. In the Print dialog box (which should look exactly like the Print Preview dialog box), click OK.

Your print job goes to the printer.

Decoding the Print Preview and Windows Print dialog box

Three cheers for simplicity! The Print Preview and Print dialog boxes in SketchUp are exactly the same. Figure 12-2 shows the former because that's the one I advocate using first every time, but the descriptions in this section apply to both.

Printer

If you used the Print Setup dialog box first, you shouldn't need to change the settings in this section. If you want, from the drop-down list, you can choose which printer to use. If you know something about printers, you can even click the Properties button to make adjustments to your printer settings. (Because settings are different for every printer on Earth, that's between you and your printer's user manual — I'm afraid I can't be of much help.)

Tabbed Scene Print Range

Use this area to tell SketchUp which of your scenes you want to print, if you have more than one. This option is really handy for quickly printing all your scenes. Select the Current View option to print only whatever's currently in your modeling window.

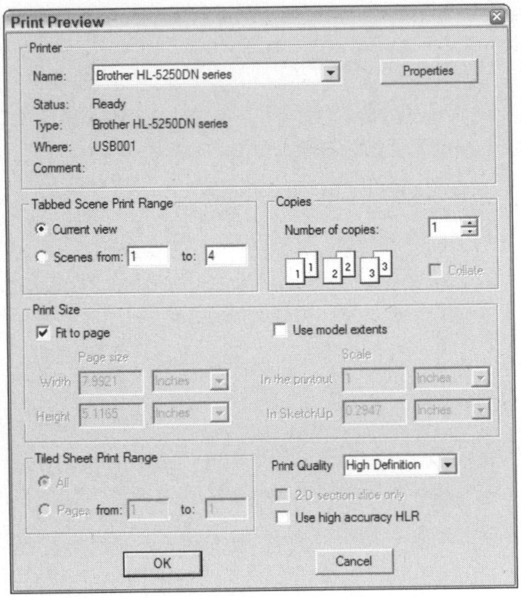

Figure 12-2:
The Print
Preview
dialog box
in Windows.
The Print
dialog
box looks
exactly the
same.

Copies

This one's pretty basic: Choose how many copies of each view you want to print. If you're printing multiple copies of multiple scenes, select the Collate check box to print *packets,* which can save you from assembling them yourself. Here's what happens when you print three copies of four scenes:

- ✔ Selecting the Collate check box prints the pages in the following order: 123412341234.
- ✔ Deselecting the Collate check box prints the pages like this: 111222333444.

Print Size

This is, by far, the most complicated part of this dialog box; Print Size controls how your model will look on the printed page. Figure 12-3 shows the effect of some of these settings on a final print.

The Print Size controls are as follows:

- ✔ **Fit to Page:** Selecting this check box tells SketchUp to make your printed page look like your modeling window. As long as the Use Model Extents check box isn't selected, you can see exactly what you see on your screen — no more, no less.
- ✔ **Use Model Extents:** I have to admit that I don't like this option; I almost never select it. All it does is tell SketchUp to zoom in to make your model (excluding your sky, ground, watermark, and whatever else may

be visible on your screen) fit the printed page. If I want this effect, I just use choose Camera⇨Zoom Extents from the menu bar before I print my model; it's easier, and I know exactly what I'm getting.

✔ **Page Size:** As long as you don't have the Fit to Page check box selected, you can manually enter a page size using these controls. If you type a width or height, SketchUp figures out the other dimension and pretends it's printing on a different-sized piece of paper.

The Page Size option is especially useful if you want to make a big print by tiling together lots of smaller pages. See the next section in this chapter, "Tiled Sheet Print Range," for more details.

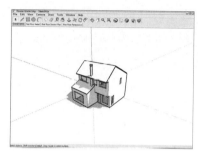

My SketchUp screen

Fit to Page

Figure 12-3:
Different
Print Size
settings
applied to
the same
view in
SketchUp.

Fit to Page and Use Model Extents

✔ **Scale:** Here's where printing gets a little complicated. To print to scale, you must do two things before you go anywhere near the Print or Print Preview dialog boxes:

• Switch to Parallel Projection mode.

• Make sure that you're using one of the Standard views.

Take a look at the section "Printing to scale (Windows and Mac)," later in this chapter, for a complete rundown on printing to scale in SketchUp.

Tiled Sheet Print Range

Perhaps you're printing at a scale that won't fit on a single page, or you've entered a print size that's bigger than the paper size you chose in the Print Setup dialog box. The Tiled Sheet Print Range area lets you print your image on multiple sheets and then attach them together later. You can get posters from your small-format printer!

Print Quality

To be honest, I think a little bit of voodoo is involved in selecting a print quality for your image. What you get with each setting depends a lot on your model, so try a couple different settings if you have time.

✔ Draft and Standard are really only useful for making sure your model appears the way you want it to on the printed page.

✔ I recommend using High Definition first and then bumping up to Ultra High Definition if your computer/printer setup can handle it.

Other settings

You can control the following odds-and-ends settings in the Print Preview dialog box, too:

✔ **2-D Section Slice Only:** If you have a visible section cut in your model view, selecting this check box tells SketchUp to print only the section cut edges. Figure 12-4 shows what the same model view would look like without (on the left) and with (right) this option selected. I use this to produce simple plan and section views that I can sketch on by hand.

✔ **Use High Accuracy HLR:** The bad news is that I have no idea what HLR stands for. The good news is that it doesn't really matter. Selecting this check box tells SketchUp to send *vector* information to the printer instead of the usual *raster* data. (Check out Chapter 13 for a description of what these terms mean.) Why should you care? Vector lines look much smoother and cleaner when printed, so your whole model will look better — with one condition: *Gradients* (those nice, smooth shadows on rounded surfaces) don't print well as vectors. If you have a lot of rounded or curvy surfaces in your model view, you probably don't want to choose this option. Try a print both ways and choose the one that looks better. Thank goodness for Print Preview, huh?

If your model view includes a Sketchy Edges style, don't use high accuracy HLR; you won't see any of the nice, sketchy effects in your final print.

Figure 12-4:
Printing only the 2-D section slice yields a simple drawing that's easy to sketch over.

 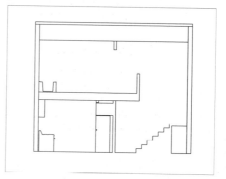

Printing from a Mac

If you're using a Mac, the printing story is a little simpler than it is for folks who use Windows computers — but only by a little. The first part of the following sections lays out a procedure for generating a simple, straightforward print of what you see in your modeling window. The second part can be called "Gross anatomy of the Mac Document Setup dialog box;" this is where I go into some detail about what each and every setting does.

Making a basic print (Mac)

Follow these steps to print exactly what you see in your modeling window on a Mac:

1. **Make sure that your modeling window contains whatever you want to print.**

   SketchUp prints exactly what you see in your modeling window, unless of course you're printing to scale. This is considerably more complicated, so I gave it a whole section at the end of this chapter.

2. **Choose File⇨Page Setup.**

   The Page Setup dialog box opens, where you decide what printer and paper size to use.

3. **In the Page Setup dialog box (see Figure 12-5), do the following:**

   a. Choose the printer you want to use from the Format For drop-down list.

   b. Choose a paper size for your print.

   c. Choose an orientation for your print.

   I usually end up using the second or third one (Landscape), because my modeling window is usually wider than it is tall.

Figure 12-5:
The Page Setup dialog box on a Mac lets you select a printer, a paper size, and a page orientation.

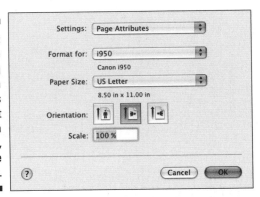

4. **Click OK to close the Page Setup dialog box.**

5. **Choose File⇨Document Setup.**

   The Document Setup dialog box opens.

6. **In the Document Setup dialog box, make sure that the Fit View to Page check box is selected.**

   Check out the next section in this chapter for a full description of what everything does.

7. **Click OK to close the Document Setup dialog box.**

8. **Choose File⇨Print to open the Print dialog box.**

9. **In the Print dialog box, click the Preview button.**

   This generates an onscreen preview of what your print will look like on paper.

10. **If the preview suits you, click the Print button to send your print job to the printer.**

    If you're not happy with the preview, click the Cancel button and start again at Step 1. Isn't printing fun?

Deciphering the Mac printing dialog boxes

Because printing from SketchUp on a Mac involves two separate dialog boxes, I describe both in the following sections.

The Document Setup dialog box

You use the settings in the Document Setup dialog box (see Figure 12-6) to control how big your model prints. Here's what everything does:

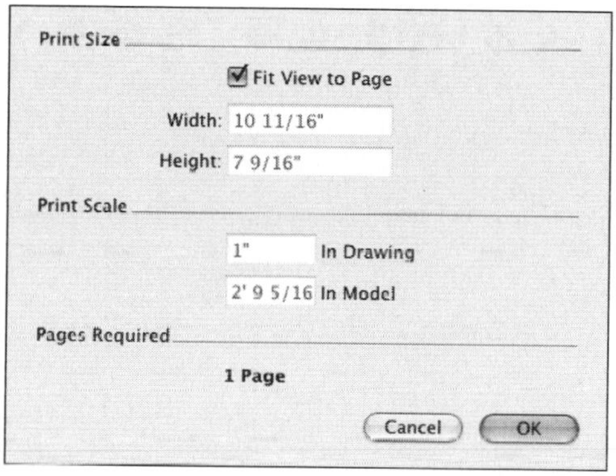

Figure 12-6:
The Mac
Document
Setup dialog
box.

> Print Size
>
> ☑ Fit View to Page
>
> Width: 10 11/16"
>
> Height: 7 9/16"
>
> Print Scale
>
> 1"   In Drawing
>
> 2' 9 5/16 In Model
>
> Pages Required
>
> 1 Page
>
> (Cancel)   (OK)

- ✔ **Print Size:** This one's pretty self-explanatory, but here are some details just in case:

    - *Fit View to Page:* Select this check box to tell SketchUp to make your printed page look just like your modeling window onscreen. It's really that simple.

    - *Width and Height:* If the Fit View to Page check box is deselected, you can type either a width or a height for your final print. This is the way to go if you want to print a tiled poster out of several sheets of paper; just enter a final size, and you'll have a poster in no time flat.

- ✔ **Print Scale:** Use these settings to control the scale of your printed drawing, if that's the kind of print you're trying to make. Because printing to scale is a bit of an ordeal, I devote the last section of this chapter to the topic. See that section for a description of what these settings do.

- ✔ **Pages Required:** This is really just a readout of how many pages you need to print. If you have selected the Fit View to Page check box, this is 1. If your print doesn't fit on one sheet, it's tiled onto the number of sheets displayed in this section of the dialog box.

The Print dialog box

The Print dialog box on the Mac is something of a many-headed beast; several more panels are hidden underneath the Copies & Pages drop-down list. Luckily, you only need to use two. Both are pictured in Figure 12-7 and described in the following list:

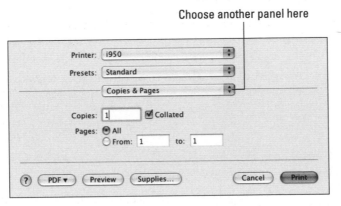

Choose another panel here

This doesn't matter unless you're using Vector Printing

Figure 12-7: The Copies & Pages and SketchUp panels of the Print dialog box.

✔ **Copies & Pages panel:** The controls in this part of the Print dialog box are pretty straightforward; use them to tell SketchUp how many copies and pages you want to print:

• *Copies:* If you're printing more than one copy of a print that includes multiple pages, select the Collated check box to tell SketchUp to print *packets,* which can save you from having to collate them yourself.

• *Pages:* If the Pages Required readout at the bottom of the Document Setup dialog box said that you need more than one sheet to print your image, you can choose to print all or some of those pages right here.

✔ **SketchUp panel:** You use the settings in this panel to control the final appearance of your print:

- *Print Quality:* I usually set this to High, but the results you get depend a lot on your printer model. In general, I avoid Draft or Standard unless I'm just making sure my page will look the way I want it to. If you have time, try both High and Extra High and see which one looks the best.

- *Vector Printing:* When you select this check box, SketchUp sends *vector* (instead of *raster*) information to the printer. Have a look at Chapter 13 for a description of these terms.

The upshot here is that vector printing makes edges look much smoother and cleaner but does a lousy job on *gradients* (the shadows on your curved surfaces). Use vector printing if your model view is made up of mostly flat faces, but try printing both ways (with vector printing on and off) to see which looks better.

If your model view includes a Sketchy Edges style, don't select Vector Printing; you won't see any of the nice, sketchy effects in your final print.

- *Line Weight:* This option works only if you've selected the Vector Printing check box. The number in this box represents the thickness of edges in your print; any edges that are 1-pixel thick in your model view will be drawn with a line as thick as what you choose for this option. The default is 0.50 points, but feel free to experiment to see what looks best for your model.

Printing to a Particular Scale

Here's where printing gets interesting. Sometimes, instead of printing exactly what you see on your screen so that it fits on a sheet of paper, you may need to print a drawing *to scale.* See the nearby sidebar "Wrapping your head around scale" for more information about drawing to scale.

Keep in mind that if you have SketchUp Pro, you can use LayOut to generate scaled views of your model very easily. Take a look at Chapter 14 for more information.

Preparing to print to scale

Before you can print a view of your model to a particular scale, you have to set up things properly. Keep the following points in mind:

- **Perspective views can't be printed to scale.** If you think about it, this makes sense. In perspectival views, all lines appear to "go back" into the distance, which means that they look shorter than they really are. Because the whole point of a scaled drawing is to be able to take accurate measurements directly off your printout, views with perspective don't work.

- **Switch to Parallel Projection if you want to print to scale.** I know, I know — this is the same as the last point. But it's important enough that I figure it's worth mentioning twice. To change your viewing mode from Perspective to Parallel Projection, choose Camera⇨Parallel Projection. That's all there is to it.

- **You have to use the Standard views.** SketchUp lets you quickly look at your model from the top, bottom, and sides by switching to one of the Standard views. Choose Camera⇨Standard and pick any of the views except Iso.

TECHNICAL STUFF

Wrapping your head around scale

When you print to scale, anyone with a special ruler (called a *scale,* confusingly enough) can take measurements from your drawing, as long as he knows the scale at which it was printed. You can use three kinds of drawing scales:

Architectural: In the United States, most people use feet and inches to measure objects. Most architectural scales substitute fractions of an inch for a foot. Three common examples of architectural scales follow:

- ½ inch = 1 foot (1 inch = 2 feet)
- ¼ inch = 1 foot (1 inch = 4 feet)
- ⅛ inch = 1 foot (1 inch = 8 feet)

Engineering: When measuring big things like parcels of land and college campuses, U.S. architects, engineers, and surveyors still use feet, but they use engineering scales instead of architectural ones. Three common engineering scales follow:

- 1 inch = 20 feet
- 1 inch = 50 feet
- 1 inch = 100 feet

Metric: Outside the United States, virtually everyone uses the metric system. Because all measurement is based on the number ten, metric scales can be applied to everything from very small things (blood cells) to very big things (countries). Metric scales use ratios instead of units of measure. Here are three examples:

- 1:10 (The objects in the drawing are 10 times bigger in real life.)
- 1:100 (The objects in the drawing are 100 times bigger in real life.)
- 10:1 (The objects in the drawing are 10 times smaller in real life.)

Printing to scale (Windows and Mac)

The steps in this section allow you to produce a scaled print from SketchUp; I give Windows instructions first and then Mac. When the user-interface elements are different for the two platforms, the ones for Mac are shown in parentheses. Figure 12-8 shows the relevant dialog boxes for printing to scale in Windows and on a Mac.

When printing to scale, don't worry about these numbers

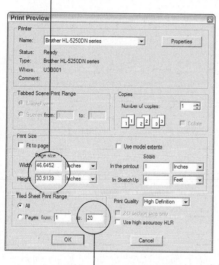
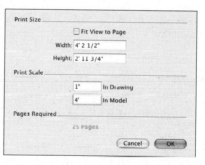

Figure 12-8: Setting up to print at 1 inch = 4 foot (¼ inch = 1 foot) scale.

To print at 1 inch = 4 feet, you'll need 20 pages

Before you begin, make sure that you've switched to Parallel Projection and that your view is lined up the right way. See the preceding section of this chapter for the lowdown on what you need to do to prepare your model view for scaled printing. Follow these steps to produce a scaled print:

1. **Choose File⇒Print Setup (Page Setup).**

2. **Select a printer, paper size, and paper orientation, and then click OK.**

3. **Choose File⇒Print Preview (Document Setup).**

4. **Deselect the Fit to Page (Fit View to Page) check box.**

5. **Windows: Make sure that the Use Model Extents check box is deselected.**

   Mac users don't have this option.

6. **Enter the scale at which you want to print your model view.**

   If you want to print a drawing at ¼-inch scale, enter the following:

   - **1 Inches** into the In the Printout (In Drawing) box
   - **4 Feet** into the In SketchUp (In Model) box

   If you want to produce a print at 1:100 scale, enter the following:

   - **1 m** into the In the Printout (In Drawing) box
   - **100 m** into the In SketchUp (In Model) box

7. **Take note of how may pages you'll need to print your drawing.**

   If you're using Windows, you can check this in the Tiled Sheet Print Range area of the dialog box. On a Mac, the number of pages you'll need appears in the Pages Required section of the Document Setup dialog box. If you want to print on a different-sized piece of paper, change the setting in the Print Setup (Page Setup) dialog box.

8. **If you want to print your drawing on a single sheet and it won't fit, use a smaller scale.**

   Using the ¼ inch = 1 foot example, try shrinking the drawing to 3⁄16 inch = 1 foot scale. To do this, enter the following:

   - **3 Inches** into the In the Printout (In Drawing) box
   - **16 Feet** into the In SketchUp (In Model) box

9. **When you're happy with how your drawing will print, click OK.**

10. **Perform the step based on your computer:**

    - *Windows:* If you like what you see in the Print Preview dialog box, click the Print button (in the upper-left corner) to open the Print dialog box.
    - *Mac:* Choose File➪Print.

11. **In the Print dialog box, click OK to send your print job to the printer.**

See this chapter's "Making a basic print" section (for your operating system) for the whole story on basic printing from SketchUp.

Chapter 13

Exporting Images and Animations

In This Chapter

▶ Creating 2D views of your model as TIFFs, JPEGs, and PNGs

▶ Reading about pixels and resolution

▶ Making sure that you export the right kind of image

▶ Exporting the kind of movie file you need

*W*ant to e-mail a JPEG of your new patio to your parents? How about a movie that shows what it's like to walk out onto that new patio? If you need an image or a movie of your model, forget about viewing or printing within SketchUp. Exporting is the way to go.

SketchUp can export both still images and animations in most of the major graphics and movie formats. Here's the part that's a little bit confusing: Which file formats you can export depend on the version of SketchUp you have. If you have regular ol' Google SketchUp (the free one), you can create *raster* image files and movies. If you've sprung for Google SketchUp Pro, you can also export *vector* files and a whole bunch of 3D formats; I talk about them all in the first online Bonus Chapter for this book. (See the Introduction for details about what's online and where to find it.)

In this chapter, I talk about the export file formats that are common to both versions of Google SketchUp. Just in case you're not familiar with the terms *raster* and *vector,* I give brief definitions of each. Then I go into some detail about the 2D, raster image formats that you can create with SketchUp. I spend the last part of this chapter talking about exporting animations as movie files that anyone can open and view.

Exporting 2D Images of Your Model

Even though the free version of SketchUp can only export 2D views of your model as *raster* images, it's helpful to know a little bit about graphics file formats in general. If you're already an aficionado about these sorts of things, or if you're in a big hurry, you can skip ahead to the section "Exporting a raster image from SketchUp."

If you have SketchUp Pro, you have a much better way to get images out of SketchUp: LayOut. In fact, LayOut may even be able to replace whatever application is the reason you're trying to export an image in the first place. Take a look at Chapter 14 for the whole story.

Pictures on your computer are divided into two basic flavors: *raster* and *vector*. The difference between these two categories of file types has to do with how they store image information. Here's the one-minute version:

✔ **Raster:** Raster images are made up of dots. (Technically, these dots are *pixels,* just like the pixels that make up images you take with a digital camera.) Raster file formats consist of information about the location and color of each dot. When you export a raster, you decide how many dots (pixels) it should include, which directly affects how big it can be displayed. SketchUp exports TIFF, JPEG, and PNG raster images; the Windows version also exports BMPs, although that's nothing to get excited about. You can read more about raster images in the sidebar "Understanding rasters: Lots and lots of dots," later in this chapter.

✔ **Vector:** Vector images consist of instructions written in computer code. This code describes *how* to draw the image to whatever software tries to open it. The major advantage of using vector imagery (as opposed to raster) lies in its *scalability* — vectors can be resized larger or smaller without affecting their image quality, whereas rasters lose quality if you enlarge them too much. The free version of SketchUp can only export raster images, but SketchUp Pro can export vectors in both PDF and EPS file formats; you can read all about it in the online Bonus Chapter 1.

Exporting a raster image from SketchUp

The process of exporting a view of your SketchUp model is fairly straightforward. Depending on which format you choose, the export options are slightly different, but I address them all in this section.

Follow these steps to export a raster image from SketchUp:

1. **Adjust your model view until you see exactly what you want to export as an image file.**

   SketchUp's raster image export is *WYSIWYG* — What You See Is What You Get. Basically, your entire modeling window view is exported as an image, so use the navigation tools or click a scene to set up your view. Use styles, shadows, and fog to make your model look exactly the way you want it to. To change the proportions of your image, resize your SketchUp window. Follow these steps to do so:

   a. *Windows only: If your SketchUp window is full screen, click the Minimize button in its upper-right corner.*

   b. *Drag the Resize tab in the lower-right corner of your SketchUp window until the modeling window is the right proportion.*

   In Figure 13-1, I want to export a wide view of a house I modeled, so I adjust the proportions of my modeling window until things look right.

Figure 13-1:
Adjust your view and your modeling window until things look the way you want them to in your exported image.

SketchUp modeling window

Exported image

You may be wondering whether *everything* in your modeling window shows up in an exported raster image. The red, green, and blue axes don't, which is good, but guides do, which is usually bad. If you don't want your guides to be visible in your exported image, deselect Guides in the View menu.

2. **Choose File➪Export➪2D Graphic.**

   The File Export dialog box opens.

3. **Choose the file format you want to use from the Format drop-down list.**

   Before you choose JPEG by default, know that this file type isn't always the best choice. For a complete description of each format (as well as recommendations for when to choose each), see the section "Looking at SketchUp's raster formats," later in this chapter.

4. **Choose a name and a location on your computer for your exported image.**

5. **Click the Options button.**

   The Export Options dialog box opens, where you can control how your image is exported. Figure 13-2 shows what this dialog box looks like for each of SketchUp's raster file formats.

Figure 13-2: The Export Options dialog boxes for TIFFs, PNGs, and BMPs (left) and JPEGs.

Export Options for TIFFs, PNGs, and BMPs

Export Options for JPEGs

6. **Adjust the settings in the Export Options dialog box.**

   Here's a description of what the settings do:

   • *Use View Size:* Selecting this check box tells SketchUp to export an image file that contains the same number of pixels as are currently being used to display your model onscreen. If you're just planning to use your exported image in an e-mail or in an onscreen presentation (such as PowerPoint), select Use View Size, but it's still better to manually control the pixel size of your exported image. If you plan to print your exported image, don't select this check box — whatever you do.

   • *Width and Height:* When you don't select the Use View Size check box, you can manually enter the size of your exported image. Because this process requires a fair amount of figuring, I've devoted a whole section to it; take a look at "Making sure that you're exporting enough pixels," later in this chapter, to find out what to type into the Width and Height boxes.

- *Anti-Alias:* Because raster images use grids of colored squares to draw pictures, diagonal lines and edges can sometimes look jagged and, well . . . lousy. *Anti-aliasing* fills in the gaps around pixels with similar-colored pixels so that things look smooth. Figure 13-3 illustrates the concept. In general, you want to leave anti-aliasing on.

- *Resolution (Mac only):* This is where you tell SketchUp how big each pixel should be, and therefore how big (in inches or centimeters) your exported image should be. Pixel size is expressed in terms of pixels per inch/centimeter. This option is available only when the Use View Size check box isn't selected. Just as with the Width and Height boxes, I go into a lot of detail about image resolution in "Making sure that you're exporting enough pixels," later in this chapter.

- *Transparent Background (Mac only, not for JPEGs):* Mac users can choose to export TIFFs and PNGs with transparent backgrounds, which can make it easier to "cut out" your model in another piece of software. Exporting your image with a transparent background is also a nice way to use image-editing programs like Photoshop to drop in a sky and ground plane later. If you're a Windows user, the only way to produce images with transparent backgrounds is to use LayOut, which is part of SketchUp Pro. Chapter 14 has all the details.

- *JPEG Compression (JPEG only):* This slider lets you decide two things at the same time: the file size of your exported image and how good the image will look. The two are, of course, inversely related; the farther to the left you move the slider, the smaller your file will be, but the worse it will look. I never set JPEG compression less than 8 — my models take too long to build for me to make them look terrible on export.

No anti-aliasing   With anti-aliasing

Figure 13-3:
A view of
the same
image with
anti-aliasing
off (left)
and on.

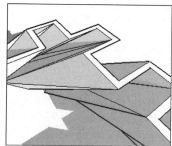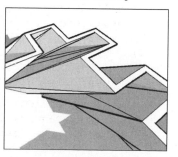

Understanding rasters: Lots and lots of dots

When you look at a photograph on your computer, you're really looking at a whole bunch of tiny dots of color, or *pixels.* These are arranged in a rectangular grid called a *raster.* Digital images that are composed of pixels arranged in a raster grid are *raster images,* or *rasters* for short. Have a look at the first image in the figure below for a close-up view of a raster image. Here are some things to keep in mind about rasters:

✔ **Rasters are everywhere.** Almost every digital image you've ever seen is a raster. TIFF, JPEG, and PNG are three of the most common raster file formats, and SketchUp exports them all.

✔ **Rasters are flexible.** Every two-dimensional image can be displayed as a raster; a grid of colored squares is an incredibly effective way of saving and sharing picture information. As long as you have enough pixels, any image can look good as a raster.

✔ **Rasters take up a lot of space.** If you think about how raster images work, it takes a lot of information to describe a picture. Digital images are made up of anywhere from thousands to millions of pixels, and each pixel can be any one of millions of colors. To store a whole picture, a raster image file needs to include the location and color of *each* pixel; the bigger the picture, the more

pixels it takes to describe it, and the bigger the file size gets.

✔ **Rasters are measured in pixels.** Because every raster image is made up of a specific number of pixels, you use a raster's *pixel dimensions* to describe its size. If I told you that I'd e-mailed you a photograph that was 800 x 600, you could expect to receive a picture that is 800 pixels wide by 600 pixels tall. (See the following figure.) Pixels don't have a physical size on their own — they're just dots of color. You determine a picture's physical size by deciding how big its pixels should be; this is referred to as *resolution,* and is generally expressed in terms of *pixels per inch* (ppi). Check out the section "Making sure that you're exporting enough pixels," later in this chapter, for the whole scoop.

Why use pixels instead of inches or centimeters to describe the size of a digital image? It all has to do with how computer screens work. Because not all screens display things at the same size, it's impossible to predict how *big* an image will look when it shows up on someone's computer. Depending on the person's display settings, an 800-x-600-pixel image may be a few inches across, or it may take up the whole screen. Giving a digital image's dimensions in pixels is the only accurate way of describing how "big" it is.

Individual pixels

600 pixels

800 pixels

7. **Click OK to close the Export Options dialog box.**

8. **Back in the File Export dialog box, click the Export button to export your raster image file.**

   You can find your exported file in whatever location on your computer you specified in Step 4. What you do with it is entirely up to you — you can e-mail it, print it, or use it in another software program to create a presentation.

   Don't be alarmed if the export process takes longer than you think it should. If you export a pretty big image (one with lots and lots of pixels), the export takes a while. Take the opportunity to call your mother — she'll appreciate it.

Looking at SketchUp's raster formats

So you know you need to export a raster image from SketchUp, but which one do you choose? You have four choices in Windows; three of them are available on the Mac. The following sections give you the details.

When you export a raster image, you're saving your current view in SketchUp to a separate file somewhere on your computer. As a raster image, that file consists of tiny, colored dots, or *pixels* — more pixels than you can shake a stick at. When you look at all the pixels together, they form an image.

Tagged Image File (TIFF or TIF)

TIFFs are the stalwarts of the raster image file format world; everyone can read them and just about everyone can create them. *TIFF* stands for Tagged Image File Format, but that's hardly important. Here's everything you need to know about TIFFs:

- ✔ **When image quality is important, choose TIFF.** Unless file size is a concern (because, for example, you need to send an image by e-mail), always export a TIFF if you need a raster image. For everything from working in Photoshop to creating a layout in InDesign or QuarkXPress, a TIFF can provide the image quality you need.

- ✔ **TIFFs don't compress your image data.** That means they don't introduce any garbage like JPEGs do, but it also means that they're really big files.

- ✔ **Pay attention to your pixel count.** If you're exporting a TIFF, you're probably looking for the best image quality you can get. And if that's the case, you need to make sure that your TIFF is "big" enough — that it includes enough pixels — to display at the size you need. Have a look at "Making sure that you're exporting enough pixels," later in this chapter, for more information.

Joint Photographic Experts Group (JPEG or JPG)

JPEG stands for Joint Photographic Experts Group, which makes it sound much fancier than it really is. Almost every digital image you've ever seen was a JPEG (pronounced *JAY-peg*); it's the standard file format for images on the Web. Check out these JPEG details:

- ✔ **When file size is a concern, choose JPEG.** The whole point of the JPEG file format is to compress raster images to manageable file sizes so that they can be e-mailed and put on Web sites. A JPEG is a fraction of the size of a TIFF file with the same number of pixels, so JPEG is a great choice if file size is more important to you than image quality.

- ✔ **JPEGs compress file size by degrading image quality.** This is known as *lossy* compression; JPEG technology basically works by tossing out a lot of the pixels in your image. JPEGs also introduce a fair amount of pixel garbage; these smudges are *artifacts,* and they're awful.

- ✔ **JPEG + SketchUp = Danger.** Because of the way the JPEG file format works, JPEG exports from SketchUp are particularly susceptible to looking terrible. Images from SketchUp usually include straight lines and broad areas of color, both of which JPEG has a hard time handling. If you're going to export a JPEG from SketchUp, make sure that the JPEG Compression slider is *never* set less than 8. For more details, see the section "Exporting a raster image from SketchUp," earlier in this chapter.

Portable Network Graphics (PNG)

Hooray for PNG! Pronounced *ping,* this graphics file format is my hero. Unfortunately, it isn't as widely used as it should be. If I had my druthers (I keep leaving them on the subway), every raster export from SketchUp would be a PNG. Why? Because, at least as far as SketchUp is concerned, PNG combines all the best features of TIFF and JPEG. Why don't more people use PNGs? Because standards are hard to change, and right now, it's a JPEG world. PNG details are as follows:

- ✔ **PNGs compress image data *without* affecting image quality.** As a *lossless* compression technology, PNGs are smaller files than TIFFs (just like JPEGs), but they don't mess up any pixels (totally unlike JPEGs). Granted, PNGs aren't as small as JPEGs, but I think the difference in image quality is worth a few extra bits.

- ✔ **If you're exporting an image for someone who knows a thing or two about computers, choose PNG.** The truth is, some software doesn't know what to do with a PNG, so there's a risk in using it. If you plan to send your exported image to someone who knows what he's doing, go ahead and send a PNG — he'll be impressed that you're "in the know." If the recipient of your export is less technologically sophisticated, stick with a JPEG or TIFF file; it's the safe choice.

The PNG file format wasn't developed to replace JPEG or TIFF; it was supposed to stand in for *GIF* (Graphics Interchange Format), which is a file type that SketchUp doesn't export. Without going into too much detail, folks use JPEG for images like photographs and GIF for things like logos. Because exported SketchUp views usually have more in common with the latter, PNG (the replacement for GIF) is the better choice. So why can't PNG replace JPEG and TIFF? For most photographs (which are the majority of images on the Web), JPEG is better than PNG because it produces smaller files, which in turn yields faster load times when you're surfing the Internet. TIFF is more versatile than PNG because it supports different *color spaces,* which are important to people in the printing industry. For reasons that are beyond the scope of this book, that isn't relevant to exports from SketchUp; PNG is still (in my opinion) the best — if not the safest — choice.

Windows Bitmap (BMP)

Windows Bitmap, or BMP, files are old school; they can only be used on Windows, and they're big. If a BMP were a car, it would be the old, rusty van in your parents' garage. As you can probably guess, I don't recommend using BMPs for anything, with a couple exceptions:

- **To send your exported file to someone with a very old Windows computer:** If the person to whom you're sending an exported image has a Windows computer that's more than about eight years old, I suppose I'd send him a BMP.

- **To place an image in an old Windows version of layout software:** If your layout person is using a copy of Word or PageMaker that's a several years old, he may need a BMP file.

Making sure that you're exporting enough pixels

With raster images, it's all about pixels. The more pixels your image has, the more detailed it is, and the bigger it can be displayed or printed. Figure 13-4 shows the same image three times. The first image is 150 x 50, meaning that it's 150 pixels wide by 50 pixels high. The second image is 300 x 100, and the third is 900 x 300. Notice how the image with more pixels looks a lot better? That's the whole point of this section.

Why not always export a truckload of pixels, just in case you need them? There are two reasons:

- Image exports with lots of pixels take a long time to process.
- Raster images are very big files.

150 x 50 pixels

300 x 100 pixels

Figure 13-4:
More pix-
els yield a
much more
detailed
image.

900 x 300 pixels

How many pixels you need to export depends on what you're going to use the image *for*. Very broadly, you can do two things with your image:

✔ Display or project it on a screen, digitally

✔ Print it

In the next two sections, I talk about each of these possibilities in detail.

Exporting enough pixels for a digital presentation

If you plan to use your exported image as part of an onscreen presentation, it's helpful to know what computer monitors and digital projectors can display:

✔ The smallest, oldest devices currently in use have images that are 800 pixels wide by 600 pixels high.

✔ At the other end of the spectrum, high-end, 30-inch LCD monitors display 2560 x 1600 pixels.

So it stands to reason that if you're exporting an image that will be viewed only onscreen, you need to create an image that's somewhere between 800 and 2500 pixels wide. Table 13-1 provides some guidelines on image sizes for different digital applications.

Table 13-1	Suggested Image Sizes for Onscreen Use
How the Image Will Be Used	*Image Width (Pixels)*
E-mail	400 to 800
Web site, large image	600
Web site, small image	200
PowerPoint presentation (full screen)	800 or 1024 (depends on projector)
PowerPoint presentation (floating image)	400

Understanding resolution: Exporting images for print

Images that you want to print need to have lots more pixels than ones that are only going to display onscreen. That's because printers — inkjet, laser, and offset — all operate very differently than computer monitors and digital projectors. When you print something, the pixels in your image turn into microscopic specks of ink or toner, and these specks are smaller than the pixels on your computer screen. To make a decent-sized print of your exported image, it needs to contain enough *pixels per inch* of image. An image's pixel density, expressed in pixels per inch (ppi), is its *resolution*. What kind of resolution you need depends on three things:

- ✔ **The kind of device you print to:** For home inkjet printers, you can get away with a resolution of as little as 150 ppi. If your image will be appearing in a commercially produced book, you need a resolution of at least 300 ppi.

- ✔ **How far away the image will be from the audience:** There's a big difference between a magazine page and a trade-show banner. For close-up applications, a resolution of 200 to 300 ppi is appropriate. Large graphics that will be viewed from several feet away can be as low as 60 ppi.

- ✔ **The subject matter of the image:** Photographic images tend to consist of areas of color that blur together a bit; these kinds of images can tolerate being printed at lower resolutions than drawings with lots of intricate detail. For images with lots of lines like SketchUp models, it's best to work with very high resolutions — 300 to 600 ppi — especially if the image will be viewed close-up.

Table 13-2 provides some guidelines for exporting images that will be printed.

Table 13-2 **Recommended Resolutions for Prints**

How the Image Will Be Used	Image Resolution (Pixels/Inch)	Image Resolution (Pixels/Centimeter)
8.5-x-11 or 11-x-17 inkjet or laser print	200 to 300	80 to 120
Color brochure or pamphlet	300	120
Magazine or book (color and shadows)	300	120
Magazine or book (linework only)	450 to 600	180 to 240
Presentation board	150 to 200	60 to 80
Banner	60 to 100	24 to 40

Keep in mind that the biggest raster image that SketchUp can export is 10000 pixels wide or tall (whichever is greater). This means that the largest banner image, printed at 100 ppi, that SketchUp can create is about 100 inches wide. To make larger images, you need to export a *vector* file; check out the details on exporting to vector formats with SketchUp Pro in Bonus Chapter 1, online.

Follow these steps to make sure that you export enough pixels to print your image properly:

1. **In the Export Options dialog box, make sure that the Use View Size check box is deselected.**

   To get to the Export Options dialog box, follow Steps 1–6 in the section "Exporting a raster image from SketchUp," earlier in this chapter.

2. **Decide on the resolution that you need for your exported image. (See Table 13-2.)**

   Keep the resolution in your head or scribble it on a piece of paper.

3. **Decide how big your exported image will be printed, in inches or centimeters.**

   Note your desired physical image size, just like you did with the resolution in the preceding step.

4. **Multiply your resolution from Step 2 by your image size from Step 3 to get the number of pixels you need to export:**

   Resolution (pixels/in or cm) × Size (in or cm) = Number of pixels

In other words, if you know what resolution you need to export, and you know how big your image will be printed, you can multiply the two numbers to get the number of pixels you need. Here's an example: 300 pixels/inch × 8 inches wide = 2400 pixels wide.

To export an image that can be printed 8 inches wide at 300 ppi, you need to export an image that's 2400 pixels wide. Figure 13-5 gives an illustration of this example.

SketchUp's default setting is to make your exported image match the proportions of your modeling window; that is, you can type only a width *or* a height, but not both. If you're on a Mac, you can manually enter both dimensions by clicking Unlink (which looks like a chain). You can always click it again to relink the width and height dimensions later.

8 inches wide x 300 ppi = 2400 pixels

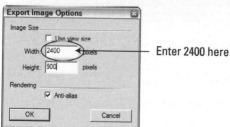

Figure 13-5:
To figure out how many pixels you need to export, multiply the resolution by the physical size.

Enter 2400 here

5. Type the width *or* height of the image you want to export, in pixels.

It's usually pretty hard to know *exactly* how big your image will be when it's printed, and even if you do, you probably want to leave some room for cropping. For these reasons, I always add 15–25 percent to the number of pixels I figure I'll need. If my image calls for 2400 pixels, I export 3000 pixels, just to be safe.

If you're on a Mac, things are a little easier because SketchUp's designers built a pixel calculator into the Export Options dialog box. Just enter your desired resolution in the appropriate spot, change the Width and Height units from pixels to inches or centimeters, and type your desired image size. SketchUp does the arithmetic for you.

6. **Click OK to close the Export Options dialog box.**

Making Movies with Animation Export

When it comes to having nerdy fun, I think exporting movie animations of your SketchUp models is right up there with iPods and store-bought fireworks. Like both these things, what's so great about animation export is how *easy* it is to do. That's not to say that animation and digital video are simple topics — they're not. It'd take a freight elevator to move the books that have been written about working with video on the computer, but I'm going to keep it simple. Because you and I are primarily interested in 3D modeling, what you find in the following sections are instructions for doing what you need to do.

Getting ready for prime time

The key to exporting animations of your SketchUp models is using scenes; if you haven't read it already, now's the time to check out Chapter 10. *Scenes* are saved views of your model that you can arrange in any order you want. When you export an animation, SketchUp strings together the scenes in your model to create a movie file that can be played on just about any computer made in the last several years.

Follow these steps to get your model ready to export as an animation:

1. **Create scenes to build the "skeleton" of your animation.**

2. **To adjust the animation settings in the Model Info dialog box, choose Window⇨Model Info and then select the Animation panel.**

   I explain all the controls in the section about moving from scene to scene in Chapter 10.

3. **Select the Enable Scene Transitions check box to tell SketchUp to move smoothly from one scene to the next.**

4. **Enter a transition time to tell SketchUp how long to spend moving between scenes.**

   If your Scene Delay is 0 (below), you can multiply your transition time by your number of scenes to figure out how long your exported animation will be.

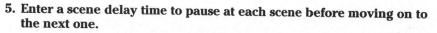

5. **Enter a scene delay time to pause at each scene before moving on to the next one.**

   If you plan to talk about each scene, use the scene delay time to pause before each one. If your animation is supposed to be a smooth walk-through or flyover, set this to 0.

6. **Adjust the proportions of your modeling window to approximate the proportions of your movie.**

   Unlike SketchUp's 2D export formats, the proportions of your exported movie don't depend on those of your modeling window; that is to say, making your modeling window long and skinny won't result in a long and skinny movie. You choose how many pixels wide and tall you want your movie to be, so to get an idea of how much you'll be able to see, make your modeling window match the proportions of your exported file (4:3 is common for video formats). Have a look at Step 1 in the section "Exporting a raster image from SketchUp," earlier in this chapter, for guidance on adjusting your modeling window.

7. **When your project is ready to go, move on to the next section to export your animation.**

Exporting a movie

Fortunately, you have only one choice if you want to export a movie from SketchUp. If you're using Windows, create an AVI file; Mac users create QuickTime MOVs.

If you're paying close attention to the available file formats for exporting movies, you'll probably notice three more choices in the drop-down list: TIF, JPG, and PNG. I don't go into detail about these formats for animation (movie) export in SketchUp because you probably won't need them; choosing to export in any of these formats will give you a pile of image files that each represent one frame in your animation. People who want to include their SketchUp animation in a Flash file should take advantage of this option, but explaining how to do so is beyond the scope of this book.

Although exporting animations in SketchUp is a pretty simple operation, figuring out how to set all the animation export controls can seem like landing the space shuttle. What follows are step-by-step instructions for generating a movie file; settings recommendations are in the next section.

Follow these steps to export a movie file from SketchUp:

1. **Prepare your model for export as an animation.**

   See the section "Getting ready for prime time," earlier in this chapter, for a list of things you need to do before you export an animation.

2. **Choose File⇨Export⇨Animation.**

   The Animation Export dialog box opens.

3. **Give your movie file a name and then choose where it should be saved on your computer system.**

4. **Make sure that the correct file format is selected.**

   In the Format drop-down list, choose AVI if you're using Windows and QuickTime if you're on a Mac.

5. **Click the Options button to open the Animation Export Options dialog box. (See Figure 13-6.)**

6. **Adjust the settings for the type of animation you want to export.**

   How you set up everything in this dialog box depends on how you plan to use the animation you create. Check out the next section in this chapter for recommended settings for different applications.

   If you're working on a Mac, there's an extra drop-down list that you may find helpful: Format includes a short list of uses for your animation. Choosing one automatically sets most of the controls for you, though (as you see in the next section) you can improve things a bit by making some of your own selections.

7. **Select the Anti-Alias check box, if it isn't already selected.**

   Choosing this doubles the amount of time it takes for your animation to export, but it makes your edges look much better in the final movie.

8. **Click the button next to Codec (Windows) or the Expert button (Mac).**

   This opens the Video Compression (Compression Settings on a Mac) dialog box. (See Figure 13-7.) Choose the correct settings for the type of animation you want to export, again referring to the next section of this chapter for details about what the options mean.

Figure 13-6:
The Windows (left) and Mac versions of the Animation Export Options dialog box.

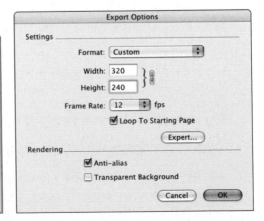

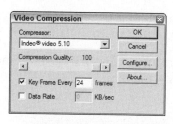

Figure 13-7:
The Video
Comp-
ression
dialog
box for
Windows
(top)
and Mac
(bottom).

9. **Click OK in the Compression dialog box and then click OK again in the Export Options dialog box.**

   You return to the Animation Export dialog box.

10. **Check to make sure that everything looks right and then click the Export button.**

    Because exporting an animation takes awhile, it pays to double-check your settings before you click the Export button. When the export is complete, you can find your animation file in the location you specified in Step 3. Double-clicking it causes it to open in whatever movie-playing software you have that can read it. On Windows computers, this is usually Windows Media Player; on Macs, it's QuickTime.

Figuring out the Animation Export options settings

As I say earlier, digital video is complicated. Lucky for you, you don't really have to know what everything means to export the right kind of movie; you just have to know how to set up everything.

What follows are a number of different things you may want to do with your animation, and recommended settings for getting good results. Feel free to experiment, but the following sections are a good place to start.

For sending an animation in an e-mail

If you're going to e-mail someone an animation file, you have to make the file as small as you can. These settings can help you do just that:

Width and Height	160 x 120
Frame Rate	10 frames per second (fps)
Codec (Windows)	Indeo Video 5.10
Compression Type (Mac)	H.264
Key Frame Every	24 frames
Compression Quality (Windows)	50
Quality (Mac)	Medium

For uploading an animation to YouTube

YouTube (www.youtube.com) is a video-sharing site that can host your animations for free. After your video is on YouTube, you can link to your video and even embed it on your own Web pages. You need to keep two things in mind when you create a video for YouTube: Videos need to be less than 1GB in file size, and they need to be less than 15 minutes in length. These settings yield a YouTubeable video:

Width and Height	1280 x 720
Frame Rate	30 fps
Codec (Windows)	Indeo Video 5.10
Compression Type (Mac)	H.264
Key Frame Every	24 frames
Compression Quality (Windows)	50
Quality (Mac)	Medium

For viewing an animation onscreen (computer or projector)

If you plan to use your animation as part of an onscreen presentation (such as with PowerPoint or Keynote), you probably want it to look good full-screen. You'll probably be using a digital projector to present, and these days, most digital projectors come in two resolutions: 800 x 600 and 1024 x 768. If you know the resolution of the projector you'll be using, you're made in the shade. If you're unsure, export at the lower pixel count, just to be safe:

Width and Height	800 x 600 or 1024 x 768
Frame Rate	15 fps
Codec (Windows)	Indeo Video 5.10
Compression Type (Mac)	H.264
Key Frame Every	24 frames
Compression Quality (Windows)	100
Quality (Mac)	Best

You want your exported animations to look smooth — the transitions from one frame to the next shouldn't be jumpy or awkward. If your camera covers a lot of ground (in other words, moves a large distance between scenes) in a very short time, you may want to experiment with increasing your frame rate to keep the movement smooth. Doing so adds more frames between transitions, which means the camera doesn't travel as far between frames.

For exporting to DV (for viewing on a TV with a DVD player)

If you need to export an animation that will be burned onto a DVD that will (in turn) be played in a DVD player, go all-in on quality and file size by using the DV format. The export process takes a long time, but you'll get the best-looking movie you can get. Try these settings first:

Width and Height	720 x 480
Frame Rate	29.97 fps
Codec (Windows)	Full Frame
Compression Type (Mac)	DV/DVCPRO
Compression Quality (Windows)	100
Quality (Mac)	Best
Scan Mode (Mac)	Interlaced

Chapter 14

Creating Presentation Documents with LayOut

In This Chapter

▶ Discovering LayOut's purpose

▶ Figuring out the tools and panels

▶ Building a simple presentation document from scratch

▶ Printing and exporting your work

*P*eople who design things in 3D have to present their ideas to other people, and most of the time, they have to present in a 2D format. Creating these presentations almost always involves the use of layout or illustration software like InDesign, Illustrator, or QuarkXPress — great programs but expensive and tricky to figure out, especially if you're not a graphic designer.

If you're lucky enough to have the Pro version of Google SketchUp 8, you have access to a whole separate piece of software — LayOut.

LayOut enables you to create documents for presenting your 3D SketchUp models, both on paper and onscreen. LayOut was designed to be easy to use, quick to learn, and tightly integrated with SketchUp. The people who built it want you to use LayOut to create all your design presentations; here are examples of what you can make:

✔ Design packs, presentation boards, and posters

✔ Simple construction drawings with scaled views and dimensions

✔ Vector illustrations and diagrams

✔ Storyboards for planning camera shots

LayOut gives you the tools to create cover pages, title blocks, callouts, and symbols — whatever needs to accompany views of your model. You can create presentations that are just about any physical size and export them as PDF files or images to send to other people. Best of all, when your design changes in SketchUp, you can easily update your model views in LayOut to reflect the changes. If you make your living designing and presenting ideas in 3D, LayOut can save you boatloads of time.

In this chapter, I give a pretty high-level overview of what you can do with LayOut. I start with a quick tour of the LayOut user interface, explaining where everything is and what it's supposed to do. Next, I take you through the process of creating a simple presentation drawing set from one of your SketchUp models — not exhaustively by any means, but it should be enough to see you through a tight deadline. Chapter 15 is dedicated to exploring LayOut in more detail — jump ahead if you're dying to know something specific.

Getting Your Bearings

Even though LayOut comes with SketchUp Pro, it's not just a SketchUp feature — LayOut is a full-fledged, gets-its-own-icon program. As such, LayOut has its own menus, tools, dialog boxes, and drawing window. A couple of versions from now, LayOut will probably have its own *For Dummies* book. (Maybe I'll even get to write it!)

Even though LayOut's user interface is pretty standard, I want to give you a quick overview of the different elements. Knowing that it's a lot like other software you've used (including SketchUp) should help you come up to speed quickly. Figure 14-1 shows the LayOut user interface. The following sections explain the various parts in more detail.

Some menu bar minutiae

Just like almost every other piece of software in the universe, LayOut has a menu bar. And just like SketchUp, you can use LayOut's menu bar to access the vast majority of its tools, commands, settings, and dialog boxes. Instead of boring you with a bunch of stuff you almost certainly already know, I skip ahead to the especially useful items:

✔ **Preferences:** You find LayOut's application-wide Preferences dialog box on the Edit menu on Windows computers, and on the LayOut menu on Macs. Preferences is where you do things like assign custom keyboard shortcuts and create new drawing scales. (Personally, I'm a big fan of ³⁄₁₆.)

✔ **Document Setup:** Located on the File menu, this is LayOut's version of SketchUp's Model Info dialog box; it's jam-packed with settings you use all the time:

- *Grid:* Not only can LayOut display a helpful grid on your pages, it also lets you control the size and color of the gridlines or points. You can also choose to display the grid *above* your drawing elements, which some people really appreciate.

- *Paper:* Right below the boring settings for paper size and margin width lies one of the most important controls in LayOut: Rendering Resolution. Both Edit Quality and Output quality are set to Medium by default, but you want to adjust them for almost every file you work on. Curiosity piqued? Head on over to Chapter 15.

- *References:* When you insert a SketchUp model or an image in your LayOut document, LayOut creates a file reference that keeps track of where it came from.

    If you edit the original file (which you probably will), this panel lets you know whether LayOut shows the most currently saved version. For people who go back and forth between design and presentation documents a lot (sound familiar?), the References panel is a gift from the heavens.

✔ **Snap settings:** These help you position elements on your page by making it easier to line up things with a grid or with other elements. Depending on what you want to do, you may choose to work with both kinds of snap settings, just one, or none at all. I switch between Object Snap and Grid Snap while I work; I rarely use both at the same time. The snap settings are at the bottom of the Arrange menu.

In both the Windows and Mac versions of LayOut, you can have more than one document open at a time. On the Mac, separate files look just like they do for other programs; they're all in different windows. LayOut on Windows is a little different, though: Your open files display as tabs across the top of your drawing window, a little bit like scenes in SketchUp. The tabbed files confuse some people who think that the tabs represent pages. Now you know — they don't.

Menu bar

Toolbar

File tabs (Windows)   Drawing window

Panels

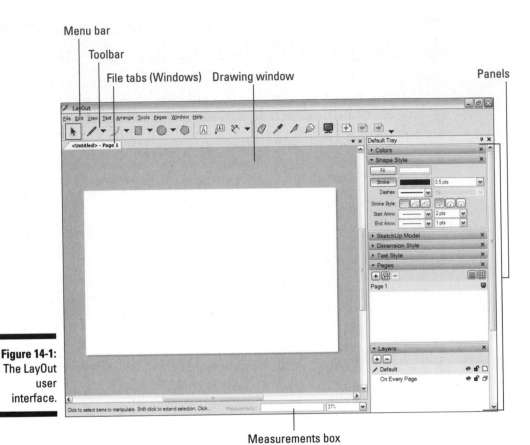

Figure 14-1:
The LayOut
user
interface.

Measurements box

Perusing LayOut's panels

You can find most of LayOut's knobs and switches in its nine panels. In Windows, most of these are contained in a "tray" that appears on the right side of your screen by default.

On the Mac, your panels float around willy-nilly, but you can snap them together if you want. Choosing Window⇨Arrange Panels tidies up things when everything's everywhere and you can't find anything. Don't you wish your house had something similar?

Switching to LayOut from similar software

If you're used to using other page-layout or illustration software, some things about LayOut are useful to know when you're just getting started. The folks who designed LayOut did things a little differently on purpose, hoping to do for page layout in 2007 what they did for 3D design seven years earlier — make it easier for motivated people with no experience to produce good work, quickly.

Here, I point out the five things to keep in mind when you explore LayOut:

✔ LayOut includes templates that help you get up and running in no time. See the nearby section "Starting with a template" for details.

✔ You can insert models from SketchUp, skipping the process of exporting your model as an image file. Importing has the added benefit of helping you automatically update model views in your presentation.

✔ The Layers feature in LayOut is a powerful tool for organizing your content. In particular, you can place content that appears on more than one of your pages on a shared layer, so you have to position the content only once.

✔ In LayOut, you have enormous flexibility to crop images, including model views, with ease using clipping masks. Find out how in Chapter 15.

✔ When your presentation is ready to go, LayOut enables you to set up digital slide shows in full-screen mode, as well as to create printouts and PDF files that you can e-mail to clients.

Here's a one-minute description of each panel:

✔ **Colors:** Just about all your LayOut documents use color in some way, so you need this dialog box most of the time. The nice thing about the Colors panel is that clicking any color well in LayOut pops it open (if it wasn't open already).

To hide a dialog box without closing it, click its title bar once to minimize it. Click again to see the whole thing.

✔ **Shape Style:** A lot of the graphic elements in your presentation can have color fills and strokes (outlines). The Shape Style panel is where you control the appearance of those fills and strokes. Check out the options in the Start and End drop-down lists — you won't find callout styles like these in most other layout programs.

✔ **SketchUp Model:** The greatest thing about LayOut (at least with respect to other software like it) is its ability to include 2D views of your SketchUp models. In the SketchUp Model panel, you can control all sorts of things about the way your placed SketchUp model looks, including camera views, scenes, styles, shadows, scale, and fog. For folks who spend a lot of time laying out presentation drawings that include SketchUp models, the SketchUp Model panel is a godsend.

✔ **Dimension Style:** LayOut in SketchUp 8 lets you draw both linear and angular dimensions. This panel is where you control what they look like. For more information, take a look at Chapter 15.

✔ **Text Style:** You should be pretty familiar with what the Text Style panel lets you do; you use it to control the font, size, style, color, and alignment of text in your document.

✔ **Pages:** You can add, delete, duplicate, and rearrange the pages in your document to your heart's content. The List and Icon buttons at the top let you toggle between views of your pages; I prefer to use the former and give my pages meaningful names as I work. The little icons on the right control visibility for full-screen presentations.

✔ **Layers:** You can have multiple layers of content in every LayOut document you create.

Use the Layers panel to add, delete, and rearrange layers in your document. The icons on the right let you hide (and show), lock, and share individual layers.

Shared layers let you automatically place elements on more than one page. For more detail, see Chapter 15.

✔ **Scrapbooks:** This one's a little trickier to explain; scrapbooks are unique to LayOut, so you probably haven't worked with anything like them before. *Scrapbooks* are LayOut files that live in a special folder on your computer system. They contain colors, text styles, and graphic elements, such as scale cars, trees, and people that you may use in more than one LayOut document. To use something in a scrapbook, just click it with the Select tool and then click again in your drawing window to stamp it in. You can also sample things like colors, line weights, and text styles by clicking with any other tool.

✔ **Instructor:** The Instructor panel works just like it does in SketchUp; it shows information on whichever tool you happen to be using. If you're just starting with LayOut, make sure that this panel is open.

Building a Quick LayOut Document

Pretend you have a major deadline looming, and you've flipped to this page because you need to turn your SketchUp model into a set of drawings. There's no time for the nitty-gritty — you need model views, page titles, basic dimensions, some annotations, and maybe a logo.

You've come to the right place. In the following sections, I walk you through putting together a bare-bones LayOut document that includes all the elements I list in the preceding paragraph. Take a deep breath, put a fresh battery in your mouse, and follow me . . .

Starting with a template

In my experience, templates are the quickest way to get up and running with a new LayOut project. Follow these steps to load a LayOut template and customize it for your own purposes:

1. **Launch LayOut.**

   Keep in mind that LayOut and SketchUp are separate software programs, so you need to launch them individually. If you've already launched LayOut, choose File⇨New to open the Getting Started dialog box. (See Figure 14-2.) If you don't see it, you can switch it on in the Startup panel of the Preferences dialog box.

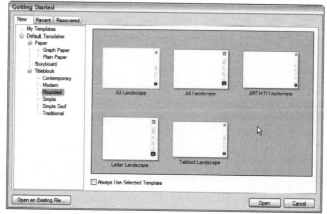

Figure 14-2: The Getting Started dialog box.

2. **In the Getting Started dialog box, click the New tab.**

   This shows a list of available templates on the left, with thumbnail previews of each template on the right. Nothing about these templates is special — they're just ready-made LayOut files you can use as a starting point for your document.

3. Choose a template to use.

Expand the items in the list on the left to see the available templates by category. Browse the list, select one you want to use, and click the Open (Choose on a Mac) button to work with that template.

If you change your mind about the template you picked, close the file you just created and choose File⇨New to pick another one.

4. Unlock all your new document's layers.

Many templates that come with LayOut have multiple layers, and some layers are locked by default so that you can't accidentally move things. In this case, you want to unlock them all so you can customize the template with your own information.

In the Layers panel, unlock all the locked layers by clicking their little lock icons one at a time. Figure 14-3 shows the Layers panel, among other things.

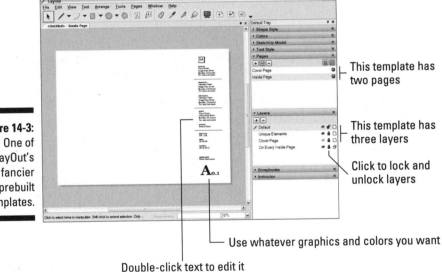

Figure 14-3: One of LayOut's fancier prebuilt templates.

This template has two pages

This template has three layers

Click to lock and unlock layers

Use whatever graphics and colors you want

Double-click text to edit it

5. Edit the default text on the page.

With the Select tool, double-click text to edit it. Click somewhere else on the page to stop editing.

Roll your scroll wheel to zoom in and out on the page, just like in SketchUp. Hold down the scroll wheel button to pan around. To fill your drawing window with the page you're viewing, choose Scale to Fit (Zoom to Fit on the Mac) from the Zoom drop-down list in your window's lower-right corner.

6. **Edit the default text on all your other pages.**

   Most of the more interesting templates include at least two pages; many templates open on the second page. Use the Pages panel to switch between pages in your document. Repeat Step 5 for any default text that needs to change.

7. **(Optional) Change colors and line styles.**

   You can edit lines and other graphic entities you select in the Shape Style panel. Clicking a color well opens the Colors panel. To change the color of text, select it and click the color well in the Text Style panel (Fonts panel on a Mac).

   Sometimes the entity you're trying to edit is buried inside a group. Double-click a group to edit it. Sound familiar? SketchUp and LayOut are, after all, siblings.

8. **Swap out the generic logo for your own.**

   Delete the generic logo wherever it appears in your document by selecting it and hitting Delete on your keyboard. Follow these steps to bring in a logo of your own:

   a. *Make sure you're not on your document's cover page.*

   b. *In the Layers panel, click the On Every Inside Page layer to make it the active one and then choose File⇨Insert.*

   c. *Find the logo image you want to use and click the Open button.*

   d. *Activate the Select tool; then resize your logo by dragging its blue corner grips and pressing down the Shift key to keep from stretching your logo while you resize it.*

   e. *Click and drag your logo to put it where you want on the page and then choose Edit⇨Copy to copy your logo to the clipboard.*

   f. *Switch to your document's cover page and make the Cover Page layer active by clicking its name in the Layers panel.*

   g. *Choose Edit⇨Paste to paste your logo on the page.*

   h. *Repeat Steps d and e to place your logo where you want it, and then make the Default layer the active one before you forget.*

Inserting SketchUp model views

With every other page-layout program in the universe, the only way to include a view of a SketchUp model is to export that view from SketchUp as an image file and then place it in the layout program. Changing the SketchUp file means going through the whole export-and-place process again, and if your presentation includes lots of SketchUp model views, it can take hours.

This brings me to LayOut's *raison d'être:* Instead of exporting views from SketchUp to get them into LayOut, all you do is insert a SketchUp file. From within LayOut, you can pick the view you like best. You can also use as many views of the same model as you want. When your SketchUp file is modified, LayOut knows about it and (using the References panel in the Document Setup dialog box) lets you update all your views at once by clicking a single button.

Follow these steps to insert a SketchUp *viewport* (model view) into your document:

1. **In SketchUp, create a scene for each view of your model that you want to show in your LayOut document (see Figure 14-4).**

   Take a look at Chapter 10 for a refresher on using scenes. Be sure to give them meaningful names, and remember to save your SketchUp file when you're done.

Figure 14-4: To save time, save a scene in SketchUp for every view you want to include in your LayOut document.

2. **In LayOut, navigate to the page where you want to insert a viewport.**

   Use the Pages panel to move between existing pages. The quickest way to add a new page is to duplicate an existing one: Just click the Duplicate Selected Page button (between Add and Delete) in the Pages panel.

3. **Insert a SketchUp model viewport:**

   a. *Choose File⇨Insert to open the Insert dialog box.*

   b. *Find the SketchUp file on your computer that you want to insert and click the Open button.*

   The Insert dialog box closes, and your SketchUp model is placed on your current LayOut document page.

4. Associate a scene with your model viewport (see Figure 14-5).

With the Select tool, right-click your viewport and choose Scenes, and then choose the name of the scene you want to associate.

If you don't see a list of scenes, you probably forgot to save your SketchUp file in Step 1. Save your SketchUp file; then right-click your viewport (in LayOut) and choose Update Reference.

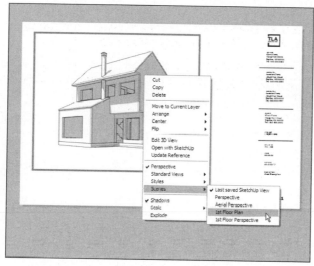

Figure 14-5:
Associate
a scene
from your
model with
a viewport
in LayOut.

5. Assign a drawing scale to your model view, if that's appropriate (see Figure 14-6).

If the scene you picked in Step 4 is an *orthographic* view (top, front, side) where perspective is turned off, it's very likely that you want to show your model at a particular drawing scale. With Select, right-click your viewport, choose Scale, and then choose one from the list that appears.

LayOut doesn't prevent you from assigning a scale to any old view, but that doesn't matter. Drawing scales apply only to nonperspectival, straight-on views of your model. If your view isn't orthographic, it isn't at scale.

If a bright yellow exclamation mark icon appears in the lower-right corner of a viewport, you need to tell LayOut to render that viewport in order for it to reflect whatever changes you've made to it. Right-click the viewport and choose Render Model from the context menu, and you're good to go. See Chapter 15 for a complete discussion of viewport rendering methods and options.

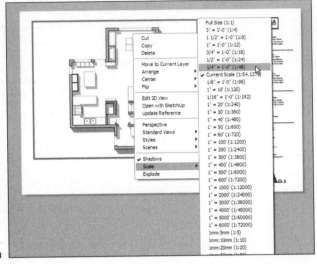

Figure 14-6:
Assign a
precise
drawing
scale to
any ortho-
graphic
viewport.

6. Use the Select tool to position, rotate, or resize your model view.

Click and drag to move any element in your document on the page. Use the Rotation Grip (the little blue stick in the center of your image when it's selected) to rotate. You can resize anything by clicking and dragging any corner.

Go ahead and repeat the preceding steps for all the additional viewports you want to add to your document. Check out Chapter 15 for lots more information about viewports.

Adding images and other graphics

Inserting images into your LayOut document is a straightforward affair. Just choose File⇨Insert and take it from there. A few more things to know about images you insert:

- ✔ **LayOut can insert raster images.** This means TIFFs, JPEGs, GIFs, BMPs, and PNGs — these are all graphics file formats that save pictures as lots of tiny dots.

- ✔ **The Mac version of LayOut can also insert PDF files.** This is indisputably the best way to bring in vector art, such as logos. You can use a program like Adobe Illustrator to save any AI (Illustrator) or EPS file as a PDF.

- ✔ **Images are a lot like viewports.** Moving, resizing, and rotating images works just like it does for SketchUp model views; use the Select tool to do everything. Remember to hold down the Shift key when you resize to keep your images from stretching.

Unfortunately, LayOut offers no easy way to import editable vector (such as AI, EPS, and SVG) graphics. If you want to use vector graphics in your LayOut document, you have two choices:

- **Make your own.** LayOut is actually a pretty fantastic vector illustration tool — I actually prefer it to Illustrator for most things I draw. Take a gander at Chapter 15 to discover all the nuances of LayOut's illustration toolset.

- **Borrow shamelessly from the Scrapbooks panel.** One of the best things about LayOut is the hundreds — maybe thousands — of pre-drawn graphical elements you can find in the Scrapbooks panel (see Figure 14-7). You find things like

  - *Symbols:* Arrows, section markers, north indicators, graphic scales, and column grids

  - *Entourage elements:* Trees, cars, and people at various scales and levels of detail

  - *Color palettes:* To help with producing attractive documents quickly

To use something you see in the Scrapbooks, just click it with the Select tool to "sample" it and then click again to stamp it onto your page. You can keep clicking to stamp more copies, or press the Esc key when you're ready to exit stamping mode.

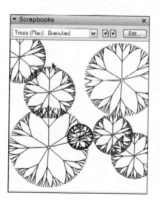

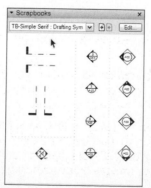
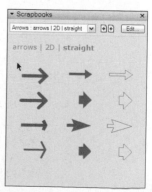

Figure 14-7: LayOut's Scrapbooks is the fastest way to add professional-looking graphics to your drawings.

Annotating with text and dimensions

LayOut has a few tools you can use to add blocks of text, titles, callouts, labels, and dimensions to your drawings. Luckily, none is terribly complicated to use. Here's a mini-section about each text tool; Figure 14-8 is a sampler of different drawing annotations:

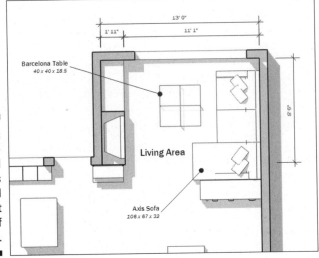

Figure 14-8: Text, callouts, and dimensions are all different forms of annotation.

The Text tool

Text boxes in LayOut are classified into two broad types, depending on how you create them:

✔ **Bounded:** If you click and drag with the Text tool, the text box you create is *bounded*. Any text you enter into it that doesn't fit isn't visible, and you get a little red arrow at the bottom. That arrow tells you that there's more in your text box; you need to use the Select tool to make the box bigger to show everything that's inside. Use a bounded text box whenever your text needs to fit into a precise space in your design.

✔ **Unbounded:** If, instead of creating a text box with the Text tool, you simply click to place your cursor somewhere on your page, the text you create is *unbounded*. It stays inside a text box, but that text box automatically resizes to accommodate whatever text you put inside it. To turn an unbounded text box into a bounded one, just resize it with the Select tool or choose Text⇨Make Unbounded.

Naturally, you control things like text size, color, alignment, and font using the Text Style panel (Fonts panel on a Mac).

This only applies to Mac folks: Choosing Text➪Show Rulers does more than just display ruled increments at the top of your drawing window. It also enables extra controls for paragraph spacing and lists — bulleted and numbered. Just select text in your document to see them appear above the ruler.

The Label tool

Use the Label tool to add *callouts* (notes with leader lines) wherever you need them. Four important points about (what I consider to be) the most useful tool in LayOut:

- **Activate, click, click, type, and click.** Activate the Label tool, click once to "pin" the end of the leader line to an element in your drawing, click again to place your text cursor, type something, and click somewhere else to finish your label.

- **Leader lines stick to drawing elements.** When you move the thing your leader line is pinned to, the line moves with it.

- **Use the Shape Style panel to edit the look of your leader lines.** You can change the color, thickness, and endpoints (arrowheads, slashes, and dots) of any leader line very easily after you create it.

- **Save time by sampling.** After you edit a label you've made already, it's easy to set up things so every subsequent label you make looks the same:

    a. *Activate the Label tool and then press the S key.*

    Your cursor changes into an eyedropper.

    b. *Click the text part of the label you sample and then click S again.*

    c. *Click the leader line of the label you sample.*

    Now every label you create looks just like the one you sampled.

- **Use the Style tool to copy styles between labels you've created already.** If you have a bunch of labels and you want to make them all look the same, follow these steps:

    a. *Activate the Style tool (it looks like an eyedropper) and then click the text part of the label whose style you want to copy.*

    b. *Apply (by clicking) that style to the text of every other label you want to change.*

    c. *Repeat Steps a and b, sampling the leader lines of your labels instead of the text.*

The dimension tools

Both dimensioning tools (Linear Dimension and Angular Dimension) work very similarly to the Label tool; all three are made of lines and text. Here's a stripped-down version of what you find in Chapter 15:

- ✔ **Turn on Object Snap before you start.** Choose Arrange➪Object Snap to make sure your dimension leader lines can "see" the points they're supposed to be attached to.

- ✔ **Creating a new linear dimension is very simple.** Activate the Linear Dimension tool, click a start point, click an end point, click to define an offset, and you're done.

- ✔ **Double-click to create a string of linear dimensions.** After you create your first dimension and while the tool is still active, double-click the next point you want to dimension. The offset you set for the first is duplicated.

- ✔ **Angular dimensions are a little trickier.** Using the Angular Dimension tool is a five-click operation. Follow these steps to make it work (see Figure 14-9):

  a. Activate the Angular Dimension tool and then click once to establish the first "pin point" for your new dimension.

  b. Click again, somewhere along the same line as the point you clicked in Step a.

  c. Click once to establish the second pin point.

  d. Click again along the same line as your second point.

  e. Click one last time to position the text of your angular dimension.

- ✔ **Use the Shape Style panel to edit your leader lines.** Thickness, color, endpoints — it's all here.

- ✔ **Use the Dimension Style panel to change formatting.** By *formatting,* I mean metric or imperial, decimal places, text position, and visibility.

- ✔ **Use the Style tool to copy formatting and other settings between dimensions.** Activate Style, click your "source" dimension, and then click each dimension you want to change.

Creating separate layers for text, labels, and dimensions saves time in the long run. In the Layers panel, click the Add Layer button to make a new one. The layer with the little, red pencil next to it is your active layer.

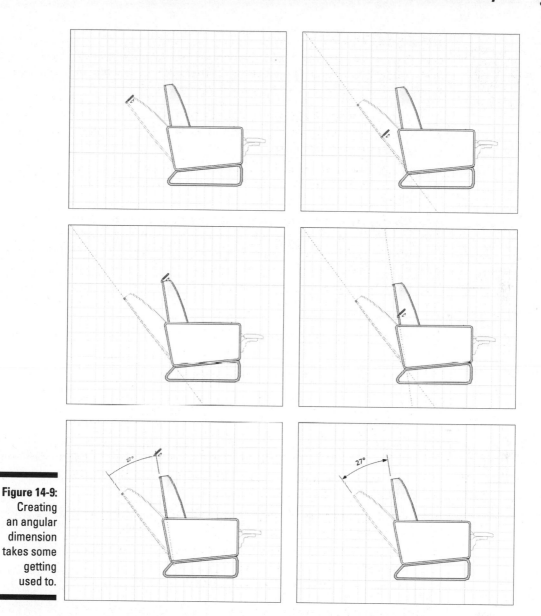

Figure 14-9:
Creating
an angular
dimension
takes some
getting
used to.

Getting Your Document Out the Door

After you create a LayOut document, you can do the following five things to show it to someone else:

- ✔ Print it.
- ✔ Export it as a PDF file.
- ✔ Export it as an image file.
- ✔ Export it as DWG or DXF (CAD) file.
- ✔ View it as a full-screen presentation.

Simple, huh? The next five sections provide more detail on each of these options.

Printing your work

Chapter 12 is about printing from SketchUp; notice that it's more than ten pages long. The instructions for printing from LayOut, on the other hand, would easily fit on a business card:

1. **Choose File⇨Print.**

   In the Print dialog box, choose which pages to print and how many copies you want.

2. **Click OK to send your document to the printer.**

And that, my dear reader, is why you should always insert your SketchUp models into a LayOut document if you need to print them.

That said, I almost never print directly from LayOut. Ninety-nine percent of the time, I export a PDF and use Adobe Acrobat (or Reader) to send the actual job to the printer. The settings in Adobe's Print dialog box give you more control over the finished product.

Exporting a PDF

Anyone with Adobe Reader software (which is free and is already loaded on millions of computers) can look at a PDF document you create; all you have to do is e-mail it to her. Follow these steps to export your LayOut document as a PDF file:

1. **Choose File⇨Export⇨PDF.**

   If you're on a Mac, choose File⇨Export and then make sure PDF is selected in the Export dialog box. This opens the Export PDF dialog box.

2. **Give your PDF file a name and figure out where to save it on your computer.**

3. **Click the Save button (in Windows) to open the PDF Export Options dialog box; click the Options (Mac).**

4. **Set the PDF options the way you want them.**

   Here's what everything means:

   - *Page:* Choose which pages you want to export.

   - *Quality:* See Chapter 15 for a brief discussion about Output Quality. Here's a good rule of thumb: For documents that are small enough to be hand-held, I recommend a setting of High. For anything bigger, go with Medium or Low.

   - *Layers:* PDFs can have layers, just like LayOut documents do. If it makes sense to do so, you can export a layered PDF so that people who view it can turn the layers on and off.

   - *Finish:* Select this check box to view your PDF after it's exported.

5. **Mac only: Click OK to close the PDF Export Options dialog box.**

6. **Click the Export button (Save button on a Mac) to export your document as a PDF file.**

Exporting an image file

You can export the pages of your file as individual raster images in either JPEG or PNG format. Take a look at Chapter 13 for more information on the differences between JPEG and PNG if you need to. Follow these steps to export your LayOut document as one or more image files:

1. **Choose File⇨Export⇨Images.**

   If you're on a Mac, choose File⇨Export, and make sure PNG or JPEG is selected in the Export dialog box. This opens the Export Image dialog box.

2. **Name your file and tell LayOut where to save it on your computer.**

3. **Click the Save button (Options on a Mac).**

   The Image Export Options dialog box opens.

4. **Set the Image Export options.**

   Here's what each option means:

   - *Pages:* Choose which pages you want to export. Each page in your LayOut document exports as a separate image file.

   - *Size:* See Chapter 13 for a complete rundown on pixel size and image resolution.

   - *Finish:* Select this check box to view your image after it's exported.

5. **Mac only: Click OK to close the Image Export Options dialog box.**

6. **Click the Export button (Save button on a Mac) to export your document as one or more image files.**

Exporting a DWG or DXF file

You'd be hard-pressed to find a piece of professional computer-aided drawing (CAD) software that can't read the DWG and DXF formats, which are the industry standard for exchanging CAD files with people who use apps like AutoCAD and Vectorworks. Here's how to turn your LayOut document into a CAD file:

1. **Set all your SketchUp viewports to vector rendering mode.**

   Here's the short version: LayOut treats your SketchUp models' edges as either *raster* (dots) or *vector* (math) information. Viewports that are rendered as rasters export to DWG/DXF as raster images. That's usually not what you want to happen — especially if you're exporting a CAD file. Follow these steps to make sure your viewports are vector images:

   a. *Select a model viewport and then click the View tab of the SketchUp Model panel (choose Window⇨SketchUp Model to open this panel).*

   b. *Change the Rendering style drop-down list from Raster to Vector.*

      Depending on the complexity of your model, LayOut may take a while to think.

   c. *Repeat the preceding two steps for each viewport.*

   If a viewport contains a view whose edges you don't want to manipulate in CAD (such as a glitzy rendering), leave it as a raster.

2. **Choose File⇨Export⇨DWG/DXF.**

   On a Mac, choose File⇨Export and make sure DWG/DXF is selected in the Export dialog box.

3. **Name your file, tell LayOut where to save it on your computer, and click the Save button (Options on a Mac).**

   The DWG/DXF Export dialog box opens.

4. **Set the DWG/DXF Export options.**

   Here's what all the knobs and switches do:

   • *Format:* Unless you know you need a DXF, export a DWG file. As for which version, stick with the latest one: AutoCAD 2010.

   • *Pages:* Choose which pages you want to export. Keep in mind that each page in your LayOut document exports as a separate file.

- *Output Space:* When you choose Paper Space, the lines in your resulting document file, when measured in the CAD program you use next, are exactly as long as they'd be on a piece of paper printed from LayOut. Choosing Model Space tells CAD to draw the lines at a particular scale. Here's an example:

  You have a viewport that shows a plan view of your building at ⅛ scale. Your building is 80 feet wide, so it looks 10 inches wide in the drawing in LayOut.

  If you export to Paper Space, open your drawing in AutoCAD and measure your building, it'll be 10 inches wide — probably not what you wanted.

  If you export to Model Space, choose ⅛" = 1'–0" as a scale, and then measure your building in AutoCAD, it'll be 80 feet wide. Most of the time, you want to choose Model Space.

- *Scale:* This setting is relevant only if you choose to export to Model Space. Pick the drawing scale that matches the scale of the viewports on the pages you're exporting.

  If your pages have viewports at different scales, you have to export them separately to make sure all the scaling is accurate. Have two viewports at different scales on the same page? Only one of them will be correct in your exported file.

- *Layers:* Compared to the preceding two settings, this one's mercifully clear. Decide which layers will appear in your exported files.

- *Ignore Fills: Fills* are shapes that are drawn in LayOut and filled with a color.

5. **Mac only: Click OK to close the DWG/DXF Export dialog box.**

6. **Click the Export button (Save button on a Mac) to export your document as one or more DWG/DXF files.**

   If your LayOut file included any inserted raster images (such as JPEGs or PNGs,) you also end up with a folder that contains copies of those. They're necessary for the DWG/DXF files you produce.

Going full-screen

Many times, design presentations for clients go beyond printed boards and booklets; they include a digital slide show that usually involves a few hours of work in a program like PowerPoint or Keynote.

LayOut helps you skip the PowerPoint step by letting you display your presentation in a full-screen view. You can move back and forth between pages with the arrow keys on your computer, and you can even double-click SketchUp model views to orbit them. Follow these tips:

✔ **Switching to Presentation mode takes less than a second.** Choose View➪Start Presentation to view your presentation full-screen. Press the Esc key to exit Presentation mode.

✔ **Specify where you want your presentation to appear.** Use the Presentation panel in the Preferences dialog box to tell SketchUp which monitor (or projector) you want to use to show your presentation.

✔ **Move from page to page.** Use the left- and right-arrow keys to flip through pages.

✔ **Choose which pages to show full-screen.** You can decide not to show certain pages in full-screen mode by toggling the Show Page in Presentations icon to the right of those page names in the Pages dialog box (make sure that you're in List view to be able to do this).

✔ **Double-click to change your view of a SketchUp model.** When you're in full-screen mode, you can double-click any SketchUp model view to orbit and zoom around inside it. Just use your mouse's scroll wheel button the same way you do in SketchUp. Click anywhere outside the view to exit.

✔ **Draw while you're in full-screen mode.** Try clicking and dragging while you're in full-screen mode; doing so lets you make red annotations right on your presentation. If a client doesn't like the porch you designed, scrawl a big, red *X* over it to let her know you understand. When you hit Esc to exit Presentation mode, you can choose to save your annotations as a separate layer.

✔ **Play scene animations in full-screen mode.** You can double-click and then right-click a model view with scenes that you've set up in SketchUp; then choose Play Animation. LayOut transitions from scene to scene, just like SketchUp does. You can read more about scenes in Chapter 10.

Chapter 15

Diving Deeper into LayOut

In This Chapter

▶ Using layers and pages to streamline your work

▶ Mastering inserted SketchUp model views

▶ Getting precise about dimensions

▶ Creating your own templates and scrapbooks

Chapter 14 lays out the basics of LayOut: What it's for, where everything is, and how to use it to when you just need to get something done. This chapter is filled with hints, recommended techniques, and minutiae about the more powerful — but less obvious — aspects of SketchUp's sister app.

I start by discussing the way LayOut wants you to organize your documents. After that, you explore the intricacies of inserting SketchUp models and getting them to look exactly the way you want. You dig in to dimensions and discover how to create your own templates and scrapbooks. Customizing LayOut for yourself (or the rest of your team) shaves hours off your next project.

Staying Organized with Layers and Pages

Here's something you already know: When you build a sophisticated document, cutting corners at the beginning of the process comes back to bite you when you need to make a last-minute change. Knowing *exactly* how LayOut's layers work gives you the confidence to use them all the time. The frustration you avoid late in the schedule (when it really counts) is easily worth the extra few minutes it takes to "work clean."

Using layers to maintain your sanity

LayOut has *layers* that (unlike SketchUp's layers) act just like layers in InDesign, Illustrator, Photoshop, and every other graphics program you've ever used. Layers let you

- ✔ Keep collections of similar elements separate and organized.
- ✔ Easily show or hide large numbers of elements at once.
- ✔ Lock elements so you can't accidentally change them.
- ✔ Stack one group of elements on top of another.
- ✔ Create design iterations by tweaking copies of the same elements.

Figure 15-1 shows a simple, one-page document with three layers. Different elements on the page are assigned to different layers. When you work with layers, keep these points in mind:

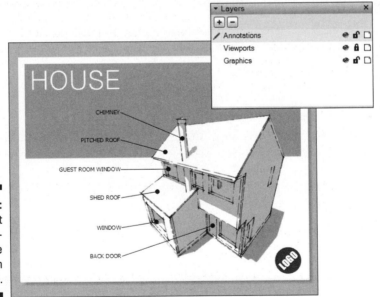

Figure 15-1: Layers let you organize the elements on your page.

- ✔ **To know which is the active layer,** look for the little red pencil icon; anything you insert, draw, or paste is assigned to the active layer.
- ✔ **To make another layer the active layer,** click its name in the Layers panel.

- ✔ **To show or hide a layer,** click the "eye" icon next to that layer's name.

- ✔ **To change the stacking order of layers,** drag them around in the Layers panel.

- ✔ **To see what layer an element is on currently,** select the element and look for the tiny blue dot in the Layers panel. If you select two elements on two different layers, you see two blue dots.

- ✔ **To change which layer something's on,** select the destination layer in the Layers panel. Then right-click the element you want to move and choose Move to Current Layer. Selecting multiple elements, right-clicking one of them, and choosing Move to Current Layer moves them all.

Without overbeating this particular dead horse, using layers is the absolute best way to work efficiently in LayOut. Check out the following tips for working with layers:

- ✔ **Give your layers meaningful names.** When you (or somebody else) open your file next year, you want to know what the heck is going on.

- ✔ **Lock layers you're not using.** I know it's annoying to unlock a layer before you can modify its contents, but it's even more annoying to accidentally move the wrong things, or even delete them. Lock a layer by clicking the lock icon next to its name in the Layers panel.

- ✔ **Improve performance by hiding layers.** Make liberal use of the hide icon next to the name of each layer; hiding layers can really improve LayOut's performance, especially on slower computers. Hide any layers you're not working with, and you'll notice the difference.

- ✔ **Duplicate a layer and its contents to save time.** I do this fairly often when I work on an illustration; it's a quick way to iterate through several different versions. Here's how you can, too:

    a. *Lock all your other layers and choose Edit⇨Select All.*

    b. *Create a new layer and name it.*

      Make sure it's the active layer.

    c. *Choose Edit⇨Paste.*

- ✔ **Move several elements from multiple layers to a single layer with Copy and Paste.** Copying elements from multiple layers and pasting them pastes them all on the same layer — the active one.

- ✔ **Group elements from different layers to create a group on the active layer.** This one bother me sometimes like when I'm trying to group a viewport and its dimensions. They start on separate layers and end up on the same one. Oh well.

Making layers and pages work together

You can use layers to make certain elements appear on more than one page in your document. LayOut has two kinds of layers:

- ✔ **Unshared:** Any element (text, graphic, or otherwise) that you put on an unshared layer exists only on one page: the page you're on when you put the element on the layer.

- ✔ **Shared:** LayOut introduces the notion of *shared layers;* anything you put on a shared layer appears on every page of your document, as long as those pages are set up to show that layer. Think logos, title blocks, arrows, and other graphics that need to be exactly the same on most pages.

Shared layers can confuse new LayOut users, so here are a few quick tips about how you organize content on layers — including shared layers — as you create presentations in LayOut:

- ✔ **You can make any layer a shared layer by clicking the sharing icon to the right of its name in the Layers panel. (See Figure 15-2.)**

- ✔ **You can make an element (such as a logo) appear in the same spot on more than one page by putting it on a shared layer.** For example, the logo and the project title need to appear in the same spot on every page; I put these two elements on the shared On Every Page layer. In Figure 15-2, note how the logo and project title appear in exactly the same place on the second, third, and fourth pages.

- ✔ **Put content that appears on only one page on an unshared layer.** Again, on the last three pages of the document shown in Figure 15-2, the image boxes and page titles are different on each page, so I put them on the unshared Default layer.

- ✔ **You decide which pages should show which layers.** For example, I don't want the logo and the project title to be on the cover (first) page. I toggle the show/hide icon beside the On Every Page layer to hide it on that page.

I like to work with at least four layers, organizing content on each as follows:

- ✔ Elements that should appear in the same place on almost every page, such as logos and project titles

- ✔ Things that appear in the same place on most pages, but that change from page to page, such as numbers and page titles

- ✔ Content (such as images and SketchUp model views) that appears only on a single page

- ✔ Unused stuff that I'm not sure I want, but that I don't want to delete

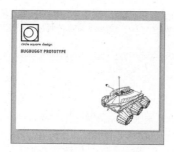

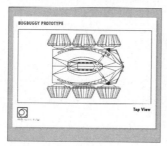

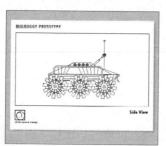

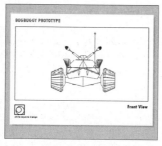

Figure 15-2:
A simple
document
with two
layers:
One that's
shared,
and one
that isn't.

Sharing icon shows
this is a shared
layer

On the Cover page,
this layer is hidden

Working with Inserted Model Views

Being able to choose views of your SketchUp models and put together documents to present them is what LayOut is all about. Text, vector drawing, raster images, and everything else aside, LayOut is a tool for presenting SketchUp models.

This section is about two things: managing the model views that you've inserted into your LayOut document and controlling how they look. You accomplish both by fiddling with the controls in the SketchUp Model panel, which you can open by choosing Window⇨SketchUp Model from the menu bar.

To insert a view of a SketchUp model into your LayOut document, all you have to do is choose File⇨Insert and pick the model you want to work with. Creating the look you want, on the other hand, is a whole lot trickier — and that's where this section comes into play.

Framing exactly the right view

A SketchUp model view that lives in your LayOut document is a *viewport*. You can have multiple viewports that show the same model. For example, you may have different viewports for a top view, a perspective, and a section through a building you're designing. They're all linked to the same model but show it in different ways.

The next few sections provide specific advice on setting up different model views in your documents' viewports.

Of course, your LayOut document can also have viewports that correspond to more than one SketchUp model. Some folks don't realize that, so I thought I'd point it out.

Seeing precisely what you want to see

When you insert a SketchUp model into a LayOut document, it shows up in a new viewport. Not only that — it shows up looking exactly the way it did in SketchUp when you saved it (see Figure 15-3).

Saving while on this view in SketchUp...

...yields this view when you insert the model into LayOut

Figure 15-3:
Newly inserted SketchUp models look just like they did when you saved them.

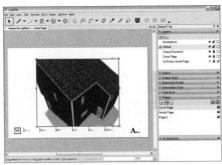

You can do a couple things to change your viewport's point of view: Use the Camera tools or edit scenes with the Model panel.

Using the Camera tools directly

Double-clicking a viewport with the Select tool is a little bit like activating SketchUp from inside LayOut. The model looks different (worse, usually) than it did — that's because you're looking at the model itself, instead of the rendered image of it that LayOut made when you inserted it. To change your point of view, you can

- ✔ Orbit, zoom, and pan around using your mouse, exactly the way you do in SketchUp.
- ✔ Right-click the viewport and choose a specific Camera tool from the context menu.

When you're done repositioning your model, click somewhere else to stop editing the viewport. LayOut re-renders the view, and your model goes back to looking nice and crisp.

Using scenes and the SketchUp Model panel

Using the SketchUp Model panel is by far my preferred method for controlling what's visible in viewports. Instead of messing around with the Camera tools, choose a scene to display from the Scenes drop-down list in the panel's View tab; see Figure 15-4.

Figure 15-4: Use the View tab of the SketchUp Model panel to control your viewport's point of view.

Of course, working this way requires that you first set up scenes in your SketchUp model, but that's not hard at all; Chapter 10 describes the whole simple process of creating and working with scenes.

Cropping with clipping masks

Cropping an image means reframing it so that you can see only part of it; every page-layout program on the planet allows you to crop images, and each one insists that you do it a little differently. LayOut is no exception.

In LayOut, use *clipping masks* to hide the parts of images — and viewports — that you don't want to see. Follow these steps to use a shape as a clipping mask; the images below provide a visual reference:

1. **Draw the shape you want to use as a clipping mask and make sure that it's positioned properly over the image you want to crop.**

2. **Use the Select tool to select both the clipping mask object and the image you want to crop.**

3. **Right-click the selected elements and choose Create Clipping Mask from the context menu.**

Here are some fun facts about clipping masks in LayOut:

- ✔ **Clipping masks work on inserted images.** This includes both raster images and SketchUp model viewports.

- ✔ **Deleting clipping masks is easy.** To see a whole image again, select the image and choose Edit➪Release Clipping Mask.

- ✔ **Edit clipping masks by double-clicking them.** When you double-click a clipping mask, you can see the whole image and the shape you used to create the mask. Now you can modify the shape, the image, or both. Clicking somewhere else on your page exits the edit mode.

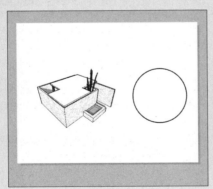

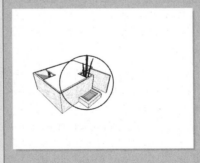

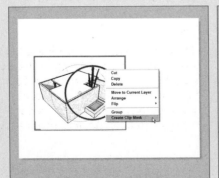

Setting up the views you want to use in LayOut by saving scenes in SketchUp makes things easier for four main reasons:

- ✔ **You can see more.** Your SketchUp modeling window is bigger than your viewport in LayOut, so it's easier to see what you're doing.

- ✔ **You can go back to a previous view.** Repositioning your model in a LayOut viewport is kind of a temporary thing; if you change things, there's no way to come back to the view you set up previously. SketchUp scenes, on the other hand, are views that you can always return to.

- ✔ **You can show section cuts.** Scenes are the *only* way to save views of your model with different section planes active.

- ✔ **You have more control over shadows, fog, and styles.** LayOut provides basic tools for fiddling with other aspects of your viewports' appearance, but they're nowhere near as easy to use as the ones in SketchUp.

If the scenes you created in SketchUp aren't visible in the SketchUp Model panel, you probably forgot to save your model before you switched applications. You also need to make sure your viewport is current; right-click it and choose Update Reference to make sure everything's up to date.

Figure 15-5 shows a LayOut page with three viewports on it. All three show the same model. Before I laid out this page, I created three scenes in SketchUp:

- ✔ **Large plan view:** To get this point of view, lop off the top of the model (temporarily, of course) by adding a section plane about 48 inches from the floor. Turn off Perspective view (Camera➪Parallel Projection) and choose a top view (Camera➪Standard Views➪Top). Apply a Hidden Line style to make it black and white and then choose View➪Section Planes to hide the section plane. Update the style and turn on Shadows to help the model read better on the page.

- ✔ **Smaller perspective views:** To create these two scenes, use a little trick: Create two section planes a couple inches apart. "Point" one down and the other up; right-clicking a section plane lets you reverse it (Edit➪Section Plane➪Reverse) — whatever was hidden becomes visible and vice versa.

Creating scaled orthographic views

With the addition of honest-to-goodness dimensions (both linear and angular) to LayOut in SketchUp Pro 8, people have started to push the limits of what LayOut was intended to do. LayOut was never supposed to be a 2D drafting tool; its toolset has always been closer to Illustrator than to AutoCAD. That said, you absolutely can put together simple, scaled drawing sets, complete with title blocks, symbols, dimensions, and other forms of annotation.

SketchUp model with Section Plane and shadows turned on

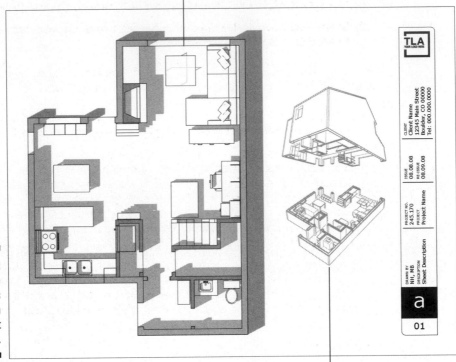

Figure 15-5:
Three
viewports
inserted in
a LayOut
document.

Model with Perspective turned on

The first step in creating a dimensioned drawing is to turn your viewport into a 2D orthographic view of your model. (See Chapter 10 for an introduction to orthographic views.) Although you can use the controls in the SketchUp Model panel to accomplish this, my favorite way is to go back to the model and create a scene.

Follow these steps to save an orthographic scene in your SketchUp model and assign it to a viewport in LayOut:

1. **In LayOut, right-click (with the Select tool) the viewport that contains your model and choose Open with SketchUp.**

2. **If you plan to have an active section cut in your view, add it to your model (if you haven't already).**

   Chapter 10 explains how to make section cuts.

3. **In SketchUp, choose Camera⇨Parallel Projection; then choose Camera⇨ Standard Views⇨Top (or any other option from this list except Iso).**

4. **Zoom and pan (but don't orbit) until you have the view you want and then choose View⇨Animation⇨Add Scene.**

5. **Save your model and close it.**

6. **In LayOut, right-click the viewport and choose Update Reference.**

7. **In the View tab of the SketchUp Model panel, choose your new scene to associate it with the viewport.**

Now that you have an orthographic view of your model, you can assign a scale to it. Here's everything you need to know about that:

- **Assign a scale using the scale drop-down list in the SketchUp Model panel (see Figure 15-6).** Don't forget to select the viewport you're working on first.

- **You can create your own scales if you want.** Need a scale that doesn't appear in the default list? Choose Edit➪Preferences (LayOut➪Preferences on a Mac) to open the Preferences dialog box; then click Scales on the left. Click the plus sign to add a new scale to the list. Scales you add are available for any LayOut file you're working on.

- **Make sure Preserve Scale on Resize is selected.** After you assign a scale to a viewport, you probably want to manually resize its boundaries with the Select tool. Before you do, make sure the Preserve Scale on Resize check box (in the SketchUp Model panel) is selected. If it's not, you change the scale of your model view when you try to resize its viewport.

Figure 15-6:
Use the
SketchUp
Model panel
to assign
a scale
to your
viewport.

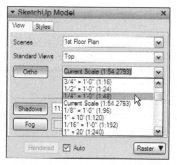

Making your models look their best

Getting your models "posed" correctly on the page is only half the battle; they also need to look readable and compelling. That's what this section is about. You discover how LayOut *renders,* or draws, your models on the page and how adjusting line weights can make your drawings look their best.

Choosing raster, vector, or hybrid

Every time you insert or edit a SketchUp model view, LayOut renders an image of your model to display in the viewport. This rendering process is just like exporting an image from SketchUp; it can produce either a raster or a vector, depending on the settings. Take a look at Chapter 13 for more information about raster and vector images.

You control how your models look by choosing which method LayOut uses to render each viewport. Simply select an option from the rendering method drop-down list in the lower-right corner of the SketchUp Model panel. You have three choices, which I illustrate in Figure 15-7:

- ✔ **Raster:** Renders your viewport as an image comprising many, many little dots. If your model is rendered as a raster, it can display sketchy styles, shadows, and other effects that make it look like it does in SketchUp. On the other hand, printing or exporting a raster image at large sizes involves truckloads of pixels, and that can make LayOut choke. See the nearby sidebar "Balancing performance and quality" to find out more.

- ✔ **Vector:** Renders your selected model view as a vector image. Lines appear smooth and crisp, but things like shadows, textures, and sketchy styles don't appear. Also, choosing vector rendering for really complex models can take a long time to process. A *very* long time.

- ✔ **Hybrid:** Combines clean vector lines with rich raster faces, shadows, and other goodies. Behind the scenes, LayOut actually renders twice — once as a vector and once as a raster. Hybrid rendering takes even longer than vector rendering, but it produces very nice results. If you have time, try hybrid rendering to see how it looks.

I tend to use raster rendering for views of my models that involve Sketchy Edges styles and for any model with a lot of geometry. I prefer hybrid or vector rendering for any plans, sections, or other views that feature a lot of line work.

Raster	Vector	Hybrid
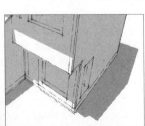	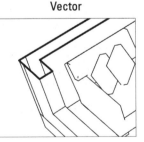	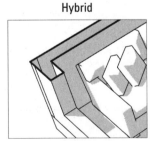
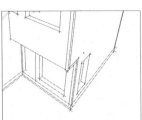		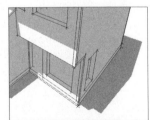

Figure 15-7: Choose a rendering method for each viewport in your LayOut document.

Balancing performance and quality

LayOut places rendered images of your SketchUp models into viewports on the page; that's why your models looks so much better in LayOut than they do in SketchUp's modeling window. But that's also why LayOut can feel so slow at times — rendering is a very time-intensive activity. Luckily, you have a few ways to manage LayOut's speed:

Manage your rendering resolution

At the bottom of the Paper pane (File⇨Document Settings), you find two settings: Edit Quality and Output Quality. They both control the pixel resolution of raster-rendered viewports in your document. Low correlates to a resolution of 72 ppi (pixels per inch), Medium to 150 ppi, and High to 300 ppi. The higher the resolution, the more pixels LayOut has to figure out — and the longer it takes to render. By default, both settings are set to Medium for every new document you create.

When I work with big raster- or hybrid-rendered viewports, I dial down my Edit Quality to Low. Doing so doesn't adversely affect the quality of my exports and prints; both of those are controlled by Output Quality. What it does is ask LayOut to draw far fewer pixels every time I fiddle with a viewport. It makes a big difference — believe me.

Be careful about choosing vector rendering

When you set a viewport to be rendered as a vector, LayOut runs through every single edge and face in your SketchUp model — even the ones you can't see. Really big models can take eons to vector-render. Another thing: Unlike rasters, vectors don't care how small your viewport is. A 1-millimeter viewport takes just as long to vector-render as a one meter one. Big viewports kill rasters, whereas big models kill vectors; that's really all you need to remember.

Here's a tip if you're using vector rendering: LayOut renders *everything* in your SketchUp model when you use vector rendering on a viewport — even the geometry that isn't visible. To speed things up, put everything you don't need LayOut to render on a separate layer (in your SketchUp model,) hide that layer, and save a scene to associate with your viewport in LayOut. Chapter 7 has everything you need to know about using layers in SketchUp.

Switch off auto rendering

Notice the controls in the lower-left corner of the SketchUp Model panel? When the Auto check box is selected, LayOut automatically re-renders a viewport every time you edit it. If your model is big and heavy, you have to wait while LayOut works, and that can get old, fast. Deselecting the Auto check box lets *you* decide when LayOut should render your viewports. Just select a viewport and click the Render button (also in the SketchUp Model panel) to tell LayOut to start cranking.

Line Weight

The SketchUp Model panel's second tab — Styles — contains what one of the most important settings in all of LayOut. In the lower-left corner, the Line Weight field lets you control how bold your models look. Take a look at Figure 15-8 to see what I mean.

The number you put into the Line Weight field tells LayOut how thick to draw the thinnest lines in your viewport. Entering **2** yields edges that are 2 points wide. Typing **0.25** makes your edges a quarter point wide — much thinner and (in many cases) much nicer.

Managing styles inside LayOut

The Styles tab of the SketchUp Model panel gives you access to all the styles included with SketchUp, plus any that you've saved with your model. You can select any viewport in your document and apply a style to it at any time. Simple, right?

Wrong. The tricky part lies in knowing which styles are actually saved with your model. If you're like me — lazy about naming the different variations of every style that you create while you model — your In Model collection of styles looks like a dog's breakfast. Add in things like section plane visibility, background colors, and transparency, and it's really, really hard to know what you have.

If you depend on styles to work in LayOut, make sure you do two things:

✔ **Create scenes.** Not the first time you've heard that one, eh? The easiest way to make sure you can get the model views you want in LayOut is to create scenes in SketchUp beforehand. As long as the style in each scene looks right, you should be just fine when you get to LayOut.

✔ **Update religiously.** Problems sometimes crop up when folks forget to update their current style before they save their model. That creates a disconnect between the styles in SketchUp and the ones in LayOut. Before you save a SketchUp model you're using in a LayOut viewport, make sure your current style doesn't need updating. If it does, its thumbnail (in the Styles dialog box) looks like the one in the following image. Click the icon to bring the style up to date.

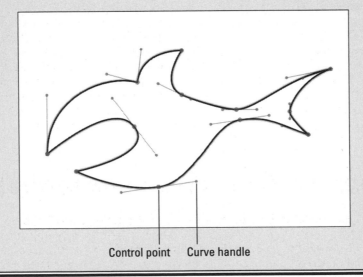

Control point   Curve handle

0.25 points

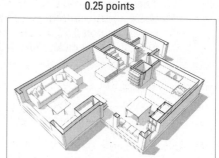

0.5 points

1 point

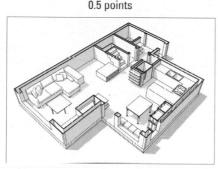

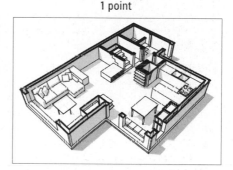

Figure 15-8:
Use the Line
Weight field
to make
your models
look their
very best.

Changing the Line Weight number is the single best thing you can do for your models in LayOut. The line weights you use depend entirely on the size of your viewports and the complexity of your drawings. Try to avoid making anything look too wispy or too chunky — the key here is *readability*.

If the style that's applied to your viewport has Profiles enabled, some edges look thicker. To change the thickness of Profiles in a LayOut viewport, you need to edit the style that defines them in the SketchUp model. Profile thickness is always a multiple: A setting of **4** produces Profiles that are four times as thick as regular edges. Check out Chapter 9 for more about styles and how to edit them, and see the nearby sidebar "Managing styles inside LayOut" to find out how they relate to SketchUp's companion application.

Discovering More about Dimensions

When Google added dimensions to LayOut in SketchUp 7.1, designers, architects, engineers, woodworkers, and all kinds of other people jumped for joy. With the addition of *angular* dimensions in SketchUp Pro 8, LayOut became a full-fledged tool for creating scaled, annotated drawings from your models.

I provide a decent-sized set of instructions for using both of LayOut's dimension tools in Chapter 14; flip to there if that's the extent of the help you need right now. In the interest of not making this book longer than it needs to be, I don't repeat that information here.

If you have trouble getting your dimension tool to "see" any of the points in a model viewport, chances are you don't have Object Snaps (Arrange⇨Object Snaps) turned on.

Editing your dimensions

After you actually draw a dimension — linear or angular — on your page, you can do an awful lot to change what the dimension looks like. To begin with, take a look at the anatomy of a dimension. Figure 15-9 shows an example of each kind.

Now that you're clear on nomenclature, here's some advice on making the kinds of changes you may want to make:

- ✔ **Use the Shape Style panel** to change colors, line styles, line weights, and arrow styles (the things at the ends of dimension lines). Basically, the Shape Style panel is for controlling everything about your dimensions except their text strings.

- ✔ **Use the Dimension Style panel** to change the format of text strings and their level of precision. Skip ahead a page or two for a more in-depth look at the Dimension Style panel.

- ✔ **Double-click a dimension to get access to all its internals.** After you've double-clicked to start editing a dimension, you can move its connections points, offset points, or extent points all you like.

- ✔ **Click and drag to move a text string.** Need to reposition a text string to make it more legible? Just drag it someplace else — after you've double-clicked the dimension to edit it, of course.

- ✔ **Double-click twice more to edit a text string.** That's three double-clicks in total; this clearly isn't something the folks on the LayOut development team thought you'd do very often.

- ✔ **Select individual lines to edit them individually.** After you double-click a dimension, you can select its constituent lines one at a time. I like to draw my dimension lines slightly thicker than my extension lines; selecting the former individually lets me do that.

- ✔ **Overshoots can be tricky.** The *overshoot* (as shown in Figure 15-9) is the part of an extension line that extends beyond the dimension line. You can adjust your overshoots' length if you like. Here's how:

    a. *Double-click a dimension to edit it.*

    b. *Click to select the extension line whose overshoot you want to adjust.*

    c. *Change the number beside the End Arrow setting in the Shape Style panel.*

Unfortunately, there's no way to alter both extension lines' overshoots simultaneously. What I recommend is to change one, choose Edit⇨Copy Style; then select the other and choose Edit⇨Paste Style.

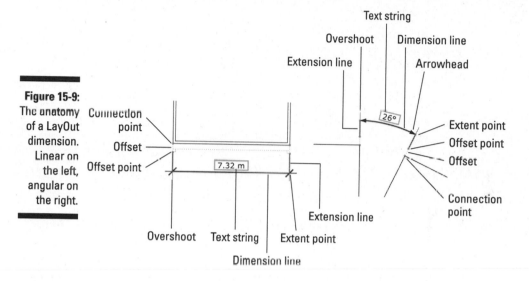

Figure 15-9: The anatomy of a LayOut dimension. Linear on the left, angular on the right.

Copying a dimension's style and applying it to your other dimensions is pretty easy. Just use the Style tool to transfer formatting from one dimension to the other. To sample a dimension's style so that every new dimension you draw matches it: Activate the tool, tap the S key, and click your "source" dimension before you draw the next one.

Take a gander at the Dimension Style panel, as shown in Figure 15-10. Most of the controls here are obvious, but some definitely aren't. Diving right in:

Figure 15-10: The Dimension Style panel is where you control your dimensions' text string format.

Text position   Text alignment   Display units

Scale drop-down

Dimension Style

Auto Scale   1/4" = 1'-0" (1:48)

Length: Architectural   Inches

Precision: 1/4"

Angle: Degrees   1°

✔ **Text position:** Choose to display a text string above, below, or right smack dab in the middle of its corresponding dimension line.

- **Text alignment:** Force a text string to always be horizontal or vertical on the page, or aligned (parallel) or perpendicular to its dimension line.

- **Display units:** People who use the Imperial system of measurement tend to show the units on their dimensions. Metric folks tend not to. You have the choice.

- **Auto Scale button:** Here's where dimensions start to get a little bit complicated. For a full discussion of what the heck this button does, see the next section.

- **Scale drop-down list:** This is available only when Auto Scale is deselected. Skip ahead to read all about model space and paper space. Getting your head around this topic takes time.

- **Length:** Different professions have different conventions for the dimensions they put on their drawings. Choose the one that suits you best.

- **Precision:** If you dimension the overall length of an airport runway, you probably don't need to be accurate the 1000th of an inch. If you design an artificial heart valve, on the other hand . . .

- **Angle:** Degrees or radians — you decide. Sometimes it's easy to forget that software is made by math nerds.

Keeping track of model space and paper space

When you place a SketchUp model viewport on your page, you end up with two different types of space in your LayOut document:

- **Paper space:** Distances that pertain to the physical sheet of paper you're working on are said to be in *paper space*. A 4" x 4" blue square in paper space is 4 inches long.

- **Model space:** Distances within a model viewport have nothing to do with the size of the sheet of paper the viewport's on. An 80' x 80' building shown at 1 inch = 8 feet scale is 80 feet long in model space. In paper space, it's 10 inches long.

A dimension you draw in LayOut is either in paper space or in model space. Which one the dimension is in by default depends on what the dimension is connected to:

- **Viewports:** When you draw a dimension between two points in a model viewport, LayOut is smart enough to presume that you want to display the length between the points *in the model* (in model space).

- **Everything else:** When you create a dimension between two points that have nothing to do with a viewport, LayOut assumes that you want to see the *actual length on the page* (in paper space).

Figure 15-11 shows what I mean. Both dimensions are exactly the same physical length on the page: 3 inches. The difference is that the dimension on the left is attached to two points on a SketchUp model that's shown at 1 inch = 8 feet scale. It displays the *model space* length of 24 feet (3 x 8) whereas the dimension on the right just shows its *paper space* length of 3 inches.

The Auto Scale button in the Dimension Style panel is automatically selected whenever you create a new dimension. If your dimension touches a point in a model viewport, the text string displays the length in model space. If it doesn't touch any model viewport at all, you get a length in paper space.

Turning off Auto Scale lets you assign a scale to the dimension you select. Choosing 1" = 60 feet for a dimension that's physically 4 inches long makes its text string read 240 feet — no matter what it's attached to.

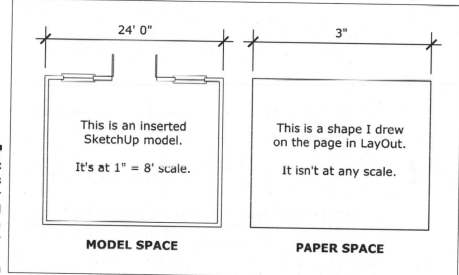

Figure 15-11: Dimensions can either show model space or paper space.

Drawing with LayOut's Vector Tools

LayOut includes a full slate of drawing tools that you can use to create logos, title bars, north arrows, graphic scales — anything you want. The drawings you create are *vectors*, meaning that you can do the following:

- Scale the drawings without losing quality
- Change the fill and stroke (outline) colors
- Split lines and then rejoin them to make new shapes

Curves are back

LayOut's Line tool has a secret: It's quite simply the most intuitive *Bézier* curve vector drawing tool I've ever used — and I've used a lot. In vector software (such as LayOut and Illustrator), you can draw curved lines freehand, but they don't usually look very good. It's hard to draw smooth, flowing curves without assistance, and that's where the Line tool comes in. Figuring out how to draw Bézier curves usually takes a little getting used to, but after you do, it's hard to go back.

So what makes LayOut's Line tool so great? Two things, actually:

✔ **The Line tool uses the inference system.** SketchUp and LayOut share a similar "guidance" system of colorful points and lines that help guide you. By turning on Object Snap when you draw, you can align things and draw more accurately.

✔ **Draw and edit with two tools.** Use the Line tool to draw curves (and straight lines, of course) and then do all your editing with the Select tool. Compared to curve tools in other software, LayOut does a lot more with a lot less.

Here are pointers on creating and editing curves with the Line tool:

✔ **Click-click-click to draw straight-line segments.** The LayOut Line tool works just like the Line tool in SketchUp.

✔ **Click-drag-release to draw curved-line segments.** You "shape" your curve while you drag.

✔ **Double-click with the Select tool to edit.** When you do, you see all your line's control points and *handles* (the antenna-looking things that poke out of your control points). Click and drag points and handles to edit your line, and then click somewhere else to stop editing.

✔ **Drag a control point on top of an adjacent point to delete it.** If you want to remove a control point while you edit a line, just drag it onto one of its neighbors.

✔ **Hold down the Ctrl key and click somewhere on your line to add a point.** Hold down the Option key on a Mac.

✔ **Hold down Ctrl and drag on a point to pull out curve handles.** That's the Option key on a Mac.

✔ **Hold down Ctrl (Option on a Mac) and drag on a handle to sharpen a curve.**

Because I don't know what you want to draw, a step list would be pretty pointless here. Instead, here are a few pointers to get you started:

✔ **Use the right kind of snaps.** Drawing exactly what you want is easier if you let the software help a bit. Just like SketchUp, LayOut includes an elaborate (but easy-to-use) *inference* system of red and green dots and lines to help you line up things. LayOut also has a grid (that you define) to keep elements in your drawing aligned:

  • *Snap to objects:* When you choose Arrange⇨Object Snap to turn on object snapping, colored hints to help you draw appear onscreen.

- *Snap to grid:* Choose Arrange⇨Grid Snap to turn on grid snapping. Now your cursor automatically *snaps* to (is attracted to) the intersection of grid lines in your document — whether your grid is visible or not. See Chapter 14 for more information on setting up grids in LayOut.

You can use any combination of snapping systems (Object or Grid) while you work, but I prefer to use one or the other, depending on what I'm trying to do. To save time, assign a keyboard shortcut that toggles each system on and off. (To do that, use the Shortcuts panel in the Preferences dialog box, which you can find in the Edit menu; on a Mac, look on the LayOut menu.)

✔ **Type measurements and angles.** LayOut has a Measurements box (in the lower-right corner of your screen), just like the one in SketchUp. Take a look at Chapter 2 for tips on working accurately with this box.

✔ **Build complex shapes out of simpler ones.** For example, Figure 15-12 shows how to draw a simple arrow. Follow these steps to build one just like it:

a. *Make sure that Grid Snap is turned off and Object Snap is turned on, and then draw a rectangle with the Rectangle tool.*

b. *Draw a triangle with the Polygon tool.*

To do so, type **3s** and press Enter before you start drawing to make sure that you're drawing a triangle. Hold down the Shift key to make sure that the bottom of the triangle is a horizontal line.

c. *Shift-click to select both shapes and then choose Arrange⇨Align⇨Vertically to line up the rectangle and the triangle vertically.*

You can always use the Undo feature to go back a step; it's in the Edit menu whenever you need it.

d. *Deselect both shapes by clicking once somewhere else on your page, and then select a shape and move it up or down on the page (by pressing the up- and down-arrow keys) until the two shapes overlap.*

e. *Use the Arc tool to draw a half-circle at the bottom of the rectangle.*

f. *With the Split tool, click and hold down the mouse button over an intersection point, and don't release the mouse button until all the lines stop flashing blue. Do this for all four intersection points to split the shapes into a series of line segments.*

g. *Use the Join tool (it looks like a bottle of glue) to connect all the line segments by clicking once on the arrowhead part, once on each half of the stem part, and once on the half-circle.*

You have one shape instead of three; verify this by clicking the shape once with the Select tool. You see one red "selected" rectangle around your new shape. If you don't have one shape, use the Join tool again.

h. *Move your new shape somewhere else and then delete the leftover line segments you don't need.*

✔ **Open the Shape Style dialog box.** Use the Shape Style dialog box to change the fill and stroke characteristics of elements in your document. In plain English, this is where you pick colors for the things you draw. The controls are pretty straightforward, so you don't need much help from me; just experiment and see what happens.

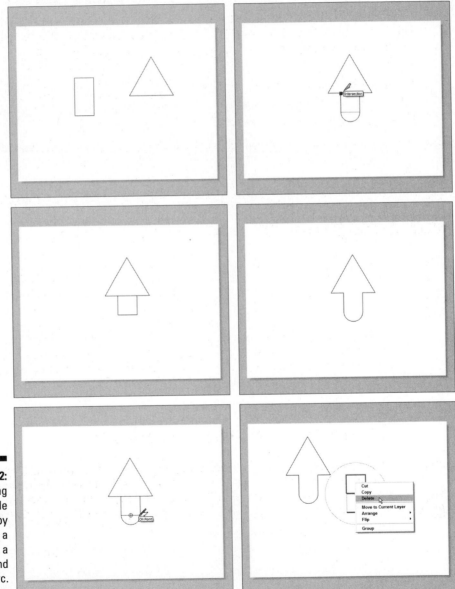

Figure 15-12:
Drawing a simple arrow by combining a rectangle, a triangle, and an arc.

Watch those defaults

All LayOut's drawing and text tools come "out of the box" with a default setting, depending on the template you use. For example, the Line tool may be set to create a single-pixel black line with a white shape fill. The Text tool may be configured to create 10-point Verdana. Tools automatically use the settings that were applied the last time they were used.

It's easy enough to change the default settings for your tools. Just follow these steps:

1. **Click the tool icon you want to use.**

2. **In the Shape Style or Text dialog box, choose the settings you want to use.**

3. **Draw or type to use the new settings.**

Here's the thing: Changing the default settings in one LayOut file doesn't change them for other files. Tool defaults stick to particular documents. If you want to change the default settings for every new document you create, you need to create your own template. Discover how in "Creating your own templates," later in this chapter.

Customizing LayOut with Templates and Scrapbooks

When you've made your own templates and scrapbooks in LayOut, you know you've arrived. Every time you need to put together a drawing set, all you have to do is open your template (which already includes your logo, title block, layout, and text styles) and insert your model.

Need to add your firm's custom symbols? Just open one of your scrapbooks and drag the symbols onto your pages. Having a collection of your own templates and scrapbooks means never starting all over again at the last minute — which is when most LayOut files are made.

Creating your own templates

Most of the design presentations that you (or your firm) put together probably look alike — after all, they're part of your brand identity. If the presentation documents you make are all variations on a couple themes, why not build your own templates and use them every time you need to start a new project?

You can set up LayOut so that your templates appear in the Getting Started dialog box, making it easier to build consistent presentations, quicker.

Follow these steps to turn any LayOut file into a template:

1. **Build a LayOut file that includes all the elements you want.**

   These elements may include a title block, a logo, a page number, and a cover page.

   Before you move to Step 2, make sure that you're viewing the page that you want to use as the thumbnail preview in the template list.

2. **Choose File⇨Save as Template.**

   The Save as Template dialog box opens.

3. **Type a name for your template and then choose a location for your new template.**

   In the list at the bottom of the dialog box, click the folder (they're all folders) in which you want to include the template you're adding.

4. **Click OK (Save on a Mac).**

   The next time the Getting Started dialog box appears, your new template will be in it.

Putting together your own scrapbooks

Most hardcore LayOut users make their own scrapbooks of scale figures, cars, trees, drafting symbols, typography — anything they need to use again and again.

Like templates, *scrapbooks* are just LayOut files that have been saved in a special folder on your system. When you open the program, it checks that folder and displays the files it finds in the Scrapbooks panel.

Follow these steps to build your own LayOut scrapbook, as shown in Figure 15-13:

1. **Build a LayOut file with the elements you want to include in your scrapbook.**

2. **Choose File⇨Save as Scrapbook.**

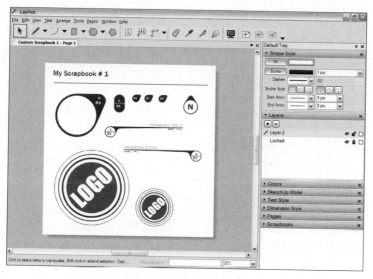

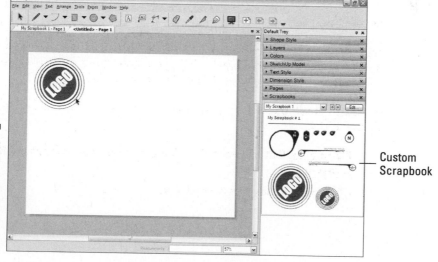

Figure 15-13:
Making
your own
scrapbooks
is easy
and ultra-
rewarding.

Custom
Scrapbook

3. **Type a name for your scrapbook.**

   The Scrapbook Folder list in the Save as Scrapbook dialog box shows the location of the folder on your system where your new scrapbook will be saved. If you prefer to use another folder, you can add one using the Folder panel of the Preferences dialog box.

4. **Click OK (Save on a Mac).**

   The next time you restart LayOut, your scrapbook appears at the top of the Scrapbooks panel.

A few notes about making your own scrapbooks:

- ✔ **A good size is 6 x 6 inches.** You can choose any paper size for the file you plan to save as a scrapbook, but smaller sheets work better. The scrapbooks that come with LayOut are six inches square.

- ✔ **Scrapbooks can have multiple pages.** In fact, just about all the default scrapbooks in LayOut do. The first page in your document becomes the cover page for the scrapbook; all subsequent pages appear below it in the list. Pay attention to your page names, which appear in the Scrapbooks panel, too.

- ✔ **Use locked layers.** Anything you put on a locked layer can't be dragged out of the scrapbook. Take a look at the People scrapbook that comes with LayOut — the word *People* and the information next to it are on a locked layer. Notice how you can't drag them into your drawing?

- ✔ **You can put model viewports into scrapbooks.** Open the Arrows ∣ 3D ∣ Curved scrapbook. Drag one of the arrows onto your page. Now double-click it — it's a model! I created that scrapbook specifically to provide story boarders with orbitable arrows that they could pose however they liked. The moral of this story is that you can put *anything* into a scrapbook: graphics, images, viewports, and text.

Part V
The Part of Tens

The 5th Wave — By Rich Tennant

"So this is your design? I didn't know Google SketchUp had an 'overkill' function."

In this part . . .

Face it; everybody loves lists. The last part of this book (and almost every *For Dummies* book out there) is dedicated to presenting useful information in short, bite-sized chunks that you can read while you stand in the elevator. Or use the bathroom. Or wait for your turn in the shower.

Chapter 16 is a list of the problems that every new SketchUp user runs into — check here when you're ready to pour acid all over your keyboard and move to Amish country.

The list in Chapter 17 is all about plugins and *Ruby scripts*: little programs you can install to extend SketchUp's functionality and usefulness.

The last chapter in this book is, fittingly, about ten ways that you can keep discovering more about SketchUp — places to go, books to read, DVDs to watch. I'm a firm believer that the best way to figure out anything is to see it presented in more than one way, so I highly encourage you to check out at least a couple of these resources.

Chapter 16

Ten SketchUp Traps and Their Workarounds

The bad news is that every new SketchUp user encounters certain problems, usually in the first couple hours using the software. I guess you can call these problems growing pains. The good news is that such predictability means that I can write a chapter that anticipates a lot of the bad stuff you'll go through. I can't prevent it from happening, but I *can* help you make sense of what's going on so you can get on with your life as quickly as possible.

SketchUp Won't Create a Face Where You Want It To

You've dutifully traced all around where you want SketchUp to create a face, but nothing's happening. Try checking whether your edges aren't all on the same plane or whether one edge is part of a separate group or component.

To check whether you have a component problem, try hiding groups or components and checking the edges to make sure that they're all in the group or component you think they're in. See Chapter 5 for details.

However, 90 percent of the time when SketchUp doesn't create a face where you think it should, an edge isn't on the *plane* you think it's on. To check whether your edges are coplanar, draw an edge that cuts diagonally across the area where you want a face to appear. If a face appears now, your edges aren't all on the same plane. To fix the problem, you have to figure out which edge is the culprit.

I call my favorite method for doing this the Color by Axis method; Color Plate 20 shows images of the steps that I describe:

1. **In the Styles dialog box, change your edge color from All Same to By Axis.**

   See Chapter 9 for details. SketchUp draws the edges in your model the color of the axis to which they're parallel; edges parallel to the red axis are red, and so on.

2. **Look carefully at the edges you wanted to define a face.**

   Are all the edges the color they're supposed to be? If they're not all supposed to be parallel to the drawing axes, this technique doesn't do much good. But if they are, and one (or more) of them is black (instead of red or green or blue), that edge (or edges) is your problem child. Fix it and switch back to All Same when you're done.

Your Faces Are Two Different Colors

In SketchUp, faces have two sides: a front and a back. By default, these two sides are different colors.

When you do certain things like use Push/Pull or Follow Me on a face, sometimes the faces on the resulting geometry are "inside out." If it bothers you to have a two-tone model (I know it bothers me), right-click the faces you want to flip over and choose Reverse Faces from the context menu. If you have lots of them, you can select them all and then choose Reverse Faces to do them all at once.

Edges on a Face Won't Sink In

This tends to happen when you're trying to draw a rectangle (or another geometric figure) on a face with one of SketchUp's shape-drawing tools. Ordinarily, the Rectangle tool creates a new face on top of any face you use it on; after that, you can use Push/Pull to create a hole, if you want.

When the edges you just drew don't seem to cut through the face you drew them on, try these approaches:

- **Retrace one of the edges.** Sometimes that works — you'd be surprised how often.

- **Select Hidden Geometry from the View menu.** You're checking to make sure that the face you just drew isn't crossing any hidden or smoothed edges; if it is, the face you thought was flat may not be.

- **Make sure that the face you drew on isn't part of a group or component.** If it is, undo a few steps and then redraw your shape while you edit the group or component.

SketchUp Crashed, and You Lost Your Model

Unfortunately, SketchUp crashes happen sometimes.

The good news is that SketchUp automatically saves a copy of your file every five minutes. The file that SketchUp auto saves is actually a *separate* file, `AutoSave_your filename.skp`. If your file ever gets corrupted in a crash, an intact file is ready for you to find and continue working on.

The problem is that most people don't even know it's there. Where is this file?

- If you've ever saved your file, it's in the same folder as the original.

- If you've never saved your file, it's in your My Documents folder — unless you're on a Mac, in which case it's here:

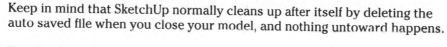

```
User folder/Library/Application Support/Google
        SketchUp 8/SketchUp/Autosave
```

Keep in mind that SketchUp normally cleans up after itself by deleting the auto saved file when you close your model, and nothing untoward happens.

To minimize the amount of work you lose when software (or hardware) goes south, always do two things:

- Save often. Compulsively, even.

- Save numbered copies while you work. I use Save As to create a new copy of my work every half-hour or so. When I'm building a big model, it's common for me to have 40 or 50 saved versions of it on my computer, dating back to when I first started working on it.

SketchUp Is Sooooo Slooooooooow

The bigger your model gets, the worse your performance gets, too. What makes a model big? In a nutshell, faces. Do everything in your power to keep your model as small as you can. Here are some tips for doing that:

- **Reduce the number of sides on your extruded circles and arcs.** See Chapter 6 for instructions on how to do this.

- **Use 2D people and trees instead of 3D ones.** Three-dimensional plants and people have *hundreds* of faces each. Consider using 2D ones instead, especially if your model won't be seen much from overhead.

Some models are just big, and you can't do much about it. Here are some tricks for working with very large SketchUp models:

- **Make liberal use of the Outliner and layers.** Explained in detail in Chapter 7, these SketchUp features were specifically designed to let you organize your model into manageable chunks. Hide everything you're not working on at the moment — doing so gives your computer a fighting chance.

- **Use substitution for large numbers of complex components.** For example, insert sticks as placeholders for big sets of 3D trees, cars, and other big components. See the tips for replacing components in Chapter 5 for details.

- **Turn off shadows and switch to a simple style.** It takes a lot of computer horsepower to display shadows, edge effects, and textures in real time on your monitor. When you're working, turn off all that stuff.

- **Use scenes to navigate between views.** Scenes aren't just for presenting your model — they're also great for working with it. Creating scenes for the different views you commonly use, and with different combinations of hidden geometry, means that you don't have to orbit, pan, and zoom around your gigantic model. Better yet, deselect Enable Scene Transitions (in the Animation panel of the Model Info dialog box) to speed up things even more.

You Can't Get a Good View of the Inside of Your Model

It's not always easy to work on the inside of something in SketchUp. You can do these things to make it easier, though:

- **Cut into your model with sections:** SketchUp's Sections feature lets you cut away parts of your model — temporarily, of course — so that you can get a better view of what's inside. Take a look at Chapter 10 for the whole story on sections.

✔ **Widen your field of view:** *Field of view* is basically the amount of your model you can see on the screen at one time. A wider FOV is like having better peripheral vision. You can read all about it in Chapter 10.

A Face Flashes When You Orbit

If you have two faces in the same spot — maybe one is in a separate group or component — you see a *Z-fighting* effect. SketchUp is deciding which face to display by switching back and forth between them; it's not a good solution, but certainly a logical one — at least for a piece of software. The only way to get rid of Z-fighting is to delete or hide one of the faces.

You Can't Move Your Component the Way You Want

Some components are set up to automatically *glue* to faces when you insert them into your model. A glued component instance isn't actually glued *in one place*. Instead, it's glued to the plane of the face you originally placed (or created) it on. For example, if you place a sofa component on the floor of your living room, you can move it around only on that plane — not up and down.

This behavior comes in handy when you deal with things like furniture; it allows you to use the Move tool to rearrange things without worrying about accidentally picking them up.

If you can't move your component the way you want to, right-click it and see whether Unglue is an option — if it is, choose it. Now you can move your component around however you want.

Bad Stuff Happens Every Time You Use the Eraser

It's pretty easy to delete stuff accidentally with the Eraser tool. Worse yet, you usually don't notice what's missing until it's too late. Here are some tips for erasing more accurately:

✔ **Orbit around.** Try to make sure that nothing is behind whatever it is you're erasing; use SketchUp's navigation tools to get a view of your model that puts you out of danger.

✔ **Switch on Back Edges.** Choose View➪Edge Style➪Back Edges when you're going to be using the Eraser heavily. That way, you can see every edge in your model, and you're less likely to erase the wrong ones.

✔ **Double-check.** I've gotten into the habit of giving my model a quick once-over with the Orbit tool after I do a lot of erasing, just to make sure that I didn't get rid of anything important. Put a sticky note on your computer monitor that says something like *Check after Erase!* just to remind you.

All Your Edges and Faces Are on Different Layers

I'll be blunt — using Layers in SketchUp is a dangerous business. Chapter 7 has tips you should follow when using layers, so I don't repeat them here, but here's the short version: Always build everything on Layer0, and only put whole groups or components on other layers if you really need to.

If you used layers and now things are messed up, here's what you can do to recover:

1. **Make sure that everything is visible.**

   Select Hidden Geometry on the View menu; then (in the Layers dialog box) make all your layers visible. Just make sure that you can see everything in your model.

2. **Choose Edit➪Select All.**

3. **In the Entity Info dialog box, move everything to Layer0.**

4. **In the Layers dialog box, delete your other layers. When prompted, tell SketchUp to move anything remaining on them to Layer0.**

5. **Create new layers and follow the rules in Chapter 7.**

Chapter 17

Ten Plugins, Extensions, and Resources Worth Getting

In This Chapter

▶ Scripts that make your life easier and add power to SketchUp

▶ Software for making your SketchUp views look like photographs

▶ Fun hardware add-ons

The really great thing about SketchUp's price is how much room it frees in your budget for nifty add-ons. This chapter is a list of ten (give or take a few) such nifty add-ons, along with a little bit of information about them and where you can go to find them. I've split them into three categories, just to make things clearer: Ruby scripts, renderers, and hardware.

Ruby Scripts

What's a Ruby script, you ask? Basically, Google provides a way for people to make their own plugins for SketchUp. These *plugins* are just mini-programs (or *scripts*) written in the Ruby computer programming language. The best thing about Ruby scripts (*Rubies*, for short) is that you don't have to know anything about Ruby, or programming in general, to use ones that other people have created.

To install Rubies, drop them into a special folder on your computer:

▶ **Windows:** C:/Program Files/Google/Google SketchUp 8/Plugins

▶ **Mac:** Hard Drive/Library/Application Support/Google SketchUp 8/ SketchUp/Plugins

The next time you launch SketchUp, Rubies you put in the preceding location become available for you to use. How you use them depends on what they do. They may show up on one of the toolbar menus or on your right-click context menu. The more complex ones even come with their own little toolbars. Most Rubies also come with a helpful set of instructions that tells you how to use them.

Luckily for those who aren't programmers, plenty of smart folks out there develop and (in some cases) sell Rubies that anyone can use. Here are three places you can go to find some:

- ✔ **Smustard.com:** Smustard.com is a Web site run by a few of these smart folks. You can choose from dozens of helpful Rubies that add functionality to SketchUp. Most are free, but the ones that aren't are well worth the money. (`www.smustard.com`)

- ✔ **Ruby Library Depot:** The Ruby Library Depot is a huge collection of Rubies from helpful software developers around the world. Everything is well-organized and thoroughly vetted. Highly recommended. (`http://rhin.crai.archi.fr/RubyLibraryDepot/`)

- ✔ **SketchUcation:** This combination how-to Web site, blog, and discussion forum is also a terrific source of Rubies. Developers post their plugins in forum discussion threads, where SketchUp über-modelers from around the galaxy gather to test them and provide feedback. The upside is that you can see instructions and examples for most Rubies. The downside is that some of the threads are 20 pages long. Typing **sketchucation plugins index** into your favorite search engine leads you to the right place on SketchUcation's extensive Web site.

Now that you know where to go to find them, which Rubies should you use? Table 17-1 lists some of my favorites.

Table 17-1	SketchUp Ruby Scripts		
Ruby Name	*What It Does*	*Author; Source*	*Free or Pay?*
CAD cleanup scripts	If you routinely import 2D CAD drawings to use as a starting point for SketchUp models, you need these scripts. Without going into any detail, here's a list of the CAD cleanup scripts to hunt for on Smustard.com: StrayLines, CloseOpens, MakeFaces, IntersectOverlaps, Flatten, and DeleteShortLines.	Todd, Burch; Smustard.com	Pay

Ruby Name	What It Does	Author; Source	Free or Pay?
Drop	Takes a bunch of groups or components that you've selected and drops them down in the blue direction until each hits a surface. If you're trying to populate a sloping hillside with trees, it's much easier to make a big, flat grid of them in the air and then Drop them to meet the ground.	Octavian Chis; Smustard.com	Free
FredoScale	Adds the ability to taper, twist, bend, and stretch 3D objects in a way you'd never be able to with plain ol' SketchUp.	Fredo6; Ruby Library Depot	Free
Fur Maker	Lets you "grow" fur — or grass — on faces in your models. More fun, and more useful, than you'd think.	tak2hata; SketchUcation	Free
Layer Tools	Allows you to add a layer that's only visible in your current scene. Great for design iterations where each iteration is on a separate layer that is linked to a unique scene.	Joe Zeh; search the Web for *layers management ruby script*	Free
Joint Push Pull	Wouldn't it be great if you could push/pull curved surfaces to give them thickness? With this plugin, you can. Even better, it comes with great documentation when you download it.	Fredo6; Ruby Library Depot	Free

(continued)

Table 17-1 *(continued)*

Ruby Name	What It Does	Author; Source	Free or Pay?
PresentationBundle	This package of five Rubies helps you use scenes to create better presentations. You can customize the transition time between individual scenes, for instance, and even create really elaborate fly-by animations.	Rick Wilson; Smustard.com	Pay
RoundCorner	Turns sharp edges and corners into smooth rounds and fillets. Shaves literally hours off the time it takes to model almost any manufactured product.	Fredo6; Ruby Library Depot	Free
Shape Bender	Lets you bend (and stretch) a 3D shape along a path you designate. Everything from spiral ramps to fancy retail signage just got a heck of a lot easier.	Chris Fullmer; SketchUcation	Free
Simplify Contours	Sometimes *contours* (topography lines) you import from a CAD file are very complex. Running this script on them reduces their complexity, which makes the terrain you use them to generate easier to work with.	Google; search the Web for *simplify contours ruby*	Free
Slicer3	Takes a model and cuts it into even, parallel slices. Indispensable for turning 3D terrain into easy-to-make site models.	TIG; Ruby Library Depot	Free

Ruby Name	What It Does	Author; Source	Free or Pay?
Soap Skin & Bubble	Make a loop of connected edges, activate this Ruby, and watch in amazement as it automatically "stretches" a surface over them — think circus tent. You can even apply pressure to inflate your new tensile structure right before your eyes.	Josef Leibinger; search the Web for *ruby soapskin bubble*	Free
SubdivideAndSmooth	If you're interested in *organic modeling* — stuff that isn't boxy or otherwise angular — look at this one. Basically, it lets you create smooth, blobby (I mean that in a good way) forms based on *proxies* (boxes, sort of) that you manipulate. It's much cooler and more versatile than it sounds.	Dale Martens; Smustard.com	Pay
SketchyPhysics	An extension that lets you apply real-world physical *constraints* (such as gravity) to your SketchUp models. You can, for instance, set up a row of dominoes, tip one over, and watch them all fall down. Or build a machine with wheels, pistons, and other mechanical parts and then set it in motion.	DarthGak; search the Web for *sketchyphysics*	Free
Tools On Surface	Use these drawing tools — Line, Offset, Circle, Rectangle, and Freehand — to draw directly on non-flat surfaces like terrain.	Fredo6; Ruby Library Depot	Free

(continued)

Table 17-1 *(continued)*

Ruby Name	What It Does	Author; Source	Free or Pay?
Weld	Takes edges you've selected and welds them together to make a single edge that you can select with a single click. This is *super* handy when you use Follow Me.	Rick Wilson; Smustard.com	Free
Windowizer	Helps you create store-front windows much more quickly than you can manually. Wicked powerful.	Rick Wilson; Smustard.com	Pay

Renderers

One thing SketchUp does *not* do is create photorealistic renderings. Its styles are great for making your models look hand-drawn, but none of them can make your work look like a photograph. Most SketchUp users are okay with that, but for those who aren't, you can find some nice solutions out there.

Of course, SketchUp Pro's 3D export formats make it possible to render SKP files with just about any of the dozens of über-powerful renderers on the market, but the ones that I describe in the following list have three important things in common: They work with the free version of SketchUp, they were developed with SketchUp in mind, and you don't have to work for George Lucas to figure them out. Here's the list:

✔ **SU Podium:** SU Podium is a plugin that lets you create photorealistic views right inside SketchUp. It's relatively inexpensive, straightforward to use, and the results are impressive. SU Podium is available for both Windows and Mac, and there's a free, lower-resolution trial version you can get to see whether it suits you. (www.suplugins.com)

✔ **IDX Renditioner:** This software evolved from another renderer — TurboSketch. Like SU Podium, IDX Renditioner is a plugin available for Windows and Mac computers, and you can try a free version that creates smaller 640-x-480-pixels images. I recommend trying both SU

Podium and IDX Renditioner, and seeing which you prefer. (www.idx-design.com)

✔ **Artlantis:** If you're really serious about making images that look like photographs, take a good look at Artlantis. Instead of running as a plugin inside SketchUp, it's a fully functional, separate piece of software that works with lots of other 3D modeling programs. Its results are out of this world. (www.artlantis.com)

Like I mention earlier, lots of rendering applications are out there, and depending on what you want to do, different ones may work better than others. If photo rendering is your thing, try plugging these names into your favorite search engine: Cheetah3D, Kerkythea, LightUp, Maxwell Render, Shaderlight, Thea Render, Twilight Render, V-Ray, and Vue.

Hardware

All you really need to use SketchUp is a computer with a decent video card, a keyboard, and a mouse. On the other hand, having specialized hardware can come in handy — especially if you use SketchUp all the time:

✔ **A better video card:** This isn't really an option if you're on a laptop, but if you use a desktop machine, upgrading your computer's video card (or *graphics card)* is the best way to improve your SketchUp experience. Your *video card* is a piece of hardware that handles the stuff that appears onscreen. Not all cards are made to be used with 3D modeling programs — not even some that are made specifically for whiz-bang video games. Look for something that supports *OpenGL 1.5* or higher and has a lot of video memory; the more, the better. I've heard good things about cards made by NVIDIA and ATI.

✔ **SpaceNavigator from 3Dconnexion:** Using a scroll-wheel mouse to fly around in 3D space works great for most people, but lots of SketchUp power users swear by dedicated 3D navigation tools like the SpaceNavigator. It looks a little like an enormous button that sits on your desk, connected to your computer via a USB cable. Use it with whatever hand isn't on your mouse; it's an add-on (and not a replacement) for any other peripheral in your system. Basically, the SpaceNavigator lets you orbit, pan, and zoom with subtle movements of your hand — it really is a much more natural way to interact with a 3D model. You'll find a bit of a learning curve, but that's nothing for serious SketchUp users. Anything that makes software easier and more fun to use is worth the time it takes to master it.

Chapter 18

Ten Ways to Discover Even More

In This Chapter

▶ Checking out some great, free SketchUp information

▶ Discovering other helpful resources

Don't get me wrong — I don't think this book is woefully incomplete. I just don't think it's possible to get too many different *forms* of information, especially about something as dynamic as SketchUp. You can find some great help resources out there, and I'd be remiss if I didn't point you to some of them.

I devote the first half of this chapter to the free stuff; it's all online and it's all available to anyone who wants it. In the second half of the chapter, I list some of the best nonfree SketchUp resources I know of. If you're willing to shell out a few bucks, you won't be sorry — nothing beats seeing the same information presented in different ways.

Incidentally, this is probably a good place to mention the dozens of free videos that accompany this book. You can link to them from this book's Web site (www.dummies.com/go/sketchup8fd), but you can also get to them directly on YouTube. To hear my (surprisingly Muppet-like) voice while I put SketchUp through its paces, check out www.youtube.com/aidanchopra.

Put Away Your Wallet

I have a confession to make: At fancy receptions, I'm the one stuffing my suit pockets with *hors d'oeuvres* wrapped in napkins. I love free stuff *that much*. So without further ado, what follows are six *complimentary* sources of SketchUp help.

Everything in this section requires that you have an Internet connection, so make sure that your computer's online before you try any of these.

- **SketchUp Training resources:** Google publishes really first-rate materials for SketchUp right on its Web site (http://sketchup.google. com/training):

  - *Video Tutorials:* When SketchUp first launched in 2000, it became known for its excellent video tutorials. I can't recommend them highly enough; there's nothing like *seeing* SketchUp in action.

  - *Self-Paced Tutorials:* These are SketchUp files that use scenes to teach different aspects of the program in a "follow along with me" style. If this is how you like to figure things out, have a look.

- **Online Help Center:** Google maintains big, extensive Help Centers (Web sites, basically) for all its products. These include hundreds of articles in question-and-answer format, created specifically to help new users along. The easiest way to get to the SketchUp Help Center is to choose Help⇨Help Center from the SketchUp menu bar.

- **SketchUp Help Forum:** The SketchUp Help Forum is an online discussion forum where SketchUp users from all over the world can get help, ask questions, and show off their work. (www.google.com/support/ forum/p/sketchup)

- **SketchUcation:** Home of the SketchUp Community Forums, this is easily the largest and most active group of SketchUp users in the world. You find discussions, tutorials, plugins, news, and piles of other good stuff at SketchUcation. (www.sketchucation.com)

- **Go-2-School Videos:** These guys have a terrific YouTube channel. The free videos are first-rate, and you can buy a couple of great DVDs, too. I talk about them in the next part of this chapter. (http://www.youtube. com/4sketchupgo2school)

- **The Official Google SketchUp Blog:** Visit the SketchUp blog regularly for news, case studies, tips and tricks, modeler profiles, plugins, and other updates. (http://sketchupdate.blogspot.com)

Now Get Out Your Wallet

Really. These resources cost a bit of money, but they're worth every penny:

- **Bonnie Roskes' books:** Bonnie's *The SketchUp Book* (published by 3DVinci) was the first one available, and now she has several new titles, including SketchUp books for kids. If you think you want to get another, bigger book about SketchUp (written with architects and other design pros in mind), check out Bonnie's books at www.3dvinci.net.

- ✔ **Daniel Tal's book:** *Google SketchUp for Site Design: A Guide to Modeling Site Plans, Terrain and Architecture* (published by Wiley) is, simply put, a great book. It contains tons of information about things I don't even begin to cover in mine: working with CAD files, using specific Rubies, managing huge models . . . When you're ready to take the next step in your SketchUp relationship, get Dan's book.

- ✔ **School DVD:** I mention School's videos in the previous section, but School's designers have also produced the world's first SketchUp educational/training DVDs, which you can order from its Web site (www.go-2-school.com). The production quality on these things is outstanding, and Mike and Alex (the School guys) do an amazing job of teaching SketchUp for both Windows and the Mac.

- ✔ **Dennis Fukai's books:** One word: jaw-dropping detail (okay — three words). Dennis's books are hard to describe. He's written four of them, each is fully illustrated in SketchUp and each teaches a different subject. If you want to discover more about using SketchUp in building construction or more about construction itself, or you just want to be completely inspired by what you can do with SketchUp, have a look at these books. Search for his name on Amazon (www.amazon.com) or go to his company's Web site, www.insitebuilders.com.

- ✔ **SketchUp Pro training:** If you think you might benefit from spending a few hours with a real-live trainer and a handful of other SketchUp students, Google Authorized Training Centers may be just the thing. They're located all over the world, so there might just be one near you. Check out this Web site for more information: http://sketchup.google.com/training/atc.html.

Index

● *F* ●

Apple & Macs

iPad For Dummies
978-0-470-58027-1

iPhone For Dummies,
4th Edition
978-0-470-87870-5

MacBook For Dummies, 3rd
Edition
978-0-470-76918-8

Mac OS X Snow Leopard For
Dummies
978-0-470-43543-4

Business

Bookkeeping For Dummies
978-0-7645-9848-7

Job Interviews
For Dummies,
3rd Edition
978-0-470-17748-8

Resumes For Dummies,
5th Edition
978-0-470-08037-5

Starting an
Online Business
For Dummies,
6th Edition
978-0-470-60210-2

Stock Investing
For Dummies,
3rd Edition
978-0-470-40114-9

Successful
Time Management
For Dummies
978-0-470-29034-7

Computer Hardware

BlackBerry
For Dummies,
4th Edition
978-0-470-60700-8

Computers For Seniors
For Dummies,
2nd Edition
978-0-470-53483-0

PCs For Dummies,
Windows
7 Edition
978-0-470-46542-4

Laptops For Dummies,
4th Edition
978-0-470-57829-2

Cooking & Entertaining

Cooking Basics
For Dummies,
3rd Edition
978-0-7645-7206-7

Wine For Dummies,
4th Edition
978-0-470-04579-4

Diet & Nutrition

Dieting For Dummies,
2nd Edition
978-0-7645-4149-0

Nutrition For Dummies,
4th Edition
978-0-471-79868-2

Weight Training
For Dummies,
3rd Edition
978-0-471-76845-6

Digital Photography

Digital SLR Cameras &
Photography For Dummies,
3rd Edition
978-0-470-46606-3

Photoshop Elements 8
For Dummies
978-0-470-52967-6

Gardening

Gardening Basics
For Dummies
978-0-470-03749-2

Organic Gardening
For Dummies,
2nd Edition
978-0-470-43067-5

Green/Sustainable

Raising Chickens
For Dummies
978-0-470-46544-8

Green Cleaning
For Dummies
978-0-470-39106-8

Health

Diabetes For Dummies,
3rd Edition
978-0-470-27086-8

Food Allergies
For Dummies
978-0-470-09584-3

Living Gluten-Free
For Dummies,
2nd Edition
978-0-470-58589-4

Hobbies/General

Chess For Dummies,
2nd Edition
978-0-7645-8404-6

Drawing
Cartoons & Comics
For Dummies
978-0-470-42683-8

Knitting For Dummies,
2nd Edition
978-0-470-28747-7

Organizing
For Dummies
978-0-7645-5300-4

Su Doku For Dummies
978-0-470-01892-7

Home Improvement

Home Maintenance
For Dummies,
2nd Edition
978-0-470-43063-7

Home Theater
For Dummies,
3rd Edition
978-0-470-41189-6

Living the
Country Lifestyle
All-in-One
For Dummies
978-0-470-43061-3

Solar Power Your Home
For Dummies,
2nd Edition
978-0-470-59678-4

Available wherever books are sold. For more information or to order direct: U.S. customers visit www.dummies.com or call 1-877-762-2974. U.K. customers visit www.wileyeurope.com or call (0) 1243 843291. Canadian customers visit www.wiley.ca or call 1-800-567-4797.

Internet

Blogging For Dummies,
3rd Edition
978-0-470-61996-4

eBay For Dummies,
6th Edition
978-0-470-49741-8

Facebook For Dummies,
3rd Edition
978-0-470-87804-0

Web Marketing
For Dummies,
2nd Edition
978-0-470-37181-7

WordPress
For Dummies,
3rd Edition
978-0-470-59274-8

Language & Foreign Language

French For Dummies
978-0-7645-5193-2

Italian Phrases
For Dummies
978-0-7645-7203-6

Spanish For Dummies,
2nd Edition
978-0-470-87855-2

Spanish
For Dummies,
Audio Set
978-0-470-09585-0

Math & Science

Algebra I
For Dummies,
2nd Edition
978-0-470-55964-2

Biology For Dummies,
2nd Edition
978-0-470-59875-7

Calculus For Dummies
978-0-7645-2498-1

Chemistry For Dummies
978-0-7645-5430-8

Microsoft Office

Excel 2010 For Dummies
978-0-470-48953-6

Office 2010 All-in-One
For Dummies
978-0-470-49748-7

Office 2010 For Dummies,
Book + DVD Bundle
978-0-470-62698-6

Word 2010 For Dummies
978-0-470-48772-3

Music

Guitar For Dummies,
2nd Edition
978-0-7645-9904-0

iPod & iTunes For
Dummies, 8th Edition
978-0-470-87871-2

Piano Exercises
For Dummies
978-0-470-38765-8

Parenting & Education

Parenting For Dummies,
2nd Edition
978-0-7645-5418-6

Type 1 Diabetes
For Dummies
978-0-470-17811-9

Pets

Cats For Dummies,
2nd Edition
978-0-7645-5275-5

Dog Training For Dummies,
3rd Edition
978-0-470-60029-0

Puppies For Dummies,
2nd Edition
978-0-470-03717-1

Religion & Inspiration

The Bible For Dummies
978-0-7645-5296-0

Catholicism For Dummies
978-0-7645-5391-2

Women in the Bible
For Dummies
978-0-7645-8475-6

Self-Help & Relationship

Anger Management
For Dummies
978-0-470-03715-7

Overcoming Anxiety
For Dummies,
2nd Edition
978-0-470-57441-6

Sports

Baseball
For Dummies,
3rd Edition
978-0-7645-7537-2

Basketball
For Dummies,
2nd Edition
978-0-7645-5248-9

Golf For Dummies,
3rd Edition
978-0-471-76871-5

Web Development

Web Design
All-in-One
For Dummies
978-0-470-41796-6

Web Sites
Do-It-Yourself
For Dummies,
2nd Edition
978-0-470-56520-9

Windows 7

Windows 7
For Dummies
978-0-470-49743-2

Windows 7
For Dummies,
Book + DVD Bundle
978-0-470-52398-8

Windows 7 All-in-One
For Dummies
978-0-470-48763-1

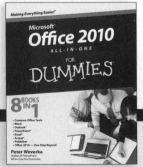

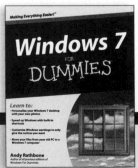